FACE VALUE

FACE VALUE

THE IRRESISTIBLE INFLUENCE OF FIRST IMPRESSIONS

ALEXANDER TODOROV

PRINCETON UNIVERSITY PRESS

PRINCETON AND OXFORD

Published by Princeton University Press, 41 William Street, Princeton, New Jersey 08540
In the United Kingdom: Princeton University Press, 6 Oxford Street,
Woodstock, Oxfordshire OX20 1TR

press.princeton.edu

Jacket design by Kimberly Glyder

Jacket art courtesy of Shutterstock

ISBN 978-0-691-16749-7

British Library Cataloging-in-Publication Data is available

This book has been composed in Minion Pro and Din

Printed on acid-free paper. ∞

Printed in Korea

10 9 8 7 6 5 4 3 2 1

To the memory of my grandmother
Todorka Alexandrova Koleva (1924–2015)
and my friend
Ivan Toshev Bashovski (1951–1998)

CONTENTS

PROLOGUE

A crew from a Korean TV station is in my office. They are literally pushing into my face large pictures of Korean politicians running for the highest office in South Korea. I am supposed to tell them who has the looks to win the Korean elections. I get these kinds of media requests all the time when there are important elections coming up. You would think that in an institution like Princeton University, you would not find "face readers." I agree with you: there shouldn't be. Because I don't have a crystal ball in my office, I always decline to provide an answer. But why is this extremely polite crew—not counting the pushing of the images into my face—in my office? More than 10 years ago, my lab conducted a series of studies testing whether first impressions from facial appearance predict important elections in the United States. The first impressions did surprisingly well in predicting the winner. In a nutshell, politicians who look more competent are more likely to win elections.

Snap judgments from pictures of politicians predict their electoral success not only in the United States but also around the world. The continually expanding list of countries where the same results have been found includes Brazil, Bulgaria, Denmark, Finland, France, Italy, Japan, Mexico, and the United Kingdom. In these studies, to demonstrate that first impressions rather than prior knowledge about the politicians predict electoral success, the participants are often from a country different from that of the politicians. My favorite study was done by John Antonakis and Olaf Dalgas in Switzerland. The participants in their study were not only from a different country but also of a very different age. Antonakis and Dalgas had 5- to 13-year-old children first play a computer game reenacting Odysseus's trip from Troy to Ithaca. Then the children were asked to imagine that they were about to sail from Troy to Ithaca, shown pairs of pictures of French politicians who ran for the French parliament, and asked to choose one of them as the captain of their boat. Just like adults' competence judgments, kids' captain choices predicted about 70 percent of the elections.

A few years ago, I visited the Exploratorium, the Science Museum in San Francisco. Like any good science museum, it was full with kids. One of the exhibits in the psychology section was called "competent candidates." It partially simulated our very first study on political elections. You see ten pairs of pictures of politicians who ran for the U.S. Senate, and you have to decide who looks more competent. My son, who was 7 years old at the time, did not have any problems doing the task, although his performance was far from stellar. He was not better than chance in predicting the winner. But the judgments of the more than 19,000 museum visitors who have done the task until that day correctly picked the winner in seven out of the ten elections. You can think of this as an informal and uncontrolled but fun replication of Antonakis and Dalgas's findings from Switzerland. Children, just like adults, are prone to using face stereotypes.

● ● ● ● ●

It is just that easy to form impressions from faces. Find out for yourself. Who would you vote for?

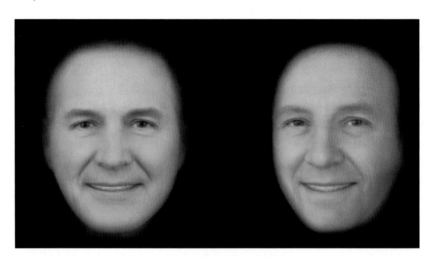

FIGURE 1. Who looks more competent? To most people, this is an easy and quick decision. The face on the left was created by morphing the faces of a few politicians perceived to be more competent than their rivals. The face on the right was created by morphing the faces of these rivals.

Most people choose the face on the left without much thought. In fact, seeing these faces for one-tenth of a second gives you enough information to make up your mind. We cannot help but form impressions of others. These impressions are closer to perception than to thinking. We don't need to think, we *see*.

As Solomon Asch, one of the founding fathers of modern social psychology, wrote in 1946: "We look at a person and immediately a certain impression of his character forms itself in us. A glance, a few spoken words are sufficient to tell us a story about a highly complex matter. We know that such impressions form with remarkable rapidity and with great ease. Subsequent observations may enrich or upset our view, but we can no more prevent its rapid growth than we can avoid perceiving a given visual object or hearing a melody." Impressions simply register on our senses. At least, this is how it appears to us. The subjectively compelling nature of impressions is the major reason we trust them even when we have evidence to the contrary.

Asch was not the first to note the immediacy of first impressions. More than 150 years before him, Johann Kaspar Lavater, the father of the pseudoscience of physiognomy—the "art" of reading character in faces—noted: "at the first advance of a stranger, we are certainly moved to declare our sentiments, in which sympathy and antipathy has a share without our perceiving it." Lavater also believed that these sentiments could be a direct readout of the stranger's character, especially if these were the sentiments of a skilled physiognomist like himself. Lavater's works on physiognomy were phenomenally popular in Europe. His musings almost caused Charles Darwin to miss the *Beagle* voyage, which enabled Darwin's revolutionary observations on evolution, on account of Darwin's nose. Apparently, the captain of the ship, "an ardent disciple of Lavater," did not think that Darwin possessed "sufficient energy and determination for the voyage." "But I think," Darwin noted in his *Autobiography*, "he was afterwards well-satisfied that my nose had spoken falsely."

The nineteenth century was the heyday of physiognomy. Cesare Lombroso, the founding father of criminal anthropology, was writing books on the criminal man and woman and how they can be identified by external, physical characteristics. Francis Galton, a talented scientist but also a purveyor of unsavory ideas like eugenics, invented a photographic technique to identify human types ranging from the ideal English type to the criminal type. All modern morphing techniques, like the one we used to create the morphs of politicians' faces in Figure 1, originate with Galton's methods to create composite photographs.

The physiognomists' ideas permeated mass culture, and many practical guides of face readings were published in the late nineteenth and early twentieth centuries. In a 1922 chapter analyzing the face of President Warren Harding, we are told that his forehead "indicates broad-mindedness, and intellectual powers that find their expressions rather scientifically." Moreover, his chin is "perhaps the strongest of any of our Presidents" indicating that "there is strong will-power and great endurance combined in one chin." You can appreciate President Harding's forehead and chin in Figure 2. The insights gained by this face analysis were ultimately summarized as "steadfastness, balance, and stern justice with a natural, practical bent of mind." Alas, these insights do not agree with the historical analysis.

FIGURE 2. President Warren Harding. He was the twenty-ninth president of the United States from 1921 until his death in 1923. In his time, physiognomists saw the signs of presidential greatness in his face.

It is a very difficult task to rank American presidents on their greatness, but when it comes to the worst, historians agree. Warren Harding, who won the U.S. presidential election in 1920, gets the dubious distinction of having been the worst American president. His administration became best known for scandals involving bribery and incompetence.

· · · · ·

We may poke fun at physiognomists, but we are all naïve physiognomists: we form instantaneous impressions and act on these impressions. This book is about why physiognomy has not disappeared and will not disappear from our lives. The physiognomists promised an easy way to solve the problem of understanding other people: knowing them from their faces. Georg Christoph Lichtenberg, one of the most unorthodox thinkers of the eighteenth century and the person most responsible for unraveling Lavater's "science," equated physiognomy with prophecy. The prophetic nature of physiognomy, its promise to figure out human nature from observing the face, was the physiognomists' promise. The appeal of this promise is as strong today as it was during Lavater's time.

Part 1 of the book explains the popular appeal of the physiognomists' promise. As physiognomists suspected, we agree on our first impressions, a fact that was established about 100 years ago in the new science of psychology. But in the search for the accuracy of these impressions, psychologists in the early twentieth century missed the significance of this fact. The agreement on first impressions makes the physiognomists' promise believable. What makes this promise appealing is that we can't help but form impressions. And we do act on these impressions. First impressions predict a host of important decisions: from voting choices to economic and legal decisions.

Part 2 is about the perceptual rules of first impressions—about visualizing the agreement of our impressions. By discovering these rules, we can understand why we form impressions. The modern science of first impressions shows that there are systematic, predictable relations between appearance and impressions. These impressions are not fundamentally "irrational." They serve our need to figure out the intentions and capabilities of others; they are grounded in shared stereotypes, subtle emotional expressions, and our own idiosyncratic experiences with other people.

Part 3 is about the illusions of first impressions: compelling yet inaccurate perceptions. Psychologists in the early twentieth century found little evidence for the accuracy of first impressions, but the past decade has seen a resurgence of physiognomic claims in scientific journals. We are told that it is possible to discern a person's political leanings, religious affiliation, sexual orientation, and even criminal inclinations from images of their face. Perhaps the physiognomists were right not only about our natural propensity to form impressions but also about the accuracy of these impressions. A closer look at the modern studies shows that the claims of the new physiognomy are almost as exaggerated as those in the eighteenth and nineteenth centuries.

Part 4 takes you on a tour of some of the most exciting discoveries in the science of face perception. For physiognomy, the face was the key to unlocking the secrets of character. For modern science, the face is the key to unlocking the secrets of the mind. Faces loom large in our social lives from the get-go. We are born with a readiness to attend to faces, and this readiness develops into an intricate network of brain regions exclusively dedicated to the processing of faces. This brain network supports our rich physiognomical inferences and provides input to other brain networks that help us understand the social world. Our brains automatically compute the social value of faces.

● ● ● ● ●

Physiognomists saw the face as a map that revealed the hidden dispositions of its owner. The value of the face was in its capacity to expose these dispositions. But the map we are reading is not the map the physiognomists envisioned. The map is in our minds, shaped by our own culture, individual histories, and biases. It emerges from our reading of the face. Although the meaning of the map is elusive, we cannot resist reading it. We are the ones creating face value—making too much out of too little information. This book is about how we create the most entertaining map in the world: the map of the face.

PART 1

THE APPEAL OF PHYSIOGNOMY

THE PHYSIOGNOMISTS' PROMISE

Agnieszka Holland's movie *Europa Europa* is based on the autobiography of Solomon Perel. As a German Jewish boy, Perel is forced to escape Nazi Germany. After a chain of events that includes stints in Poland and Russia, he is captured by German soldiers. To save his life, he pretends to be Josef Peters, a German from Baltic Germany. Eventually he wins the admiration of the soldiers and their commanding officer and is sent to a prestigious Hitler Youth School in Berlin. One of his scariest moments at the school occurs during a science lesson on racial purity. Next to the giant swastika flag hang three large posters showing faces overlaid with measurements. The teacher walks in and asks, "how do you recognize a Jew?" and then continues, "that's quite simple. The composition of Jewish blood is totally different from ours. The Jew has a high forehead, a hooked nose, a flat back of the head, ears that stick out and he has an ape-like walk. His eyes are shifty and cunning." In contrast to the Jewish man, "the Nordic man is the gem of this earth. He's the most glowing example of the joy of creation. He is not only the most talented but the most beautiful. His hair is as light as ripened wheat. His eyes are blue like the summer sky. His movements are harmonious. His body is perfect." The teacher continues, "science is objective. Science is incorruptible. As I have already told you, if you thoroughly understand racial differences, no Jew will ever be able to deceive you." This is where the frightening moment for Perel/Peters really begins. The teacher turns toward Peters and asks him to come forward. Horrified, Peters reluctantly goes to the front of the room. The teacher pulls out a measuring tape and starts measuring his head—first from the chin to the top of the head, then from the nose to the top of the head, and then from the chin to the nose. While the measurement continues, there is a close up on Peters's face as he anxiously tracks the actions of the teacher. The teacher continues with his measurement. He measures the width of Peters's head and then compares his eyes with different eye colors from a table. "The eyes. Look at his skull. His forehead. His profile [turning Peters's head, who is visibly blushing]. Although his ancestors' blood, over many generations mingled with that of other races, one still recognizes his distinct Aryan traits." On hearing this, Peters almost jerks his head toward the teacher's face. "It's from this mixture that the East-Baltic race evolved. Unfortunately, you're not part of our most noble race, but you are an authentic Aryan."

The "objective science" of physiognomy was not invented by Nazi scientists. It has a long history originating in ancient cultures. The physiognomists' claims reached scientific credibility in the nineteenth century, although this credibility came under attack by the new science of psychology in the early twentieth century. Their claims were wrong, but the physiognomists were right about a few things: we immediately form impressions from appearance, we agree on these impressions, and we act on them. These psychological facts make the physiognomists' claims believable, and the claims have not disappeared. A surge of recent scientific studies test hypotheses that the physiognomists would have approved of. An Israeli technology start-up is offering its services in facial profiling to private businesses and governments. Rather than using a tape to measure faces, they use modern computer science methods. Their promise is the old physiognomists' promise: "profiling people and revealing their personality based only on their facial image." We are tempted by the physiognomists' promise, because it is easy to confuse our immediate impressions from the face with seeing the character of the face owner. Grasping the appeal of this promise and the significance of first impressions in everyday life begins with the history of physiognomy and its inherent connections to "scientific" racism.

• • • • •

The first preserved document dedicated to physiognomy is *Physiognomica*, a treatise attributed to Aristotle. The major premises of the treatise are that the character of animals is revealed in their form and that humans resembling certain animals possess the character of these animals. Here is one of many examples of applying this logic: "soft hair indicates cowardice, and coarse hair courage. This inference is based on observation of the whole animal kingdom. The most timid of animals are deer, hares, and sheep, and they have the softest coats; whilst the lion and wild-boar are bravest and have the coarsest coats."

The logic is also extended to races: "and again, among the different races of mankind the same combination of qualities may be observed, the inhabitants of the north being brave and coarse-haired, whilst southern peoples are cowardly and have soft hair."

In the sixteenth century, Giovanni Battista della Porta, an Italian scholar and playwright, greatly expanded on these ideas. Humans whose faces (and various body parts) "resembled" a particular animal were endowed with the presumed qualities of the animal. His book is filled with illustrations like the one in Figure 1.1.

FIGURE 1.1. An illustration from Giovanni Battista della Porta's *De Humana Physiognomia*. Della Porta's book, in which he inferred the character of people from their supposed resemblance to animals, was extremely popular and influenced generations of physiognomists.

This particular illustration appears four times in the book in analyses of different facial parts, yet the message is consistent. People who look like cows—whether because of their big foreheads or wide noses—are stupid, lazy, and cowardly. There is one positive characteristic: the hollow eyes indicate pleasantness. As you can imagine, those who "look like" lions come off much better.

Della Porta's book was very popular in Europe and enjoyed multiple translations from Latin into Italian, German, French, and Spanish, resulting in twenty editions. The book influenced Charles Le Brun, one of the dominant figures in seventeenth-century French art. Le Brun, appointed by Louis XIV as the first Painter of the King, was also the Director of the Royal Academy of Painting and Sculpture. In 1688, Le Brun delivered a lecture on the facial expressions of emotions: the first attempt in human history to systematically explore and depict such expressions. After Le Brun's death, the lecture—discussed, admired, and hated by artists—was published in more than sixty editions. Le Brun also delivered a second lecture on physiognomy. Unfortunately, this lecture was not preserved, but some of the illustrations survived. Compare della Porta's Lion-Man in Figure 1.2 with Le Brun's Lion-Man in Figure 1.3.

FIGURE 1.2. Another illustration from Giovanni Battista della Porta's *De Humana Physiognomia*. Compare this illustration with Figure 1.3.

Le Brun's drawings are more beautiful and true to life, and it is apparent that he was trying to develop a much more sophisticated system of comparisons between animal and human heads. Le Brun experimented with the angles of the eyes to achieve different perceptual effects. He noted that the eyes of human faces are on a horizontal line and that sloping them downward makes

FIGURE 1.3. After Charles Le Brun, lion and lion-man. Le Brun was developing a system for comparing animal and human faces.

the faces look more bestial. This is illustrated in his drawing of the Roman emperor, Antoninus Pius, in Figure 1.4.

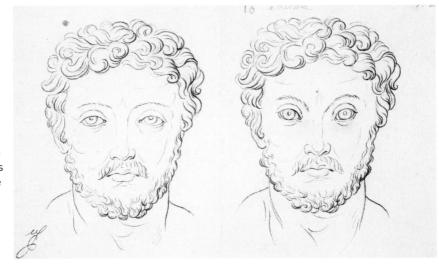

FIGURE 1.4. Charles Le Brun, Antoninus Pius with sloping eyes. Le Brun experimented with the angle of the eyes to make humans look more like animals.

Alternatively, making the eyes of animals horizontal makes them look more human, as in Figure 1.5. These kinds of experiments are not that different from modern psychology experiments testing how changes in facial features influence our impressions.

FIGURE 1.5. Charles Le Brun, horse and lion with horizontal eyes. Le Brun experimented with the angle of the eyes to make animals look more like humans.

The theme of comparative physiognomy would continue to run through physiognomists' writings and appear in the work of many caricaturists throughout Europe and America for the next 300 years. Some of the most talented caricaturists, like Thomas Rowlandson in England and Honoré Daumier and J. J. Grandville in France, would exploit this theme to achieve humorous effects. But other authors took the theme seriously. Many national stereotypes and prejudices of the day find their expression in a book titled *Comparative Physiognomy or Resemblances between Men and Animals,* published in the United States in 1852: Germans are like lions, Irish are like dogs, Turks are like turkeys, and the list goes on.

● ● ● ● ●

Johann Kaspar Lavater, the real superstar of physiognomy, highly recommended della Porta's book, although he was critical: "the fanciful Porta appears to me to have been often misled, and to have found resemblances [between men and beasts] which the eye of truth never could discover." Prior to Lavater, physiognomy was closely associated with suspect practices like chiromancy (palm reading), metoposcopy (reading the lines of the forehead), and astrology. There were even laws in Britain stating that those "pretending to have skill in physiognomy" were "rogues and vagabonds," "liable to be publicly whipped." Lavater engaged in debates with some of the greatest minds of the eighteenth century and legitimized physiognomy. Reviewing the history of physiognomy at the end of the nineteenth century, Paolo Mantegazza, an Italian neurologist and anthropologist, summarized it this way: "plenty of authors, plenty of volumes, but little originality, and plenty of plagiarism! Who knows how often we might have been dragged through the same ruts if towards the middle of the last century Lavater had not appeared to inaugurate a new era for this order of studies." For Mantegazza, Lavater was "the apostle of scientific physiognomy."

Born and raised in Zurich, Switzerland, Lavater showed early inclinations toward religion. After receiving a theological education, he rose through the ranks of the Zurich Reformed Church to become the pastor of the Saint Peter's church. By many accounts of the day, he was extremely charming. His sermons were popular, and he entertained hundreds of visitors. Lavater was also a prolific author. He managed to write more than 100 books and maintain an extremely large correspondence. Ironically, he was reluctant to write about physiognomy, although he was continually urged to do so by Johann

Georg Ritter von Zimmermann, another Swiss who was the personal physician of the King of England and a European celebrity. Zimmermann would remain Lavater's greatest promoter and supporter.

Lavater's first publication on physiognomy was unintentional. As a member of the Society for Natural Sciences in Zurich, Lavater was asked to deliver a lecture of his own choosing. He gave a lecture on physiognomy, which ended up being published by Zimmermann, who "had it printed wholly without my knowledge. And thus I suddenly saw myself thrust into public as a defender of physiognomics." Being thrust into this role and aware of the strong feelings that physiognomy provoked, Lavater approached many celebrities of the day to help him with the writing of his *Essays on Physiognomy*. By then, he was a famous theologian, and support was coming from all directions—from encouragement to requests for portraits to be analyzed. None other than Goethe helped Lavater edit the first volume, and some of the best illustrators worked on the books. The four-volume work was published between 1775 and 1778, and the result was "a typographical splendor with which no German book had ever before been printed." And in fact, the large format, richly illustrated books are beautiful even by today's standards.

The success of the books was phenomenal despite the exorbitant price. It helped that the books were distributed by subscription to many aristocrats and leading intellectuals, some of whom were lured by Lavater's promise to analyze their profiles. More importantly, societies formed to buy and discuss the books. Within a few decades, there were twenty English, sixteen German, fifteen French, two American, one Russian, one Dutch, and one Italian editions. As the author of the Lavater obituary in *The Gentleman's Magazine* in 1801 put it, "in Switzerland, in Germany, in France, even in Great Britain, all the world became passionate admirers of the Physiognomical Science of Lavater. His books, published in the German language, were multiplied by many editions. In the enthusiasm with which they were studied and admired, they were thought as necessary in every family as even the Bible itself. A servant would, at one time, scarcely be hired but the description and engravings of Lavater had been consulted in careful comparisons with the lines and features of the young man's or woman's countenance."

● ● ● ● ●

Lavater defined physiognomy as "the talent of discovering, the interior man by the exterior appearance." Although his ambition was to introduce physiognomy as a science, there was not much scientific evidence in his writings. Instead he offered "universal axioms and incontestible principles." Here are some of the axioms: "the forehead to the eyebrows, the mirror of intelligence; the cheeks and the nose form the seat of the moral life; and the mouth and chin aptly represent the animal life." The "evidence" came from counterfactual statements peppered with what now would be considered blatantly racist beliefs: "who could have the temerity to maintain, that Newton or Leibnitz might resemble one born an idiot" or have "a misshapen brain like that of Laplander" or "a head resembling that of an Esquimaux."

The other kind of "evidence" came from the many illustrations, which served as Rorschach's inkblots on which Lavater (and his readers) could project their knowledge and biases. The knowledge projection came from describing famous personalities. Analyzing the profile of Julius Caesar, Lavater noted that "it is certain that every man of the smallest judgment, unless he contradict his internal feeling, will acknowledge, that, in the form of that face, in the contour of the parts, and the relation which they have to one another, they discover the superior man." Analyzing the profile of Moses Mendelssohn, a brilliant philosopher known as the "German Socrates" and Berlin's most famous Jew, "I revel in this silhouette! My glance welters in this magnificent curve of the forehead down to the pointed bone of the eye. . . . In this depth of the eye a Socratic soul is lodged!"

And there are the illustrations of particular human types like the "horrible face" in Figure 1.6, described by Lavater in the following way:

FIGURE 1.6. An illustration of a "horrible face" from Johann Kaspar Lavater's *Essays on Physiognomy*. Lavater's richly illustrated books on physiognomy were immensely popular in the eighteenth and nineteenth centuries. Image courtesy Princeton University Library.

"It is not virtue which that horrible face announces. Never could candour, or a noble simplicity, or cordiality, have fixed their residence there. The most sordid avarice, the most obdurate wickedness, the most abominable knavery, have deranged those eyes, have disfigured that mouth." Lavater also illustrated and described "national types." Naturally, Europeans, especially the Germans and English, fared much better than the rest of humanity. Many of the non-Europeans could hardly pass for humans in his book.

Lavater was just as popular as his books. One of his aristocratic friends wrote in a letter that she would keep his visit to Bern a secret "so as not to have the entire local population round our necks asking for physiognomical reading." The Emperor Joseph II did not miss a chance to meet Lavater while visiting Switzerland. After the meeting, the emperor wrote to him: "the fact that you can see into people's hearts puts one on one's guard when one comes too close to you." Joseph actually suggested that physiognomy should become an academic discipline to be taught at universities. Wisely, Lavater politely declined: "well, let's put off of a system of physiognomy for another forty or fifty years. Meanwhile, [we can] make daily observations, confirm and define the old ones more precisely, add new ones, and not draw up our armies until we have recruited enough hardy individual soldiers."

• • • • •

In the end, the phenomenal success of Lavater's "science" was short lived. The person most responsible for its demise was Georg Christoph Lichtenberg. Lichtenberg, the son of a Protestant clergyman, studied mathematics and physics at the University of Göttingen, one of the most liberal universities in Germany. Shortly after his graduation, he was appointed as a professor there. His lectures on experimental physics were famous and attended by luminaries like Alessandro Volta, Goethe, Karl Friedrich Gauss, and Alexander von Humboldt. Elected to the most prestigious science societies in the world, he was highly respected. But he is remembered more for his contributions to literature and philosophy than to the natural sciences. Goethe referred to his writings as "the most wonderful divining rod," and Lichtenberg is credited with the introduction of the aphorism in German literature.

Lichtenberg was remarkably modern in his ideas, not buying into the prevailing racist prejudices of his day. To Lavater's claim that it is impossible to imagine "that Newton or Leibnitz might resemble" somebody from an "inferior" ethnic origin, he responded, "this shallow and passionate youthful declamation can be arrested forever with a simple *and why not?"* With respect to the worst prejudices about the people of Africa, he wrote, "I just want to put in a word for the Negro, whose profile one has drawn to be the downright ideal of stupidity and stubbornness and, so to speak, the asymptote of the line marking the stupidity and stubbornness of Europeans."

Lichtenberg was just as fascinated with faces as Lavater, "From my early youth, faces and their interpretation were one of my favorite pastimes." But he was suspicious of Lavater's physiognomy, which "instead of cultivating the intellect, gives every feeble mind the opportunity to marshal its own confused ideas under the banner of a notorious man." Lichtenberg set out to show that Lavater's physiognomy was not a science and hastily wrote an essay that was published in the *Göttinger Taschen Calendar.* Although the first edition of this almanac was poorly printed, all 8,000 copies sold out. Soon many personal threats followed, and Lichtenberg was warned by Zimmermann, the main promoter of Lavater's books, that "antiphysiognomics would be *roughly* and *forcefully* refuted." Lichtenberg was surprised by the hostile reaction and expanded his essay in a second edition. In brief, he argued that our behavior is just as much a product of our life circumstances as of our dispositions. "What do you hope to conclude from the similarity of faces, especially the fixed features, if the same man who has been hanged could, given all of his dispositions, have received laurels rather than the noose in different circumstances? Opportunity does not make thieves alone; it also makes great men." For Lichtenberg, it was impossible to draw conclusions from the constant features of the face "about people, who are always changing." He wondered what to make of "beautiful rogues" and "smooth swindlers." Physiognomy was "an unfathomable leap from the surface of the body to the recesses of the soul!"

Except for Zimmermann, none of Lavater's friends stepped up to defend him. It was hard to argue against Lichtenberg's arguments, and some of these friends were unhappy with Lavater's interpretations of their portraits. Goethe had already parted ways with Lavater, offended by his exuberant "Lavaterian" style and his Christian fervor.

Despite Lavater's fall from grace, his ideas permeated nineteenth-century culture, the heyday of popular physiognomy. This was the time of great industrial migrations, bringing together people with profoundly different backgrounds, who often did not even share a common language. The physiognomists' ideas promised an easy, intuitive way to deal with the uncertainty generated by this diversity. Countless books supplied physiognomic recipes for reading character, including pocket Lavater editions and pocket editions entirely dedicated to reading character from noses. An extremely popular genre—physiologie, which depicted the appearance and manner of different social types—appeared in France. During its peak popularity, about half a million copies of books in this genre were sold in Paris, which had a population of 1 million, only half of whom were literate. The most popular journals devoted to caricature were founded at this time, and caricatures of social types were consumed with "the news and the morning coffee." Physiognomic descriptions of characters became standard in European novels. Lavater's ideas influenced not only easily forgotten authors but also greats like Balzac, Dickens, and Stendhal. After seeing the cast of the head of an executed prisoner, Dickens noted, "a style of head and set of features, which might have afforded sufficient moral grounds for his instant execution at any time, even had there been no other evidence against him." The physiognomists' ideas were self-evident.

· · · · ·

Although Lavater's ambition was to introduce physiognomy as a science, he himself thought of physiognomy as an art form that only a few gifted individuals could practice: "perhaps more than in any other science, much must be left to genius and to sentiment." He did not introduce any replicable empirical methods to study physiognomy. He did sketch in his books an instrument for cranial measurement, which he called "Stirnmaaß," which preceded Franz Gall's phrenology by decades, and had ambitions to make physiognomy as exact as mathematics, but none of this was realized. All that Lavater offered were appeals to the power of observation and his "expert" testimony. Without empirical methods, it was hard to make the case for physiognomy as a science. Francis Galton changed this with the invention of composite photography at the end of the nineteenth century. In contrast to Lavater, Galton was an established and respected scientist. He was also obsessed with measurement.

Galton, to whom we owe the phrase "nature versus nurture," was a polymath, a cousin of Charles Darwin, and a hero to many scientists in the twentieth century. He made scientific contributions to geography, meteorology, biology, statistics, and psychology. He was the first European to explore parts of West Africa and to provide detailed maps of the region; he discovered the anti-cyclone in weather patterns and created the first meteorological map published in *The Times* in 1875; he developed the concepts of correlation and regression, which are indispensable tools for statistical analyses of empirical data; he did the first systematic studies of fingerprints, eventually transforming police practices for identifying people.

Galton's contributions to psychology were numerous, and many psychologists admired him. A prominent American psychologist, Lewis Terman, who studied intelligence and gifted children in the beginning of the twentieth century, estimated "that between the ages of three and eight years, at least, Francis Galton must have had an intelligence quotient not far from 200." Terman also noted that "little Francis was known to be as remarkably conscientious as he was intelligent." Galton was the first to use questionnaires for psychological studies, to measure family histories, and to explore individual differences in mental imagery. He came up with the free association test long before Sigmund Freud did. He was the first to study heredity using twins.

Galton was also a pioneer in inventing unorthodox measures of behavior. A classic book from the 1960s on unorthodox research methods in psychology, *Unobtrusive Measures: Nonreactive Research in the Social Sciences*, is dedicated to Galton. The research problem that this book was trying to solve was how to measure human behavior without influencing it, a problem that Galton had already considered. If you know that you are being observed, you could change your behavior accordingly, jeopardizing the validity of the observation and any inferences about the causes of your behavior. Things are much easier scientifically, if not ethically, if you don't know that you are being observed and studied. To study the "inclination of one person toward another," Galton suggested a pressure gauge attached to the legs of the chairs on which the people are sitting. By measuring the stress of the chair legs, one can quantify the physical inclinations of the people. As the authors of *Unobtrusive Measures*, Eugene Webb, Donald Campbell, Richard Schwartz, and Lee Secherest, put it, "it is obvious that such a device may be a substitute for human observers when their presence might contaminate the situation, and where no convenient hidden observation site is available."

Galton also had ideas about how to measure boredom. "Let this suggest to observant philosophers, when the meeting they attend must prove dull, to occupy themselves in estimating the frequency, amplitude and duration of the fidgets of their fellow sufferers." And he created "beauty maps" of the British islands by using "a needle mounted as a pricker, wherewith to prick holes, unseen, in a piece of paper . . . classifying the girls I passed in streets or elsewhere as attractive, indifferent, or repellent." He found "London to rank highest for beauty; Aberdeen lowest."

● ● ● ● ●

Galton would have been celebrated today as one of the greatest scientists of the nineteenth century were it not for his preoccupation with heredity and eugenics during the second part of his life. This is what finally made him internationally famous at the end of the nineteenth century and infamous after his death in the second half of the twentieth century. Eugenics was Galton's understanding of how to use Darwin's evolutionary ideas to better the human world. The "positive" side of eugenics involved the selective breeding of super humans—those with the highest abilities. The negative side involved the restriction of the breeding of those deemed to be less capable. In his final days, Galton worked on a novel *Kantsaywhere*, in which he laid out his utopian vision. In the land of Kantsaywhere, those who pass the examinations in the Eugenics College with high distinction are incentivized to marry early. Those who fail are sent to labor camps where they have to remain celibate. To be fair to Galton, at the time, eugenics was endorsed across the ideological spectrum. The list of notable supporters included George Bernard Shaw, H. G. Wells, Havelock Ellis, and the prominent Marxist scientist, J. B. S. Haldane.

Galton's obsession with eugenics was what led him to the study of faces and fingerprints. Both promised to provide a means of identifying individuals and, ultimately, distinguishing the allegedly more from the allegedly less capable by identifying specific human types. In the 1870s, Galton was approached by Edmund Du Cane, the director-general of prisons. Du Cane was interested in identifying criminals from their facial features. This was a popular idea at the time. Cesare Lombroso, a contemporary of Galton and the founder of criminal anthropology, argued that "each type of crime is committed by men with particular physiognomic characteristics . . . thieves are notable for their expressive faces and manual dexterity, small wandering eyes that are often oblique in form, thick and close eyebrows, distorted or squashed noses, thin beards and hair, and sloping foreheads." Lombroso wrote books on identifying the "criminal man" and the "criminal woman," and provided his "scientific" testimony at several criminal trials. But empirical methods for identifying criminals were lacking.

Du Cane provided thousands of photographs of prisoners, which Galton examined and eventually settled on three groups of photographs. As Galton explained, "the first group included murder, manslaughter, and burglary; the second group included felony and forgery; and the third group referred to sexual crimes." Galton scored the photographs on a number of features, but no obvious differences emerged. As he would later reflect, "the physiognomical difference between different men being so numerous and small, it is impossible to measure and compare them each to each. . . . The usual way is to select individuals who are judged to be representatives of the prevalent type, and to photograph them; but this method is not trustworthy, because the judgment itself is fallacious. It is swayed by exceptional and grotesque features more than by ordinary ones, and the portraits supposed to be typical are likely to be caricatures."

Galton's creative solution was composite photography. The idea of blending facial images was in the air. Mr. L. A. Austin, a gentleman from New Zealand, wrote a letter to Darwin describing how he discovered that putting two facial images of similar size and orientation in a stereoscope appears to blend the faces, "producing in the case of some ladies' portraits, in every instance, a *decided improvement* in beauty." Herbert Spencer discussed with Galton a method of combining face drawings by tracing them on transparent paper and then superimposing the drawings to find commonalities. Galton's idea was to blend photographic portraits on the same photographic plate. The first device that Galton designed with this objective in mind is shown in Figure 1.7.

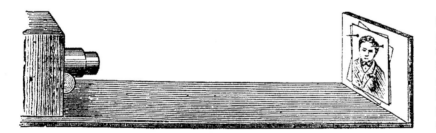

FIGURE 1.7. The first composite photography device designed by Francis Galton. Galton blended different photographic images on the same plate to create "pictorial averages."

Composite photography was an empirical method of deriving "pictorial averages," a way of establishing the essence of a group of images by discarding things that were idiosyncratic to specific faces while preserving the commonalities. Galton and his followers in Britain and the United States conducted systematic studies to improve the technique—experimenting with the order of images, they concluded that the order did not matter as long as each image was exposed for the same amount of time—and build better and more precise devices.

Galton had lofty goals for composite photography. Based on the assumption that characters have specific appearances, it was possible to classify humankind in innumerable ways. The composite photography was the tool for identifying common types ranging from the ideal English man to the criminal. It was also the tool of eugenics, Galton's "science" of selective breeding. Galton believed that each race had an "ideal typical form" or "central type" and that only those conforming to this type should be encouraged to breed. Composite photography was the "method of discovering the central physiognomical type of any race or group."

And Galton moved forward with composite portraits of families, privates and officers, people suffering from tuberculosis, people in prisons, and people in asylums. Collecting photographs occasionally carried risks. An asylum patient, considering himself a great man, was insulted that he was the second person to have his picture taken and "when the photographer had his head well under the velvet cloth, with his body bent, in the familiar attitude of photographers while focusing, Alexander the Great slid swiftly to his rear and administered a really good bite to the unprotected hinder end of the photographer."

Composite photography was favorably received by scientists. An editorial in *Science* magazine from 1886 noted that "with this great contribution of Galton well in hand, we may at length hope that we shall be able to enter upon the study of that unexplored realm of the human face, and physiognomy become a tolerably exact science." In the same issue, the technique was illustrated with a composite portrait of thirty-one members of the National Academy of Sciences, as shown in Figure 1.8. Although this may not be obvious to you (it is not to me), the author observed: "the faces give to me an idea of perfect equilibrium, of marked intelligence, and, what must be inseparable from the latter in a scientific investigator, of imaginativeness." We can recognize the style of Lavater: like Lavater's analysis of the profiles of famous personalities, the *Science* author was projecting his knowledge of the qualities of the people to their composite face image. Regardless, the classification of human types that was once left to artists was now in the hands of scientists.

Galton was ultimately disappointed by the composites of prisoners, where it all started: "I have made numerous composites of various groups of convicts, which are interesting negatively rather than positively. They produce faces of a mean description, with no villainy written on them. The individual faces are villainous enough, but they are villainous in different ways, and

FIGURE 1.8. A composite portrait of thirty-one members of the U.S. National Academy of Sciences from 1886.

when they are combined, the individual peculiarities disappear, and the common humanity of a low type is all that is left." But the methods Galton invented continue to thrive. All modern morphing techniques derive from his composite photography. The first digital composites were created in the 1980s by the artist Nancy Burson in collaboration with scientists from the Massachusetts Institute of Technology (MIT). You can see one of her composites, "Warhead I," in Figure 1.9. It is a morph of the heads of governments in possession of nuclear weapons.

FIGURE 1.9. "Warhead I" by Nancy Burson (1982). A digital composite of the faces of Ronald Reagan (55 percent), Leonid Brezhnev (45 percent), Margaret Thatcher (less than 1 percent), François Mitterrand (less than 1 percent), and Deng Xiaoping (less than 1 percent). The percentages correspond to the proportion of nuclear weapons in possession of the respective countries at the time (the percentages add to more than 100 because of rounding).

Today, anyone with a computer can obtain decent morphing software and manipulate facial images. Morphs of faces are regularly used in the media to illustrate concepts like the new face of America: a morph of faces representing the ethnicities living in the United States. And Galton's project is alive and well. In the past decade, a few psychologists have been working on creating composites of different character types. Galton would have been pleased.

• • • • •

Both Lavater and Galton saw physiognomy as a tool to better humanity. The subtitle of Lavater's *Essays on Physiognomy* was *For the Promotion of the Knowledge and the Love of Mankind*. In Lavater's theology, every human was a product of God's design. Physiognomy simply revealed God's intentions, promoting human love and understanding. At the end, Lavater's physiognomy did not promote human love, but he did his best as a pastor and citizen of Zurich. His funeral in 1801 was attended by thousands of Zurich's citizens.

Galton's betterment of humanity involved the breeding of super humans and restricting the breeding of "suboptimal humans." Spending the second half of his life promoting the "science" of eugenics, he was eventually successful. The first organized eugenics society was founded in Germany in 1905 and was called the Race Hygiene Society. Galton was the honorary president. Similar societies sprang up in the United Kingdom and the United States. A few decades later, H. F. K. Günther, also known as "Rassen-Günther" (Race-Günther), closely followed Galton's logic in his writings on identifying the ideal and "superior" Nordic type. His inaugural lecture at the University of Jena was attended by Adolf Hitler and Hermann Göring. Physiognomy and phrenology were the main tools in Günther's empirical approach of differentiating the Nordic from "lesser" humans. During the Third Reich, one of his books was a required reading in all German schools. Nazi Germany realized Galton's eugenics utopia. This utopia was also realized on a smaller scale in the United States. In 1907, the state of Indiana passed the first involuntary sterilization law. The targets of the law were people in state institutions: prison inmates and those considered mentally deficient or mentally ill. Within 20 years, twenty-three other states had similar laws.

In contrast to Lavater and Galton, Lichtenberg saw physiognomy not as a tool for the betterment of humanity but as a tool for creating and justifying prejudices. As he put it, "I wanted to prevent people from practicing physiognomy to promote the love of man as they previously singed and burned to promote the love of God." But Lichtenberg knew that it was not possible to prevent people from "practicing physiognomy." This is where he saw the danger in Lavater's writings. Lavater's books simply licensed our natural impulses to form impressions from appearance and removed any social controls on and doubts about these impressions. As Lichtenberg noted, "if physiognomy becomes what Lavater expects of it, then one will hang children before they have done the deeds that merit the gallows; a new kind of confirmation will thus be undertaken each year. A physiognomic auto-da-fé." This was no exaggeration. About 100 years later, Lombroso, whose ideas were hugely influential in Europe, advocated for separating children based on face and body measurements: "anthropological examination, by pointing out the criminal type, the precocious development of the body, the lack of symmetry, the smallness of the head, and the exaggerated size of the face explains the scholastic and disciplinary shortcomings of children thus marked and permits them to be separated in time from their better-endowed companions and directed towards careers more suited to their temperament."

Lavater's and Galton's conceptions of human nature were remarkably similar. For Lavater, everything in one's life was determined by God's purpose. For Galton, it was determined by heredity. Their task was to decipher those determining forces from the face. They took it for granted that there was a perfect correspondence between character and facial appearance. The same dangerous assumption underlies the modern versions of physiognomy that try to pass for scientific. The dressing is different, but the substance is the same. The "science" behind the Israeli facial profiling start-up is based on the facts that some of our character and some of our appearance are inherited. But these two facts do not logically imply a correspondence between character and facial appearance. Following their logic, hand and big toes profiling should do just as well in revealing personality. But what gives the veneer of legitimacy to facial profiling is our natural propensity to form impressions from faces.

Like Lavater and Galton, modern physiognomists want to go straight from the face to the essence of the face bearer, but they miss the crucial fact that what we see in the face are our own impressions. The science of first impressions is the study of our natural propensity to form impressions. This propensity is part of our essence, though not the essence Lavater and Galton were after. It is part of our quest to know and understand others.

2

SINGLE-GLANCE IMPRESSIONS

I am looking at a game: "Faces, The Hilarious Game of First Impressions." According to a sticker on the box, the game is a multiple award winner: Creative Child, Parent's Choice (for the record, this would not be my choice), *Family Fun Magazine*, Major Fun. There are piles of cards with faces (men, women, and animals) and piles of cards with impressions like "the hero," "the cheater," "the know-it-all," "the librarian," "the plumber," "the criminal mastermind," "the millionaire," "the communist," "the one who sees nothing funny," and so forth. The goal is to match faces and impressions. A few faces are randomly selected, an impression card is drawn, and then each player decides which face fits the impression best. And this goes on for a few rounds. The winner is the player whose matches are most similar to the other players' matches. The game is about agreement on first impressions.

A quick Internet search turns up reviews of the game like "extremely funny" and "one of the most popular party games I've ever introduced—groups continually want to play it over and over." The game involves "lots of chatter and uproarious laughter . . . just the sort of thing a party game is supposed to involve." You can almost sense the enjoyment of the members of the societies formed a couple of centuries ago to buy and discuss Lavater's books on physiognomy. The game's appeal comes from something that Lavater knew: it is easy to form impressions. And it is fun, especially when we agree. The agreement is never perfect, but it is there, which makes the game interesting and physiognomy appealing.

Matching pictures of people to "social types" is something that psychologists have studied extensively. The first studies were done almost 100 years ago. In a 1933 study, the researcher selected pictures of men and women from *Time* magazine. Participants were shown these pictures and asked to match them to the correct social type. The social types for the men were "college president, newspaper editor, political boss, U.S. senator, bolshevik, member of royalty, financier, bootlegger and gunman, actor, and humorist." The social types for the women were "prima donna, member of royalty, politician, bolshevik, actor, lawyer, university professor, and newspaper woman." These categories are not that different from the categories used in the "Hilarious Game of First Impressions."

Participants guessed the "social types" better than what would be expected by random guessing but not by much. The "prima donna" was identified accurately 18 percent of the time—random guessing would have resulted in 12.5 percent—but she was more than twice as likely to be misidentified as a "lawyer" and just as likely to be misidentified as a "university professor" or an "actress." Participants were at their best identifying the "bolshevik," which the author attributed to the "coarse dress" that "distinguished this woman from those women bedecked with modern clothes, furs, and articles of display."

Whatever pitfalls one can find in this study, the author was right to argue that we share appearance stereotypes: "pictures in our heads." We easily and consistently clump images of unfamiliar people into arbitrary categories. In another study conducted half a century later, the researchers selected images of Caucasian, middle-aged men from a casting directory. These were front headshots of faces with neutral expressions without facial hair, scars, or glasses. Participants were asked to choose the pictures of the "mass murderer, armed robber, and rapist" and the "medical doctor, clergyman, and engineer." The choices were highly consistent across participants. When it came to "mass murderer," most of the pictures were never selected, but one of the pictures was selected almost 31 percent of the time, and the top five choices were selected about 80 percent of the time. The top choices for criminals were never the top choices for high prestige occupations.

The "pictures in our heads" tell us who looks like a good guy and who looks like a bad guy. They even tell us the looks of different kinds of good and bad guys. If we did not have these pictures, the "Hilarious Game of First Impressions" would not exist. The implicit or explicit endorsement of physiognomy would not exist either. For first impressions to be compelling, they need to be grounded in two psychological facts. The first fact is what feels like their quasi-instinctive nature. Darwin, who read Lavater with a "very cautious" mind, wondered whether there is "anything in these absurd ideas." But he wrote down Lavater's thought "that every man is born with a portion of physiognomical sensation, as certainly as every man who is not deformed is born with two eyes" and added, "I think this cannot be disputed." The second psychological fact is the existence of shared appearance stereotypes, the existence of agreement on impressions. Without this agreement, even if partial, first impressions will not persist. We need the validation of others to believe our impressions. Physiognomy can only thrive when the "pictures in our heads" are shared. At the time of Lavater and later Darwin, these facts were not established. But they would be in the new science of psychology.

● ● ● ● ●

In the early twentieth century, physiognomy and phrenology were firmly established as part of the popular culture. Books with titles like *A System of Practical and Scientific Physiognomy*, *Analyzing Character*, *Characterology*, and *Vaught's Practical Character Reader* abounded; private institutions promised to teach you how to read faces and judge character "accurately, quickly, scientifically." But physiognomy and phrenology were facing the skepticism of the newly founded science of psychology. Psychologists were taking the physiognomists' and phrenologists' claims seriously and putting them to the test. As a result, most early psychology studies were focused on the accuracy of first impressions. Psychologists in the early twentieth century were skeptical about this accuracy. After reviewing the existing empirical evidence, the famous behaviorist Clark Hull concluded, "the results as a whole certainly look very bad for the judgment of character on the basis of photographs." Hull even tried to test a famous phrenologist, who wisely declined.

The psychologists did not find much evidence for accuracy, but they did find evidence for consensus on impressions. As the authors of a paper from 1924 noted, "it is noteworthy that casual observation right or wrong is nevertheless fairly consistent. Whatever physical signs go to impress a casual observer seem similarly to impress other casual observers." In a study notable for its methodological rigor, Stuart Cook asked experienced personnel managers and social workers—presumably those with good judgment of character—to judge 150 photographs of students on intelligence. The correlations of the judgments with the measured intelligence of the students, as well as their grades, were barely above zero. In other words, the judges could not predict the intelligence of the students. But despite this lack of predictability, they agreed with one another in their judgments. Cook also compared the photographs of the ten highest and the ten lowest ranked individuals on intelligence. He found that those judged to be intelligent had more typical facial features, pleasant expressions (in contrast to the puzzled expressions of the other group), and more neat appearances. These are some of the cues that trigger our shared stereotypes of what an intelligent face looks like.

Consensus on impressions was noted in these early studies, but it remained a side finding unworthy of further attention. The social psychologist Paul Secord and his colleagues changed that in the 1950s. Rather than searching for correspondence between facial appearance and actual character, they started searching for correspondence between facial appearance and impressions of character. The focus was on perception, on understanding the "pictures in our heads." The change in focus might have been facilitated by broader changes in psychology. This was the time of the cognitive revolution, the gradual displacement of behaviorist approaches by cognitive approaches. For behaviorists, the unobservable contents of the black box between external stimuli and behavioral responses were of no interest. But for cognitive scientists, this was the main interest. To them, perception was not a direct readout of sensory information coming from the world but a transformation of this information into mental representations. These representations were what psychologists needed to study and identify. And what were first impressions if not a specific set of mental representations?

In an impressive set of studies, Secord and colleagues started the modern work on first impressions in psychology. First, they observed high levels of agreement on impressions of faces for dozens of personality traits like conscientiousness, friendliness, honesty, and intelligence. The agreement was not only high among people from the same culture but also among those from different cultures. Second, the agreement on impressions for many traits was higher than the agreement on perceptions of directly observable facial characteristics like grooming of hair, wrinkles at eye corners, and distance between the eyes. As the art historian Ernst Gombrich put it, "we respond to a face as a whole: we see a friendly, dignified, or eager face, sad or sardonic, long before we can tell what exact features or relationships account for this intuitive impression." Third, faces that were similarly rated on personality traits like trustful, kind, honest, and friendly tended to have similar configurations of features, such as shallow-set eyes, light eyebrows, light complexion, and a medium width face. Secord and his colleagues were starting to identify the configurations of features that account for this "intuitive impression." Fourth, judges had little awareness of what physical features influenced their impressions. These findings form the foundation of modern research on first impressions. We effortlessly form impressions, we agree on these impressions, and these impressions are based on physical differences in appearance, even though we may not be aware of the exact differences driving our impressions.

• • • • •

Establishing the existence of shared impressions or face stereotypes is one thing. Demonstrating that by changing features of the face you can manipulate impressions is another. That gets you much closer to finding the content of the stereotypes and to understanding what really drives these stereotypes. Long before psychologists, skilled artists knew that subtle variations in faces lead to different impressions, and they experimented with these variations. Leonardo da Vinci was probably the first face experimenter. He was fascinated by grotesque heads, and his drawings of such heads were widely copied by other artists across Europe. One of his famous drawings is shown in Figure 2.1.

One interpretation of this drawing is that it was a physiognomic treatment, depicting the then-popular four temperaments—sanguine, choleric,

FIGURE 2.1. Leonardo da Vinci, five grotesque heads. According to one historical interpretation, the four heads surrounding the most normal-looking head represent (from left to right) the sanguine, choleric, melancholic, and phlegmatic temperaments.

melancholic, and phlegmatic—surrounding the most normal looking head. Leonardo owned books on physiognomy and by some accounts intended to write his own book. But he distanced himself from physiognomy: "I will not enlarge upon false physiognomy and chiromancy, because there is no truth in them, and this is made clear because such chimeras have no scientific foundation." However, in the same paragraph he argued, "it is true that the signs of faces display in part the nature of men, their vices and their temperaments," and he proceeded with a few examples like "those who have facial features of great relief are bestial and wrathful men of little reason."

The more plausible interpretation of Leonardo's drawings of grotesque heads is that he simply experimented with combinations of facial features. He was an excellent draftsman and was known to use the same motifs but achieve different results by experimenting with combinations of these motifs. On "how to make a portrait in profile after seeing the subject only once," he advised, "commit to memory the variations of the four features in profile, which would be the nose, the mouth, the chin and the forehead" and then proceeded with a classification of different types of noses: straight, concave, and convex, each type further subdivided into subtypes. The painter would simply have to note the types of features in the profile to quickly reproduce it. Studies of Leonardo's grotesque heads suggest that they are different combinations of the same types of facial features like types of noses (hooked vs. pug) combined with types of foreheads (flat vs. bulging). This includes his famous bearded "self-portrait."

The first artist to systematically experiment with variations in the appearance of faces was the British painter Alexander Cozens. In an essay, *Principles of Beauty, Relative to the Human Head*, published in 1778, he distinguished between simple beauty ("a beautiful face unmixed with character") and compound beauty ("beauty to which some character is annexed"). Cozens argued "that a set of features may be combined by a regular and determinate process in art, producing simple beauty" and that many other kinds of beauty can be derived from arrangements of the features. He provided tables with the principal variations of the human features—forehead (four variations), nose (twelve), mouth (sixteen), chin (two), eyebrow (twelve), and eyes (sixteen)— and illustrated all these variations. Then using different combinations of these variations, he created the face of simple beauty and the faces of sixteen different characters. Figure 2.2 shows five of these faces.

FIGURE 2.2. Illustrations from Alexander Cozens's *Principles of Beauty*. Cozens experimented with drawings to create different kinds of beauty. The head in the middle is simple beauty. Clockwise starting from the upper left corner: steady ("a quality founded on resolution of being firm"), languid ("delicacy of constitution"), artful ("keenness, with a little self-gratification"), and penetrating ("keenness, or quickness of perception") beauty.

The idea of systematically changing facial features to achieve different effects on impressions was found in guides on drawing both beautiful and humorous forms. Francis Grose in his *Rules for Drawing Caricaturas*, published a decade after Cozens's essay, advised artists to learn to draw perfect, beautiful heads and then to amuse themselves by distorting the drawings "whereby he will produce a variety of odd faces that will both please and surprise him." Like Cozens, he enumerated variations of features and commented on how combinations of features produce different effects: "convex faces, prominent features, and large aquiline noses, though differing much from beauty, will give an air of dignity to their owners; whereas concave faces, flat, snub, or broken noses, always stamp a meanness and vulgarity."

The greatest artist-experimenter on the effects of appearance on impressions was Rodolphe Töpffer, the inventor of the comic strip. He had nothing positive to say about phrenology—it "has never yielded one immediate, dependable result; it has no useful, profitable, or even workable application"—but endorsed physiognomy as an artistic device: it has "profited from the student's pen and artist's pencil to reach a wealth of immediate, dependable results, a host of workable, valuable, useful applications." Like Grose, Töpffer urged artists to experiment with drawing different faces and compare the impressions evoked by these faces. Moreover, Töpffer knew that faces always have meaning: "any human face, however poorly and childishly drawn, possesses necessarily, by the mere fact of existence, some perfectly definite expression." He did not believe that this definite expression was the key to the face bearer's moral character and intelligence, but he knew that this expression could manipulate impressions as the artist intended.

Adopting "the style of schoolboys," Töpffer demonstrated that even "the most elementary form of the human head" couldn't exist without being perceived as having a character. Take a look at Figure 2.3.

FIGURE 2.3. Illustrations from Rodolphe Töpffer's *Essay on Physiognomy*. Using simple alterations in the drawings of faces, Töpffer could easily manipulate our impressions.

The face on the left has "the look of a stupid stammering fellow, not even too sad about his lot." With a few changes, the face on the right is "less stupid, less stammering, and if it is not blessed with wits, at least it has a certain capacity for concentration." Töpffer did more systematic studies.

Starting from the same face, he generated multiple variations. Figure 2.4 illustrates some of his experiments. The faces on the top row have identical upper parts. If you don't believe me, take a piece of opaque paper and cover the faces from the bridge of the nose down. Using very simple variations, he "can modify, transform, or diminish the intellectual faculties" and "can do the very same with the moral faculties." Similar effects can be obtained by keeping the lower part of the faces the same and changing the upper parts, as demonstrated in the bottom row of Figure 2.4. Töpffer also experimented with changing only the nose and the upper lip, only the nostril, only the eye, and only the eyebrows. In all cases, our impressions of the faces change. He concluded, "in art you can combine these signs among themselves and with others to indicate, successfully and at will, qualities of intelligence and character quite plain enough for your purpose." But he warned against taking physiog-

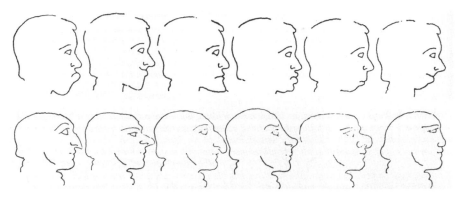

FIGURE 2.4. Illustrations from Rodolphe Töpffer's *Essay on Physiognomy*. The faces on the top row have identical upper parts (from the eye up). The faces on the bottom row have identical lower parts (from the lips down). Despite these identical parts, the impressions from the faces are very different.

nomy at face value, "because here art is plying its legitimate trade, in skillful magic and diverting tricks, we must not take its games as authority for erecting systems that are sometimes as pernicious, philosophically speaking, as they are rash."

● ● ● ● ●

Da Vinci, Cozens, Grose, and Töpffer all experimented with combinations of facial features but relied on their intuitions about the effects of these combinations on impressions. Cozens was aware of this fact, leaving "the ultimate decision of the principles to the feelings and experience of mankind." Psychologists are in the business of measuring these feelings and experience. In our business, intuition never constitutes sufficient evidence.

The first experimental study that manipulated features of schematic faces and measured their effects on impressions was conducted by Egon Brunswik and Lotte Reiter in 1937. Just like Cozens, they started by manipulating features like height of the mouth (three variations), height of the forehead (three), distance between the eyes (three), and length and position of the nose (seven). Unlike Cozens, they created all possible combinations of these features, resulting in 189 (3 × 3 × 3 × 7) drawings of schematic faces, and measured their effects on impressions by having participants rank the drawings on mood (happy to sad), age (young to old), beauty (beautiful to ugly), character (good to bad), likeability (likeable to dislikeable), intelligence (intelligent to unintelligent), and energy (energetic to unenergetic).

This is what constitutes a proper experiment. Once the researchers decide on the important variations, they create all possible combinations and then measure their effects on impressions. Although the effort is more boring than amusing oneself with distorting face features in seemingly random ways, it enables researchers to identify the importance of the variations of every single feature. Confirming the artists' intuitions, Brunswik and Reiter found that judgments changed systematically rather than randomly as the facial features changed. The height of the mouth, for example, was the most important feature, with high mouths leading to impressions of happiness, youth, unintelligence, and lack of energy. All these differences in impressions emerged from differences in extremely simple drawings.

Take a look for yourself. Which of the two faces in Figure 2.5 is more energetic?

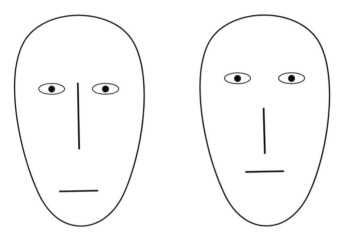

FIGURE 2.5. We easily form impressions from schematic faces. Which of the two faces is more energetic?

In a partial replication of Brunswik and Reiter's findings, Myra Samuels selected the drawings most consistently ranked at the extremes (the most energetic face had a high forehead, normal mouth, long nose, and eyes close together; the least energetic face had a low forehead, high mouth, short nose, and eyes close together), and asked participants to pick the "correct" face. Note that in both drawings the eyes are close together (you did not find a typo in the sentence above), although they seem farther apart in the "unenergetic" face. This is part of the strange effects of face perception, a topic we will return to in Chapter 4. In Samuels's study, the overwhelming majority of participants picked the "correct" face—the one on the left—as being more energetic. Samuels went on to show similar effects for real faces matched as best as possible to the schematic faces, although the agreement on the photographs was far less impressive.

These studies using overly simplistic stimuli don't quite identify the content of the "pictures in our heads." And experimental methods, as systematic as they are, may not be the best way to discover this content. This discovery, the topic of the second part of the book, would have to await the development of modern methods. But the studies show that our face stereotypes are not random or completely subjective. We agree on our first impressions, and these impressions can be manipulated.

• • • • •

The skillful, experimental manipulation of facial features to evoke different impressions had to wait for the next generation of researchers after Secord. These researchers moved beyond establishing agreement on impressions and proposed theories about the origins and content of these impressions. The most influential among them was Leslie Zebrowitz from Brandeis University. She introduced a distinctly theoretical perspective with great explanatory power.

Take a look at Figure 2.6. Can you pick out the profile of the baby or the boy? Three-year-olds can do this task. These profiles were not drawn by an artist but generated by a mathematical algorithm simulating how our heads change as we age. Relative to the rest of the face, our foreheads become smaller, and our chins larger and more prominent. The relative position of our eyes also moves upward.

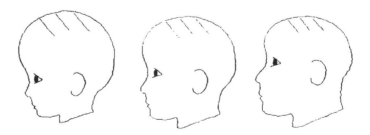

FIGURE 2.6. Can you pick out the baby? As we age, the shape of our faces changes.

Zebrowitz and her colleagues have shown that we are highly sensitive to these changes. Moreover, we attribute different characteristics to people whose faces resemble the faces of younger or older adults, even when these people are of the same age. "Babyfaced" adults are perceived as physically weak, naïve, submissive, honest, kind, and warm. Zebrowitz had an elegant theory to explain all this. We are attuned to differences in faces that matter in our social environments. Age is one such difference that carries a lot of information about the mental and physical capabilities of an individual. Babies are not as smart as adults, they are physically weak, need protection, and cannot hurt us; adults are smart, they are physically strong, can take care of themselves, and can hurt us. Because the detection of age differences is important for our normal social functioning, we are extremely sensitive to these differences. As a result, even when people are of the same age, we base our impressions on the similarity of their faces to the facial prototypes of different ages. In the language of the theory, we overgeneralize.

We can use Zebrowitz's theory to understand persistent physiognomic beliefs. While Grose advised artists in the eighteenth century on how to use convex and concave profiles to achieve humorous effects, physiognomists in the early twentieth century took these profiles to reveal character. In almost every book on physiognomy, the convex and concave shapes of faces and various facial parts are discussed. Here is a description by two of the more famous "character analysts" of the time, Katherine Blackford and Arthur Newcomb: "the significance of the pure convex type is energy, both mental and physical. Superabundance of energy makes the extreme convex keen, alert, quick, eager, aggressive, impatient, positive, and penetrating." The pure concave, of course, is the opposite: "The keynote of his character is mildness. His concave nose is an indication of moderate or deficient energy. He is slow of thought, slow of action, patient in disposition, plodding." Hull took these ideas so seriously that he designed a special instrument to measure the convexity of face profiles. Alas, there was little evidence that convexity reveals character. But where are these ideas coming from? Take another look at Figure 2.6. As we age, the shape of our profiles changes from relatively concave to relatively convex. And some of the characteristics that the physiognomists attributed to these shapes go along with our knowledge of what babies and adults are like. Zebrowitz's theory can explain not only why we form these impressions but also the origins of persistent physiognomic beliefs.

This is even clearer when the theory is applied to other physiognomic beliefs. Let's take the chin: "a small deficient chin stands for weakness of will and physical endurance." In contrast, "the strong, large but well-proportioned chin stands for mental backbone . . . and also tremendous physical energy and endurance." Take a look at Figure 2.7. Our chins do get stronger and larger as we age, and the physiognomic attributions follow these changes.

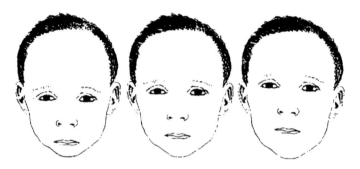

FIGURE 2.7. As we age, our chins become larger and more pronounced.

Whether the differences in our adult chins reveal our endurance is another matter. Remember the chin of the worst American president—Warren Harding—"perhaps the strongest [chin] of any of our Presidents," indicating that "there is strong will-power and great endurance combined in one chin."

Most of us like babies, puppies, kittens, and all kinds of beasty babies in general. Across many species, these babies share similar head features: bulging foreheads, receding chins, and large eyes. The famous ethologist Konrad Lorenz argued that observing such juvenile features automatically triggers nurturing responses. We generalize from our response to human babies not only to adults with "babyfaced" appearance but also to beasty babies. These responses also go with our impressions. Recently, Zebrowitz has shown that we perceive adult lions, Labradors, and foxes with more babyfaced appearances than their peers to be less dominant than those peers. These impressions also shape cultural creations. In an essay on the "evolutionary" transformation of Mickey Mouse, Steven Jay Gould documents how the Disney character has acquired more juvenile features over the ages. Mickey from the 1950s has a larger head (relative to his body), a larger cranium, and larger eyes than Mickey from the 1930s. As he acquired a more pleasing and proper personality than the troublemaker from the 1930s, he also changed his appearance.

When Zebrowitz started her work on first impressions, this was not a hot topic in psychology. But she persevered despite her nonprominent chin. Here I have singled out our sensitivity to age differences as revealed in faces, but the list of our attunements to facial differences is much larger. Whether the face is masculine or feminine shapes our impressions of the person. This comes from the importance of knowing the sex of others and all the associations we have about the different sexes. Whether the face wears a welcoming or disgruntled expression shapes our impressions, too. This comes from the importance of knowing the emotional states of others and our expectations of the behaviors associated with these states. After more than 30 years, Zebrowitz's perspective continues to be one of the dominant perspectives in the field.

· · · · ·

It is easy to discard the physiognomists, but they were on to something. Deep down, their intuitions align with ours. We have an immediate "gut" response to the appearances of others. Here is a little demonstration of how easy it is to make a decision based on appearance. Take a look at Figure 2.8. You are walking into a party, and these are the first two people you see.

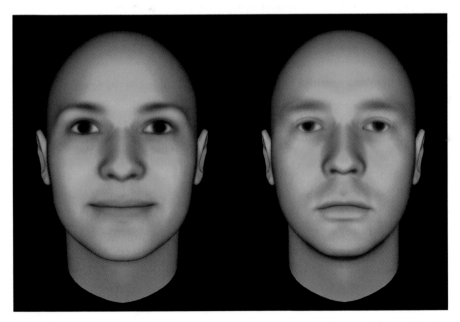

FIGURE 2.8. Visualizing impressions of extroverted and introverted faces. This work is described in Chapter 6.

Who would you approach? If you are like most people and you are at the party to have fun and not to console others, the choice is obvious and immediate. The person on the left appears extroverted and ready to have fun. It is hard to imagine a better companion for the party. The images are compelling, because they capture the consensus on impressions of extroversion and introversion. These images were not produced by an artist but by brute empirical force. Nick Oosterhof, a Dutch computer scientist who later became a neuroscientist, and I created a computer model of this consensus. As long as there is agreement on impressions, we can build precise models of these impressions and visualize them.

Agreement on first impressions emerges surprisingly fast from remarkably little information. In one of our first studies on first impressions, the one predicting the outcomes of the U.S. Senate elections, participants were asked to make competence judgments of pairs of politicians after a 1-second presentation of their faces. Judging faces in 1 second may seem ridiculous, but 1 second, the time to pronounce "twenty-one," is an exceedingly long time for automatic, perceptual processes. Prompted by our initial findings, we then tested whether people can form impressions after seeing faces for much shorter durations. We presented our participants with faces flashed for 100 milliseconds (a tenth of a second), 500 milliseconds, or a full second just as in our previous study. We thought that people would be able to make such character judgments as trustworthiness, aggressiveness, and competence only after longer presentation of the faces. After all, one-tenth of a second is just one-tenth of a second. We were wrong. One-tenth of a second of viewing provided ample face information for our participants to make up their minds. The effect of additional time was to simply increase confidence in their judgments.

In Princeton, all undergraduate students write a senior thesis with a faculty advisor of their choosing. The work described above was the thesis of Janine Willis. In the rush of excitement and the confines of the short academic year, we did not do the best possible job, technically speaking. If you want to be sure that an image is presented for a specific amount of (short) time, the image should be replaced by another image like a meaningless gray cloud after the intended time expires. In psychology lingo, this is called perceptual masking. Were you to present the same face for 100 or 500 milliseconds without a masking image, you would barely notice the difference in duration. The image persists in your awareness. Were you to present the face with a mask, the difference is striking. Experimental psychologists spend a lot of time thinking and worrying about these kinds of issues. In our studies, we had text (a question about the impression) replacing the face immediately after the intended presentation time, but this was not a proper perceptual mask covering the image.

Our study was published in 2006. That same year, the neuroscientist Moshe Bar and his colleagues published another study. They used proper masking and even shorter presentations of faces—26 and 39 milliseconds. After 26 milliseconds, participants' judgments did not show much agreement with judgments made after a substantially longer presentation of almost 2 seconds. But after 39 milliseconds, the agreement was substantial. The difference is that perceptually masked images presented for 26 milliseconds are below the visual awareness of most people. We simply don't see the images. Images presented for 39 milliseconds are in the visual awareness of most people. We did not know that Moshe was working on a similar problem, but that made the convergent findings even more rewarding. Since then many subsequent replications of our findings have been done. You need as little as 30 to 40 milliseconds of exposure to a face to form an impression of it. This is so fast that the face is barely visible. These impressions do not change with face presentations longer than about 200 milliseconds. Impressions from faces are literally single-glance impressions.

Agreement on first impressions emerges not only fast but also early in development. Emily Cogsdill, Liz Spelke, and Mahzarin Banaji from Harvard University and I studied the impressions formed by kids as young as 3 to 4 years old. The kids were shown pairs of face images like the ones in Figure 2.9 and asked to point to the person "who is very nice." The faces were generated by a model of impressions of trustworthiness based on adult judgments. Adults judge the face on the left as trustworthy and that on the right as untrustworthy even after as little as 33 milliseconds' presentation of the face.

We did not torture the kids with super short presentations of faces. We were only interested in whether their impressions are like adults' impressions. They were. Just like adults, more than 75 percent of the kids pointed to the "trustworthy" face when asked to identify the nicer person. The findings were similar when the kids were deciding who is strong (faces were generated by a model of impressions of dominance) or who is smart (faces were generated by a model of impressions of competence).

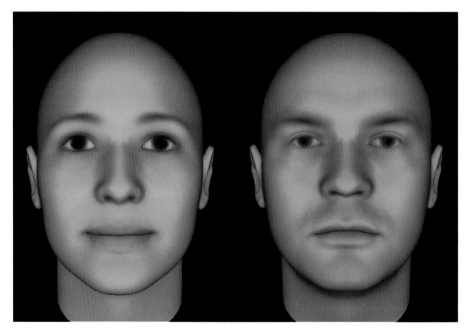

FIGURE 2.9. Visualizing impressions of trustworthy and untrustworthy faces.

It turned out that 3-year-olds are already too old to study when it comes to understanding the emergence of first impressions. Recently, the German psychologists Sarah Jessen and Tobias Grossmann studied 7-month-old infants. To be precise, the infants' average age was 213 days. The venerable behavioral measure of attention in babies (and monkeys) is looking time. As babies are nonverbal and have trouble following instructions, researchers need to revert to studying their spontaneous behaviors in controlled settings. In the preferential looking paradigm, infants are typically presented with a pair of images. The proportion of time they spend looking at the images indicates their relative interest. At the very least, different looking times indicate that infants discriminate between these images. So Jessen and Grossmann had the infants look at pairs of faces generated by the model of impressions of trustworthiness (Figure 2.9). As shown in Figure 2.10, the infant was comfortably seated on the lap of their parent in front of a board with two images of faces attached to it. Before the beginning of each trial, the two faces were covered with black cloth. After the cloth was removed, the infant had 30 seconds to look at the faces. During this time, the parent either closed his or her eyes or looked away to avoid influencing the behavior of the

FIGURE 2.10. Studying the visual preferences of 7-month-old infants for trustworthy vs. untrustworthy looking faces. The infants had 30 seconds to look at a pair of faces. The researchers measured the proportion of time they spent looking at each of the faces.

infant. If the infant was distracted and looked away, the experimenter tapped on the middle of the board. The infants preferred to look at the "trustworthy" rather than at the "untrustworthy" faces.

In a different experimental situation, Erik Cheries, Ashley Lyons, and Rachel Rosen from the University of Massachusetts Amherst and I obtained similar findings for slightly older infants. In our study, 11-month-old infants were placed in a crawling position facing two equally distant buckets. One of the buckets had a "trustworthy" face attached to it and the other an "untrustworthy" face, both faces generated from our model of impressions of trustworthiness (Figure 2.9). Once the infant was facing the two buckets with faces, the experimenter showed a graham cracker to him or her, exclaimed "Look what I have. I have a yummy graham cracker," and ate the cracker. After this demonstration, the experimenter placed three crackers in each of the buckets, and the infant was allowed to crawl and retrieve the crackers. As we expected, the majority of infants crawled toward the bucket with a "trustworthy" face.

These studies show that the cues identified by the model of impressions of trustworthiness were sufficiently strong to be picked up by the infants. Some of these cues have to do with subtle differences in expressions (did you notice the differences in Figure 2.9?). By 7 months, infants have observed enough positive and negative expressions to be able to discriminate among them.

· · · · ·

Physiognomists got a few things right. Faces immediately capture our attention. Studies recording eye movements show that when we look at scenes containing faces, the vast majority of the first eye fixations are on the face. And it takes a little more than one-tenth of a second for our eyes to land on the face. There is no other object that attracts our attention so rapidly. Attention to faces is reflexive. Faces are so important to us that we even see them in clouds and random objects. The demonstrations of how we tend to see faces in random objects range from cute books for children showing various vegetables formed as animated faces to artsy books showing everyday objects, like the ones in Figure 2.11.

FIGURE 2.11. The photographers François Robert and Jean Robert take pictures of objects that resemble faces. We see these objects not only as faces but also as having distinct personalities.

Our immediate attention to faces is accompanied by attributions of likes or dislikes, of emotional and mental states, and of character. We don't simply see the objects in Figure 2.11 as faces. The "earphones fellow" is a happy, excitable, talkative dude. The "yellow fellow" is distressed and unhappy. Not so for the "red fellow," who is ready to play like a puppy. The "mop fellow" is skinny, serious, and tired. As Töpffer argued long ago, by virtue of its existence, every facial image is meaningful.

The agreement on our first impressions makes physiognomy possible. The ease with which we dispatch impressions makes the physiognomists' promise appealing. Physiognomists used the wrong methods and reached the wrong conclusions, but they were right that we can't help but form impressions. Unfortunately, even if forming impressions based on looks may be hilarious, their consequences often are not. We explore these consequences in the next chapter.

3

CONSEQUENTIAL IMPRESSIONS

In the early twentieth century, Katherine Blackford and Arthur Newcomb devised a "scientific plan of employment" to find the best employees for the job. Many of their arguments, if not their methods, were quite sensible, and they advocated for the creation of employment departments, the equivalent of Human Resources today. Blackford and Newcomb's solution for the problem of finding the best employees was to match the character of the employee to the character of the job. The tool was physiognomy, although they preferred to refer to the science of "character analysis."

Describing the interview selection process, they advised the interviewer to be extremely courteous and friendly. After making you feel comfortable and briefly discussing your qualifications, the interviewer would ask you to fill out an application form for the position. While you are doing this, the most important part of the selection process begins. The expert interviewer, trained by Blackford and Newcomb, "does not know what you are writing. But from external signs and indications which you cannot conceal he is learning something about your natural aptitudes, about your character, and about the use you have made of the talents with which nature has endowed you. In making these notes he uses Blank No. 3, Analysis." Check out Blank No. 3 in Figure 3.1.

The interviewer does not simply check the color of your hair and the shape of your head. She analyzes your character. The process is secretive, and the objective of making you comfortable in the beginning of the interview is to preclude your suspicions. You are not supposed to know that you are being analyzed. Blank No. 3 is "filled out in cipher so that it is unintelligible to any except the employment supervisor and his staff. In general, it is a complete

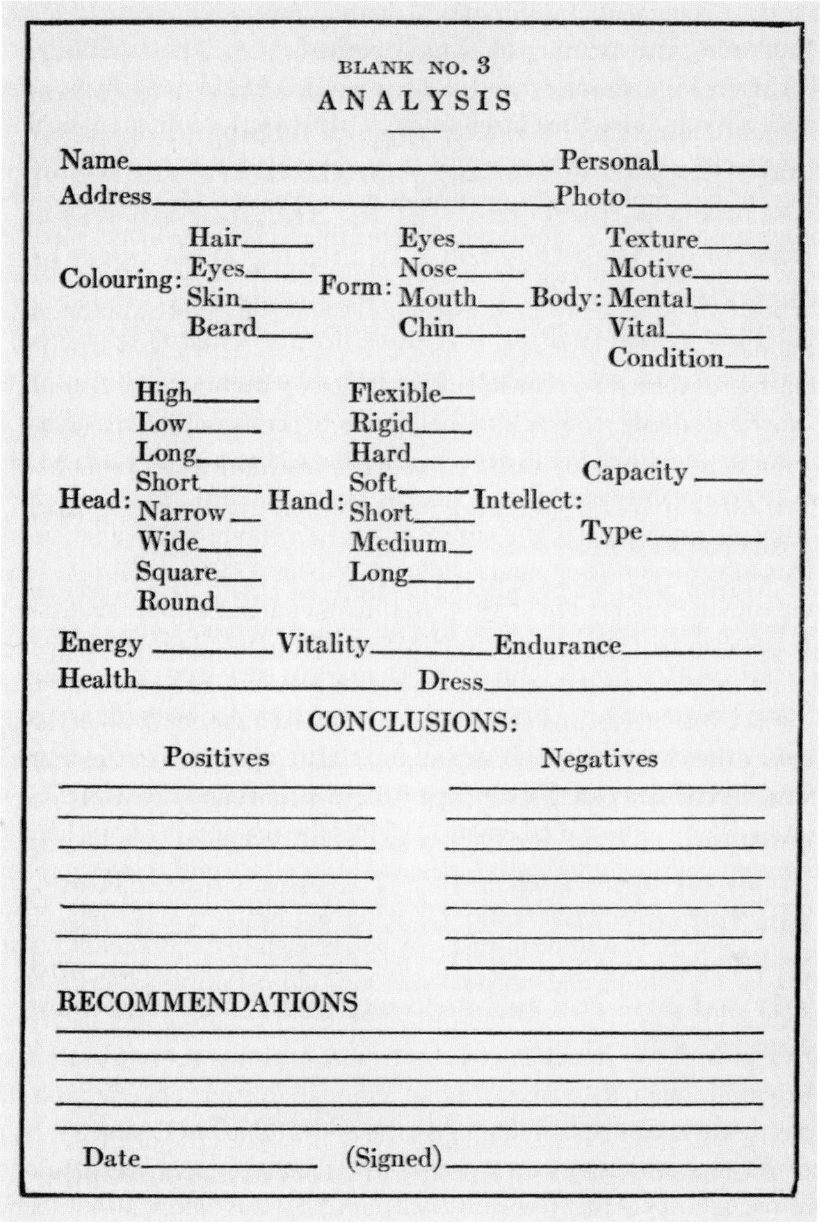

BLANK NO. 3
ANALYSIS

Name_____ Personal_____

Address_____ Photo_____

Colouring: Hair_____ Eyes_____
Eyes_____ Form: Nose_____ Texture_____
Skin_____ Mouth_____ Body: Motive_____
Beard_____ Chin_____ Mental_____
Vital_____
Condition_____

High_____ Flexible—
Low_____ Rigid_____
Long_____ Hard_____
Short_____ Soft_____ Capacity_____
Head: Narrow_____ Hand: Short_____ Intellect:
Wide_____ Medium_____ Type_____
Square_____ Long_____
Round_____

Energy _____ Vitality_____ Endurance_____

Health_____ Dress_____

CONCLUSIONS:

Positives   Negatives

_____   _____
_____   _____
_____   _____
_____   _____
_____   _____
_____   _____
_____   _____

RECOMMENDATIONS

_____
_____
_____
_____

Date_____ (Signed)_____

FIGURE 3.1. The form to record the physical features of job applicants in Blackford and Newcomb's "scientific" plan of employment. Blackford and Newcomb believed that they could identify the best employees from a character analysis of faces.

but concise statement of your physical, mental, and psychical characteristics and aptitudes, your training and your experience."

For many jobs, an interview was not even needed. In one instance, there was a request for hire of eighteen workers to fill fourteen different positions like carpenter, crane operator, and a man for assembly work. An expert assistant in the employment department took the list and "walking quickly through the hundred or more men gathered there, chose the men wanted, one by one." Another expert assistant could immediately tell who was chosen for what position. Apparently, these assistants were well trained by Blackford and Newcomb.

Blackford worked as a consultant for large corporations. She also worked for Harrington Emerson, one of the leaders of the "scientific management" movement, who hired her to develop selection techniques for his firm. More than 200 companies used the services of Emerson's firm. Blackford was not the only physiognomist in the service of business. There was Holmes Merton and his Institute for Vocational Guidance, William Kibby and The Personnel Company, and many others. More and more companies were requesting a photograph as part of the application process. From the photograph, they can not only see the race and gender of the candidates but also read their physiognomies. Blackford considered photographs far superior to interviews in revealing the character of job applicants. Unaffected by the style of the applicant, the character analyst can "apply the principles and laws of the science relentlessly and almost mathematically." Despite the efforts of psychologists to discredit physiognomy, the business world and the world at large remained receptive to physiognomic ideas. As psychologists Donald Laird and Herman Remmers put it, "that some insight may be gained into mental characteristics by the facial contour and expression is [an] almost universal belief at the present day."

The "present day" was 1924. I am not aware of any large-scale applications of "scientific character analysis" today, although this must be the marketing dream of the Israeli facial profiling start-up mentioned in Chapter 1. In any case, the analysis has not disappeared from business practices. One of the front-page stories of the *New York Times* on Christmas day in 2014 was about the hiring of a face reader by the Milwaukee Bucks, an NBA team. The face reader had already worked for NFL and college teams. The Bucks were hoping that he could help them with the selection of players. The team psychologist called him their "secret weapon." By the end of the season, the Bucks won as many games as they lost. They managed to make the playoffs, but lost in the first round. Things might be better for them in the next season, but I would not bet my money on their secret weapon. I would bet my money on unorthodox sports managers like Billy Beane, the general manager of Oakland A's, one of the poorest MLB teams with one of the best winning records. Beane's secret weapon was to exploit the prejudices of appearance: to select baseball players who did not look the part but had outstanding performance records. These players consistently failed to impress scouts and were chronically undervalued in the market of players. In the words of Michael Lewis, who describes the unlikely success of the Oakland A's in his fascinating book *Moneyball*, "what begins as a failure of the imagination ends as a market inefficiency: when you rule out an entire class of people from doing a job simply by their appearance, you are less likely to find the best person for the job."

• • • • •

I became interested in studying first impressions after my students and I discovered that such impressions can predict the outcomes of important political elections. First impressions mattered. I was in my first few years as an assistant professor at Princeton with a tiny lab consisting of one half-time research assistant and two graduate students. There was no easy way to collect data online at the time, so we participated in one of the Questionnaire days organized by the department of psychology. These Q-days were advertised among students on campus, and those willing to trade 1 hour of their time for $10 or so were handed a thick bundle of questionnaires to fill out. Buried among those were some of our questionnaires presenting pairs of images of the winner and the runner-up from all Senate races in the United States for 2000 and 2002, excluding races with highly recognizable politicians like Hillary Clinton and John Kerry. Different students were assigned different questions like "Who looks more competent?" and "Who looks more honest?" We were hoping that some of these questions would predict who won the elections. When we analyzed the data, our hopes were surpassed. Judgments of who appeared more competent predicted about 70 percent of the elections. A general rule of science is that results should be replicable, especially if these results are surprising. So we put everything else on hold and started preparing new questionnaires. I even hired an undergraduate student to help with the preparation. Then the results came back, and it looked like our appearance judgments predicted nothing. They were at chance. That is, on average the winner was judged to be more competent than the runner-up in 50 percent of the cases. Flipping a coin to decide who won the race would give you the same result.

I could not sleep that night. I was thinking that we simply got lucky the first time, and it was time to cut our losses and move on to new projects. But I could not think of anything else in the next couple of days. I started going over the images in the questionnaires, trying to figure out why the new results were so different from the old ones. It turned out that the undergraduate student I hired to help made a mistake. When you do a computer-based experiment, you typically randomize the order of the stimuli for each participant to rule out the possibility that whatever effects are observed result from the specific order. This is trivial to do when the experiment is programmed on a computer, but much more difficult for paper-and-pencil questionnaire studies. In this particular case, I generated a few random orders of the Senate races, say, in order 1 the Senate race for Minnesota is first, the New Jersey race is second, and the Rhode Island race is fifteenth. The task of the student was to prepare several sets of questionnaires, each set with a particular order of the Senate races. Copying and pasting many images could be confusing, and the orders that the student produced were different from the ones I asked her to produce. Because the statistical analyses were based on my order, the results were at chance. In essence, it was like taking the judgments from the faces of the New Jersey politicians and trying to predict from these judgments the outcome of the race in Minnesota. After taking the correct order into account, we had a nice replication of our initial results. I have never been so happy to discover a serious error by one of my research assistants. After a couple of other replications, we eventually wrote up the findings, and the paper was published in *Science*. The publication spurred replications by different research groups and in different countries. This phenomenon was not limited to American elections.

• • • • •

Before our findings were published, I applied for funding for this research. The way funding applications work is that you write a research proposal and the proposal is reviewed by anonymous reviewers. The reviews covered the whole range from the very positive to the very negative. You can guess which ones are weighted more heavily in funding decisions. One of the reviewers basically wrote that the kinds of effects we had documented—naïve judgments from facial appearance predicting political elections—must only occur in my lab. In their words, "before I would find these proposed studies at all compelling, I would like to see some evidence that this situation occurs anywhere outside of the P.I.'s laboratory." The "P.I." stands for me, the principal investigator. Needless to say, I did not get the funding.

After the findings were published, I received my first hate e-mail. I still don't understand what instigated it, but its author was irritated by our "trivial" results. Buried among the profanities, he actually had a plausible alternative explanation of our findings. According to him, it was patently obvious that the observed effects were due to media exposure. Although our participants did not explicitly recognize the faces of the politicians, they must have been exposed to these faces and this exposure made them rate more familiar politicians as more competent. If more familiar politicians are more likely to be the winners, this could explain our results. Though plausible, this hypothesis turned out to be false.

The right way to question unexpected findings is to conduct replication studies and test alternative explanations. In this case, political scientists were the first to test trivial explanations that had to do with differences in image quality of the pictures or campaign spending. Such differences could not explain the appearance effects on election outcomes. Differences in gender and race also could not explain them. In fact, we obtained our best results when the prediction was limited to elections in which the candidates were matched on race and gender. Familiarity with the candidates' faces could not explain the effects. As mentioned in the Prologue, my favorite replication was the study of Antonakis and Dalgas, in which Swiss children's judgments predicted the outcomes of past French parliamentary elections. Some of the kids in the study were not even born when these elections were conducted. In other replications in Europe, judgments of American and Swedish participants predicted the outcomes of Finnish elections. Abby Sussman, one of my graduate students, Kristina Petkova, a Bulgarian colleague, and I used judgments of Americans to predict the 2011 presidential elections in Bulgaria, the country where I grew up. These elections are interesting, because there is a very low threshold for entering the race and, as a result, many candidates take part: eighteen in this particular year. It was sad to see one of my professors from Sofia University doing very poorly in terms of both appearance judgments and electoral votes. Finally, the political scientists Gabriel Lenz and Chapel Lawson had American and Indian participants rate the faces of Mexican and

Brazilian politicians. Although the cultures of the raters and the politicians were deliberately chosen to be very different, the raters agreed in their judgments of the politicians, and these judgments predicted the outcomes of the elections.

· · · · ·

But how does this really work in the real world? For one thing, participants in psychology experiments and certainly kids are not representative of those who actually vote. For another, it is hard to imagine that political partisans are voting based on the appearance of candidates. What they care about is the political affiliation of these candidates, not their looks. Lawson and Lenz have done great research to figure out how it might work in the real world. Studying real voters, they found that appearance only affects those who know next to nothing about politics. Being glued to the TV most of the time makes the effect of appearance even stronger. In other words, appearance has its biggest effects on politically ignorant couch potatoes. Some of them are the swing or undecided voters.

Lenz and Lawson's findings make perfect sense to psychologists. One of the successful metaphors describing the mind is "cognitive miser." When we need to make a decision, particularly when we have little knowledge, we rely on shortcuts: hunches, "gut" responses, stereotypes. We use shortcuts because it is easy. We are ready to leap to conclusions, especially when we are too lazy or busy to look for hard evidence. And most of us are cognitively lazy or busy some of the time. When it comes to decisions about strangers, the easiest, most accessible shortcut is our first impression. Unknowledgeable voters go for this shortcut.

Do the effects obtained in contrived lab demonstrations make a difference in the real world? In close races, unknowledgeable or "appearance-based" voters can sway the outcome of the races. Lenz and Lawson estimated that candidates who appear slightly more competent than their opponents can get as much as 5 percent more votes from unknowledgeable, TV-loving voters. Recently, Lenz and his students conducted experiments with voters in California and eighteen other states. In the 2 weeks before election day, voters were shown ballots either with or without pictures of the candidates and were asked to express their intention to vote. Depending on the race—primary or general—when the voters saw the pictures, the best looking candidates got a boost of between 10 and 20 percent over the appearance-disadvantaged candidates. Lenz estimated that the looks of the candidates could have changed the outcomes of 29 percent of the races in primary elections and 14 percent of those in the general elections. These results are quite remarkable, because the experimental design rules out the possibility that factors like candidate effort and spending can explain the effects of appearance. The only difference between the voters in the two experimental conditions was the presence or absence of pictures on the ballot.

One uninteresting explanation of these experimental results is that once presented with the candidates' pictures, the voters find their influence irresistible and this irresistible, immediate influence inflates the effect of appearance on votes. We should be grateful that ballots in the United States—unlike in Brazil, Belgium, Greece, and Ireland—do not include pictures of the candidates. But for all we know the effect of appearance may have been underestimated. Many voters in the no-picture ballot group knew how the candidates look, which should have minimized the difference between their choices and the choices of voters in the picture ballot group. This possibility is testable. Lenz and colleagues reasoned that as the campaign gets closer to election day, the effect of appearance should increase in the control group (the group that did not have pictures on their ballots). The reason is that voters should be more and more likely to be exposed to images of the candidates. This is what Lenz and colleagues found. If anything, the effect of appearance seemed to decrease in the experimental group, which had pictures on the ballot, presumably because voters are finding other information about the candidates that influences their choices. These secondary analyses suggest that the effects of appearance on votes cannot be completely explained by the fact that the voters in the experimental group saw the candidates' pictures; and that the actual effects can be even larger than the estimated effects. Another depressing finding was that political knowledge did not inoculate voters against appearance in congressional primaries where multiple candidates from the same party were competing against one another.

Occasionally, Abraham Lincoln is described as "appearance-disadvantaged," with the implication that he would not have been a successful politician in modern times. This is a debatable point. Lincoln was the first presidential candidate to use pictures in the electoral campaign, and he paid attention to the potential effects of his appearance. He grew a beard to improve his appearance, possibly on the advice of a group of fellow Republicans who "have come to the candid determination that these medals would be much improved in appearance, provided you cultivate whiskers and wear standing colors."

● ● ● ● ●

One of the most surprising findings in our studies was the specificity of the appearance effect. One particular judgment—competence—was by far the best predictor of the election outcomes. Before our work, there was some research suggesting that more-attractive politicians are more likely to be elected. But more-competent looking candidates on average tend to be more attractive, too. When you pit these two against each other, perceived competence is a much stronger predictor of electoral success than attractiveness is. As it turned out, we were not the first to discover that competence judgments predict elections better than other judgments. When we were describing our findings, we conducted a thorough search of the literature to make sure that we did not miss relevant studies. In a 1978 paper in the *Australian Journal of Psychology*, D. S. Martin reported that judgments of competence, but not of pleasantness, from faces predicted the outcomes of a local Australian election. Our "original" findings were not that original after all.

About 30 years ago, another pioneering study was conducted by the political scientist Shawn Rosenberg and his colleagues. After showing that people easily rank photographs of middle-aged men on their suitability for congressional office ("the kind of person you would want to represent you in the United States Congress"), they created voting flyers with photographs of "highly suitable" and "less suitable" candidates. Incidentally, attractiveness was not part of the package of Congress suitability: the "highly suitable" were no more attractive than the "less suitable" candidates. The flyers presented not only the candidates' photographs but also information about their party affiliation and policy positions. Despite the presence of this information, the appearance-advantaged candidates garnered about 60 percent of the votes of the experimental participants.

But why is perceived competence so important? Voting choices even by uninformed voters are not completely irrational. When you ask people about the most important characteristic of their ideal political representative, competence is on the top of the list. How well these perceived characteristics predict elections depends on the assigned importance to them. Voters don't care one way or another whether their representative is extroverted, and judgments of extroversion do not predict who is going to win the election. But voters care about whether their representative is competent, and judgments of competence do predict the winner. What appearance-influenced voters are doing is substituting a hard decision with an easy one. Finding out whether a politician is truly competent takes effort and time. Deciding whether a politician looks competent is an extremely easy task. Appearance-influenced voters are looking for the right information in the wrong place, because it is easy to do so.

● ● ● ● ●

In psychology, we make a distinction between relatively automatic, effortless processes and relatively deliberate, controlled processes. The Nobel laureate Daniel Kahneman describes the many ways in which these processes differ in his wonderful book *Thinking, Fast and Slow*. Like perceiving objects and orienting to a loud sound, forming impressions from faces is an example of an automatic process. There are many ways to demonstrate the automatic nature of these impressions. One is to present faces for a very brief time; another is to force participants to form impressions much faster than they would ordinarily do. None of this prevents the forming of impressions or changes their nature.

From Janine Willis's thesis (see Chapter 2), we already knew that people could form impressions after extremely brief presentations of faces. A couple of years later, Chas Ballew, another talented undergraduate student, continued this line of work. For his thesis, we revisited our earlier political election studies. We flashed pairs of pictures of the winners and runner-ups in gubernatorial elections—the most important elections in the United States next to the presidential election—for 100 milliseconds, 250 milliseconds, or until the participant responded. Just like in the work of Janine, one-tenth of a second was enough for participants to make competence judgments, and these judgments predicted the election outcomes. In fact, predictions did not get better with longer presentation of the images. When given unlimited time to look at the images, participants took 3.5 seconds on average to decide whom of the two politicians looked more competent. In our second study, we made them respond within a 2-second window. Their judgments predicted the outcomes of the elections just as well as when they had unlimited time to respond. The participants' judgments were particularly poor at predicting the outcomes for only one condition: asking them to deliberate and make a good judgment. This may seem surprising at first sight, but there wasn't really anything for the participants to deliberate about. We don't form first impressions by deliberating; they come to us spontaneously. These instructions simply added noise to participants' judgments.

Occasionally, appearance is explicitly evoked as a reason for a candidate endorsement. As Bob Dole—a runner-up against Bill Clinton in the 1996 presidential election—commented on the 2012 Republican presidential nomination, "so it looked to me like it would be either Romney or Newt [Gingrich] for the nomination, but . . . Romney *looks* like a president." Our findings suggest that the influence of appearance may be less explicit and not easily recognized by voters. Character judgments from faces occur remarkably quickly and operate with minimal input from controlled processes. And they matter most under conditions that lead to greater reliance on shortcuts in decisions. In the case of elections, these conditions include lack of knowledge, low stakes, high costs of obtaining information when there are many candidates rather than two, and candidate-centered rather than party-centered elections. All these conditions increase the effect of appearance on voters' choices.

• • • • •

Competence is perceived as the most important characteristic of politicians. But what people perceive as an important characteristic can change in different situations. Imagine that it is wartime, and you have to cast your presidential vote today. Would you vote for the face on the left or the one on the right in Figure 3.2? Most people quickly go with the face on the left. What if it is peacetime? Most people now go with the face on the right. This preference reversal is so easy to obtain that I often use it in class demonstrations.

These images were created by Anthony Little and his colleagues in the United Kingdom. The face on the left is perceived as more dominant, more masculine, and as that of a stronger leader; attributes that matter in wartime. The face on the right is perceived as more intelligent, forgiving, and likeable; attributes that matter more in peacetime. Now look at the images in Figure 3.3. You should be able to recognize past President George W. Bush and former Secretary of State John Kerry. Back then when the study was done, John Kerry was the Democratic candidate running against George W. Bush for the American presidency. Can you see some similarities between the faces on the left in Figures 3.2 and 3.3, and between the faces on the right in Figures 3.2 and 3.3? The teaser is that the images in Figure 3.2 show what makes the faces

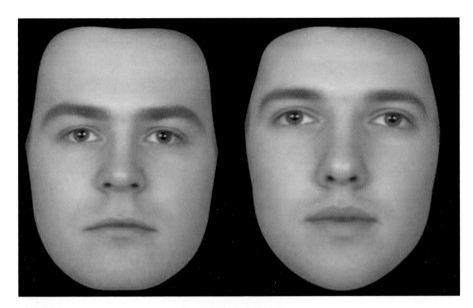

FIGURE 3.2. Who would you vote for in wartime? Who would you vote for in peacetime?

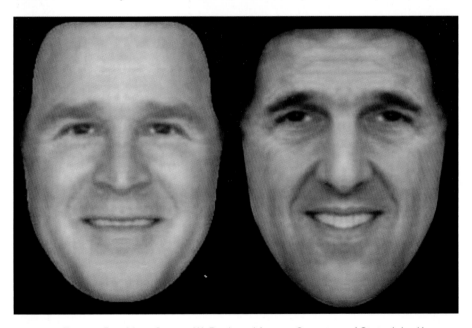

FIGURE 3.3. Former President George W. Bush and former Secretary of State John Kerry. Do you see the similarity between the face on the left in Figure 3.2 and Bush's face; and between the face on the right in Figure 3.2 and Kerry's face? The faces in Figure 3.2 visualize what makes the faces of Bush and Kerry distinctive relative to a typical male face.

of George W. Bush and John Kerry distinctive. To obtain the distinctiveness of a face, you only need to find out what makes it different from an average face—in this case, a morph of about thirty male faces. The faces in Figure 3.2 were created by accentuating the differences between the shapes of Bush's and Kerry's faces and the shape of the average face. At the time of the election in 2004, the United States was at war with Iraq. I will leave the rest to your imagination.

What we consider an important characteristic also depends on our ideological inclinations. Take a look at Figure 3.4. Who would make a better leader?

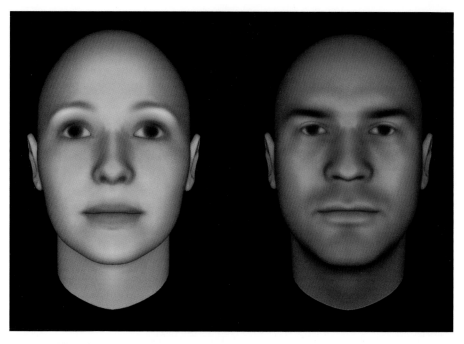

FIGURE 3.4. Visualizing impressions of nondominant and dominant faces. This work is described in Chapter 6.

The Danish researchers Lasse Laustsen and Michael Petersen used faces generated by our computer model of impressions of dominance and showed that whereas liberal voters tend to choose the face on the left, conservative voters tend to choose the one on the right. These preferences reflect our ideological stereotypes of right wing, masculine, dominant-looking leaders and left wing, feminine, nondominant-looking leaders. Turning to real elections in Denmark, Laustsen and Petersen replicated the competence effect: an appearance of competence benefited political candidates across the ideological spectrum. But the benefit of dominant appearance depended on the ideological orientation of the candidates. Whereas dominant-looking conservative candidates gained in votes, dominant-looking liberal candidates lost in votes, but only when they were men. Dominant looks were bad news for women candidates regardless of whether they were conservative or liberal. Gender stereotypes are hard to beat.

Laustsen and Petersen also manipulated the faces of actual politicians to look less or more dominant (Figure 3.5).

FIGURE 3.5. A Danish politician (original image in the middle) whose face is manipulated to look less (image on the left) or more dominant (image on the right).

When the politicians were not well known, this manipulation made a difference. Liberal participants were more receptive to the policy position of the candidate when he was made to look less dominant. In contrast, conservative participants were more receptive when he was made to look more dominant. The political situation or our ideological inclinations can change what we consider important, but they don't change our propensity to form impressions and act on these impressions.

• • • • •

Impressions shape not only our political decisions but also our economic decisions. J. P. Morgan heavily relied on character judgments when making loan decisions. As he put it, "a man I do not trust could not get money from me on all the bonds in Christendom." In long-term economic transactions, we can rely on reputation, which is established over repeated transactions. But many economic transactions are one-shot exchanges. The large majority of eBay transactions, for example, are one-shot. You may have feedback about the person you are trading with from other users, but this feedback is far from perfect. Not all users provide feedback; most of it is positive; and the rate of negative feedback is suspiciously low, because it is costly. Even services that thrive on providing accurate information to consumers, like Angie's List, have built-in mechanisms to bias this feedback. A negatively rated provider can try to appease the displeased customer, who in turn is expected to increase the rating of the service.

Just as in the case of electing politicians, appearance plays a large role in deciding whether to trust another person—especially in one-shot transactions where information about past behavior is sparse. Take a look at Figure 3.6. If you have to make an investment decision, whom would you entrust with your money?

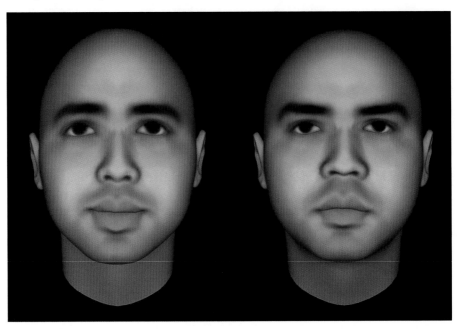

FIGURE 3.6. Applying a computer model of impressions of trustworthiness to a face to make it appear more (image on the left) or less (image on the right) trustworthy.

To most people, the face on the left appears more trustworthy and, hence, is more likely to receive the money. A research group in the United Kingdom, including one of my former graduate students, Chris Olivola, used faces generated by our model of impressions of trustworthiness to run an investment experiment. Participants played a series of online investment games with what they believed were real people represented by the faces on the screen. The game was a standard risky, economic game. If you decide to invest in your partner, your investment is tripled but is in the hands of your partner, who decides what to do with the money. A truly trustworthy partner should reciprocate and return half or more of this tripled amount to you. A truly untrustworthy person would keep all the money. The experimenters took unusual care to make sure the participants believed that they played with real people. The participants' pictures were taken and uploaded into a computer program that generated a computerized image of their face without hair that was not much different from the images of their "partners" in the games. If the participants were late by more than 5 minutes for the experiment, they were rescheduled for another session, presumably because they missed their appointment with their online partners. As expected, participants invested more in their trustworthy-looking partners. Surprisingly, this was the case even when participants were provided with information about the past investment behavior of their partners, the only useful piece of knowledge in this economic transaction.

We already saw that kids' impressions of faces parallel adults' impressions. In the study with my Harvard colleagues, 3- to 4-year-olds chose the trustworthy-looking faces as the nicer ones. An Australian research group led by Gillian Rhodes studied the trust behavior of 5- and 10-year-olds. The kids played "Token Quest." This game had the same structure as the investment experiment in the United Kingdom study, except that the kids "invested" tokens that looked like pieces of pirate treasure. Just like adults, both 5- and 10-year-olds invested more tokens in trustworthy-looking partners. The researchers also included rounds of the game in which the players could pay to see the faces of their partners. More than one-third of the adult participants paid. The kids were even more willing to see these faces.

These appearance effects are not confined to the lab. Field studies show that appearance matters a great deal in real economic transactions. One of my Princeton colleagues and friends, Eldar Shafir, conducted a study in South Africa where a bank sent loan applications to potential customers. Some of the loan applications included a picture of an attractive woman. The inclusion of the picture increased the participation of men, and the effect was equivalent to that of decreasing the interest rate of the loan by 3 percent. When he first told me about this finding, I exclaimed, "we [meaning men] are so shallow," to which he responded, "no, we are profoundly stupid." A study by economists on Prosper, one of the leading peer-to-peer lending sites in the United States, also finds large effects of appearance on lending behavior. On Prosper, borrowers submit loan requests, which can vary from $2,000 to $35,000, and lenders submit bids. If there are enough bids, the loan is funded. Borrowers are not expected to upload pictures of themselves, but some do. Apparently it is a good idea, as borrowers with pictures are more likely to receive loans. But not all pictures are created equal. Borrowers who look more trustworthy, but not necessarily more attractive, are more likely to get loans and to get lower interest rates on these loans. This is quite remarkable, as the site contains rich information about the borrowers, including credit history, debt-to-income ratio, income, and employment status.

Appearance can help or hurt not only people who need loans but also CEOs. Several studies have found that CEOs who look more competent (as measured by naïve judgments just like those in the election studies discussed earlier) lead more successful firms. Although these findings are often interpreted to mean that looks of competence reflect real competence, a more careful analysis of the data shows that the more successful firms simply hire better-looking CEOs. Economists from Duke University showed that the lucky CEOs with competent appearance were able to secure more profitable positions for themselves. Importantly, the competent looks only predicted the executives' compensation, *not* their firms' performance. In other words, these looks benefit the face owner but not the people hiring him or her. As the authors put it, "what you see is not necessarily what you get."

● ● ● ● ●

Impressions from facial appearance also shape legal decisions. The "Hilarious Game of First Impressions" described in Chapter 2 had quite a few impression cards related to criminality: the con artist, the criminal mastermind, the evil genius, the fugitive, the mobster, the one from that FBI poster at the post office. Finding the features of the face that diagnose devious personalities has been a longstanding physiognomic quest. Galton's invention of the composite photography was motivated by this quest. The first application of his technique was to photographs of prisoners.

In the 1920s and 1930s, following in the footsteps of Galton and Lombroso, the Harvard anthropologist Earnest Hooton collected extensive physical measures of more than 14,000 prisoners, about 1,200 "insane civilians," and about

2,000 "sane civilians" from ten different states. Just for the head and the face, twelve different measurements were made, ranging from the obvious ones like head circumference and face height to obscure ones like the maximum diameter between the zygomatic arches. Two books came out of this effort in 1939. The first one, *The American Criminal, Volume 1* (no other volumes came after that), weighs a little over 5 pounds and in the words of the author was "a desperately dull statistical work upon a depressing subject." The book indeed contains a number of statistics, and you can find, for example, that the prisoners in the Southwest had much more hair than those in Massachusetts. The latter, though, had much thicker beards and the highest percentage of concave profiles. As for body hair, Kentucky and Texas topped the list.

The second book, *Crime and the Man*, was meant to translate the dull statistical work into something regular folks could understand and was richly illustrated. You can see the sketch of the first-degree murderer in Figure 3.7.

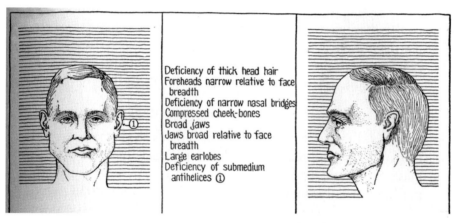

Deficiency of thick head hair
Foreheads narrow relative to face breadth
Deficiency of narrow nasal bridges
Compressed cheek-bones
Broad jaws
Jaws broad relative to face breadth
Large earlobes
Deficiency of submedium antihelices ①

FIGURE 3.7. An Illustration from Hooton's *Crime and the Man* (1939). The sketch is meant to represent first-degree murderers based on their distinctive morphological features.

Hooton was not just a random guy off the streets who claimed to know how to read character from faces. He was an eminent scientist, credited after his death for the training of the first generations of physical anthropologists in the United States. He was a member of the most prestigious scientific societies and a prolific writer, perhaps one of the first academics trying to reach the general public. He was more sophisticated than Lombroso and did not believe in the existence of clear criminal types: "no one but an anthropological ignoramus and a mathematical ass would conceive it possible to utilize for purposes of practical criminal diagnosis any rigid multiple combination of morphological features supposed to constitute a criminal type." But his illustrations like the one in Figure 3.7 were conveying the opposite idea. And ultimately, "a skillful and experienced anthropological observer" could identify such types. Identifying criminal types was important to stop "the degenerative trends in human evolution which are producing millions of animals of our species inferior in mind and in body." Identifying the criminals was just a small, first step. As in Galton's land of Kantsaywhere, the "habitual criminals who are hopeless constitutional inferiors should be permanently incarcerated and, on no account, should be allowed to breed." Although Hooton did not pay homage to Galton, Galton would have been pleased with Hooton's ultimate objective to "direct and control the progress of human evolution by breeding better types and by the ruthless elimination of inferior types."

• • • • •

Even if we find the quest for criminal physiognomic types distasteful, the "pictures in our heads" include such types. Take a look at Figure 3.8. Which face looks more criminal to you?

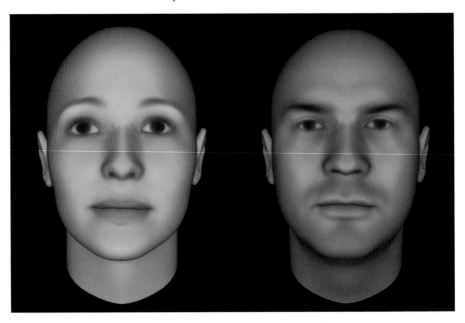

FIGURE 3.8. Visualizing impressions of noncriminal and criminal faces.

Just as we can build computer models of impressions of extroversion and trustworthiness, we can also build a model of impressions of criminality. If the faces in Figure 3.8 remind you of the faces from the model of trustworthiness (Figure 2.9) and the faces from the model of dominance (Figure 3.4), this is not a coincidence or a result of sloppy modeling. Impressions of untrustworthiness and dominance are essential components of the criminal stereotype. We can also apply these models to real faces and create "criminal" and "noncriminal" versions of the same face. Can you identify the criminal-looking version of the face in Figure 3.9? Most people quickly pick the face on the right.

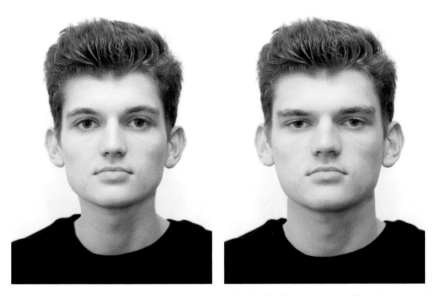

FIGURE 3.9. A face manipulated by using a model of criminal appearance. The face is made to look less (image on the left) or more (image on the right) criminal.

We agree with one another not just about who looks like a criminal but also about the looks of different types of criminals. Remember the study in which faces of actors were classified into different criminal types (Chapter 2)? In another study from the 1980s, the researchers used pictures of their friends and asked both naïve participants and police officers to match the pictures to different crimes. The choices of the two groups were similar, and they assigned different faces to different crimes. In the very first study from 1973 demonstrating the existence of visual criminal stereotypes, Donald Shoemaker and his colleagues also showed that these stereotypes mattered. The extent to which faces "fitted" different crimes predicted whether the face bearers would be found guilty of committing these crimes. Subsequent studies have replicated and extended this "face-to-crime fit" effect.

The influence of impressions of criminality on legal outcomes starts before the evaluation of the crime-related evidence and the decisions about guilt. It starts from the moment of identifying the possible culprit. Two British researchers examined faces from real police lineups. When participants were shown the lineups and asked to pick the most likely culprit, they tended to pick the "criminal-looking" faces. An analysis of the lineups also suggested that they were inadvertently biased: the police officers had selected face foils that were less criminal looking than the suspect. Eyewitness identification is notoriously prone to errors, and the criminal pictures in our heads can contribute to these errors, especially when the initial face memory is weak and the lineup is biased.

Many of these studies were laboratory studies, and we can question whether they generalize to the real legal world. Zebrowitz and McDonald studied 506 cases in small claims courts in Massachusetts. These are courts in which private citizens sue each other for damages and the court is presided over by a judge without a jury. Not surprisingly, the amount of legal support, like having a lawyer, influenced whether the defendant was judged guilty. But the appearance of plaintiffs and defendants also mattered, almost as much as having legal support. Babyfaced defendants—as opposed to mature-faced defendants—were less likely to lose the case when the case was about intentional harm. But babyfaced defendants were more likely to lose the case when the case was about accidental harm. When babyfaced plaintiffs won the case, they received larger awards if the defendant was mature faced. This all goes along with the "face-to-crime fit" effect. We expect babyfaced individuals to be more honest but also more negligent than their mature-faced peers; we also want to protect babyfaced individuals. The judges' decisions seemed to follow the stereotypes that Zebrowitz had already established.

Recently the psychologists John Paul Wilson and Nicholas Rule tested whether impressions of trustworthiness predict death sentences. They selected all male prisoners convicted of first-degree murder and sentenced to death in Florida. Florida was chosen because its Department of Corrections maintains a publicly available database of photographs of all inmates. Wilson and Rule compared the impressions of the faces of the prisoners on death row with those of the faces of prisoners convicted of first-degree murder and sentenced to life imprisonment. The prisoners sentenced to death were perceived as less trustworthy by naïve participants. As in Zebrowitz and McDonald's study, the effects of these impressions could not be explained by the usual suspects: attractiveness and race. In a follow-up study, Wilson and Rule collected photographs of innocent people who were falsely convicted of murder and subsequently exonerated. Once again, the unlucky people who were perceived as less trustworthy were more likely to be wrongfully sentenced to death.

We may frown on the physiognomists' beliefs about criminality, but their pernicious influence has not disappeared from our judicial system. When the goddess of justice is not blind to appearance, appearance influences legal decisions from small civil court awards to death sentences. In 1895, Havelock Ellis noted, "in the Middle Ages there was a law by which, when two persons were suspected of a crime, the ugliest was to be selected for punishment. At the present day judges are, consciously or unconsciously, influenced by physiognomy, and ordinary human beings, who also in a humble way sit in judgment on their fellows, are influenced in the same manner." The present day now is not so different from the present day in 1895.

· · · · ·

In the early twentieth century, Lavater was no longer popular. Some of the "scientific" character analysts did not even refer to him. They preferred to dress their arguments in evolutionary terms. Since then much has changed, but we have not abandoned Lavater's ways. Physiognomists' beliefs are insidious. We may not explicitly endorse them, but that doesn't mean that we are not acting like physiognomists, at least from time to time.

First impressions are not only fast and easy but also consequential. Evaluating people—whether their abilities or moral character—is a difficult business. When the information is limited or the evidence is ambiguous, stereotypes and inferences from appearance can sway us one way or another. If the situation calls for figuring out the competence of others, our impressions of competence come in handy. If the situation calls for figuring out their dominance, our impressions of dominance come in handy. These impressions shape our decisions and actions. If we have to decide whether a person is a violent criminal, their dominant looks will hurt them. If we have to decide whether the same person would make a good military officer, the looks will help them. Our impressions always fit the situation.

But what drives our first impressions? Part 2 of this book is about the perceptual rules of first impressions, the rules that explain why we can't help but form impressions. Physiognomists believed in systematic, predictable relations between appearance and character, although they did not find them. The modern science shows that such relations exist, *but* they are between appearance and impressions, not between appearance and character.

PART 2

UNDERSTANDING FIRST IMPRESSIONS

THE PSYCHOLOGIST'S TRADE

The magic of faces—"the most entertaining surface on earth" in the words of Lichtenberg—is that we never fail to see them as meaningful. As he put it, "the human face is a slate where every line is assigned transcendental meaning; where a slight cramp can look like mockery and a scratch like deceitfulness." This magic makes the study of impressions both fascinating and difficult. Within the uniformity of human faces, there is a bewildering complexity. As Grose noted in his eighteenth-century guide for drawing caricatures, "on a slight investigation it would seem almost impossible, considering the small number of features composing the human face, and their general familiarity, to furnish a sufficient number of characterizing distinctions to discriminate one man from another; but when it is seen what an amazing alteration is produced by enlarging one feature, diminishing another, increasing or lessening their distance, or by any way varying their proportion, the power of combination will appear infinite."

The power of combination not only makes faces different but also creates different impressions. This was the insight of Töpffer. With a few pencil strokes, he could easily transform our impressions of the person from "a stupid stammering fellow" to "less stupid, less stammering, and with . . . a certain capacity for concentration." And these were the early findings of Secord: the same facial feature in different combinations creates different impressions. Lips with the same thickness create the impression of meekness in one combination, and the impression of excitability and conceitedness in another.

The combinations of facial features are unlimited, and our minds can ascribe meaning to each one of them. The psychologist's task is to find out whether there are general rules that simplify the bewildering complexity of combinations. Demonstrating agreement on our impressions is not enough. We need to find out the combinations of features that lead to this agreement. If we know the rules that generate these combinations, we will be in a better position to understand where our impressions are coming from. For the next four chapters, let's put on the experimental psychologist's hat and dig into the psychologist's toolbox. Our objective is to make the invisible content of the mind visible. To do this, we will test our intuitions, design simple experiments, explore face illusions, and think of new ways of deconstructing our impressions.

Let's make the problem—finding the combinations of features that create our impressions—specific. Take a look at the faces in Figure 4.1.

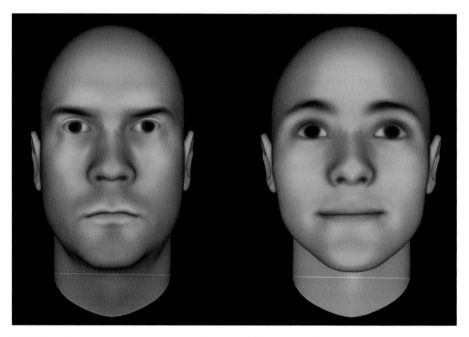

FIGURE 4.1. Whom would you approach at a party? Whom would you choose to be on your pick-up basketball team?

I don't need to tell you to form impressions, because you already have done so. These impressions have consequences. If this were a party, most people would approach the person on the right. What if it were a pick-up basketball game in an urban neighborhood? In these games, the captain has to choose four other players from players he or she may have never seen before. It is important to choose good players, because the winning team stays on the court until it is defeated. If you were the captain, whom would you choose? Assuming equal height, most people would choose the person on the left. These impressions may be completely inaccurate—the current best 3-point NBA shooter, Stephen Curry, is known as the "babyface assassin"—but this is beside the point.

Something in faces triggers these impressions. How do we capture what it is that makes us think that the fellow on the right is more likeable and the fellow on the left more dominant? There are so many differences between the faces: their shapes, the eyes, the shape of the eyebrows, the nose, the thickness of the lips, the complexion of the face, the distance between the different features, and so on. How do we reduce our complex impressions to a physical description of faces?

● ● ● ● ●

One way to go is to rely on our intuition. When we think of faces, what is the first feature that comes to mind? The eyes, of course. Are the eyes or the eyebrows more important for recognition of emotional states? Le Brun knew the right answer back in the seventeenth century: "the eyebrow is the part of the face where the passions are best distinguished, although many have thought that it was the eyes." Following the French philosopher René Descartes, he believed that the soul was expressed in the pineal gland in the brain. While raising the eyebrows toward the brain expressed "the gentlest and mildest passions," sloping the eyebrows toward the heart expressed "the wildest and cruelest passions." The reasoning was false, but the observation more or less right. Much modern research shows that the eyebrows are more important than the eyes for expressing emotions. When we express emotions, our eyebrows move in specific ways, helping other people read our emotional states. Fear is the one emotion that the eyes make easier to detect. During genuinely fearful states, we open our eyes wide, and this makes the whites of the eyes (the sclera) appear larger.

How about facial recognition? Take a look at Figure 4.2. Can you recognize this face?

FIGURE 4.2. Do you recognize this face?

Let me give you a hint. It is the face of a well-known American president. Did you get it? The vision scientist Pawan Sinha and his colleagues have shown that removing the eyebrows of a familiar face makes it harder to recognize than removing the face's eyes. If you are surprised, take a look at Figure 4.3. Is the face more recognizable?

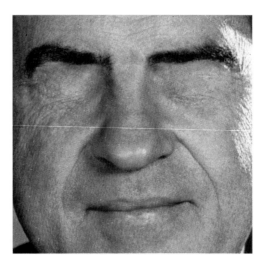

FIGURE 4.3. Do you recognize this face? It is easier to recognize a face when the eyes are removed than when the eyebrows are removed (see Figure 4.2).

It is easier to recognize Richard Nixon when his eyes are removed than when his eyebrows are removed from the image. And if you think this is because of the distinctive eyebrows of Nixon, the researchers used faces of many other celebrities like Winona Ryder, who does not have particularly distinctive eyebrows. To be sure, the eyes are important but not as important as we think. Our intuitions about what facial features are important are insufficient at best and misleading at worst.

Asking experimental participants about what facial features are important for their impressions at the moment of forming these impressions does not help much either. In Chapter 2, you read about Samuels's study, where she manipulated the features of faces and tested how this manipulation changes impressions. She also asked her participants to list the reasons for their impressions. They rarely mentioned any of the features that were actually manipulated and affected their impressions. Samuels concluded, "frequent cross-outs and blank spaces left on the page, as well as contradictory and vague statements made about the features of the faces, indicated the difficulty with which the students accounted for their judgments. There is reason to believe that rationalization is responsible in large measure for the frequent mention of the eyes." None of this should be surprising in light of the studies showing that we can form impressions after seeing a face for as little as 40 milliseconds. This is barely enough time to notice the face and certainly not enough to notice tiny differences between face features. We have little awareness of what drives our impressions.

The faultiness of our intuitions seems to be a general characteristic of how we explain our judgments and behaviors. In 1977, Richard Nisbett and Timothy Wilson published a famous but back then controversial paper "Telling more than we can know." Their main argument was that we have no introspective access to the cognitive processes that produce our judgments. We are, of course, aware of the products of these judgments but not of how we got there. Nisbett and Wilson documented many instances in which people would provide an explanation of their behavior without any actual bearing on the causes of this behavior. In one of their many studies, participants were asked to memorize word pairs like "ocean-moon." Subsequently, the participants were presented with words like "detergent" and asked to respond with the first word that comes to mind. As expected, after memorizing "ocean-moon," the response of many participants to "detergent" was "Tide." But when asked why they came up with this particular response, the participants almost never mentioned the learning of the word pairs. Instead, they provided idiosyncratic reasons like "Tide is the best-known detergent" or "my mother uses Tide."

In some extreme cases, we can see this disconnect between behavior and explanations even more clearly. The neuroscientist Michael Gazzaniga has done fascinating work with split-brain patients. In these patients, the corpus callosum—a bundle of axons that connects the two brain hemispheres—is severed, preventing the hemispheres from communicating with each other. Because of this condition, it is possible to make the patients perform actions without understanding the causes of these actions. A patient presented with the word "laugh" in his left visual field, information that is processed in the right hemisphere, starts laughing. Although the patient is unaware of the reason for his behavior, when asked by the experimenter why he is laughing, he readily replies: "you guys come up and test us every month. What a way to make a living!" Our brains—in this particular case our left hemispheres—are compelled to generate explanations of our behaviors even if these explanations are completely detached from reality.

We are all a little bit like split-brain patients. Similar effects can be demonstrated with perfectly normal people when making face choices. Look at the experimental setup in Figure 4.4. An experimenter shows two pictures to a participant. The participant is asked which face is more attractive. After the participant points to one of the faces, the experimenter, a trained magician

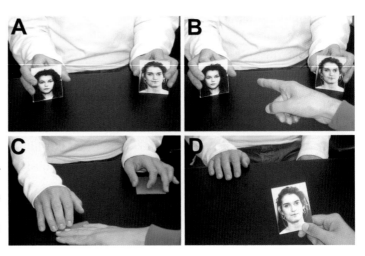

FIGURE 4.4. A trained magician is substituting the face that the participant just chose as more attractive. Would the participant notice the change?

who has copies of the pictures hidden in his sleeves, replaces the preferred picture with the picture of the face the participant just rejected. At this point in the experiment, the participant is asked to explain their choice. Our intuition tells us that the participant should immediately detect the cheap trick. In fact, they not only fail to detect the change of faces on many experimental trials, but also happily generate explanations. Their "preferred" face has "just a nice shape of the face, and the chin."

●　●　●　●　●

Since Nisbett and Wilson's seminal paper, psychologists have been suspicious of self-reports. Instead, we design experiments to find out what actually affects behavior. This is what Sinha and his colleagues did to test whether the eyes or the eyebrows are more important for face recognition. They designed a simple experiment in which only the presence or absence of the eyes and the eyebrows was manipulated. Even in such simple experiments, you have to pay attention to details. If the participants had been presented with the faces of the celebrities in the same order as presented in Figures 4.2 and 4.3—faces without eyebrows first, faces without eyes second—the experiment would have been biased. You might not be sure about the first image, but you get some information. This information can help you identify the second image. The researchers controlled for this, as well as many other things (like recognition of the intact images), by presenting some celebrities without eyebrows and others without eyes. This experimental approach works really well when you have a simple, specific hypothesis.

But when you have an open question like trying to identify the combinations of facial features that drive our impressions, things rapidly get complicated. Let's start with a simple but open question: what makes a face appear trustworthy? The standard, experimental approach is to start with a specific hypothesis. For the sake of the example, our hypothesis is that being in a positive mood makes the face appear trustworthy. Hence, we predict that smiling faces will be perceived as more trustworthy than neutral faces. We take pictures of people showing them either smiling or with neutral expressions. Ideally, the pictures are taken under the same standardized conditions, and the smile is the only difference between them. Next, we randomly assign participants to see either the smiling or the neutral faces and to rate them on trustworthiness. After we collect data from a sufficient number of participants, we conduct a proper statistical test of the differences in ratings to test whether smiling faces are rated as more trustworthy than their counterparts. In this particular case, unlike the importance of the eyes and the eyebrows, chances are that our hypothesis will be confirmed. But did we really figure out what makes a face appear trustworthy? Sure, we identified one factor that changes our impressions of trustworthiness, but is this the most important factor or the only factor that we need to know to explain these impressions? Unlikely.

Let's make the problem slightly more complicated. In addition to smiling, let's manipulate the shape of the eyebrows. For simplicity, we would manipulate the eyebrows to take on only one of two positions: pointing either like this \/ or like this /\. As good experimental psychologists, we create all combinations of the mouth and eyebrows, and we end up with four combinations. This is what psychologists call a 2 by 2 factorial design. Each unique combination is called an experimental cell, and in most experiments an equal number of participants is assigned randomly to each cell. Our experimental design is still super simple. Remember the first experimental study that manipulated features of schematic faces from Chapter 2? Brunswik and Reiter, who conducted the study, created 189 unique combinations of features. We have four. With this simple design, we are able to measure not only the effect of smiling but also the effect of the eyebrows' shape on impressions of trustworthiness. Even more importantly, we can measure their combined effect.

Let's start with schematic faces, because these are simple and researchers have already done experimental work with such faces. Take a look at the four faces in Figure 4.5 that exemplify the four combinations of features.

FIGURE 4.5. Schematic faces manipulated to have different eyebrow and mouth shapes. Some eyebrow/mouth combinations have surprising effects on impressions. Can you identify the "scheming" face?

When the faces are not smiling, the different eyebrows make them look different. Whereas the face in the upper left corner appears sad, the face in the upper right corner appears angry. This is not a perceptual illusion, because when we express these emotions, this is how our eyebrows and mouth move. When we add a smile, the face with "sad" eyebrows now seems genuinely happy and trustworthy, but it is difficult to make the same attribution to the face with "angry" eyebrows and a smile. In an early study on the emotional meaning of schematic faces, the author of the study found that the most appropriate label for this face is "scheming," a label that doesn't go well with trustworthy. Notice how this "result" qualifies our initial "finding" that smiling increases face trustworthiness. It depends on the facial configuration in which you see the smile. Let's see how our combination of eyebrows and smiling plays out in more realistic faces (Figure 4.6).

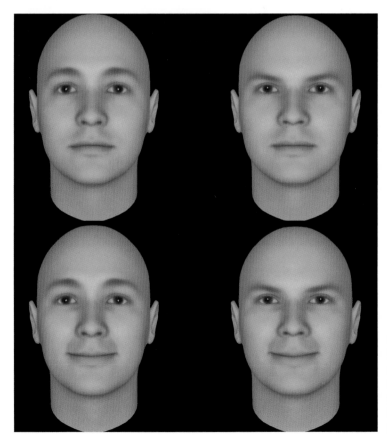

FIGURE 4.6. Faces manipulated to have different eyebrow and mouth shapes. Some eyebrow/ mouth combinations have surprising effects on impressions. Can you identify the "scheming" face?

It is easy to see who looks most like the "scheming" type. This could be the face of a sinister character in a thriller. This impression is created by the combination of incongruent features: a "happy" mouth and "angry" eyebrows, as if the face were expressing both emotions simultaneously. But we do not see this face as weird or atypical. We can readily attribute meaningful characteristics to it, like untrustworthiness.

• • • • •

Even with this trivial combination of features, we are running into strange and complex effects. This is part of the magic of perceiving faces. In psychology, we think of face perception as holistic. The same feature can look quite differently placed among other features. Take a look at the faces in Figure 4.7.

FIGURE 4.7. The eyes in the image on the left seem to smile. Now cover the lower part of the faces. The eyes in the two images are identical.

Focus on the eyes. In the image on the left, they seem to light up with the smile. Now cover the mouth in both images. You should be able to see that the eyes are identical. The two images are indeed identical with the exception of the inserted smile in the image on the left. This smile makes the same eyes look like they are smiling too.

Perception of faces is unlike perception of any other object. Although we are used to talking about facial features like mouths and eyes, we see faces as unique configurations that are not reducible to their constituent features. The same features spaced in a slightly different way make a completely different face. We see faces holistically as perceptual gestalts—integrated structures in which individual features fuse into unique combinations. Look at the composite face illusion in Figure 4.8.

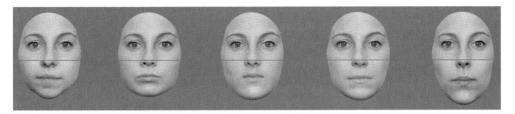

FIGURE 4.8. The composite face illusion: it is difficult to see that the top halves of the faces are identical.

The illusion is that the top halves of the five faces look different, although they are the same. The illusion is caused by the bottom halves, which are different. Our brains seamlessly align features from different faces to create a new face. This effect is particularly powerful when we align parts from different faces horizontally. If we misalign the halves of the faces, the composite face illusion disappears (Figure 4.9).

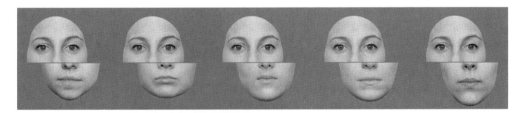

FIGURE 4.9. Once the face halves are misaligned, it is easy to see that the top halves of the faces are identical.

If you were ever in a situation where you have to shred face images so the people cannot be identified, it is best to shred the images horizontally. It seems that this might have come into play during the Iran hostage crisis in 1975. The movie *Argo*, directed by Ben Affleck, starts with a disturbing scene of street protests in Tehran that eventually escalate in the storming of the American embassy. The embassy employees are frantically trying to burn or shred all possible documents. One of the documents they shred contains the pictures and names of the embassy's employees. In a later scene, we see an army of children meticulously matching the shredded pieces of paper to re-create the faces of the employees. Eventually, they succeed. Had the employees shredding the faces taken a class on face perception, they would have shredded the faces horizontally, not vertically. This would have made the task of re-creating the faces much more difficult, if not impossible.

The composite face illusion works for highly familiar faces too. Who is the person in Figure 4.10?

FIGURE 4.10. A face created by aligning the upper and lower parts of the faces of two celebrities. Do you recognize the celebrities?

If you cover the lower part of the face, you should be able to recognize Justin Bieber. If you cover the upper part of the face, perhaps you would be able to recognize Beyoncé. Even if you know that the "face" is a hybrid of two familiar faces, your recognition would be slowed down compared to seeing only half of the face. Our brains immediately see a novel, distinct face.

The composite face illusion was discovered in the 1980s by the cognitive psychologist Andy Young and his colleagues in the United Kingdom. Combining facial halves of different celebrities the way we did it for Justin Bieber and Beyoncé, they showed that the recognition of the celebrities from these halves became harder. Participants are slower to recognize Bieber from the upper half of the face when the facial halves are aligned than when misaligned (compare Figures 4.8 and 4.9). For a long time, the illusion of how the fusion of the parts creates a new face was discussed in the context of person recognition. But you have already seen demonstrations of the illusion in the context of first impressions: how the fusion of the parts creates a new impression. These were the artistic experiments of Töpffer (see Figure 2.4). He is the artist who discovered the holistic nature of face perception. As he put it, "permanent signs are changeable and always unreliable as indicators of intelligence and character. Take a head and study separately the shape of the forehead, eye, or nose, as permanent signs. Or, again, the mouth, the chin, the back of the head. From any sign taken alone you cannot possibly estimate the effect of all together or, in other words, the measure of intelligence and morality in the subject." Töpffer meant that we couldn't predict the effect of single facial features like a concave nose on our impressions, unless we know the configuration of all features.

The artistic experiments of Töpffer were right on target. Take a look at Figure 4.11. Focus on the upper part of the faces and ignore the lower part. Which upper part looks more trustworthy?

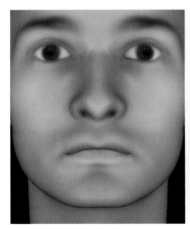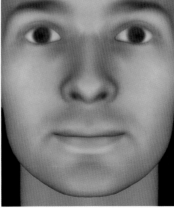

FIGURE 4.11. Ignore the lower parts of the faces and focus on the upper parts. Which upper facial part looks more trustworthy?

Most people go with the upper part on the right. But did you notice that the upper parts are identical? The lower parts that you had to ignore are different. And it doesn't really matter whether you are asked to ignore the lower or the upper part.

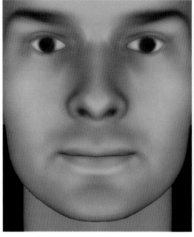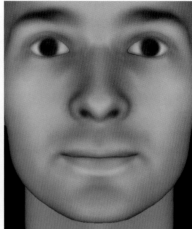

FIGURE 4.12. Ignore the upper parts of the faces and focus on the lower parts. Which lower facial part looks more trustworthy?

When asked to judge the lower parts of the faces in Figure 4.12, ignoring the upper parts, most people judge the lower part on the right as more trustworthy. In this case, the lower parts of the faces are identical, and the upper parts are different. To create these "composite" faces, we used our computer model of impressions of trustworthiness. We generated "trustworthy" and "untrustworthy" versions of the same faces, cut them into lower and upper parts, and then recombined the parts. Our judgments of the identical facial parts are influenced by the part they were combined with. If the latter part comes from a "trustworthy" face, we go for trustworthy. If it comes from an "untrustworthy" face, we go for untrustworthy. We simply cannot ignore the part we are being asked to ignore.

• • • • •

We need not combine two different faces to dramatically alter our impressions. By subtly manipulating the skin surface of a face, we can "change" its gender. Who is the woman and who is the man in Figure 4.13?

FIGURE 4.13. Who is the woman and who is the man? By changing the facial contrast, we can make a face look like a man or like a woman.

It is easy to identify the woman in the image on the right and the man in the image on the left. But the two images are almost identical with one subtle difference: the skin surface in the image on the left is a little bit darker. The eyes and lips of the faces are identical, but the rest of the image on the left was darkened, and the rest of the image on the right was lightened. This manipulation makes the face on the left look masculine and the face on the right look feminine. This is one way to induce the gender illusion. Here is another one in Figure 4.14.

 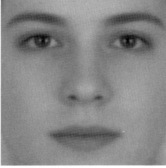

FIGURE 4.14. Who is the woman and who is the man? By changing the facial contrast, we can make a face look like a man or like a woman.

The two images are identical except that the eyes and lips were lightened in the image on the left and darkened in the image on the right. This manipulation makes the face on the left look masculine and that on the right look feminine. What makes the difference in both figures is the increased contrast between the eyes and the mouth and the rest of the face. By the way, this illusion explains why makeup is so popular: it increases this contrast and makes the face look more feminine.

The artist Nancy Burson, who created the first digital composites of faces, has achieved similar effects by morphing the faces of men and women and using either a greater percentage of male faces ("He with She," the image on the left in Figure 4.15) or a greater percentage of female faces ("She with He," the image on the right in Figure 4.15).

FIGURE 4.15. "He with She. She with He." Digital composites by Nancy Burson (1996).

Different combinations of hair and facial features can change our impressions too. Take a look at the face in Figure 4.16. What is the ethnicity of the person? Most people see the face as belonging to a Hispanic person.

FIGURE 4.16. What is the ethnicity of this face?

How about now?

FIGURE 4.17. What is the ethnicity of this face? By changing the hairstyle, we can make the same face appear to be of different ethnicities.

Most people see the face as belonging to an African-American. The only difference between the faces is the hairline and hairstyle. When a Hispanic hairstyle is added to a racially ambiguous face, most people see the face as Hispanic. When an Afro hairstyle is added to the same face, most people see the face as African-American.

Studying faces for a living does not make these effects disappear. A few years ago, my wife and I were about to watch *I'm Not There*, a movie in which actors like Christian Bale and Heath Ledger impersonate Bob Dylan. The movie starts with still screen shots of the different actors appearing as Bob Dylan. After seeing a shot of what I believed was the real Bob Dylan, I exclaimed that I did not realize how handsome he was. My wife politely pointed out that this was the face of Cate Blanchett. Framing the beautiful face of Blanchett with the hairstyle of Bob Dylan was sufficient to fool my perception (Figure 4.18).

● ● ● ● ●

The complexity of face perception, the fact that the meaning of features changes in the context of other features, is the main reason we need to conduct experiments that create all possible feature combinations. But we run out of steam pretty quickly once we increase the number of studied features. With

FIGURE 4.18. Cate Blanchett as Bob Dylan in the movie *I'm Not There.*

more than two features, the possible combinations rapidly proliferate. This is one of the reasons many psychologists prefer simple experimental designs: their results are much easier to interpret. You will rarely see a study with Brunswik and Reiter's complex design, testing the effects of 189 combinations of features on impressions.

To appreciate the rapidly increasing complexity of combining features, let's revisit the artistic experiments of Cozens, described in Chapter 2. To create his drawings of different kinds of beauty, he worked with simple and relatively few variations of features in profile: forehead (four variations), nose (twelve), mouth (sixteen), chin (two), eyebrow (twelve), and eyes (sixteen). Both Lavater and Cozens preferred profiles because of their simplicity. Cozens was aware that there are too many combinations of features to permit easy analysis and that different combinations would result in different impressions:

"many thousands of different combinations of the features may be made, among which there will be many void of character and beauty, but exhibiting certain ideas of mixed countenance." But how many combinations are really there? Almost 300,000; to be precise, with his simple variations, Cozens could have created 294,912 different profiles.

A proper experiment to find out what combinations create impressions of particular kinds of beauty would require 294,912 experimental cells. If we assigned each unique combination of features to different participants and if we needed only 10 participants per experimental cell (a very small sample size for most behavioral studies), we would need almost 3 million participants. Even in the age of online experiments, we would have a hard time running an experiment with 3 million participants. An alternative would be to recruit a small number of highly dedicated participants who would make judgments of all these combinations. If it takes them only a second to make a judgment of each feature combination, they will need to do our experiment for about 82 hours. And this is for a single judgment of beauty. Unless they are on some sort of drug that kills tediousness, it is hard to imagine such dedicated participants.

To make things worse, we do not even know what constitutes a proper facial feature, especially when it comes to real faces rather than simple drawings of profiles. Our intuition points to things like the eyes and mouth, but each of these features could be broken down further into a number of smaller features. Think of pupil size, sclera size, sclera coloration, thickness of the lips, shape and bushiness of eyebrows, and so on. And any of these can take more than two values. Hair can be blond, black, brown, curly, straight, etc. Finding the combinations of features that lead to agreement on impressions is not that easy after all.

Moses Mendelssohn, the German Socrates, expressed his misgivings about Lavater's physiognomy in an unpublished essay: "the empirical approach requires cool-headed circumspection. . . . It soon vanishes altogether in the heat of Lavater's imagination." But Mendelssohn realized that studying physiognomy was challenging: "however, the fault may not be Lavater's alone. It seems to me that our language and our psychology are as yet not sufficiently developed for physiognomy." More than 150 years later, discussing their findings of complex relations between combinations of features and different impressions, Secord and his colleagues, who started the modern work on first impressions, echoed these sentiments: "these results suggest that the conventional 'elementalizing' used by psychologists in seeking to explain their data is simply inappropriate for physiognomy, and that new ways of conceptualizing physiognomy need to be found if it is to be fully understood." The next two chapters are about tools that do not "elementilize" faces—tools for discovering the power of combinations that create the pictures in our heads. With these tools, we can make the invisible pictures visible.

5

MAKING THE INVISIBLE VISIBLE

In his famous essay, "What is it like to be a bat?", the philosopher Thomas Nagel argued that understanding consciousness and by extension the mind is scientifically impossible, because what defines consciousness is its inherently subjective nature. Science by its nature strives to explain events by describing them in objective terms that are not dependent on any subjective point of view. This is what constitutes facts. But if what defines consciousness or the unique experience of any species is its particular subjective point of view, this would make it impossible to reduce it to objective terms. We can imagine what it is like to be a bat, but we will never know the experience of what it is like to be a bat, because we are ultimately limited by our human point of view. We simply cannot take the point of view of the bat.

Nagel's essay was published in 1974. In the same year, Davida Teller and her colleagues from the University of Washington published an article with the much less interesting title "Visual acuity for vertical and diagonal gratings in human infants." In their experiment, they used a simple procedure in which an infant is presented with a homogeneous gray circle and a striped circle, as shown in Figure 5.1. In this situation, infants prefer to look at the striped circle. Through a peephole, an adult observer, who doesn't see the circles, guesses the location of the striped circle from the infant's head orientation and looking behavior. When the striped circle is very different from the gray circle, the observer's guesses are very good. But when the striped circle becomes more and more similar to the gray circle—as in the progression at the bottom of Figure 5.1—the observer's guesses become progressively worse until they are no better than chance. Nowadays, we can use sophisticated electronic devices like eye trackers that track and record the exact position and timing of the infants' eye movements, but the logic of the pro-

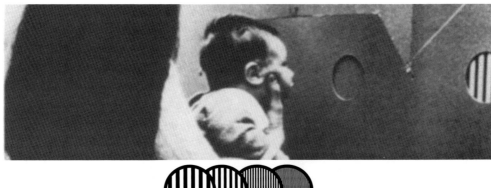

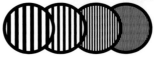

FIGURE 5.1. An experimenter is holding an infant who is presented with a gray circle and a striped circle. Infants prefer to look at the striped circle. An observer looking through a peephole (located between the two circles) is trying to guess the location of the striped circle from the infant's gaze. By presenting circles that become more and more similar to the homogeneous gray circle (shown in the bottom image), it is possible to estimate the visual acuity of infants.

cedure—a version of the preferential looking paradigm described in Chapter 2—is essentially the same. When the observer can no longer guess better than chance the location of the striped circle, we can infer that the infant does not see a difference between the gray and the striped circles. By manipulating systematically the wideness of the stripes, we can describe the grating acuity of the infant: the finest stripes she can see.

If you are not a vision scientist, this may not sound exciting to you. What we see in the world are rich scenes full of people and objects, not circles filled with stripes. This is true, but any visual scene can be decomposed into a multitude of different stripes. Removing the very narrow stripes in a scene—in vision science jargon, the high spatial frequency of an image—makes the scene look grainy, like a low-resolution photo that has been enlarged too much, or how the scene would look to you from a great distance. Removing the very wide stripes—the low spatial frequency—makes the scene look like a fine detailed pencil drawing without any shading. Figure 5.2 shows an image of former President Barack Obama rendered in low spatial frequencies (the coarse visual components of the image) and high spatial frequencies (the fine-detail components of the image). The image in the middle combines the low and high spatial frequencies.

FIGURE 5.2. The image of former President Obama rendered in low spatial frequency (left) and high spatial frequency (right).

We can even create illusions by playing with the spatial frequencies of images. Take a look at Figure 5.3. You can instantaneously recognize Albert Einstein. Now place the book far away from you and look at the images again. Or simply squint your eyes. Or if you are reading the digital version of the book, reduce the size of the images on the screen.

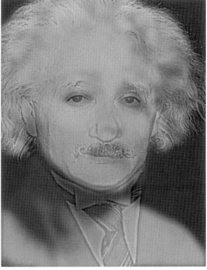

FIGURE 5.3. Do you recognize Einstein? But is it only him in the images? Squint your eyes or view the image from a long distance to find out.

Did Einstein mysteriously disappear? You should be able to see Sigmund Freud in the image on the left and Madonna in the image on the right. This illusion is based on the fact that when we are looking at an image up close, our vision and awareness are dominated by high spatial frequency information—the image of Einstein. From a far distance, we are unable to see high spatial frequency information and only see low spatial frequency information—the images of Freud and Madonna. If you make the images sufficiently small, it will be impossible to see Einstein. To create this illusion, one simply needs to superimpose two images with different spatial frequencies and play with the distance from the images or their size.

But let's get back to babies. Davida Teller's procedure allows us to figure out the infants' sensitivity to different spatial frequencies. In the language of psychophysics, we can trace how sensation (seeing) changes as physical stimuli (spatial frequency) change. From Teller's and many other studies, we know that infants younger than 6 months, and especially newborns, are particularly poor at seeing high spatial frequency information. If we now take a visual scene and remove all the spatial frequency information that infants are unable to see, we are left with what the scene looks like in their eyes. This is exciting. Using a simple psychophysical procedure, we are able to see the unseeable. In the case of faces, we are left with the image presented in Figure 5.4. To a newborn—even from a close distance—a face looks like a blurred blob with few discernible details.

FIGURE 5.4. How a newborn sees a face from a distance of 12 inches. Newborns cannot see high spatial frequency information.

We can apply the same techniques to nonhuman species. As long as we can elicit a behavioral response to a pair of stimuli, we can figure out the visual sensitivity of our nonhuman subjects. We may not be able to know what it is like to be a bat or a newborn infant or a congenitally blind person, but we can figure out what they sense. This gets us one step closer to knowing their minds.

The objective of psychophysics is to find lawlike relations between changes in physical stimuli and changes in psychological sensations. By changing the physical properties of stimuli from the outside world, we can map the corresponding changes in the inner world. While most textbook examples are about simple stimuli like light intensity, sound loudness, and weights of objects, we can use the same methods to find out things that seem impossible to know. These range from what newborns see in faces to the configuration of facial features that lead to complex impressions like trustworthiness.

●　●　●　●　●

Remember the experiment in which the researchers tested whether the eyes or the eyebrows were more important for face recognition? They manipulated the presence or absence of these features and compared the recognition of celebrities without eyes or without eyebrows. But what if we want to know which features are important without manipulating them and without relying on subjective reports? In the 1980s, the British researcher Nigel Haig introduced a technique that does not make any assumptions about the importance of features or what constitutes a proper feature. Rather than manipulating features, he would present faces that are partially occluded. Think of seeing small segments of a face through tiny apertures. This is shown in Figure 5.5.

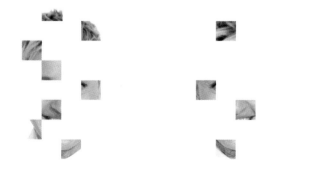

FIGURE 5.5. Participants' task is to recognize faces from partial information. Do you recognize this American celebrity?

Participants in the experiment were first familiarized with four faces. After this familiarization, the real experiment began. On each trial, the computer would randomly select a face, then select between one and eight apertures, and randomly assign the apertures to predetermined square segments covering the face (Figure 5.5). The participants' task was to recognize the face from this partial information. There are quite a few ways of assigning the apertures, and the four participants, including Haig himself, heroically did the experiment for twenty sessions each lasting 20 minutes.

The payoff of this procedure is that we can find which features are important for face recognition without biasing our search. These features emerge from the accuracy of recognition responses. If a segment helps us identify the face, the features matter. If, for example, most of the time we recognize the face when the segment reveals the outside corner of the left eyebrow, we can infer that this information is important for face recognition. If a segment does not help us identify the face, the features in the segment do not matter. If, for example, we are no better than chance at recognizing the face when the segment reveals part of the right cheekbone, we can infer that this information is not important for face recognition. Haig found that the segments covering the eyes and eyebrows, the hairline, and the top of the forehead were most informative about face recognition.

Almost all psychophysical techniques discussed in this chapter are a variation of Haig's procedure. Using these techniques, we can find out what information in the face is important for identifying gender, recognizing emotional expressions, and forming impressions. On a typical experimental trial, participants are presented with a face image, which is degraded either by presenting only parts of it or by blending the face with a meaningless image. We can call the latter "visual noise." We can manipulate the blending of face and visual noise by making the face more or less visible, as in Figure 5.6.

FIGURE 5.6. Degrading the quality of a face image while preserving low-level image properties, like luminance.

Using these degraded images, we can ask participants to guess the gender of the face, its identity, emotional expression, and even the character of the face bearer. The features that emerge from the noise are the ones that matter for the decision at hand. This may sound too abstract, but let's make it concrete by considering a few applications of noise-based techniques.

Frederic Gosselin and Philippe Schyns introduced a version of these techniques, which they called "bubbles." The technique works by mixing different kinds of noise patterns, each one containing different sizes of "bubbles." If you were a participant in a bubbles experiment, you would be shown an image like the one in Figure 5.7 and asked to make a decision, such as guessing the gender of the face.

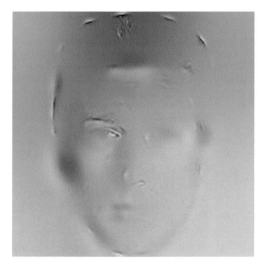

FIGURE 5.7. An example of the bubbles technique, which makes only some parts of the image visible. By using this technique, it is possible to find the information people use when making decisions like whether a face is that of a man or a woman.

You can see parts of the forehead, the right eye, the right cheekbone, and the right corner of the mouth. The function of the bubbles is to control the information that is available to you when making your decision. The bubbles vary from trial to trial, and hence, different parts of the image are revealed. By randomly varying the location and the size of the bubbles and then sorting them according to the accuracy of the participants' decisions, it is possible to identify the information in the image that is critical for the decision. If your gender decision is consistently accurate when the right corner of the mouth is revealed, we can infer that this part of the image is important for your decision. Figure 5.8 shows all the information we need to guess the gender of a face.

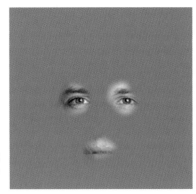

FIGURE 5.8. Information that is useful for deciding whether the face belongs to a man or a woman.

By the way, the fact that the image shows no hair doesn't mean that hair is not important. In this particular experiment, the hair was identical for faces of both men and women and, hence, completely uninformative for identifying gender.

Figure 5.9 shows the information we use to identify different emotional expressions.

Happy	Surprised	Fearful	Angry	Disgusted	Sad	Neutral

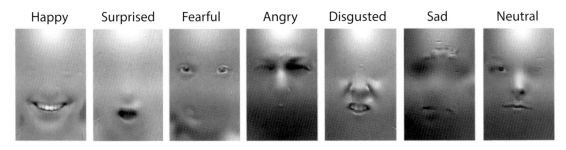

FIGURE 5.9. Information that is useful for identifying different emotional expressions.

You can see the systematic differences between emotions. The mouth region is important for identifying happiness, surprise, and disgust; the eyes for identifying fear; the eyebrows for identifying anger; the nose bridge for identifying disgust; and the forehead for identifying sadness.

The bubbles technique is superb for identifying the information we use for making perceptual decisions. To do this, we need to know which decision is accurate and which is not. This is easy to do with relatively well-defined categories, like gender and emotional expressions. If a male face covered with bubbles is classified as male, we know that the decision is accurate; and we can infer that the visible information in the image is useful for the decision. The bubbles technique reveals the information that helps us make accurate decisions. But what about categories that are not well defined, like the perceived trustworthiness of a face? Can we use these noise-based techniques if we don't know the right decision ahead of time?

• • • • •

Consider ambiguous facial expressions. Leonardo's *Mona Lisa* is one of the most celebrated paintings in the history of art. What makes Mona Lisa so special? Art historians point out that Leonardo's radically new technique of painting Mona Lisa's face without sharp lines created the feeling of the portrait being alive, in stark contrast to other portraits of that time. The other distinctive characteristic of Mona Lisa is her illusive smile. We simply cannot pinpoint her emotional state. Sometimes she seems happy and sometimes she seems sad. Capitalizing on this ambiguity, the vision scientists Leonid Kontsevich and Christopher Tyler superimposed visual noise on the intact image and asked participants to classify the face as happy or sad. Figure 5.10 shows some examples of images with superimposed noise.

FIGURE 5.10. Images of Leonardo's *Mona Lisa* with superimposed visual noise, which distorts her expression.

In some ways, this noise masking technique looks like an extreme application of the sfumato technique that Leonardo introduced in the Renaissance. More to the point, notice how the randomly generated noise masks subtly change the expression of the face. In the blurred images, our minds can read different things. The most interesting part of the experiment comes when we average the noise masks from all judgment trials on which the participant said "happy" or "sad." If we superimpose this new and nonrandom noise mask on the original image, we can see how participants constructed the two emotional states from the slight noise distortions of the image (Figure 5.11).

FIGURE 5.11. Averaging the distorted images (see Figure 5.10) in which participants see sad Mona Lisa results in the image on the left. Averaging the distorted images in which participants see happy Mona Lisa results in the image on the right.

We can also discover the parts of the image that make a difference in the participants' perceptual decisions. In this particular case, it is the corners of the mouth. And notice again how the slight difference in the mouth creates the illusion that the eyes in the two images are different. They are not. The illusion is the same as the one illustrated in Chapter 4 (Figure 4.7).

It seems that part of the secret of Mona Lisa is locked in her mouth. But how is it that our visual experience of Mona Lisa's face dynamically changes when we look at the painting? The Harvard neurobiologist Margaret Livingston argued that this all depends on where we look at the painting. When we gaze at Mona Lisa's eyes, her mouth is at the periphery of our vision and images at the periphery are primarily seen in the low spatial frequency band of information. Take a look at Mona Lisa rendered in different spatial frequencies from the lowest to the highest (Figure 5.12). She looks happiest in the lowest-frequency image. And this is why, when we gaze at her eyes, she looks happy. But when we gaze at her mouth, the smile seems to disappear, and she

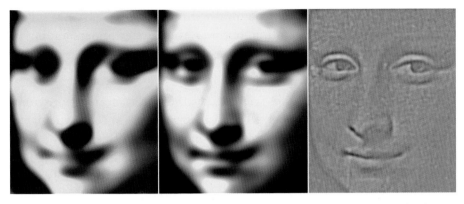

FIGURE 5.12. Mona Lisa rendered in different spatial frequencies from the lowest (left) to the highest (right).

no longer looks happy. German researchers provided an experimental demonstration of Livingstone's hypothesis. They asked participants to alternately gaze at the eyes and mouth of faces. Whenever participants moved their gaze from the mouth to the eyes, the researchers changed the mouth of the face from neutral to smiling. Because the change occurred while participants were moving their eyes, they were unaware of the change. Nevertheless, because the smile appeared in the periphery of their vision, this change made the face look happier and more attractive.

Let's retrace the investigative steps so far. Unlike the feature manipulation experiments from Chapter 4, Kontsevich and Tyler did not manipulate anything in the image in a systematic way. They did generate noise masks and superimposed them on the Mona Lisa image, but the noise patterns were completely random. The researchers did not have prior hypotheses about which features differentiate the emotional states of sadness and happiness. In other words, their search for these features did not single out any particular feature or a combination of features ahead of time. Instead, they let participants' decisions lead them to the right features. Like Haig's recognition procedure and the bubbles technique, this is an example of a data-driven approach in which our prior hypotheses do not constrain participants' behavior. By sorting the noise masks according to the participants' perceptions of sadness and happiness, Kontsevich and Tyler identified the parts of the image that differentiated these perceptions. This finding guided more theory-driven research that identified the conditions under which our perception of Mona Lisa can dynamically shift. We surely have not solved the mystery of the great painting, but we have a better understanding of some parts of it.

• • • • •

Notice that in Kontsevich and Tyler's study, there were no right or wrong answers. The noise patterns helped us visualize what is in the participants' heads when they were seeing Mona Lisa as happy or sad. This could be done for all sorts of categories. The psychologists Michael Mangini and Irving Biederman have done it for emotional expressions, gender, and identity. For perceptions of gender, they started with an androgynous face created by morphing an equal number of male and female faces. Then they subtly distorted the image by superimposing noise masks on it and asked participants to decide whether they were looking at a male or female face. Notice that in this task, there is no "correct" decision—what participants are seeing is an androgynous face distorted by visual noise. Yet their gender decisions resulted in the images shown in Figure 5.13.

FIGURE 5.13. Averaging noise-distorted images of a morph of male and female faces in which participants see a woman results in the image on the left. Averaging the distorted images in which participants see a man results in the image on the right.

In a sense, participants' minds built these images from visual noise. These are the gender pictures in our heads. Besides the subtle shape differences around the nose, the mouth, and the eyes, you may notice that the eyes and the mouth are darker in the image of the woman than in that of the man. This should remind you of the gender illusion (see Figures 4.13 and 4.14).

This particular technique has been called "superstitious perception." The term "superstitious" is used because nothing in the images besides the superimposed noise truly differentiates the two categories, whether these are a man or a woman, or emotional states like happiness and sadness. All the differentiation comes from the participants' minds, which shape the meaningless visual noise into meaningful images. But there is nothing superstitious about the method. It is one of the best methods to reveal what is inside people's heads.

This is particularly good news if our objective is to discover the visual representations of ill-defined categories like trustworthiness. Unlike the case of gender or emotional expressions, there are no well-defined examples of, say, trustworthy and untrustworthy faces. Our objective is to find exactly those examples.

Ron Dotsch, a Dutch psychologist who was a post-doctoral fellow in my lab and is now a professor at Utrecht University in the Netherlands, was the first social psychologist to apply the "superstitious perception" methods to questions in social psychology. In his first study, he searched for what stereotypes and prejudice look like in our heads. Like Mangini and Biederman, he used the same base face—a morph of Caucasian male faces—and superimposed noise masks on this face. Figure 5.14 shows the face and a randomly generated mask.

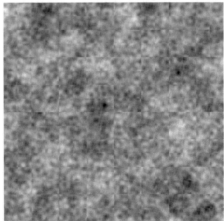

FIGURE 5.14. An "average" male face (left), created by morphing many male faces and a randomly generated noise mask (right), which is imposed on the face image to distort it.

In each trial, participants would see two images like the ones in Figure 5.15.

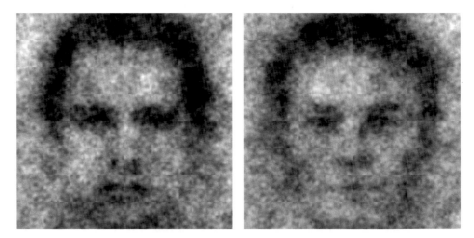

FIGURE 5.15. The images resulting from combining the same face with two different noise masks.

As a proof of concept, Ron asked participants to decide who looks more like a Moroccan man and who looks more like a Chinese man. Although the base face was a morph of Caucasian faces, the resulting faces—averaged from the few hundred trials in which the participants made guesses—looked like a Moroccan and a Chinese man, respectively (Figure 5.16).

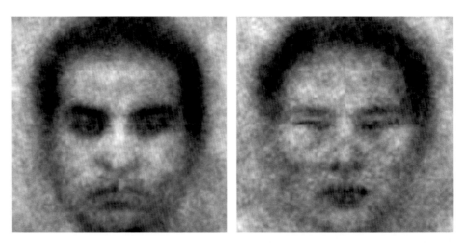

FIGURE 5.16. The image on the left results from averaging noise-distorted images of a Caucasian morph in which participants see a Moroccan face. That on the right results from averaging the distorted images in which participants see a Chinese face.

Ron was interested in the representation of Moroccans, because this is a highly stereotyped group in the Netherlands. In the most interesting part of the experiment, he compared the pictures in the minds of Dutch participants who were either more or less prejudiced against Moroccans. As shown in Figure 5.17, the pictures looked different. Can you guess which one comes from more prejudiced participants?

FIGURE 5.17. The perceptual decisions of Dutch participants who are more prejudiced against Moroccans result in the image on the left. The decisions of Dutch participants who are less prejudiced result in the image on the right.

When these images were shown to a new group of participants, they found the image on the left to look more criminal and less trustworthy. This was the image reconstructed from the choices of the more prejudiced participants. As Ron's findings illustrate, the noise-based technique can be used as a litmus test of hidden biases. After all, participants are not asked whether they are prejudiced, something that most people will deny, but only asked to report whether they see a typical member of an ethnic group in the noisy image.

In other applications of the superstitious perception technique, members of different European nations see the "typical" European face as more similar to the typical face of their own nation. And closer to home, the reconstructed image of Mitt Romney (the Republican challenger who ran against Barack Obama in 2012) from judgments of Democratic voters was perceived as less trustworthy than his image as reconstructed from judgments of Republican voters. Our biases shape the pictures in our heads.

After joining my lab, Ron turned his interest toward identifying what first impressions look like. Using the same procedures, we asked participants to decide for each pair of noisy faces (see Figure 5.15) which one looks more trustworthy. Figure 5.18 shows the resulting images.

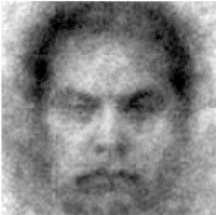

FIGURE 5.18. Averaging noise-distorted images (see Figure 5.15) in which participants see trustworthiness results in the image on the left. Averaging images in which participants see untrustworthiness results in the image on the right.

These two images capture the pictures in our heads of trustworthiness and untrustworthiness. Not surprisingly, when these images are shown to a new group of participants, they rate the trustworthy image as more trustworthy than the untrustworthy image. Note that the "trustworthy" and "untrustworthy" images did not need to turn out the way they did. If we don't have any mental representations of what trustworthy and untrustworthy faces look like, the study would not have gotten any meaningful images. The trustworthiness decisions of participants would vary randomly from trial to trial, and the average of these trials would look like nothing meaningful to us. We would not be able to point to the face on the left in Figure 5.18 and say that it is the more trustworthy one in the pair. But this is not what happens. The decisions do not vary randomly but systematically, shaping the noise into meaningful images.

We can create such images for any impression. Figure 5.19 shows the images for impressions of dominance and submissiveness.

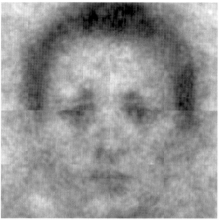

FIGURE 5.19. Averaging noise-distorted images (see Figure 5.15) in which participants see dominance results in the image on the left. Averaging images in which participants see submissiveness results in the image on the right.

Again, it is easy to see which face image resulted from dominance decisions and which one from submissiveness decisions. Comparing the untrustworthy image with the dominant image, you can see that they are similar but not the same. The similarity of the images reflects the similarity of the impressions. We can illustrate this with decisions of threat. You can see the resulting image in Figure 5.20.

FIGURE 5.20. This image results from averaging noise-distorted images (see Figure 5.15) in which participants see threat.

This image is similar to both the untrustworthy image (Figure 5.18, right) and the dominant image (Figure 5.19, left). In fact, if we were to average these two images, we would get an image indistinguishable from the image of threat (Figure 5.20). This is because our mental picture of a threatening face is a picture of a dominant, untrustworthy face.

• • • • •

Both the standard experimental approach for hypotheses testing and the data-driven approach rely on participants' behavior to find out what information they use when forming impressions. But unlike the standard approach, the data-driven approach does not start with a specific hypothesis about this information. Such hypotheses constrain the search to specific features like mouth and eyebrows, which have to be experimentally manipulated. In contrast, there is no explicit manipulation of facial features in the data-driven approach. Instead, the features are randomly distorted or degraded by noise masks. This does not constrain the search to specific features. I should note that the distinction between approaches that are inductive and data driven and those that are deductive and theory driven is not clear-cut. Much thinking and theory goes into devising data-driven techniques, and theories are built on available data and meant to explain such data.

The important point is that by using techniques like the noise-based ones, we can start with the data, unburdened by our prior conceptions of what counts as a feature and which features are important. These techniques make invisible mental representations visible. By following the psychophysical approach—tracing how our impressions change as the noise masks distort the face—we can find features and unique combinations of features that we may not even expect to matter for first impressions. Starting from noise patterns, we arrive at the meaningful patterns of our visual representations of first impressions. In the case of trustworthiness (Figure 5.18), we found meaningful images without manipulating any specific features in the face. We can consult the resulting images to list the combinations of features that differentiate trustworthy- from untrustworthy-looking faces. We can see, for example, that the eyebrows and mouth of the trustworthy and untrustworthy faces are different. These combinations of features make the trustworthy face looks calm and happy, and the untrustworthy face angry. In the case of dominance (Figure 5.19), we can see that the dominant face is more masculine than the submissive face. In the case of threat (Figure 5.20), we can see that the threatening face is an angry, masculine face.

We can do even better by building mathematical models of impressions. Using these models, we can increase or decrease at will the specific impressions of a face, whether of trustworthiness or dominance or any other impression. More importantly, by discovering the configurations of features that matter for first impressions, we can find out what is behind the irresistible influence of these impressions.

6

THE FUNCTIONS OF IMPRESSIONS

Take a look at Figure 6.1. How would you rate this face on trustworthiness? How would you rate it on dominance?

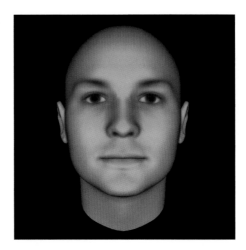

FIGURE 6.1. A synthetic face randomly generated by a statistical model.

How about the face in Figure 6.2?

Most people don't have a problem placing the faces on a scale that measures our impressions of trustworthiness and dominance. If we were to collect experimental data and the scale ranges from 1 (not at all) to 9 (extremely), the face in Figure 6.1 would be around 5 on the trustworthiness scale and around 6 on the dominance scale. The face in Figure 6.2 would be around 3.5 on the trustworthiness scale and around 8.5 on the dominance scale. Your numerical ratings might be different, but chances are that the relative ranking

FIGURE 6.2. Another synthetic face randomly
generated by a statistical model.

of the faces would be preserved. The second face would be perceived as more
dominant and less trustworthy than the first face.

By now, none of this should be surprising. But we can do more than just
measure and record impressions. We can build mathematical models of these
impressions, models that capture the unique configurations of features that
evoke specific impressions like trustworthiness and dominance. The faces in
Figures 6.1 and 6.2 were randomly generated by a statistical model, created
from three-dimensional laser scans of real faces. Using this model, we can
generate as many novel faces as we like. Each face is a set of numbers that
completely determines its shape and reflectance (skin surface and texture).
Different sets of numbers correspond to different looking faces. Once we have
this mathematical representation of faces, it is straightforward to create models of first impressions. The construction of these models follows the data-
driven logic of the noise-based techniques discussed in Chapter 5. Just as in
these techniques, we do not manipulate any facial features—instead of randomly distorting features, we randomly generate faces. Then we collect impressions of these faces, as we did for the faces in Figures 6.1 and 6.2. If the
impressions are consistent across participants, we can build a model of these
impressions: we simply relate one set of numbers—ratings of faces—to another set of numbers—those determining the shape and reflectance of the
faces. The resulting model captures the differences in shape and reflectance

of faces that lead to differences in impressions: what makes one face look more trustworthy than another. This is how we created the models that you have already seen: extroversion (see Figure 2.8), trustworthiness (Figures 2.9 and 3.6), dominance (Figure 3.4), and criminality (Figures 3.8 and 3.9).

Having a model of impressions, we can figure out the features that drive these impressions. We can visualize and exaggerate the combinations of features that drive our impressions. Exaggerating these combinations is very much like creating a caricature of our impressions—finding out what makes them distinctive. The models are our tools for discovering the perceptual sources of agreement on impressions. Knowing what goes into our impressions, we can make informed guesses about the functions of these impressions.

• • • • •

There is a reason we have spent so much time discussing impressions of trustworthiness and dominance. Impressions of different character attributes are highly similar. Faces that are perceived as trustworthy are also perceived as attractive, emotionally stable, intelligent, less aggressive, less threatening, and so on. If I continue with the list of similar impressions, I would fill up a few pages. The fact that impressions are so similar is not necessarily a bad thing. It indicates that a lot of redundancy exists in our impressions and that a simple structure might be able to organize all these impressions. We can find this structure by statistically analyzing the similarity of impressions. As it turns out, impressions of trustworthiness and dominance form the basis of the structure of impressions.

The most important dimension on which we evaluate faces is their badness or goodness. This fundamental dimension is related to any impression with an evaluative component, which means pretty much all impressions. Impressions of trustworthiness come closest to this badness/goodness evaluation. The second dimension on which we evaluate faces is their power. This dimension is related to impressions like aggressiveness and confidence. Impressions of dominance come closest to this power evaluation.

To obtain the structure of impressions, which can be represented in a simple geometrical space, we analyze the correlations between different impressions like attractiveness, dominance, threat, and trustworthiness. These correlations indicate the similarity of impressions. Figure 6.3 illustrates the resulting structure of impressions.

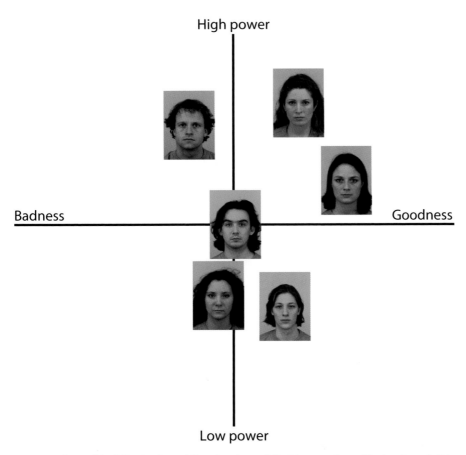

FIGURE 6.3. A graphical illustration of the structure of first impressions. Moving from left to right on the *x*-axis, faces are perceived more positively. Moving up the *y*-axis, faces are perceived as more powerful. The location of the faces indicates their perceived value on goodness/badness and power.

The badness/goodness dimension is represented by the (horizontal) *x*-axis. Moving from left to right along this axis increases the positive value of faces. In Figure 6.3, the rightmost woman is perceived more positively than the other faces. The power dimension is represented by the (vertical) *y*-axis. In the figure, the man and the woman at the top are perceived as more dominant than the other faces. You can also see that the woman is perceived more positively than the man. The important point is that to understand first impressions, we need to start with impressions of trustworthiness and dominance.

• • • • •

Having models of impressions of trustworthiness and dominance, we can examine what information goes into these impressions. Let's start with the model of trustworthiness. To create this model, my colleagues and I had participants rate a few hundred faces like the ones in Figures 6.1 and 6.2 on trustworthiness. If participants consistently use the same facial cues to form impressions of trustworthiness, we can capture these cues in our model. If most participants, for example, rate faces with eyebrows pointed like this "\/" as untrustworthy, this would be captured in the model; we should be able to see how the eyebrows change as we change the trustworthiness of faces. In contrast, if participants inconsistently use facial cues to form impressions, our model would be completely useless. We can test whether the model captures meaningful representations of trustworthiness by asking a new group of participants to rate faces manipulated by the model. Faces that are "trustworthy" according to the model should look trustworthy to us; and faces that are "untrustworthy" should look untrustworthy.

So let's see whether you are convinced. Take a look at Figure 6.4. If you think that the trustworthiness of the faces increases as we move from left to right, you are like most people who "agree" with the model of trustworthiness. Here, using this model, we are gradually increasing the changes in face shape that make the faces look trustworthy.

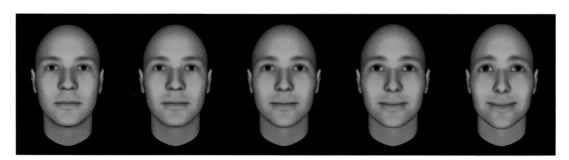

FIGURE 6.4. Increasing the changes in shape that make faces appear trustworthy.

You can think of the model as an amplifier of the signal in impressions. We can visualize and exaggerate the shape cues, which people consistently use to decide whether a person looks trustworthy. There are quite a few changes in the face, but the most striking is the emergence of positive emotions. As the face becomes more trustworthy, it also becomes happier. We can repeat the same exercise to visualize the shape changes that make faces look untrustworthy. Take a look at Figure 6.5.

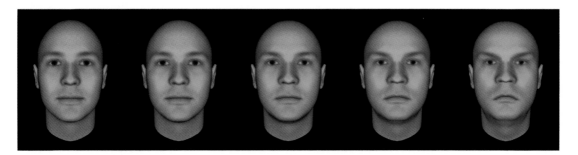

FIGURE 6.5. Increasing the changes in shape that make faces appear untrustworthy.

This time, as the face becomes more untrustworthy, it becomes angrier. The changes in expressions are most prominent in the rightmost faces: we ramped up the signal so much that the faces look grotesque. At this point of grotesque exaggeration, we don't see the faces as emotionally neutral. And we learned something in the process: emotional expressions are one of the determinants of impressions of trustworthiness. We use the momentary emotional states of others to draw inferences about character.

Note, though, that emotional expressions need not emerge in our model of trustworthiness. Before we created the model, we had no idea what would come out at the end. This is the nature of data-driven methods. Just as in the noise-based techniques described in Chapter 5, we did not manipulate anything in the rated faces. Instead, we let the features of these faces (see Figures 6.1 and 6.2) vary randomly. If anything, we were extremely careful to make sure that all these faces were "emotionally neutral" with no detectable expressions. But the model is showing that to form impressions of trustworthiness, participants were relying on the similarity, however subtle, of the faces to emotional expressions. Faces with an inkling of positive expressions are rated as more trustworthy; faces with an inkling of negative expressions are rated as less trustworthy. When Nick Oosterhof implemented the model, he came to tell me that he was not happy, because exaggerating the faces in the model—as we did in Figures 6.4 and 6.5—resulted in emotional expressions. Consequently, we could not manipulate faces on trustworthiness without changing their expressions. It took me a second to realize that this was the coolest finding I have had in my lab so far. Emotional expressions naturally emerged in the model of impressions of trustworthiness! These findings converge with Ron's findings from the last chapter (see Figure 5.18). Although the methods were very different, similar expressions emerged in the models of trustworthy and untrustworthy faces.

From these findings, we can infer that when forming impressions of trustworthiness, we rely on the resemblance of neutral faces to positive or negative emotional expressions. These expressions, among other things, signal behavioral intentions. An angry person can do many unpleasant things, and it is wise to avoid them. The one thing that is on our minds when we are about to interact with a stranger is figuring out their intentions. Do they have good or bad intentions? In most circumstances, we will approach a stranger with a happy face and avoid a stranger with an angry face. Impressions of trustworthiness are our attempt to read the intentions of others.

Besides expressions, many other differences between "trustworthy" and "untrustworthy" faces emerged in the model. You probably noticed that as the face became more trustworthy, it became more feminine (Figure 6.4), and as it became more untrustworthy, it became more masculine (Figure 6.5). These changes are even more apparent in the reflectance of the faces. In Figures 6.4 and 6.5, we kept the reflectance the same and only changed the shape of the face. Let's change the reflectance, keeping the shape the same. Figure 6.6 shows the changes in reflectance that make the faces look more trustworthy.

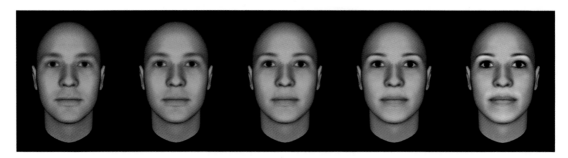

FIGURE 6.6. Increasing the changes in reflectance that make faces appear trustworthy.

Did you notice the gradual change in gender? As the face becomes more trustworthy, it transforms into a woman. Figure 6.7 shows the changes in reflectance that make the faces look untrustworthy. As the face becomes more untrustworthy, it becomes more masculine.

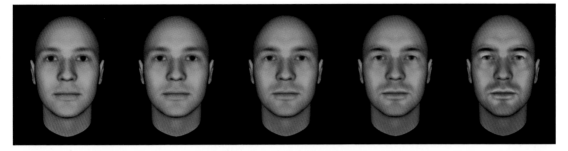

FIGURE 6.7. Increasing the changes in reflectance that make faces appear untrustworthy.

Let's put the changes in shape and reflectance together and zoom in on the extreme versions of untrustworthiness and trustworthiness (Figure 6.8).

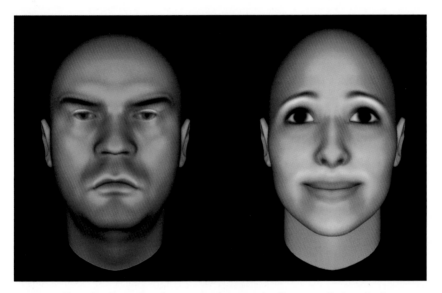

FIGURE 6.8. Zooming in on the changes in shape and reflectance that make faces appear untrustworthy or trustworthy.

Our caricatures of untrustworthiness and trustworthiness turned into a disgruntled, dominant man and a happy, relaxed woman. All these differences emerged from judgments on the trustworthiness of randomly generated faces, not from our theoretical preconceptions. Remember the study described in Chapter 2, where 7-month-old infants looked longer at trustworthy than at untrustworthy faces generated by our model? Now that we know what drives these impressions, the infants' findings should not be that surprising. By 7 months, infants can tell positive from negative expressions, and they prefer female faces, because most of the time their primary caregiver is a woman.

Let's move to the model of dominance. We created this model the same way we created the trustworthiness model, except for the fact that participants rated the few hundred faces (see Figures 6.1 and 6.2) on dominance. Figure 6.9 shows the changes in facial shape that make the faces look dominant.

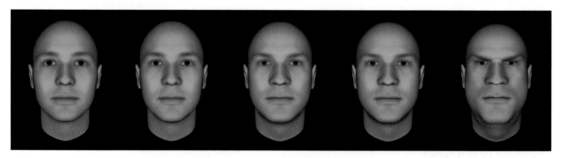

FIGURE 6.9. Increasing the changes in shape that make faces appear dominant.

As the face becomes more dominant, it becomes more masculine. The chin is tremendously enlarged, the eyes become smaller, the eyebrows change their shape, and the distance between the eyebrows and the eyes is diminished.

Figure 6.10 shows the changes in facial shape that make the faces look submissive.

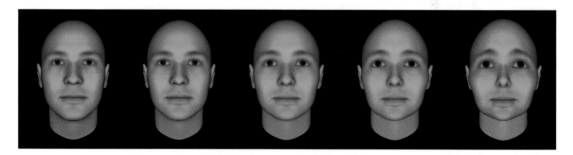

FIGURE 6.10. Increasing the changes in shape that make faces appear submissive.

As the face becomes more submissive, it becomes more babyfaced. The chin becomes smaller, the eyes and the forehead become larger, the eyebrows change their shape, and the distance between the eyebrows and the eyes is increased. These findings confirm Zebrowitz's insights about the importance of babyfaced appearances (see Chapter 2).

Let's change the reflectance of the faces while keeping the shape the same. Figure 6.11 shows the changes in face reflectance that make the faces look dominant.

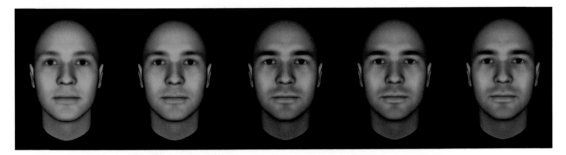

FIGURE 6.11. Increasing the changes in reflectance that make faces appear dominant.

Once again, as the face becomes more dominant, it becomes more masculine. The face becomes darker (remember the gender illusion described in Chapter 4?), the eyebrows more prominent, and the facial hair more visible.

Figure 6.12 shows the changes in face reflectance that make the faces look submissive.

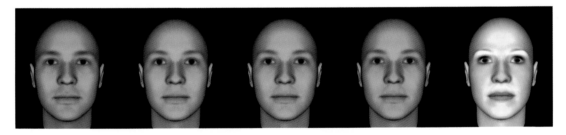

FIGURE 6.12. Increasing the changes in reflectance that make faces appear submissive.

As the face becomes more submissive, it transforms from a man into a woman. Finally, let's put the changes in shape and reflectance together and zoom in on the extreme versions of dominance and submissiveness (Figure 6.13).

This time the changes in gender and facial maturity are unmistakable. Masculine appearance matters a great deal for our impressions of dominance. These impressions might have a kernel of truth, because judgments of masculinity from faces tend to be associated with physical strength. But it is just

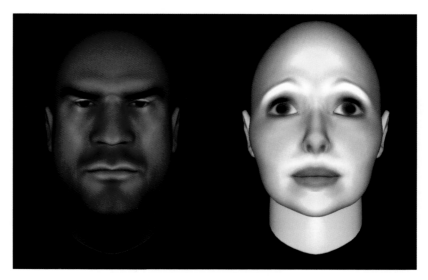

FIGURE 6.13. Zooming in on the changes in shape and reflectance that make faces appear dominant or submissive.

a kernel, as most dominance hierarchies that matter in modern times are not based on physical strength. Yet physical strength is the most important ingredient of our impressions of dominance. We discovered this after Hugo Toscano, a visiting graduate student from Portugal, decided to compare impressions of dominance and physical strength. The model of impressions of physical strength was virtually indistinguishable from that of impressions of dominance. Physical strength is what primarily drives our impressions of dominance. Impressions of dominance are our attempt to read the ability of others to physically harm us.

As illustrated in Figure 6.3, the structure of impressions can be represented as a simple two-dimensional space. We can plot any specific impression within this space. Figure 6.14 plots the axis representing impressions of threat. If we were to plot impressions of trustworthiness, their axis would be indistinguishable from the goodness-badness axis. Similarly, the axis of impressions of dominance is very close to the power axis. This is how we know that these are the two most important impressions from faces. One implication of the simple structure of impressions is that we can re-create many other specific impressions from these two fundamental impressions. What that means is that we can increase the threat of faces by simultaneously increasing their

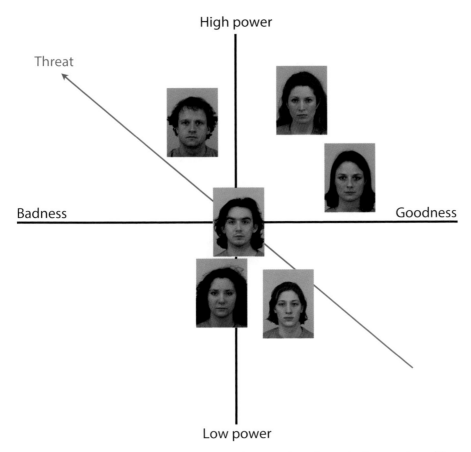

FIGURE 6.14. We can represent specific impressions, such as threat, in the structure of impressions. The arrow indicates the direction in which the perceived threat of faces increases.

untrustworthiness and dominance. We can create a model of impressions of threat or simply use the existing models of trustworthiness and dominance to manipulate threat. The results are practically identical.

Remember the model of impressions of criminality (see Figure 3.8)? The two key ingredients of the criminal stereotype are impressions of untrustworthiness and dominance. This agrees with behavioral studies: ratings of untrustworthiness and dominance of faces are highly predictive of criminal appearance; they are also highly predictive of ratings of threat. As shown in Figure 6.15, the model of impressions of threat is virtually indistinguishable from that of criminal appearance.

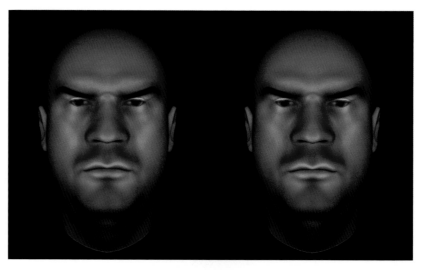

FIGURE 6.15. Visualizing impressions of criminality (left) and impressions of threat (right).

Both of these models, built from judgments of criminality and threat, respectively, can be perfectly re-created by the models of trustworthiness and dominance. Not specifying the type of crime, we typically think of a violent crime, and our stereotype of the criminal is a threatening face: one that looks dominant and untrustworthy.

Impressions of trustworthiness and dominance are not completely independent: we tend to see untrustworthy faces as dominant and dominant faces as untrustworthy. To a large extent, this is because the masculinity of faces is an input to both impressions of untrustworthiness and dominance. But we can differentiate these impressions. Experiments show that whereas impressions of trustworthiness are more dependent on emotion cues, those of dominance are more dependent on masculinity and facial maturity cues. Impressions of trustworthiness and dominance are the most important impressions, because they are our best effort, when only appearance information is available, to figure out the goodness or badness of the intentions of others and their ability to act on these intentions.

• • • • •

The similarity of impressions, though convenient when trying to figure out the structure of impressions, is pretty inconvenient when trying to figure out the unique combinations of features that lead to specific impressions.

Similar impressions will always be based on similar combinations of features. But using the models of impressions, we can find out what makes one impression different from a highly similar impression. Let's look at what happens with impressions of trustworthiness and competence when we remove the combinations of features that make a face attractive.

We learned from controlled experiments that we are more willing to invest money in trustworthy-looking others. But you probably noticed that "trustworthy" faces are more attractive than "untrustworthy" faces, mainly because the former are more feminine than the latter. This suggests an alternative interpretation of the findings, namely, that we are more willing to invest in attractive people. When we think of appearance, we usually think of attractiveness. In psychology jargon, we refer to the effects of attractiveness on decisions as "attractiveness halo" effects. From this "halo" perspective, we can argue that participants in trust experiments are responding not to the trustworthiness of faces but to their attractiveness. In experimental lingo, trustworthiness is confounded with attractiveness, and this confound can explain the data. But what if you have to make an investment choice based on the faces in Figure 6.16?

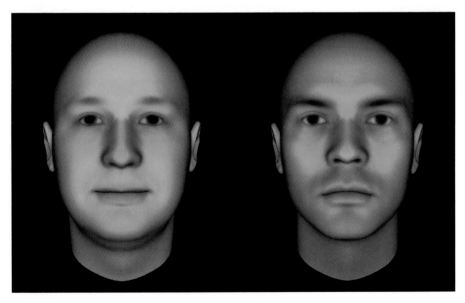

FIGURE 6.16. Who would you trust with your money? Visualizing the difference between impressions of trustworthiness and attractiveness.

Most likely, your preferred choice is the face on the left, although this face is less attractive than the one on the right. I generated these faces by simply removing their attractiveness from their trustworthiness. This is a trivial operation once we have models of these impressions. The attractiveness halo is used to explain just about any effect of appearance in both academic psychology and everyday life, but this is a fairly limited view. As the physiognomists suspected, there is much more to appearance than attractiveness. We form specific impressions from faces that are suited for the particular situation.

By removing attractiveness from other models of impressions, we can also find hidden biases in our impressions. Take a look at the faces in Figure 6.17. These faces were generated by a model of impressions of competence, an attribute that we have learned is extremely important for many decisions (see Chapter 3).

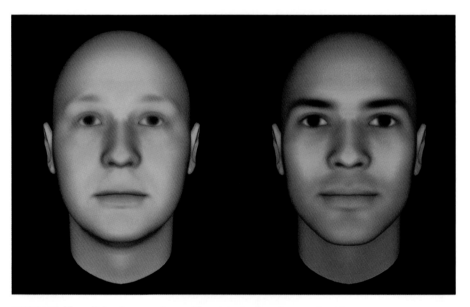

FIGURE 6.17. Visualizing impressions of incompetent and competent faces.

The "competent" male face (on the right) is more attractive than the "incompetent" male face (on the left). Look what happens in Figure 6.18 when we remove attractiveness from the competence model. Whereas the "competent" face turns into a man with a confident look, the "incompetent" face turns into a woman with an unconfident look.

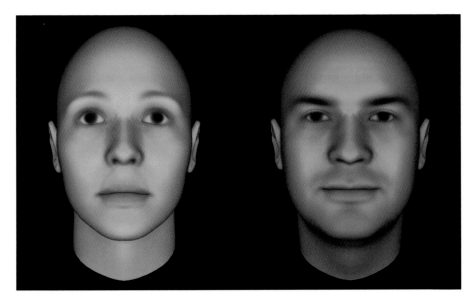

FIGURE 6.18. Visualizing the difference between impressions of competence and attractiveness.

Deconstructing the model of competence, we can see that impressions of competence are constructed from facial cues of attractiveness, masculinity, and confidence. These impressions appear to be male biased, although the bias was not immediately obvious. There are many ways in which we can refine the models of impressions and, as a result, isolate more and more specific combinations of features that shape our first impressions.

• • • • •

Other data-driven methods can be used to discover the cues that go into first impressions. A group in the United Kingdom led by Andrew Young, one of the pioneers of modern face perception research, used a high-tech version of the technique that Galton invented in the nineteenth century. The researchers started with images of 1,000 non-famous faces collected from the Internet. The faces were deliberately selected to be as different from one another as possible, in terms of age, expression, pose, and so on. The images were rated on many different characteristics, and subsequent statistical analyses confirmed the importance of impressions of trustworthiness and dominance.

To find out the cues that go into the different impressions, the researchers morphed the faces, which elicited the most extreme impressions. Just as in composite photography, morphing the faces creates "pictorial averages" that get rid of some cues, which are used inconsistently by observers, and preserve other cues, which are used consistently by observers. As a result, the final morphs represent the typical types for the corresponding impressions. Figure 6.19 shows the morphing continuum of impressions of trustworthiness.

FIGURE 6.19. A morphing continuum between composites of untrustworthy- and trustworthy-looking faces.

As we move from left to right, the faces become more trustworthy. Notice the changes in gender and expression. Just as in our models developed from computer-generated faces, as the face becomes more trustworthy, it becomes happier and transforms from a man into a woman (see Figures 6.4 and 6.6).

Figure 6.20 shows the morphing continuum of impressions of dominance.

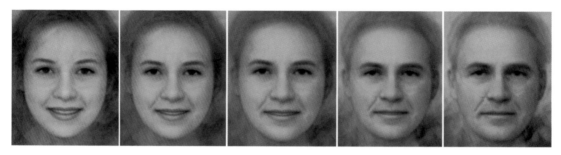

FIGURE 6.20. A morphing continuum between composites of submissive- and dominant-looking faces.

As we move from left to right, the faces become more dominant. Once again, as in our model of dominance, as the face becomes more dominant, it becomes more masculine and transforms from a woman into a man (see Figures 6.9 and 6.12). This method is another version of a data-driven approach. The researchers did not manipulate anything in the face images. In fact, these images were deliberately left to vary freely. Then the images were sorted based on participants' first impressions, and the morphing technique revealed the cues driving these impressions.

The cues identified in our models and those identified in the morphing models converge nicely. But there were a few cues that we didn't observe in our models. The morphing shows that age is an important ingredient of first impressions. As the faces become more trustworthy and more dominant, they also age. One reason we did not see this in our models is that the computer-generated faces did not vary as much in age. This is one of the major weaknesses of data-driven methods. If cues that are important for impressions do not vary in the faces used to construct the models, we will not be able to discover them. Because the age variation was low for the computer-generated faces, participants did not rely on age cues to form impressions. In the end, our computer-generated faces are simplified representations of real faces.

Using richer face stimuli that varied on age, Young and his colleagues discovered not only that age cues are important for impressions but also that the structure of impressions is a bit more complicated. In what we believed was this structure, depicted in Figures 6.3 and 6.14, attractiveness was not a fundamental dimension along with trustworthiness and dominance. It was just another specific impression that could be re-created, as we did for threat, from the perceived trustworthiness and dominance of faces. This turned out not to be true. Youthfulness-attractiveness emerged as an impression dimension independent of trustworthiness and dominance. To visualize this, imagine the axis of attractiveness sticking out of the page in Figure 6.3 or Figure 6.14. Figure 6.21 shows the attractiveness continuum.

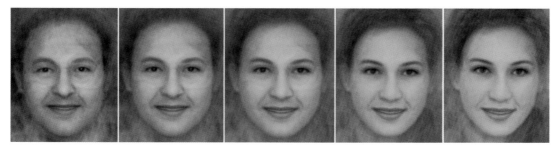

FIGURE 6.21. A morphing continuum between composites of unattractive and attractive faces.

As the face becomes more attractive, it transforms from a man into a woman. Sadly but predictably, it also becomes younger. We evaluate faces on three fundamental dimensions: attractiveness, trustworthiness, and dominance. Age, masculinity/ femininity, and emotional expressions are the most important ingredients of these impressions.

●　●　●　●　●

Mendelssohn and Secord were unhappy with the methods available at their time to study physiognomy. Secord did not appreciate the standard approach of "elementalizing" used by psychologists. This approach could not handle the holistic impression effects described by artists like Töpffer. But psychologists came up with new approaches to study first impressions—approaches that do not make any assumptions about which features are important and which are not; approaches that are capable of finding the combinations of features that shape our impressions. As illustrated by the research described in Chapters 5 and 6, none of our impressions are reducible to single features. Many, many features—including overall facial shape, eyebrows, eyes, mouth, nose, and cheekbones—change as we compare the appearance of the trustworthy- and untrustworthy-looking faces, or the appearance of the submissive- and dominant-looking faces. The changes are better described as changes in global face properties that capture things like masculinity, age, and emotional states. First impressions are constructed from multiple visual cues, ranging from fleeting expressions to invariant features, such as facial maturity. We combine these cues to form coherent impressions.

We can create mathematical models of any impression and apply these models to novel faces, including images of real faces. We can take an image of a face and make it look more attractive or more trustworthy, or more dominant, or whatever attribute we care about. But most importantly, these models help us understand first impressions. Once we have a model, we can discover the combinations of facial features that lead to these impressions. We can understand why impressions of trustworthiness and dominance are so important. These impressions are about figuring out other people: their intentions and abilities.

THE EYE OF THE BEHOLDER

Take a look at the face in Figure 7.1. This is not a face you are likely to ever see. I generated it to be very different from a typical face. But if you were to meet a person with such a face, would you trust him?

FIGURE 7.1. A synthetic face generated to be very different from a typical face.

Chances are that you wouldn't, not because the face was manipulated to be untrustworthy in one of our models, but because it is very different from what you see as a typical face. How about the face in Figure 7.2?

FIGURE 7.2. A synthetic face similar to the atypical face in Figure 7.1.

This face looks quite normal, but only because you first looked at the highly atypical face in Figure 7.1. If you stare at weird faces, what you see as typical shifts toward the weird faces. Psychologists call this "adaptation": your brain gets used to the novel, strange stimuli; consequently, stimuli similar to the strange ones don't look that strange. If you were to see the face in Figure 7.2 without seeing the atypical face first, it would not seem that typical. Or if you were to see the face in Figure 7.3 first, the face in Figure 7.2 would look extremely atypical. You can try this experiment on your own. Stare for 1 minute at the face in Figure 7.1 and then look at the face in Figure 7.2. Take a break and repeat the procedure but staring at the face in Figure 7.3 first (and then look at the face in Figure 7.2 again to experience the effect of adaptation).

Face typicality is important because it shapes our impressions. We can think of all the faces we have encountered in life as populating a large sphere, with the most typical face at the center of the sphere. All faces on the periphery are atypical faces. The faces in Figures 7.1 and 7.3 are both on the periphery but are diametrically opposite each other. We tend to distrust atypical faces. But as adaptation experiments show, what we see as typical can be easily

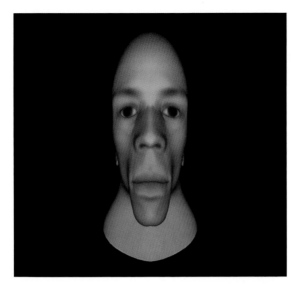

FIGURE 7.3. A synthetic face generated to be very different from a typical face.

shifted, even though the shift may be temporary. More importantly, we all have different mental face spheres—the memories of the faces we have seen—because different faces populate our environments. A person growing up in Asia has a different visual diet of faces than a person growing up in Europe or the Middle East. These different diets shape what we perceive as typical or atypical and this, in turn, shapes our impressions.

We differ not only in what we consider as typical but also in what we know about the people around us. If you know somebody who looks like the face in Figure 7.2 and you trust them, you are going to trust people with similar faces. But if you distrust them, you are going to distrust people with similar faces. Lichtenberg thought of this as "the law of our thinking that the moment we see someone, the most similar character we know immediately comes to mind, and commonly also immediately determines our judgment." It's also the case that if your face happened to have a shape similar to the face in Figure 7.2, you are also going to trust people with similar faces. We generalize our knowledge of others and ourselves to physically similar others.

The models of impressions discussed in the previous chapters identify the facial cues that we consistently use to form impressions, but they don't identify the cues that come from our cultures and our unique experiences. To build our models of impressions, we aggregate impressions across individuals. That is, we average the judgments of many individuals. Using these aggregated impressions, we can capture the shared meaning of facial cues. But aggregating across individuals masks individual differences—the unique contributions that each of us brings to our impressions. As a general statistical rule, agreement between aggregated judgments is always higher than agreement between individual judgments. Here is a specific example. If we were to collect judgments of the trustworthiness of faces from about thirty people, we would obtain a very reliable measure of the average perceived trustworthiness. This simply means that if we ask another thirty people to judge the same faces, the expected correlation between the average judgments of the two groups would be high, typically around .90. This is almost as good as it gets (when two measures are perfectly related, their correlation is 1; when they are completely unrelated, their correlation is 0). But the high correlation between the average judgments of the two groups doesn't mean that the correlations between individual judgments are also high. These correlations are much more modest, hovering around .25. That is, if you select randomly two of the judges, you would expect the correlation between their judgments to be around .25. Although we generally agree when we form impressions from faces, our agreement with one another is far from perfect. Our potential disagreements in impressions originate in our idiosyncrasies—the unique, individual contributions to first impressions.

To fully understand first impressions, we need to account for all cues that shape these impressions: not only those cues with widely shared meaning but also those that are unique to each individual. This chapter is about how our idiosyncrasies—what we consider a typical face, the appearances of our friends and foes, and our own faces—contribute to impressions. These idiosyncrasies result from living in specific cultures, belonging to specific groups, and having unique individual experiences with others.

• • • • •

Galton believed that each race had "some ideal typical form"—to be discovered by the method of composite photography—and the way to improve the race was to encourage the breeding of those similar to the typical form and discourage the breeding of the dissimilar ones. We may disagree with Galton's eugenics prescriptions, but his prejudices are deeply ingrained in us. We trust people who are similar to our tribe and distrust people who are dissimilar. This prejudice has a long history. Describing the emergence of chiefdoms—consisting of thousands of individuals—around 7,500 years ago, Jared Diamond wrote, "people had to learn, for the first time in history, how to encounter strangers regularly without attempting to kill them." We may have learned not to kill strangers, but we have preserved our first gut response not to trust them.

For Galton, the ideal, typical type was the British type. But if he had been Japanese, his ideal, typical type would have been different. To demonstrate how what we perceive as typical influences impressions of trustworthiness, Carmel Sofer, an Israeli psychologist working with Ron Dotsch, Daniel Wigboldus, and me, created morphs of a typical young Israeli woman and a typical young Japanese woman. To create these "typical" faces, he followed Galton's prescriptions: morphing the faces of a few dozen young women from their respective countries. Carmel also created a series of interpolated faces between the two typical faces. As you can see in Figure 7.4, the faces transform from a typical Japanese (on the left) to a typical Israeli face (on the right).

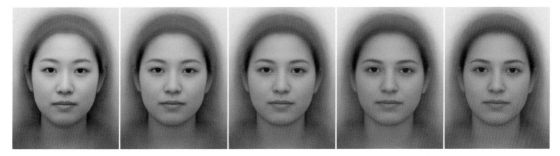

FIGURE 7.4. Morphs of a typical young Japanese woman (on the left) and a typical young Israeli woman (on the right). The faces in between are the interpolated faces.

When Israeli and Japanese women rated these faces on trustworthiness, their impressions were predictably influenced by what they considered typical. As the face became more similar to the typical Israeli face, Israelis trusted it more and more and Japanese trusted it less and less. As the face became more similar to the typical Japanese face, the opposite occurred. We trust those who look like members of our own tribe.

Experimental psychologists are always happier if we can reproduce effects from the real world in the lab under tight experimental control. This guarantees that the observed effects—changes in impressions of faces—are caused by the experimental factors we manipulated—exposure to specific faces—rather than by the many other factors that we cannot possibly control in the real world. We cannot control your exposure to faces in real life, but we can manipulate this exposure in experiments and, consequently, what you see as a typical face. Psychologists have known for a long time that when presented with novel faces, our brains seem to automatically extract their "average" or typical face (the prototype of the set of faces). You can think of the "average" face as the morph of the seen faces. There are many different ways to demonstrate this phenomenon. One is to present participants with faces without ever presenting their average. Subsequently, these participants perceive the average face as more familiar than faces that were actually presented. Remarkably, even 3-month-old infants show similar effects. After staring at faces, the infants become familiar with the faces. When presented with a novel face and a familiar face, the infants look longer at the novel face. They prefer novel stimuli. But when presented with a familiar face and the average of the familiar faces, they look longer at the familiar face. The latter is more novel to them than the average of the familiar faces. From early on in development, we effortlessly form a representation of the typical face in our environment.

Based on Carmel's work, we would expect that seeing different faces would change not only what participants perceive as typical but also what they perceive as good or bad. To test this hypothesis, with Ron Dotsch and the Israeli psychologist Ran Hassin, we had participants look at hundreds of faces. Importantly, using a statistical model for representing and generating faces, we generated faces that originated from different "average" faces. In essence, we created different spheres of faces for different groups of participants. For some participants, the average face (the one at the origin of the face sphere) might look like the face on the left in Figure 7.5; for others it might look like the face on the right. The differences are subtle, but as you will see, they are sufficient to influence impressions of novel faces.

During the first stage of the experiments, on each trial, participants saw a face generated from their sphere of faces. In total, they saw 500 different faces. To keep their attention on the faces, once every few trials, the face was fol-

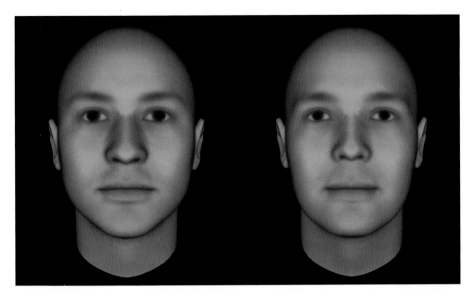

FIGURE 7.5. After being presented with a few hundred faces that are similar to the face on the left, participants started perceiving this face as more typical than did participants presented with faces similar to the one on the right.

lowed by a silhouette, and the participant decided whether the silhouette matched the face. Participants were not asked to learn anything about the faces or to rate them on any characteristic. But we expected that they would learn their respective "average" face. And they did. In the second stage of the experiment, participants were shown a novel set of faces and asked to rate each face on typicality. They rated their respective average face as more typical. They also rated faces that were more similar to their average face as more typical than faces that were less similar. So within half an hour, we managed to change what participants perceived as typical.

But we were mostly interested in how this change affects impressions. As in the case of typicality, participants perceived their average face as more trustworthy. Those who were presented with faces originating from the face on the left in Figure 7.5 rated this face as more trustworthy than those who were presented with faces originating from the face on the right. And the latter rated the face on the right as more trustworthy. Moreover, this effect generalized to other faces. Take a look at the face in Figure 7.6. Which group of participants would find this face more trustworthy?

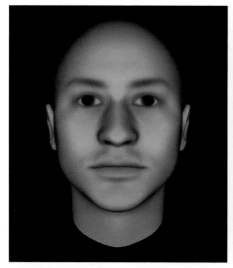

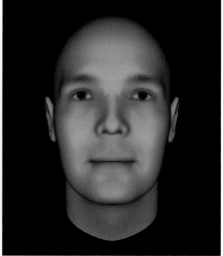

FIGURE 7.6. Which group of participants (those exposed to faces originating from the face on the left in Figure 7.5 or those exposed to faces originating from the face on the right in Figure 7.5) would find this face more trustworthy?

FIGURE 7.7. Which group of participants (those exposed to faces originating from the face on the left in Figure 7.5 or those exposed to faces originating from the face on the right in Figure 7.5) would find this face more trustworthy?

How about the face in Figure 7.7? To answer these questions, you need to notice the similarity of these faces to the average or typical faces of the two groups. Figure 7.8 makes this clear.

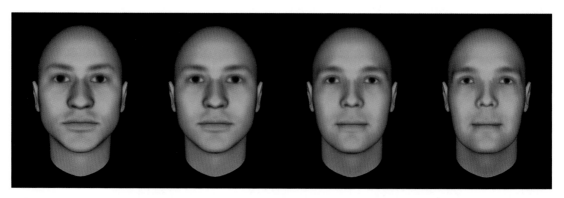

FIGURE 7.8. For participants whose typical face had a slightly wider nose (second face from the left), faces with wide noses (the face on the left) were considered more trustworthy. For participants whose typical face had a slightly thinner nose (third face from the left), faces with thin noses (the face on the right) were considered more trustworthy.

The face with the wide nose is more similar to the face next to it (the second face from the left in Figure 7.8). Participants, for whom the latter was the typical face, found the wide-nosed faces (and other similar faces) to be more trustworthy than participants for whom the typical face was the other face (the third face from the left). The latter participants found the face with the thin nose to be more trustworthy, because it was more similar to their typical face.

Note that this trust does not come from the shape of the nose per se or from any other facial features. It comes from the fact that these faces more closely resemble what participants perceived as the typical face. Although the differences between the two faces in Figure 7.5 are subtle, once they become our typical faces, they shape whether we trust novel faces. This trust originates in our experience with faces, the experience that determines what we consider typical, and not in some inherent trustworthy properties of the face. This is an experimental demonstration of Carmel's cross-cultural effect. Different people, different social groups, or even the same persons at different times in their lives, are likely to have different typical faces, which would accordingly shape their impressions of novel faces. Lichtenberg foresaw this: "there is no physiognomy for one people to another, one tribe to another, and one century to another."

· · · · ·

Each of us has our own set of idiosyncratic biases, and these biases, just like what we see as typical, shape our impressions. At first sight, we like and trust people who resemble people whom we already like and trust. As Lichtenberg put it, "the face of an enemy thus makes a thousand other faces ugly to us, just as the face of a loved one in contrast spreads its appeal to a thousand others."

The psychologist Susan Andersen has conducted many studies showing that we form impressions of people who resemble our significant others along similar lines. Not surprisingly, facial resemblance is a powerful trigger of these impressions. If your father is a warm person, you are likely to see people whose faces resemble your father's face as warm too. But it is not only resemblance to significant others that triggers these impressions. Resemblance to any person we have knowledge about is sufficient to shape our impressions.

One of my former students, Sara Verosky, now a professor at Oberlin College, and I tested whether subtle similarities to people we have learned to trust or distrust shape our trust of novel faces. Sara had participants learn evaluatively charged facts about faces. When shown a face like the one in Figure 7.9, they may learn something positive like "he provided food and clothing for flood victims" or something negative like "he made an obscene gesture at an old lady." We are remarkably good at learning such facts. Even after seeing as many as 500 faces and unique behavioral descriptions, participants are able to tell the "good" from the "bad" faces when the faces are subsequently presented alone. They don't remember the exact facts, but they do remember the evaluative gist of the facts.

FIGURE 7.9. In our experiments, participants learned to associate faces like the one shown here with positive or negative behaviors. Photo © Alex Kayser, from the book *Heads by Alex Kayser*, Abbeville Press, 1985.

Sara and I were interested in whether such learning would affect the impressions of novel faces. In our experiments, after participants learned to associate faces with positive or negative facts, they were asked to judge the trustworthiness of novel faces. Unbeknownst to them, some of these faces were manipulated to be similar to the learned faces. We manipulated the similarity by morphing learned and novel faces: the faces in Figure 7.10 are all morphs of novel faces with the face in Figure 7.9. The morphing is subtle to prevent participants from explicitly recognizing the learned face. Yet despite the lack of recognition, participants trusted faces resembling those associated with positive facts and distrusted faces resembling those associated with negative facts. The influence of face similarity was fairly automatic. Explicitly telling participants about the similarity between learned and novel faces and asking them to ignore it did not make much of a difference in their judgments. We can't help but generalize the knowledge of familiar faces to similar novel faces.

FIGURE 7.10. Morphs of the face from Figure 7.9 with four novel faces. Base photos © Alex Kayser, from the book *Heads by Alex Kayser*, Abbeville Press, 1985. Adapted in Verosky & Todorov 2010.

The influence of face similarity extends to hiring decisions and consumer choices. Participants judged job applicants whose faces resembled former successful employees as more qualified than applicants whose faces resembled former unsuccessful employees, even though the applicants' resumes contained plenty of relevant information. Before the scandal of Tiger Woods's many sexual relationships broke, participants were more willing to buy goods from the salesman on the left in Figure 7.11—a morph of Woods and an unfamiliar face—but after the scandal, their preferences reversed: the salesman on the right—a morph of two unfamiliar faces—was the one to be trusted.

FIGURE 7.11. Morphs of an unfamiliar face with the face of Tiger Woods (on the left) and with another unfamiliar face (on the right).

Similarity to our own faces is just as important as similarity to faces of liked or disliked others. There is a little Narcissus in each of us. Leonardo considered one of the greatest faults of painters to paint faces that "resemble their master." Reflecting on this human fault, he wrote: "the very soul which rules and governs each body directs our judgment before it is our own. Therefore it has completed the whole figure of a man in a way that it has judged looks good, be it long, short, or snub-nosed." He advised painters when selecting beautiful faces to "let their beauty be confirmed by public renown than by your own judgment. You might deceive yourself and choose faces which conform to your own, for often, it seems such conformities please us."

Modern research confirms Leonardo's insights. We are more willing to invest money in people and to vote for politicians whose faces have been manipulated to resemble our own faces. There is evidence that we are more likely to marry people who look like us and even choose purebred dogs who "resemble" us for pets (Figure 7.12). We try to shape our environments.

FIGURE 7.12. Several studies suggest that the faces of purebred dogs resemble the faces of their owners.

The effects of self-similarity go both ways. The very first study that Sara did in my lab was to show that people are more likely to recognize themselves in trustworthy than in untrustworthy morphs of themselves. Another study found that after economic exchanges, people perceived the faces of those who reciprocated their trust as more similar to their own faces. Nice people seem to look like us. How we look and whom we already like and trust shape our impressions of novel faces.

• • • • •

When forming impressions from faces, we use multiple cues. Some of these cues—identified by the models described in the previous chapters—are used by most of us. And some—described here—are unique to each of us. This distinction between what is shared among us and what is unique is often described as a dichotomy between the features of the face that lead to "objective" impressions and the features that are only in the eye of the beholder. But this is a false dichotomy. Everything is in the eye of the beholder, but some of it is seen by most, some of it is seen by many, and some of it is seen by few.

The models of impressions identify the shared meaning of the facial cues that we consistently use to form impressions: positive expressions indicate trustworthiness, negative expressions indicate untrustworthiness, masculinity indicates aggressiveness and dominance, and so on. But not all meaning is shared. In many Western cultures, people see smiling as indicating social bonding, but in other cultures, they see it as indicating superiority. As a result, while genuine smiles can signal good intentions in Western cultures, they may signal dominance rather than affiliation in other cultures. In some cultures, people see masculine faces as aggressive, but in others they don't. Until recently, it was taken for granted that masculine appearance is a universal signal for dominance. But recent findings show that this "universal" signal is unambiguous only in industrialized cultures. The cues that we use to infer intentions and abilities vary across cultures.

The meaning of facial cues varies not only from culture to culture but also from group to group in the same culture, and from individual to individual in the same group. In the same culture, people from the same race agree more in their impressions than do people from different races. In the same culture and race, siblings, close friends, and spouses agree more than strangers do. And even the most genetically and socially similar people, twins, have their own idiosyncratic face preferences. To estimate the genetic and environmental contributions to idiosyncratic face preferences, an international group of researchers studied more than 500 pairs of identical twins and over 200 pairs of non-identical same-sex twins. Because both identical and non-identical twins share similar family environments, but identical twins share on average twice as much of their genetic variation, it is possible to estimate the genetic and environmental contributions to abilities and preferences. Previous studies, for example, have shown that face recognition ability is mostly explained by genetic variation. In this particular study, the researchers were interested in whether agreement on the idiosyncratic components of impressions—the part of the impressions not shared with the average impression of all participants—was higher for identical than for non-identical twins. This result would have indicated that some of the idiosyncratic preferences are due to genetic influences. This was not the case. The agreement on impressions of non-identical twins was comparable to that of identical twins. And this agreement was fairly low. It was low because idiosyncratic face preferences were mostly explained by the unique environments of the individuals—those environments not shared by the twins. As the authors concluded, "individual life history and experience are a driving force behind individual face preferences."

We form impressions to infer the goodness or badness of the intentions of others and their ability to implement these intentions. When all we have is information about appearance, we rely on various facial cues—the shared meaning of expressions and unchangeable features of faces in our cultures, the similarity to what we perceive as typical and to familiar others—to make these uncertain, error-prone inferences. The meaning of facial cues is not universal, but the function of impressions is: figuring out the intentions and capabilities of others.

Physiognomists were right about our natural propensity to form impressions. The modern science of first impressions is charting the rules of these impressions: the systematic relations between appearance and impressions. In a sense, with the tools described in this part of the book, we are fulfilling half of the physiognomists' promise. We can identify our visual stereotypes of any human type or characteristic. But this is only half of the promise. The more important half of the physiognomists' promise was that these visual stereotypes are accurate, that there are systematic relations between appearance and character. Perhaps, if the old physiognomists had the right tools, they would have discovered these relations. In the past two decades, some psychologists have taken up their cause: finding the right facial cues to character. Much of this research has been fueled by advances in the study of first impressions: if we can figure out the cues that lead to agreement on our impressions, perhaps these cues also lead to actual character. The next four chapters are about the claims of the new physiognomy. Because the vast majority of studies on the accuracy of first impressions rely on still images of faces, the next chapter is about the misleading nature of images and the psychology that makes us put so much faith in these images.

PART 3

THE (MIS)ACCURACY OF FIRST IMPRESSIONS

MISLEADING IMAGES

In *Criminal Man*, Lombroso argued that criminals were qualitatively different from other humans. They were evolutionary degenerates, anomalous creatures closer to lower primates than to humans. Their difference was expressed in a number of physical anomalies, including facial appearance. The typical criminal had "jug ears, thick hair, thin beards, pronounced sinuses, protruding chins, and broad cheekbones," and there were distinctive characteristics of specific kinds of criminals: "habitual murderers have a cold, glassy stare and eyes that are sometimes bloodshot and filmy; the nose is often hawklike and always large;" rapists "often have jug ears" and "nearly always have sparkling eyes, delicate features, and swollen lips and eyelids." Lombroso's theory was hugely influential. It was discussed at international conferences attended by judges, lawyers, government officials, and scientists. Lombroso's name appeared in such different literary works as Lev Tolstoy's *Resurrection* and Bram Stoker's *Dracula*. By some accounts, the first description of Count Dracula in the book was based on Lombroso's description of the born criminal.

Lombroso included only four illustrations in the first edition of the *Criminal Man*, but the number kept increasing with every subsequent edition, reaching 121 in the last, fifth edition. These images of criminal faces and bodies were important for adding "objectivity" to Lombroso's arguments. But historical analyses suggest that the process of transforming photographs to drawings to engravings was not that objective. Some of the criminal faces became more distinctive and ugly. You can see one of these transformations in Figure 8.1. The image on the left shows the portrait of a person convicted of rape. The portrait was meant to illustrate some of the distinctive features

FIGURE 8.1. Drawings of the same person in different editions of Lombroso's *Criminal Man*.

of rapists. This was the image in the first edition of the *Criminal Man*. In the second and subsequent editions, the portrait (the image on the right) acquired more distinctive features, with more jug-like ears and more marked wrinkles. Whether these are some of the alleged features of criminals or not, modern research shows that we see more distinctive faces as more criminal. There is no evidence that Lombroso intentionally transformed the faces to become more distinctive. Most likely his convictions shaped what he saw as a typical criminal appearance.

Havelock Ellis, a progressive intellectual who supported eugenics, compared Lombroso's influence to Darwin's: "the influence of *L'Uomo Delinquente* in Italy, France, and Germany seems to have been as immediate and as decisive as that of *The Origin of Species*." In his 1895 book, *The Criminal*, Ellis discussed at length studies purporting to demonstrate the physiognomic distinctiveness of criminals, reiterating the distinctions outlined by Lombroso. He also included sketches of prisoners' profiles, "illustrating in a very remarkable manner many of the peculiarities noted." Many of the profiles drawn by Vance Clark, a governor of Woking Prison in England, were indeed peculiar, but Ellis assured the reader that "the specimens given are evidently by no means very exceptional." About two decades later, Charles Goring, using Galton's composite methods, demonstrated that the specimens were, in fact, evidently very exceptional. What Clark and Ellis saw as a typical criminal appearance was not typical at all. Just as in the case of Lombroso, the drawings were more reflective of their biases than of the essence of criminal appearance.

The first monumental statistical study of prisoners was not Hooton's study, *The American Criminal*, described in Chapter 3. It was Goring's *The English Convict*. The origin of this work was a challenge issued by Lombroso at the Congress of Criminal Anthropology held in Paris in 1889. Lombroso asked for what is now called an adversarial collaboration: a study designed, conducted, and interpreted by representatives of opposing theoretical views in an attempt to find out which view is the correct one. Three samples of born criminals, people with criminal tendencies, and noncriminal people were to be compared to test Lombroso's ideas. Although a committee, which included Lombroso, was formed, the study was not carried out. But a few years later, the deputy medical officer at Parkhurst Prison in England initiated a study in the spirit of Lombroso's challenge. Charles Goring succeeded the medical officer at Parkhurst Prison in 1903 and continued his work. The large amount of data from more than 4,000 prisoners required new methods of analysis, and Goring worked under the guidance of Karl Pearson (one of the greatest statisticians of the twentieth century and a favorite of Galton), the chair of the Biometrics Laboratory, established by Galton at University College London. Goring's conclusions were unambiguous: "no evidence has emerged confirming the existence of a physical criminal type, such as Lombroso and his disciples have described."

Goring opened his book with two composites of faces. The first one was a composite of the profiles from Ellis's book. To create the composite, he first adjusted the size of the drawings so that the distance between the base of the nose and the center of the ear was the same for each profile. Goring also obtained a random sample of profile photographs from the official photographs of the prisoners at Parkhurst. The photographs were traced to obtain the profiles' outlines, and these outlines were adjusted in the same way as the drawings. Both types of profiles—from drawings and photographs—were then traced successively on a carbon paper. Figure 8.2 shows the two composites. Can you guess which one resulted from the drawings of the handpicked criminal faces and which one from the random sample of photographs?

The more normal looking composite was the one from the randomly sampled photographs. As Goring noted, "an examination of these contrasted outlines shows most strikingly the difference between 'criminal types,' as regis-

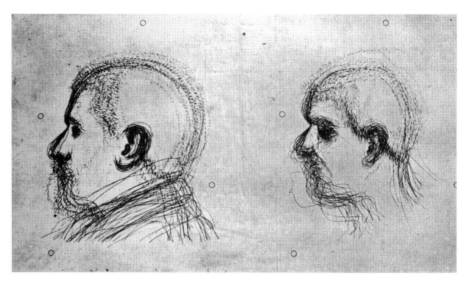

FIGURE 8.2. Two composites created from successive tracings of a random sample of thirty photographs of prisoners (image on the left) and a nonrandom sample of drawings of prisoners (image on the right).

tered by the mechanical precision of a camera, and as viewed by the imagination of an enthusiastic, but uncritical, observer." Goring's composites confirmed Galton's intuition that impressions can be "swayed by exceptional and grotesque features more than by ordinary ones."

This swaying of impressions was the reason Galton turned to composite photography. But he was aware that the mechanical precision of a camera was not sufficient to produce typical portraits. If the faces were handpicked because of their exceptional and grotesque features, "the portraits supposed to be typical are likely to be caricatures." Galton identified one of the problems of making inferences from images about reality: the problem of selection. A biased selection of weird, distinctive faces would lead to the wrong inferences. It is like polling people from the most Democratic district in the country and drawing inferences about the political opinions of the entire country. We can solve this selection problem if we select the right faces, those representative of the human types we are trying to identify. But the selection problem is bigger than that: different images of the same person lead to different impressions.

Yet most of us, including psychologists who study faces, have acted on the assumption that each image is a faithful representation of the person's face. And if we believe this assumption, we can also believe that each image captures the character of the face-bearer. In fact, the claims of the new physiognomy are mainly based on inferences from still images of people's faces. A slew of recent studies claim to demonstrate that we can accurately guess sexual, political, and religious orientations, mental health problems, violent tendencies, and even criminal inclinations from facial photographs alone, prompting headlines like "How your looks betray your personality" (*New Scientist*) and "Facial profiling: Can you tell if a man is dangerous by the shape of his mug?" (*Slate*). Like Ellis, these modern studies seem to show that we can see "many of the peculiarities" that distinguish prisoners from law-abiding citizens, gay from straight people, religious devotees from atheists, and so on. But the observed peculiarities in many of these studies can be simply explained by a biased sampling of images. Still images capture particular moments in a person's life, not the person's character. If anything, these images can be deeply misleading when it comes to inferring character.

● ● ● ● ●

We believe in the truth of photographic images. As the documentary filmmaker Errol Morris put it, "we imagine that photographs provide a magic path to the truth." Skilled artists do not imagine this. They know that there are many paths that images can take us down but not necessarily to the truth. Artfully created images can easily sway our impressions and make us see the same person as having completely different characters.

Cindy Sherman, one of the most accomplished contemporary artists, has had only one model since 1975: herself. For her work, she is the model, the makeup artist, the costume designer, the stage designer, and the photographer. In 1975, as part of a class assignment, she created twenty-three hand-colored photographs transforming her face from a plain girl to a seductive vamp (Figure 8.3). Since then, Sherman has created hundreds of different characters, ranging from seemingly lost young women to rich middle-aged socialites. Every one of them has a distinctly different face.

Like Töpffer, Sherman is a master of manipulating our impressions. Sherman became famous with her series of 8 × 10 black and white movie stills (Figure 8.4). After seeing the stills, many people would falsely remember the movie they have seen the still from or the director who made the movie. Antonioni and Hitchcock are often mentioned. But the movie stills are not from

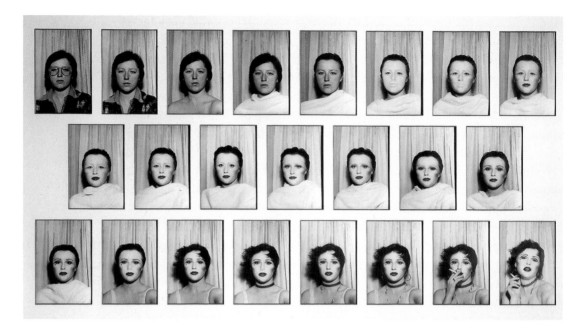

FIGURE 8.3. The photographer Cindy Sherman uses her own face to create different impressions. Cindy Sherman, Untitled #479, 1975. Set of 23 hand colored gelatin prints. Each: 4 3/4 x 3 1/2 inches; 12 x 8.8 cm. Overall: 20 1/2 x 33 1/2 inches; 52.1 x 85.1 cm (MP# CS—479). Courtesy of the artist and Metro Pictures, New York.

FIGURE 8.4. The photographer Cindy Sherman uses her own face to create different impressions. *Left*: Cindy Sherman. Untitled Film Still #21, 1978. Gelatin silver print, 8 x 10 inches (MP# CS—21). *Right*: Cindy Sherman. Untitled Film Still #30, 1979. Gelatin silver print, 8 x 10 inches (MP# CS—30). Courtesy of the artist and Metro Pictures, New York.

movies but from Sherman's imagination. She doesn't pretend that her characters are real. Yet she creates "prototypical characters," which we seem to recognize and, depending on our recognition and the feelings associated with it, they either amuse or disturb us like the characters in Figure 8.5.

FIGURE 8.5. The photographer Cindy Sherman uses her own face to create different impressions. *Left*: Cindy Sherman. Untitled #463, 2007/2008. Chromogenic color print, 68.6 x 72 inches; 174.2 x 182.9 cm. (MP# CS—463). *Right*: Cindy Sherman. Untitled #475, 2008. Chromogenic color print, 92 x 76.5 inches; 233.7 x 194.3 cm (MP# CS—475). Courtesy of the artist and Metro Pictures, New York.

Our impressions of faces can be manipulated without Sherman's theatrical exaggeration. This is what people in the digital retouching industry do. As in the art world, the retouching world has its superstars. Pascal Dangin has a long list of celebrity clients and has worked for the most important fashion magazines. Museum curators say that they can recognize his prints, although he is never credited for his work in fashion magazines. The famous photographer Annie Leibovitz said of him, "just by the fact that he works with you, you think you're good. If he works with you a lot, maybe you think, well, maybe I'm worthwhile." Dangin is able to transform the images of fashion models and celebrities with a few artful strokes. He can make them not only more beautiful, but as he puts it, "change someone's character just by doing work on the eyes."

You need not be as talented as Sherman or Dangin to successfully manipulate impressions by altering images. We can use the techniques, described in Chapters 5 and 6, to create different impressions. We can take the mathematical models of first impressions and apply these models to images of real faces; a technique developed by Mirella Walker and Thomas Vetter from the University of Basel in Switzerland. You have already seen in Chapter 3 how these models can manipulate the criminal appearance of a real face (see Figure 3.9). Figure 8.6 shows the application of a model of impressions of extroversion to an image of another real face. The original image is in the middle of the figure. We can gradually increase the extroversion of the face, resulting in the images on the right, or decrease the extroversion, resulting in the images on the left. As you can see, the differences are slight but detectable.

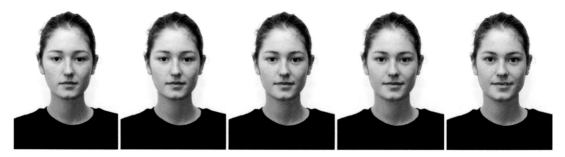

FIGURE 8.6. Applying a model of impressions of extroversion to an image of a real face. The original image is in the middle. Decreasing extroversion results in the two images on the left; increasing extroversion results in the two images on the right.

If participants are asked to rate the images, they rate the images with increased extroversion as more extroverted than the original image and the images with decreased extroversion as less extroverted. The face remains emotionally neutral, but its expressions change in subtle ways. This is easily seen in the images with most and least extroversion. You can detect the smile in the face with most extroversion and slight sadness in the face with least extroversion.

We can even change first impressions by just playing with the lighting of the face without retouching any features. Remember the bubbles technique from Chapter 5? It isolates parts of the facial image that are important for such tasks as recognizing a familiar face or an emotional expression. Using this technique, Daniel Fiset and his Canadian colleagues had participants judge the trustworthiness and dominance of faces. This allowed them to identify the parts of the image that increase or decrease the perceived trustworthiness and dominance of faces. Once this was done, all they needed to do to increase the "trustworthiness" of a face was to make the information that makes a face appear trustworthy more pronounced. The same goes for dominance. You can see the results applied to a face in Figure 8.7.

Lower trustworthiness

Original

Higher trustworthiness

Higher dominance

Lower dominance

FIGURE 8.7. Making the parts of the image that influence a face's perceived trustworthiness and dominance more or less visible.

The face needn't be unfamiliar for the technique to work. Here are the results applied to the face of former President Barack Obama (Figure 8.8). Although we can see that it is the same face in each of Figures 8.7 and 8.8, the changes in lighting induce different impressions. We are not distorting the shape of the face, just subtly manipulating the appearance of the skin surface. This is more than sufficient to change our impressions.

Lower trustworthiness

Higher trustworthiness

Original

Higher dominance

Lower dominance

FIGURE 8.8. The same technique used in Figure 8.7 applied to the face of former President Barack Obama.

● ● ● ● ●

Long before the widespread use of digital manipulation, newspaper editors used a much simpler tool for impression manipulation: image selection. The accuracy of judgments in the early twentieth-century studies, described in Chapter 2, of matching pictures of people to "social types" most likely reflected such biases in image selection. The pictures from *Time* magazine of "bootlegger and gunman" are simply different from those of "member of royalty" or "financier." But if we don't like the member of royalty or the financier, we can always choose an unflattering image to publish.

Take a look at Figure 8.9. Who is more attractive? In the top pair, most people go with the face on the left. In the bottom pair, most people go with the face on the right. But did you notice that the more attractive person in the top pair is the less attractive one in the bottom pair (and that the less attractive person in the top pair is the more attractive one in the bottom pair)? Images of the same face can be very different.

FIGURE 8.9. In the top pair, most people find the person on the left to be more attractive; in the bottom pair, they find the person on the right more attractive. But the images on the left are different images of the same person; similarly, the images on the right are different images of the same person.

Rob Jenkins, Mike Burton, and their colleagues had British participants rate the attractiveness of unfamiliar Dutch celebrities. The key was that for each of the twenty celebrities, there were twenty different images. If you average these ratings across the twenty images of each celebrity, an attractiveness ranking emerges, with some celebrities being more attractive than others. But for any two celebrities, including the least and most attractive, you can find a pair of images where one of the celebrities looks more attractive, and another pair where the other celebrity looks more attractive. In other words, the images did not represent the attractiveness of the celebrities equally. As the authors put it, "no face casts the same image twice."

Different images of the same face can change our impressions even when the differences in images are more or less random. Take a look at the images in Figure 8.10.

FIGURE 8.10. Images of the same person from a database used to train computer algorithms for face recognition. Although the differences in images are subtle, they are sufficient to evoke different impressions.

These pictures were taken from a database of face images used to train and test computer algorithms for face recognition. The ultimate success of these algorithms is recognizing a person from any image of their face. The people for this database were photographed on multiple occasions and were not instructed to pose with any specific expressions. For all practical purposes, the differences between images of the same person could be treated as random.

Yet these random image differences translated into systematic differences in impressions. Participants saw the person as trustworthy in the first image from the left, but saw him as cunning in the second image from the left. Are any of these impressions accurate? There is no way of knowing unless you already have some knowledge of the person. Given that impressions of the same person vary across different images, they can hardly be accurate assessments of the person's character. But the impressions from these images are consequential. When participants were asked to choose the image that was most fitting for a particular situation, clear preferences emerged: if the person in Figure 8.10 were to run for mayor of a local town, the first image (from the left) was the favorite choice; if he were to apply for a highly paid consulting position, the second image (from the left) was the favorite choice; and if he were to post a picture on Facebook, the third image was the favorite choice. Not surprisingly, a biased selection of images led to biased decisions: in a political campaign context, a new group of participants were more likely to vote for the person when they saw the most fitting campaign image (the leftmost image for the person in Figure 8.10) than when they saw another image. Participants did not need much time to fall for these image-induced biases: seeing an image for 40 milliseconds provided enough information to form an impression.

Not knowing how the images were produced and whether they are representative of the person, we cannot say anything about the accuracy of image-based impressions. Consider studies that purport to show accurate inferences of sexual orientation from a brief presentation of face images. Many of these studies have drawn their images from online dating websites. It is reasonable to assume that most website users did not randomly select which of their many images to post on these sites. And given that the users of these websites have different audiences in mind, it is also reasonable to assume that the images posted on gay websites are a bit different from those posted on straight websites. From this perspective, findings that participants can accurately infer the sexual orientation of the website users may simply reflect that the users did a good job of selecting the proper image to post online, communicating what they intended to communicate to their respective audiences. In other words, the so-called accurate judgments in studies on sexual orientation may have to do more with the selection of the images rather than with faces signaling sexual orientation. In fact, researchers from the University of Wisconsin–Madison recently showed that these "accurate" judgments can be explained by a simple confound: the photographs of gay men and lesbian women are of a higher quality than the photographs of straight men and women. Once the photographs of these two groups are matched for quality, guesses of sexual orientation are no better than chance.

The same problems plague studies on the accuracy of impressions of criminal inclinations, because those studies have compared mug shots with photographs of students on campus, or images of America's Most Wanted with images of Nobel Peace Prize winners. None of the control images in these studies were taken in the threatening and humiliating context of police arrest. As Raynal Pellicer, who has published a fascinating book on mug shots, describes, "you will not find any comments here [in the book] on a smile, a look, or an expression shown on the photographed faces. These would mean nothing in any case, since according to the police officers I met in the course of my research, the moment when each of these photographs was taken was intensely stressful for the person being photographed; it was the moment of arrest, captured at 1/125 second." Again, so-called accurate judgments of criminal dispositions may have to do more with the selection of the images rather than with faces signaling criminal inclinations.

It is worth mentioning a study from 1928, which is better than many of the modern studies. Discussing earlier studies on judgments of intelligence from photographs of children, Carney Landis and L. W. Phelps noted that these studies might "have overlooked the fairly obvious point that it would be possible so to select the photographs that the bright children looked 'bright' and the dull ones looked 'dull,' or vice versa." To test whether judgments from photographs predicted professional success, Landis and Phelps used an alumni book published at the twenty-fifth anniversary of the graduation of 850 men. The pictures from both the graduation and the anniversary were published, accompanied by biographical sketches. Based on the sketches, Landis and Phelps classified the men as successful or unsuccessful (a lawyer who is one of the chief attorneys of a large company vs. a lawyer who is a clerk in a large law firm), and identified the five most and the five least successful men in law, medicine, education, and engineering. Once the forty men were identified, their pictures were selected and shown to students who guessed whether the men were relatively successful or unsuccessful in their profession. On average, the students guessed that about fourteen out of the twenty successful men were successful. This rate seems pretty good, but they also guessed that about thirteen out of the twenty unsuccessful men were successful. This was the case whether the students rated the pictures of young college graduates or the pictures of the older men. The students had a general bias to perceive all men as relatively successful. When another group of students was presented with the pictures, but this time told that some of the men were successful and some were unsuccessful, the students' guesses were about 50 percent accurate for both the successful and unsuccessful. This was despite the fact that Landis and Phelps selected the most extreme representatives of successful and unsuccessful men, making it easier to detect any possible physiognomic differences between them if these were to exist. In the end, they were confident of two things: "any study conducted along similar lines will give the same result," and "it would be possible to select a group of photographs of successful men which would show a very high percentage in correctness of judgment or to select a group which would show a marked lack of accuracy."

● ● ● ● ●

Even if we accept that images can distort our impressions, aren't there some images that do provide "a magic path to the truth"? Take a look at the mug shot of Jared Lee Loughner in Figure 8.11. Isn't it obvious that he is an evil criminal?

FIGURE 8.11. An image of Jared Lee Loughner. How we see this image depends on what we know about him.

It is obvious only if you know what he did. Loughner planned to kill Gabrielle Giffords, a member of the U.S. Congress representing Arizona's eighth congressional district. On January 8, 2011, in Tucson, Arizona, he shot her in the head during a public constituent meeting and continued shooting at other people. In the carnage, six people were killed, including a 9-year-old girl, and thirteen people were seriously injured. Giffords miraculously survived but has not been able to fully recover. In the days following the shooting, the mug shot in Figure 8.11 made the front page of many newspapers. It covered the entire front pages of the *New York Post* (with the headline "Mad Eyes of a Killer") and the *New York Daily News* (with the headline "Face of Evil"). It was on the front pages of the *New York Times* and the *Washington Post*. It was the perfect shot of the face of evil. As Bill Keller, the editor of the *New York Times*, put it, "it was intense and arresting. It invited you to look and study, and wonder. The unflinching gaze. That crooked smile. That bruise around his left eye. Just as articles are meant to be read, photos are meant to be looked at, not looked past."

But it is the perfect shot only if you know about the horrendous crime Loughner committed. Four years after the crime, few Princeton students knew who he was. Out of thirty-one students, nobody remembered his name, and only four remembered that he had committed a bad crime (two of them mistook him for another mass murderer from Colorado). But we were not interested in the memory of the students. We were interested in their impressions of Loughner's face. Unsurprisingly, those who knew that he was a murderer saw him as untrustworthy, threatening, criminal, and insane. Those who did not know about him saw him as a kind of middle of the road guy, a bit more on the untrustworthy than on the trustworthy side of the road, but nothing extreme. If we were to use a different image of him like the one in Figure 8.12—the shot used by the *Guardian* in the United Kingdom—the impression would have been even more favorable. He looks like a normal young man.

FIGURE 8.12. Another image of Jared Lee Loughner.

Which of the two images better represents the "real" Loughner? Surely, the first one, but the only way we know this is because we already know what he did. We imagine that this image provides the "magic path to the truth." But we cannot know which is the "right" image before knowing the person. What we see in images is informed by our knowledge and feelings. This knowledge and these feelings make the images appear truthful, but this is just an illusion of truth.

Lavater, too, relied on this illusion when analyzing the faces of famous people. Analyzing the profiles of people like Caesar, Goethe, and Mendelssohn, he projected onto these profiles his knowledge of the people. According to Lavater, "every man of the smallest judgment" should have been able to see the superior man in the profile of Caesar. But this is only possible if "every man" knows who Caesar is. Remember the composite portrait of the members of the National Academy of Sciences from 1886 (see Figure 1.8)? The author of the portrait pointed out how the composite face expressed qualities like "perfect equilibrium," "marked intelligence," and "imaginativeness." But you can see these qualities only with the foreknowledge of what went into this portrait. Galton created not only composites of the criminal type but also of the sickly type. He could not shake off the knowledge of the pictures he used to create his composites. As he put it, the consumptive patients consisted of many hundred cases, including a considerable proportion of very ignoble specimens of humanity. Some were scrofulous and misshapen, or suffered from various loathsome forms of inherited disease; most were ill nourished. Nevertheless, in studying their portraits the pathetic interest prevailed, and I returned day after day to my tedious work of classification, with a liking for my materials. It was quite otherwise with the criminals. I did not adequately appreciate the degradation of their expressions for some time; at last the sense of it took firm hold of me, and I cannot now handle the portraits without overcoming by an effort the aversion they suggest.

Our knowledge cannot be dissociated from what we see. This creates the illusion that images contain much more than we are able to see.

• • • • •

When we don't have real knowledge about a face image, our minds readily supply assumptions that shape how we see the face. In the studies with Sara Verosky, described in Chapter 7, we used the faces of bald men. The reasons were purely pragmatic. First, we needed images of real natural faces and, second, morphing of bald faces is easy because different hairstyles do not get in the way. At the time, we did not know the source of the faces, except that they had already been used for research. For a few years, we believed that these were the faces of prisoners. You can see one of the faces in Figure 8.13.

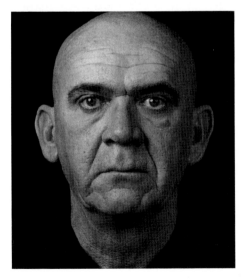

FIGURE 8.13. Photo © Alex Kayser, from the book *Heads by Alex Kayser*, Abbeville Press, 1985.

The belief was certainly plausible: stern, unsmiling faces shot in black and white were looking at us. Eventually, I decided to get hold of the original source of the images. *Heads* is a wonderful book presenting the work of the photographer Alex Kayser. The book contains 184 images of bald men and women from all walks of life, but certainly not from prison. The face in Figure 8.13 belongs to Adrian Kellard, a policeman from Westchester County, New York.

Knowledge, whether accurate or false, shapes not only how we see images but also how we create them. This was likely one of the biases in Vance Clark's drawings of prisoners. The lab group of Canon Australia recently demonstrated how this bias shapes photographic portraits. Six professional photographers were invited to make a portrait of a man called Michael. They were given 10 minutes to get to know him and "flesh out the essence of who he is." Unbeknownst to the photographers, each of them was given different information about Michael. He was described as a self-made millionaire, an ex-inmate, a former alcoholic, a commercial fisherman, a psychic, or a hero who saved somebody's life. The resulting photographs were beautiful and seemed to capture the different "essences" of Michael. Michael, the self-made millionaire, is staring into the future with an insightful look. Michael, the ex-inmate, seems withdrawn, skeptical, and full of regret. (Unfortunately, I was not able to obtain the rights to show you the photographs of Michael, but you can watch the video of the experiment on YouTube.) Acting on their false knowledge about Michael, the photographers captured those expressions and postures that conformed to what they imagined the essence of Michael was. But the resulting images are nothing more than samples of Michael's expressions, samples biased by the false beliefs of the photographers.

● ● ● ● ●

The face is not a still image frozen in time but a constantly shifting stream of expressions. Yet snapshot images of different expressions predictably shape our impressions. As Lichtenberg put it, "every movement of the soul corresponds with different degrees of visibility to movements of the facial muscles, which is why we are inclined to attribute to resting faces that resemble moving faces the significance of the latter, thus expanding the rule too far." In modern parlance, this is the emotion overgeneralization hypothesis, formulated in psychology almost 200 years later by Secord. Secord noted that we jump from the momentary states of others to impressions of character: a smile is "temporarily extended" to signify their good temper. We overgeneralize, or in the words of Lichtenberg, we expand "the rule too far." Studies confirm that we perceive smiling people as more trustworthy and angry people as less so. But as Lichtenberg argued, the emotional expressions need not be explicit. All that is needed is that the resting, emotionally neutral face has some similarity to an expression. Lichtenberg's hypothesis was that the resemblance of emotionally neutral faces to emotional expressions should predict the impressions of the faces. This may not be intuitive, but take a look at Figure 8.14. Both faces are emotionally neutral, but the face on the right resembles an angry expression more than does the face on the left.

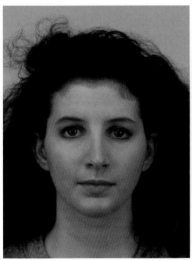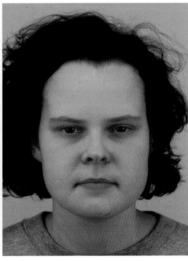

FIGURE 8.14. Emotionally neutral faces have different degrees of resemblance to emotional expressions. The face on the right has a greater resemblance to an angry expression than does the face on left.

To estimate this resemblance, my former student Chris Said, now a data analyst at Twitter, decided not to rely on participants' judgments, because these are biased by our preconceptions of how emotions are related to personality. If we believe that negative expressions and untrustworthiness go together, we may rate a face that appears to us untrustworthy as similar to an angry expression, although they may not be objectively similar. Instead, Chris relied on the "judgments" of a vision algorithm, trained to classify facial expressions as neutral, happy, angry, disgusted, fearful, sad, or surprised. The algorithm, blind to our preconceptions, provides an objective measure of the similarity of emotionally neutral faces to emotional expressions. This is how we know that the face on the right in Figure 8.14 has a greater resemblance to an angry expression than the face on the left does. Although the algorithm classified both faces as emotionally neutral, it also estimated that the face on the right was more likely to express anger than the one on the left. These estimates of similarity to expressions were highly predictive of participants' impressions. Faces that resembled happy faces were perceived as emotionally stable, sociable, responsible, and trustworthy. Faces that resembled angry faces were perceived as aggressive, dominant, mean, and threatening. Faces that resembled fearful and disgusted faces were perceived as unintelligent. These were faces of different people, but the same logic applies to different images of the same face. You already saw a demonstration of this in Figure 8.6: changing the impression of the face involved changing its expression.

The existence of emotionally neutral faces is a fiction. To paraphrase Töpffer on face drawings, any face image "possesses necessarily, by the mere fact of existence, some perfectly definite expression." Faces are imbued with affect, which can change from moment to moment. On our emotionally neutral days, we can be tired or rested, satisfied or dissatisfied, pleased or displeased with ourselves. If our pictures are taken at these different moments, we will look different. After a good night's sleep, people look healthier and more attractive in their photographs. They also look more intelligent. Women whose face pictures were taken while they were wearing clothing they liked looked more attractive than when their pictures were taken while wearing clothing they disliked. Our states change our appearance, and our friends can tell whether we are having a bad or a good day, or that something is wrong at the moment. In our good moments, we just look better, even if we are not grinning. First impressions from images are shaped not only by our momentary states but also by seemingly irrelevant things like head posture and the angle of the camera. The same face with a bowed head is perceived as submissive, but with a raised head as dominant. Tilts of the head to one's left make the face appear more approachable and attractive. And we have not even started listing the effects of bodies, posture, clothing, makeup, and various contextual prompts. All these influence impressions. The result is that still images of faces capturing people at single moments in their lives are a poor source of accurate impressions of character.

Lavater and Lombroso saw the face image as a magic path to the truth. But the magic path exists only in the tunnel of our knowledge. Once you're familiar with a face and have developed a liking or disliking of the face-bearer, this knowledge and associated feelings emerge extremely rapidly the moment you see the face. The face provides the path to this knowledge. But first impressions are about unfamiliar faces, faces for which we have no knowledge. Extrapolating from our experience with familiar faces, we erroneously assume that images of unfamiliar faces also provide a path to knowledge. They don't. Each image leads to a different impression.

Putting aside that the majority of recent studies on accuracy rely on still images of faces, many of these studies seem to find evidence that first impressions are accurate. The evidence is that these impressions are better than chance. The next chapter shows that this is hardly a reason to celebrate the accuracy of first impressions. Better-than-chance is a poor criterion for measuring accuracy. We can often do better if we completely ignore information from the face.

9

SUBOPTIMAL DECISIONS

During the 2012 Republican presidential primaries, David Brooks from the *New York Times* was interviewed by Stephen Colbert on the *Colbert Report*. Referring to my lab's research on how impressions of competence from faces predict electoral success, Brooks argued that this research indicates that "we are pretty good at judging competence." But this argument confuses the fact that we rapidly form impressions of competence with the accuracy of these impressions. The findings of the political scientists Lenz and Lawson that only unknowledgeable voters are influenced by politicians' appearance should give pause to those who think that our impressions of competence reflect real competence. If anybody knows about politicians' actual competence, it should be the knowledgeable voters, but those are the ones who are *not* influenced by appearance.

To find out whether impressions of competence are accurate, we need to know the actual competence of politicians. But measuring politicians' competence is hard and open to many alternative interpretations that depend (among other things) on one's political orientation. It is easier to measure the accuracy of impressions against less ambiguous criteria, such as sexual or political orientation or specific behaviors (including cooperating or cheating in an experimental game or being aggressive in the hockey rink). In the past decade, many researchers have been doing that. Whenever these researchers find that guesses—say, of sexual orientation—from faces are better than chance, they argue that first impressions are accurate. This chapter examines the accuracy claims of the new physiognomy.

In his critique of Lavater's physiognomy, Lichtenberg was dismissive of the accuracy of physiognomic judgments. The way he saw it, the physiognomists "are so horrendously mistaken in wanting to judge people whom they do not know from silhouettes or portraits that if one saw their hits compared with their misses, the chance nature of the game would be immediately evident." In the past decade, many psychologists have been counting the hits and misses, and some of them are coming to a different conclusion than Lichtenberg did. These psychologists might be right—the hits are a bit more than the misses—but there is more to count than hits and misses. We can do much better than chance by simply relying on general knowledge about the social world. The criterion for accuracy should be whether impressions from faces make us do better than relying on general knowledge and ignoring the faces. Let's find out.

· · · · ·

As described in Chapter 8, many studies on guesses of sexual orientation from images of faces have poorly controlled the selection of the images. In one of the better-controlled studies, instead of using online dating images posted by the website users themselves, the researchers used Facebook pictures of men who self-identified as gay or straight, but the pictures were posted by the men's friends. Presumably, this takes care of biased selection of images. This is still not quite perfect, but let's take the results at face value. Participants who were asked to guess the sexual orientation of men from their Facebook pictures did significantly better than chance. How much better? Not much: they guessed accurately 52 percent of the time, where chance is 50 percent. The accuracy of these guesses is much more dismal than that. Typically, when analyzing the accuracy of guesses, psychologists take into account two different measures. The first one is the hit rate, in this particular case the proportion of gay men accurately identified as gay. The second one is the false alarm rate, in this case the proportion of straight men misidentified as gay. The false alarm rate is extremely important when the category we are trying to guess is much smaller than the alternative category, because even a small false alarm rate can result in a huge number of false alarm errors. How this works is elaborated in the example below.

According to Gallup surveys, only 3.8 percent of Americans identify as lesbian, gay, bisexual, or transgender. If you find this estimate very low, you are not alone. Most Americans' estimates are much higher. But let's stick to the data. The percentage for gay men is a bit lower than 3.8 percent, but for simplicity let's use 4 percent. How would the better-than-chance participants fare if they were to guess the sexual orientation of a random sample of 1,000 men? Take a look at Figure 9.1. Using the 4 percent estimate of gay men, there will be 40 gay and 960 straight men.

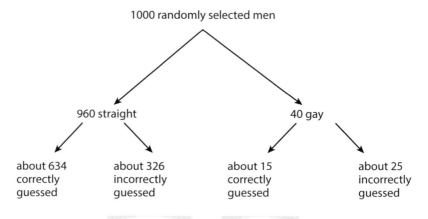

1000 randomly selected men

960 straight

40 gay

about 634 correctly guessed

about 326 incorrectly guessed

about 15 correctly guessed

about 25 incorrectly guessed

FIGURE 9.1. In a random sample of 1,000 men, we would expect to find about 40 who identify as gay and 960 who identify as straight. Applying the hit rate of .38 (taken from a study on guessing the sexual orientation of men from their pictures) to the 40 gay men, we would expect about 15 of them to be correctly identified as gay. Applying the false alarm rate of .34 to the 960 straight men, we would expect about 326 of them to be misidentified as gay.

Now let's apply the hit rate and the false alarm rate of the participants to these numbers. Their hit rate was 38 percent. So on average they would correctly identify about fifteen out of forty gay men. The more worrisome number, statistically speaking, is the false alarm rate, which was 34 percent. Our participants would misidentify more than 300 straight men as gay. But maybe it *is* the case that the Gallup estimate significantly underestimates the proportion of gay men. For many people, being gay is still stigmatized. So, let's increase the estimate to 10 percent. In this case, our participants would accurately identify 38 out of 100 gay men, and still misidentify more than 300 straight men as gay. This kind of accuracy is not going to get you too far in the real world. The logic of this analysis applies to "identifying" any rare category of people like future superstars in sports or music or people with criminal inclinations. In such cases, even a small rate of false alarm errors results in a huge number of false identifications.

We might not be very accurate in estimating the proportion of gay people, but very few think that there are more gay than straight people. From many experiments, we know that knowledge of the frequency of the members of the categories affects our guessing strategy. When we know that we are trying to guess a rare category, we tend to be conservative and more likely to guess the alternative category. This is most likely the reason the hit rate was so low in the above study: participants knew that they were trying to guess a rare category, and accordingly, they were more likely to guess that the faces belonged to straight rather than to gay people. This is a good strategy in the real world. The most accurate decisions result from combining information about the frequency of the members of the category and information about the person whose membership in the category we are trying to guess.

The real test of the accuracy of impressions is not whether they are better-than-chance but whether they are better than what we would have guessed just from our knowledge of the frequency of the members of the category. Knowing that about 4 percent of the men in the sample of 1,000 are gay, we could simply always guess straight. This would give us 96 percent accuracy, even though we won't identify a single gay man as gay. An alternative strategy is to close our eyes and randomly choose 40 out of the 1,000 pictures as depicting gay men. It is not a good strategy, but we would still be about 92 percent accurate. And what is the accuracy of our hypothetical participants in Figure 9.1? It is about 65 percent (634 correct straight guesses and 15 correct gay guesses out of 1,000). This 65 percent accuracy is actually better than in the real experiment, because in the latter the proportions of gay and straight men were the same. Is 65 percent really good? If the images contained really useful information over and above our knowledge of the relative frequency of gay and straight men, then we should do better than 96 percent.

Perhaps this example is too hypothetical, loaded with too many assumptions. But we can test empirically whether having a picture of a person helps us make more accurate judgments about the person. Chris Olivola, my former graduate student and now a professor at Carnegie Mellon University, did exactly that. It just so happened that during his time at Princeton, four undergraduate students created a website called "What's my image?" for a class project in one of their computer science classes. The objective of the website was to help people find out what first impressions strangers form of them. Those curious about the strangers' first impressions could upload images of themselves and report information such as sexual orientation, whether they have ever been arrested, ever gotten into a fist fight, used drugs, own a gun, and so on. The strangers, visiting the website, would see an image and would be asked a question, such as whether the person is gay or straight. Within 1 year of the existence of the website, more than 900 people had uploaded images, and there were more than 1 million guesses based on these images. This is when Chris approached the creators of the website and asked for their permission to analyze the accuracy of these guesses.

The guesses were better than chance, but by now you should know that better-than-chance is not a very good criterion. For every single characteristic but one, the website guesses were worse than guesses based on the frequency of the most prevalent category (for example, choosing "heterosexual" in guesses of sexual orientation). The one exception was whether the person had a college degree. The trivial explanation here is the age of the people in the images: very young people are unlikely to have finished college.

In a second experimentally controlled study, Chris and I asked participants to guess the political affiliation of members of the House of Representatives. We excluded the pictures of highly recognizable representatives like Jesse Jackson and Ron Paul, and each participant was presented with sixty randomly sampled pictures of either men or women. There was one constraint of the sampling procedure, and this was the most important part of the study. Participants were presented with different proportions of Democrats and Republicans. If you were a participant in the 90 percent Democrat scenario, you would be told that 90 percent of the faces belong to Democrats and, in fact, fifty-four of the sixty pictures would be of Democrats. In this case, your guess should be heavily biased toward guessing Democrat. There was one condition in which this proportion was completely uninformative about political affiliation: when 50 percent of the images were of Democrats and 50 percent of Republicans. In this scenario, participants guessed accurately about 55 percent of the time. This is not stellar but it is good, indicating that there is information in the pictures predictive of political affiliation. Some of this information might have been in the clothing and hairstyles of the candidates and some in their ethnicity. In the current House of Representatives, members from the three largest minorities in the United States (African-American, Asian, and Hispanics) are more than six times more likely to be Democrats than Republicans. But let's not dwell on this.

If participants are making optimal decisions, they should be able to combine information from the images with the information about the proportion of Democrats (when different from 50 percent) to make a guess better than this proportion. Alas, these guesses were always worse than any informative proportion. Much worse. Consider the 90 percent Democrats scenario. If you close your eyes and keep pressing "Democrat" for every face except for six blindly selected faces, you would be right about 82 percent of the time. And how well did people do? They were below 70 percent. These studies tell us that we are better off completely ignoring our first impressions when we have other valuable information.

In fact, there is valuable information in the face that can make guesses of political affiliation better than chance, but it is general information about the demographics of political affiliation, like ethnicity, gender, and age. Using such generally known information, which is easily readable from the faces of politicians, we can do much better in guessing political affiliation than do experimental participants. In one of our studies with Chris, participants saw more than 250 pairs of images of rival Republican and Democratic candidates who had competed in a U.S. election; the participants guessed who was the Republican (or Democrat) in each pair. As in many other studies, participants were better than chance (56 percent accuracy), but they could have done even better by using general demographic information. To make this point, Chris used simple dumb algorithms to guess political affiliation. Here is how one of the algorithms works. If only one of the two candidates is Caucasian, the algorithm guesses Republican; if the candidates are of the same ethnicity, the algorithm looks up their gender: if it is a woman running against a man, the algorithm guesses that the man is a Republican; if the candidates are of the same gender, the algorithm looks up their age: if one of the candidates is much older, the algorithm guesses that this is the Republican; if the ethnicity, gender, and age cues fail to differentiate the candidates, the algorithm makes a random guess by flipping a coin. Obviously the algorithms are not perfect and their guesses are only accurate about 62 percent of the time, and yet these dumb algorithms are still better than humans who have access to all this information plus presumably more face information indicative of the political affiliation of the candidates. We are so confident in our appearance-based impressions that these impressions trump good information and lead to suboptimal decisions.

● ● ● ● ●

Let's see whether our impressions do better when it comes to predicting specific behaviors, such as cheating in economic exchanges. The ability of Bernie Madoff, the person behind one of the largest financial frauds in the history of the United States, to defraud people and organizations for billions of dollars should make us skeptical, but let's look at experimental studies. In the investment experiment described in Chapter 3, participants were more likely to invest in trustworthy-looking partners. The experiment was a version of a standard trust game. Economists love these games, as do some psychologists, because they measure monetary outcomes rather than less "real" judgments. Here is how a round of the game goes. You are given $10 and have to decide whether to invest all of it in another player. If you invest it, the investment automatically triples and now the other player has $30 at her disposal. The risk is in this player. She can either give you back $15—this is a fair split and you have a nice return of $5—or keep all the money for herself—you lost your $10. If you have information about the past behavior of this player, the game strategy is simple: invest in players with a history of cooperation and don't invest in players with a history of cheating. But you don't have this information. If you have a choice, would you play without any information about the player—imagine a big letter X on the computer screen—or would you rather see the face of the person? The temptation is to opt for seeing the face. As described in Chapter 3, many people playing this game are willing to pay money to see the face. After all, there is more information in the face than in a big X or, at least, this is what we think.

If looks translate into behaviors, it is a good idea to invest in trustworthy-looking faces. But how good is the "trustworthiness" signal? A group of European economists and psychologists had participants play a standard trust game like the one described above. In each round, the participants would see a face and decide whether to invest or not in the face-bearer. Before the experiments, the researchers determined whether the face-bearers were potential cheaters or cooperators by describing the game and asking them what they would do. If they said they would keep the entire pot of money, they were deemed cheaters. If they said they would return half of the tripled amount, they were deemed cooperators. In the actual experiments, participants were more likely to invest in cooperators than in cheaters. These results suggest that the "trustworthiness" signal is better than chance, but there is another signal in the game that is more useful: the frequency of cooperative and cheating behaviors. The former vastly outnumbers the latter. Your initial expectations may be different, but you can quickly update them during the first few rounds of the game. Let's simulate 100 rounds of the trust game with 100 different players. Note that repeatedly playing with the same person is much simpler. If they cooperate, you invest. If they don't, you don't. We learn quickly about each other and adjust our behaviors accordingly to maximize the gains. Playing one-shot games with different players is much riskier. Based on empirical data, we would expect to play with about 85 cooperators and 15 cheaters. This is depicted in Figure 9.2. In the actual experiments, participants invested in 47 percent of the cooperators. So they failed to increase their gains for more than half of the cooperators. This lack of investment in cooperators results in a total loss of $225.

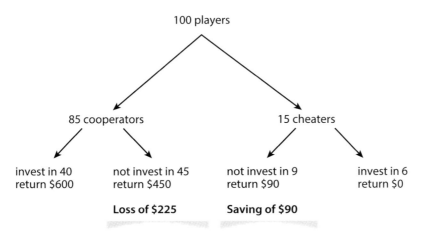

FIGURE 9.2. In a trust game with 100 people, we would expect about 85 to cooperate and 15 to cheat. Applying the investment rate in cooperators of .47 (taken from empirical studies) to the number of cooperators, we would expect to lose $225. Applying the investment rate in cheaters of .41, we would expect to save $90.

Participants invested in 41 percent of the cheaters. The small difference between the investment rates in cooperators and cheaters is the supposed evidence that people can tell them apart from their faces. The low investment rate in cheaters is a good thing: the resulting total saving (from not investing in the majority of cheaters) is $90.

How good is the overall performance in terms of money? Consider investing indiscriminately in everybody. You would have earned $135 more if you didn't pay any attention to the faces. Yes, you lost your savings of $90, because you gave your money to the few cheaters, but you gained $225 by investing in all the cooperators. If you are absolutely perfect at detecting the cheaters, you would have saved $150, but this cannot offset the loss of $225 resulting from insufficiently trusting the cooperators. The bottom line is that in an environment where cooperative behaviors are prevalent, you are better off ignoring the face information and investing your money. In the long term, this strategy brings higher payoffs.

Still the fact remains that people were less likely to invest in cheaters than in cooperators. But this difference in investment rates emerged only under very specific and unnatural conditions: when the pictures of the players were cropped to remove hair and clothes and converted to black and white. When another group of participants was shown the intact, color pictures, they rated the faces of cheaters and cooperators as equally trustworthy and, consequently, invested in cheaters and cooperators equally. One of the implications is that in a real life trust situation, the face would not give us any useful information.

There are even more qualifications of the result that people can distinguish cheaters from cooperators based on their faces. The experiments included a third group of "neutral" players. These players stated that they would only return the invested $10, so the investment neither pays off nor vanishes. Participants were more likely to invest in the cheaters than in the neutrals, even when the pictures were cropped and converted to black and white. This shows complete lack of ability to detect cheaters. Finally, we don't know whether the so-called cheaters would consistently cheat in games with different people or in repeated games with the same person. We don't even know whether they would cheat at all in actual games. Remember that their cheating status was determined from their stated intentions of what they would do in a hypothetical game.

But what we state we would do may be quite different from what we end up doing. Consider a classic study conducted in the 1930s by Richard LaPiere. He traveled more than 10,000 miles across the United States with a Chinese couple. Many Americans were prejudiced against the Chinese at the time, and he was interested in whether this Chinese couple would be refused service because of their ethnicity. Out of the 251 times they asked for service, including at hotels and restaurants, they were refused service only once. It did not seem to matter whether he was with the couple for the initial booking or order. Six months after visiting these places, LaPiere sent a letter asking whether they would "accept members of the Chinese race as guests in your establishment." Of those who responded, more than 90 percent said they would not. The rest said they were undecided, because it depended on the circumstances. There was only 1 positive response "accompanied by a chatty letter describing the nice visit she had had with a Chinese gentleman and his sweet wife during the previous summer." The overwhelming refusals could not be due to a possible negative experience with the Chinese couple. The responses of similar establishments not visited by the couple, and unlikely to have been visited by other Chinese couples, were pretty much the same. What we think we would do in a given situation can be quite different from what we actually end up doing in a real interaction with real people.

Instead of relying on stated intentions, two economists from the University of Zurich, Switzerland, measured actual behavior in a trust game. Their first experiment was conducted in Munich, Germany. Not surprisingly, they found that if the first player invested money in the second player, the second player was very likely to reciprocate. Our behavior is contingent on the behavior of others. But the economists were mostly interested in whether another group of participants could use information from the face to predict behavior in the trust game. After the trust game in Munich, the pictures of the participants were taken and used in a second experiment. In this second experiment, participants in Konstanz, Germany, were shown the pictures of the second players from the first experiment—those who cooperated or defected—and were asked to guess whether these players had cooperated or defected. The Konstanz participants' guesses were better than chance, but only because they were told whether the first player had invested in the second player. They used this piece of information to accurately infer that most players who received money would reciprocate. But they also used information from the faces to *inaccurately* infer the behavior of the players. The Konstanz participants were paid for accurate guesses: each accurate guess brought more money. Had they completely ignored the faces, they would have made more money.

Predicting specific behaviors like cooperating in a trust game is much more difficult than predicting relatively stable characteristics like political orientation. Behavior is changeable and is determined by many factors other than our character traits. The result is that it is much less predictable than we expect. How we behave in one situation may be completely uninformative about how we would behave in another situation. In the 1920s, Hugh Hartshorne and Mark May undertook a very ambitious study of deceptive behaviors. They studied schoolchildren who were given many opportunities to cheat and who believed that it was impossible to be caught. There were dozens of cheating situations, ranging from falsifying one's test results to stealing money and lying to win approval. It turned out that cheating in one type of situation—falsifying test results—is not very predictive of cheating in another type of situation—stealing money. Subsequent research has made it abundantly clear that the low generalizability from one situation to another is a general fact of life. The one way you can spuriously inflate this generalizability is to ask people what they would do in the different situations. We expect that people are much more consistent than they really are, ourselves included. Life is just messier than our expectations make it out to be.

Predicting character is a difficult business even when we have a significant amount of information about the person. As Lichtenberg argued long ago, character decisions are "very difficult, and perhaps impossible to say in any particular case whether someone is a villain; and it is audacity verging on insanity to say that someone who looks like the man whom this or that city takes to be a villain is also one." Predicting character from a person's face indeed approaches "audacity verging on insanity." We can often predict specific acts, but we would be better off ignoring faces and instead relying on our knowledge of what most people would do in that particular situation. If most people cooperate, expect that the next person would cooperate too. Every now and then, you will be wrong, but not as often as if you were to rely on your first impressions.

• • • • •

Professional sports provide an excellent domain to examine the accuracy of first impressions. In sports, specific behaviors like being aggressive in the hockey rink are frequently repeated and readily observable. This makes the behaviors predictable and good criteria against which to measure impressions from faces.

In the past few years, some psychologists have been really excited about an extremely simple face measure: the facial width-to-height ratio (fWHR). To obtain this measure, you simply divide the distance between the left and right cheekbones by the distance between the upper lip and the brow. This is illustrated in Figure 9.3. We are sensitive to differences in this face ratio, as we perceive people with high ratios to be more aggressive and less trustworthy. But what these psychologists are truly excited about is the possibility that this simple measure predicts character traits. Dozens of papers have used this measure, claiming that men with a higher fWHR are more aggressive and less cooperative. One of these papers even had the title: "Bad to the bone: Facial

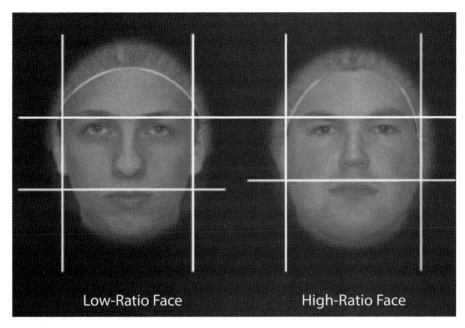

Low-Ratio Face   High-Ratio Face

FIGURE 9.3. Two faces with different width-to-height ratios. This measure has been extremely popular in the past decade. The measure is extensively discussed in Chapter 10.

structure predicts unethical behavior." This measure soon ran into many problems. Because the measure features in evolutionary hypotheses, we will postpone the discussion of these problems to Chapter 10. For now, let's consider the very first study that put this measure on the map of face perception research. The Canadian psychologists Justin Carré and Cheryl McCormick found that professional hockey players with a higher fWHR are more likely to be in the penalty box, a nice straightforward measure of aggressive behavior in an already aggressive sport.

Bob Deaner, an evolutionary psychologist, was doubtful of these results. The reason was that professional hockey players are a peculiar group; they all have been selected for their exceptional athletic ability, aggressiveness, and toughness. In a world where everybody is aggressive, it becomes difficult to predict small preexisting differences in aggression, especially from the face. Deaner and his colleagues conducted a large and careful replication of the hockey study using all NHL players except goalkeepers. They found no evidence that the fWHR predicts penalties directly linked to aggressive behavior in the rink. What predicted these penalties was the size of the players: unsurprisingly, bigger players (heavier and taller) tended to be more aggressive in the hockey rink.

And even if we were to discover that our impressions or simplistic face measures predict aggressive behavior in the hockey rink, we should not expect to observe the same aggressive behavior outside the rink. The writer and illustrator Bruce McCall recounts his encounter with one of his most hated hockey players: "it was like running into Nosferatu at the prom. Lindsay was a bad-boy left-winger whom everybody in a three-thousand-mile radius outside Detroit—even my gentle-souled mom—loved to hate: mean as a drill sergeant, almost pathologically aggressive, with a Dead End Kids kisser and zero grace, who not only racked up a lot of penalties but also an infuriating number of goals, the bastard." The encounter took place shortly after McCall's favorite team, the New York Rangers, lost the Stanley Cup to the Detroit Red Wings, in the 1949–1950 season. Collecting his strength, the teenager McCall approached Ted Lindsay and said, "I'm a Rangers fan!" expecting the worst to happen, like being grabbed by the throat and slammed into tomorrow. Instead, Lindsay smiled and responded, "great team, the Rangers. We were lucky to beat them." This confusing episode for McCall eventually led him "to digest the truth that would forever alter my fandom in sports and all other forms: the public and private personas of stars, just like the rest of us, seldom perfectly jibe and, in fact, they can actually be opposite."

● ● ● ● ●

Across several domains—predicting sexual and political orientation, cheating, and aggressive behaviors—we find little evidence that our impressions are accurate. But if these impressions are not accurate, why don't we learn to minimize their effects on our decisions? Part of the answer might be gleaned from another one of McCall's insights that "knowing too much robs you of the elemental pleasures of blind partisanship." It is easier to pigeonhole people than to see them as multifaceted human beings. But another part of the answer is that we rarely get unambiguous feedback about whether we are right or wrong. We may never find out whether the people we branded as unfriendly are actually unfriendly. Once we have decided that they are unfriendly, there is no need to approach them. There are so many other friendly people to talk to. Furthermore, we may be accurate in predicting the behavior of a person in a specific situation and be completely wrong about the person.

This was part of the confusing experience of the teenage McCall: the aggressive hockey player in the rink was a nice guy outside the rink.

Social psychologists have a term for this phenomenon: the fundamental attribution error. It refers to our willingness to explain the behavior of others in terms of their character rather than in terms of other factors, like being in a specific social role, being in a particular situation, or having a bad day. If we keep running into the same unfriendly clerk in the crowded Department of Motor Vehicles, we may form an accurate expectation that she is going to be unfriendly. The attribution error is to also assume that she is an unfriendly person, spreading her unfriendliness outside the DMV office to her home, and beyond her clients to her friends and colleagues. We will never find out if this is actually the case (chances are it is not), though we will be accurate in predicting her behavior in the specific situation in which we encounter her. In the limited context of the DMV interaction, our impression is accurate. And hence, it becomes a piece of evidence for the accuracy of our impressions.

Similar processes are at work when we form impressions from faces. With the help of the context, most of the time we can tell how another person is feeling at that particular moment. Just as in the case of the clerk, we can accurately predict whether the person is anxious, disgruntled, or relaxed. But this momentarily accurate inference is a poor guide to what the person is like in general. As Secord and Zebrowitz have argued long ago, we overgeneralize from the momentary state to the character of the person. In Lichtenberg's words, we are "expanding the rule too far." We overgeneralize not only from temporary emotional states but also from many other facial attributes that trigger associations in our minds. This was the story of Zebrowitz's research and the story of the models of impressions described in Chapter 6. Trustworthy-looking faces look happier than untrustworthy-looking faces, and they also look more feminine and older. We use the emotional state and our stereotypes about gender and age to form inferences about the person. These overgeneralizations can be completely wrong, as Zebrowitz has shown for babyfaced boys: they are more intelligent and more likely to get in trouble than their mature-faced peers. But if we don't have opportunities to observe the people—whose faces we have judged—in other situations, we can never find out whether our first impressions are right or wrong.

To make better predictions in the face of ambiguous feedback, we need to think like statisticians: appreciating the role of uncertainty and realizing that small samples of observations are bound to generate highly unstable results. We have a general intuitive understanding of statistical principles and readily apply these to chance devices like the flipping of coins and throwing of dice. Occasionally, we apply these principles to human domains where there are many repeated events. Think of sport statistics, like the percentages of free throws in basketball: we are (rightly) more confident in predicting that a basketball player who makes 90 percent of his free throws will make his next free throw than a player who makes 50 percent of his free throws. But when it comes to human psychology, we are much less willing to apply statistical principles. This is particularly true for first impressions, where we violate every principle of sound statistical thinking. We form impressions after seeing a face for a fraction of a second and are ready to act on these impressions.

The character analysts from the early twentieth century took it for granted that these impressions were more valuable than other information, such as letters of reference. As Blackford and Newcomb put it in their "scientific" plan of employment: "he [the job interviewer] is not interested in other people's opinion of you. He knows that the average employer, even if he were to state his honest convictions, would be guided by his own personal feelings and opinions or purely by guesswork, and not by reliable records of your performances. He would, therefore, far rather trust easily observable and infallibly dependable external signs of your character and habits than to take the word of a man who might or might not be sincere, and who, if he were sincere, might be utterly mistaken." But if anybody is utterly mistaken, it is Blackford and Newcomb. We saw in the Landis and Phelps study (described in Chapter 8) that "infallibly dependable external signs" are a worthless predictor of professional success. As for letters of reference, they are more predictive of professional success than are interviews, because the letters summarize more than just impressions from appearance. Interviews turn out to be a very weak predictor of professional success: the typical correlation between impressions from interviews and job performance is below .15. If you find this surprising, you are not alone. When people are asked to estimate this correlation, they predict it to be about .60. The discrepancy between reality and expectations about the utility of interviews is what the social psychologists Richard Nisbett and Lee Ross call the interview illusion. Letters of reference do much better than interviews, because they summarize a much larger sample of observations. In the world of available evidence, first impressions are of little value.

Töpffer, who endorsed physiognomy as a tool for depicting characters in comic stories, did not put much faith in the accuracy of physiognomic signs. Instead he believed that what "emanates directly from" a person's mind "is an infinitely, incomparably more reliable criterion of his moral and intellectual faculties than all the physiognomic signs of his face, examined one by one or taken all together." If anything, the physiognomic signs can get in the way of appreciating the value of people.

Anna Lelkes was the first woman to become a member of the Vienna Philharmonic Orchestra, one of the best in the world. It took her more than 20 years playing as a "non-member." Until recently, prestigious orchestras were exclusively populated by men. Then suddenly came an influx of women. What made the difference was the introduction of blind auditions: prospective candidates performed behind closed curtains, so the hiring committee could not see them and could not judge them by their gender. Had Anna Lelkes been evaluated in a blind audition at the very beginning rather than being discriminated against because of her gender, she would not have had to wait 20 years to become a member of the Vienna Philharmonic. If we care about fairness and better outcomes, we should structure decisions to increase access to valid performance-based information and limit access to appearance-based information.

Before Billy Beane became a successful baseball manager, he was a major league player who did not live up to expectations. While still in high school, everybody believed that Beane was destined for baseball greatness. It was not only his athleticism, but also his looks. In Michael Lewis's memorable description, "The boy had a body you could dream on. Ramrod-straight and lean but not so lean you couldn't imagine him filling out. And that face! Beneath an unruly mop of dark brown hair the boy had the sharp features the scouts loved. Some of the scouts still believed they could tell from the structure of a young man's face not only his character but his future in pro ball. They had a phrase they used: 'the Good Face.' Billy had the Good Face." You would not be surprised that in the movie based on Lewis's book, Brad Pitt rather than Jim Carrey starred as Billy Beane. Beane's career as a player was a disappointment. After being traded to several teams and never fulfilling his potential, he decided to end his career as a player. He was not asked to leave. He decided to leave and take a job in the front office of the Oakland A's. This decision and much that followed was a surprise to most people in baseball. Learning from his own experience that appearance is not a good predictor of success on the field, he spearheaded a revolution in the scouting decision-making process. He did not allow himself or his scouts "to be victimized by what we see." Decisions were based on good statistical evidence and not on impressions from appearance. Beane was looking for "those guys who for their whole career had seen their accomplishments understood with an asterisk. The footnote at the bottom of the page said, 'He'll never go anywhere because he doesn't *look* like a big league ballplayer.'" But they did go far and they succeeded, because Beane was able to see beyond their appearance. He was looking for "young men who failed the first test of looking good in uniform," those young men who were undervalued. This is what made Beane so successful as a general manager. He could have a great team while having a much smaller budget than the rich teams.

When reading character or level of talent in faces, we are making too much out of too little information. As Lichtenberg put it, we are lending "the smallest possible knowledge the greatest possible appearance of it." This may not be consequential in some situations—deciding that your DMV clerk is unfriendly—but may be consequential in others—deciding that your neighbor is untrustworthy or that a stellar prospect is incompetent. When these impressions are consequential, the right course of action is to consult other, more useful, non-facial information. In judgments of people, we should follow Lichtenberg's advice: "consider someone wise who acts wisely and righteous who acts righteously, and do not be misled by irregularities on the surface."

But if forming impressions from faces is universal, it is possible that they are rooted in our evolutionary past and, hence, are adaptively useful. From this perspective, impressions must deliver accurate signals. In other words, if our proclivity to form impressions is a product of evolution, these impressions must have a kernel of truth. Following this reasoning, many studies on the accuracy of first impressions are inspired by evolutionary ideas. The next chapter is about the conclusions that we can draw from these studies.

10

EVOLUTIONARY STORIES

On a beautiful sunny day in March, I was having breakfast with a friend in a café in Tel Aviv. We were chatting about the projects we were working on. At the time, I was working on this book, and somehow we ended up talking about the accuracy of first impressions. He asked me about the evidence for such accuracy and I said, as I have explained in Chapters 8 and 9, that these impressions are not accurate. At this point, my friend gently confronted me, "OK, let's put aside the political correctness. Do you really believe that these impressions are not accurate? Evolution would not design us that way." My friend is not an evolutionary psychologist, but like most scientists, including myself, he believes that we are a product of evolutionary processes. The "we" here refers not only to our bodies but also to our minds.

But starting from this evolutionary premise doesn't guarantee that we'll arrive at the right conclusions. Character analysts in the early twentieth century also believed in evolution. For Blackford and Newcomb, the science of character analysis was "based upon three very simple scientific truths." They believed that "man's body is the product of evolution through countless ages," "man's mind is also the product of evolution through countless ages," and "man's body and man's mind profoundly affect each other." These perfectly reasonable premises led Blackford and Newcomb to some unreasonable conclusions. Illustrating their evolutionary thinking, they discussed differences in the appearance of noses of people from different parts of the world. They noted that whereas people living in hot-humid climates have low and flat noses, people living in cold-dry climates have high and thin noses. Blackford and Newcomb suggested that these nose differences are evolutionary adaptations to living in different climates. They were most likely right about that.

There is a correlation between the shape of noses and the climate of one's ancestors, and this correlation can be explained by the physiological function of the nose. The nose is like an air conditioner for the lungs: it warms the air to body temperature and humidifies it; if it fails to perform its function, the lungs will be damaged. In cold-dry climates the nose needs to work much harder—the air needs to be warmed and humidified to a larger extent—than in hot-humid climates. Larger, more projecting noses are better suited for cold-dry climates, because they increase the contact between the air and the walls of the nasal cavity (mucosal tissue), making the air conditioner more efficient. Smaller, flatter noses are better suited for hot-humid climates, because they are more efficient for heat dissipation. This suitability has to do with the nasal morphology inside the nose, not with the outside appearance of the nose per se. The respective morphologies minimize the energy expenditure of the bodies.

From their evolutionarily correct inference, Blackford and Newcomb leaped to the following conclusion: "the low, flat nose is everywhere the nose of indolence and passivity, while the large nose, high in the bridge, is everywhere an indication of energy and aggressiveness." To reach this conclusion, they supplied an extra assumption—hot-humid climates abound with food and people can afford to be lazy, whereas in cold-dry climates people cannot afford to be lazy—and a large dose of ethnocentrically motivated prejudice. Their discussion of differences in skin color followed the same logic. A long history of living in different climatic environments not only leads to differences in skin color but also, they argued, to differences in character. People with ancestors from tropical climates are "slow, easy-going, hateful of change, introspective, philosophical and religious." In contrast, people with ancestors from northwestern Europe are "aggressive, active, restless, fond of variety, and, because of their fierce struggle for existence, exceedingly practical, matter-of-fact, and material."

Modern evolutionary psychologists are much more sophisticated than character analysts and collect data to test evolution-inspired hypotheses, but making evolutionary inferences is just as hard today as it was 100 years ago. The problem evolutionary psychologists face is inferring from observations today what happened thousands and even millions of years ago. In contrast to paleontologists, who can use bones from distant times to make inferences about the evolution of the body, evolutionary psychologists don't have bones to make inferences about the evolution of the mind. This makes figuring out which of our current perceptual and cognitive biases are evolutionary adaptations far from trivial.

Yet many people, laypersons and scientists alike, assume that if a perceptual or a cognitive bias is pervasive, it must be adaptively useful. Impressions from faces fall easily into this category of potentially adaptive biases. Here is the underlying logic: because of evolutionary pressures related to reproductive success or survival, we have evolved facial characteristics that signal our biological (and perhaps our character) qualities to potential mates or competitors. These qualities are reflected in the "honest signals" in our faces. For these "honest signals" to matter, they should be readable. So we have also evolved perceptual and cognitive biases to form impressions that successfully pick up these signals. This perspective doesn't assume that all impressions are accurate, but some should be to the extent that they are about honest signals of character.

This chapter examines the evidence for so-called honest signals in the face that indicate character. The emphasis is on facial masculinity, and particularly the fWHR (see Figure 9.3) as an index of masculinity, because this has been a topic of intensive theorizing and research from an evolutionary point of view. In a nutshell, the claim is that men with masculine faces are not only perceived as dominant, aggressive, and threatening but also that they *are* dominant, aggressive, and threatening. All this indicates that facial masculinity is an honest signal of aggressive qualities that evolved due to sexual selection pressures. To provide empirical support for this hypothesis, the best one can do is to demonstrate, first, that people from different cultures form similar impressions from masculine faces and, second, that these impressions conform most closely to evolutionary predictions in the few remaining non-industrialized, small-scale societies in the world. The second demonstration is very important, as these small-scale societies should be more representative of our ancestral societies than modern, industrialized, large-scale societies. As we will see, a close reading of the evidence finds little support for evolved honest signals of character in the face.

● ● ● ● ●

You read about the fWHR in Chapter 9. It was the ratio of the distance between the left and right cheekbones and the distance between the upper lip and the eyebrows. People with "narrow heads" have a low ratio, and those with "wide heads" have a high ratio. The ratio measure was introduced about

10 years ago by researchers who compared skulls of men and women. These researchers found that the skulls started differing around puberty, with men having wider faces and hence a higher fWHR. They hoped that such differences in skulls could be used to identify the gender of fossil skulls of our ancestors. More importantly, because the gender difference in fWHR could not be simply explained by the increased body size of men, the researchers suggested that these differences might have resulted from differential sexual selection pressures acting on facial parts. According to the sexual selection perspective, sexually dimorphic features—differences between the two sexes—emerge as a result of competition for mates. Features that lead to or signal reproductive success become exaggerated over time (on the evolutionary time scale).

The suggestion that differences in the fWHR are a result of sexual selection pressures fueled the interest of psychologists, and they ran with the fWHR measure. The simplicity of using the measure might have contributed to this interest. Although the original measures were collected from skulls, they were illustrated on photographs of faces, and most researchers proceeded with measuring the fWHR from photographs. In less than 10 years, more than sixty peer-reviewed papers were published using the fWHR measure. You read about the very first paper that put this measure on the map in Chapter 9—this was the study measuring the fWHR of Canadian hockey players. The finding—at least until Bob Deaner collected those measures for all NHL players—was that players with a higher fWHR are more aggressive. This finding was extended to regular participants in psychology experiments, and the list of negative behaviors grew: men with a higher fWHR are not only more aggressive and dominant but also more untrustworthy, uncooperative, and prejudiced. This ratio was now heralded as "part of an evolved cueing system of intra-sexual threat, dominance, and aggressiveness in men" and "an honest signal of superiority in intra-sexual conflict."

At the basis of these statements is the assumption that the fWHR is sexually dimorphic—higher for men than women. But just how sexually dimorphic is the fWHR? Even in the original paper that introduced this measure, the gender differences seemed small, especially relative to the very large variations in each gender (just like men, some women have very high fWHRs and some have very low fWHRs). To test the sexual dimorphism of the fWHR, an international group of researchers analyzed skull measurements of over 4,500 individuals from more than ninety different populations around the world. By comparison, in the original paper, the researchers analyzed just over 100 skulls originating from a single population in South Africa. The new study found remarkably little evidence for sexual dimorphism in the fWHR. A group of psychologists, who had used the fWHR in previous studies, did not like this conclusion and analyzed all published data on gender differences in the fWHR. These differences were statistically significant. But statistical significance is easy to achieve with very large samples. The important question is whether the size of the difference is large enough to matter in any real sense. The correlation between gender and the fWHR was .05, which is barely distinguishable from zero, and implies that gender can only explain up to one-quarter of 1 percent of the variation in fWHR across individuals. The gender differences in fWHR are miniscule relative to much more obvious gender differences in height, weight, and muscle mass. The correlation between gender and either height or weight is above .30—not surprisingly, men are taller and heavier than women on average—while the correlation between gender and muscle mass is above .80. Alas, the evidence—that the fWHR is not sexually dimorphic enough to matter—did not lead to the abandonment of the measure.

There are two distinct evolutionary hypotheses for why the fWHR could be an honest signal of reproductive success. The first one is that the choosiest sex—women in the case of humans, because they invest more time and resources in raising children—is attracted to facial features indicating masculinity like the fWHR, because these features signal good genetic qualities. The complex version of this hypothesis is that this only applies to short-term mating, as masculinity may also signal a lack of willingness to invest in child rearing. Regardless, the underlying assumption is that facial masculinity signals good genes. The standard story for why women would prefer masculine faces is called immunocompetence. Here is how it goes. Too much testosterone is bad for you, because it suppresses the body's immune functions. Testosterone is associated with both muscle and facial growth, leading to masculine appearance. Given all this, men with very masculine faces must have really good genes, because they can afford that much testosterone. This may sound a bit counterintuitive, but the story is inspired by animal research (large antlers and peacock tails may be burdensome but attract mates, because they signal good genes that allow the animal to survive in spite of those burdens). Not all scientists agree with the immunocompetence story. There is little evidence that masculine men have better heritable health, and the role of testosterone may be more sophisticated than simply suppressing immune function.

Irrespective of how the final evidence for the immunocompetence story works out, women have to be attracted to masculine faces for the first evolutionary hypothesis to be true. For years, evolutionary psychologists have argued about what makes faces attractive. One issue of heated disagreements is the role of masculinity/femininity. Everybody agrees that women with feminine faces are more attractive. The standard evolutionary story for this preference is that femininity is a signal of fertility. But the evidence on the attractiveness of men with masculine faces is split. In some studies, women find men with masculine faces more attractive. In others, they find men with feminine faces more attractive. Chris Said, who showed how resemblance to emotional expressions predicts first impressions (see Chapter 8), built a model of face attractiveness and discovered that what women find attractive in men's faces depends on whether masculinity is expressed in the shape or the reflectance of the face. Take a look at the faces in Figure 10.1. These faces have the same reflectance, but the face on the right has a more masculine shape (and a higher fWHR). On average, women find this more masculine face *less* attractive.

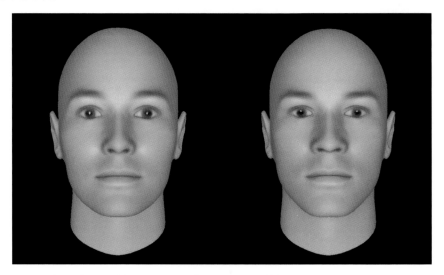

FIGURE 10.1. Male faces with the same reflectance but different shapes. The face on the right has a more masculine shape. On average, women do not find male faces with masculine shapes attractive.

Now take a look at Figure 10.2. These faces have the same shape, but the face on the right has a more masculine reflectance. On average, women find this more masculine face more attractive.

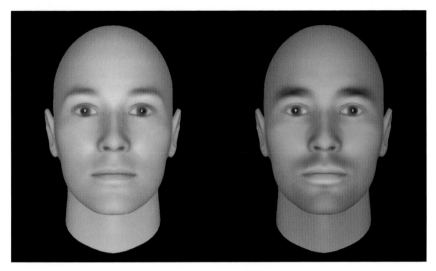

FIGURE 10.2. Male faces with the same shape but different reflectances. The face on the right has a more masculine reflectance. On average, women find male faces with masculine reflectances attractive.

These findings resolved prior inconsistencies in the literature: whereas studies showing that women find masculine faces more attractive had predominantly manipulated reflectance cues, those showing the opposite had predominantly manipulated shape cues. The fWHR is only related to face shape and, consequently, women do not find men's faces with a high fWHR attractive.

Studies using real faces support the conclusion that women do not find faces with a masculine shape attractive. But women are sensitive to the color of faces. In all cultures studied, men tend to be darker than women, and reflectance could be a reliable signal of gender. Further, as we will learn in Chapter 11, such color hues as yellow and red are indicative of our current health status. These hues are part of the reflectance of faces. What women find attractive are men's faces that have color hues associated with good health. That is, women's attractiveness preferences are better predicted by fluctuating cues for health than by stable sexually dimorphic cues, such as masculinity. This observation is consistent with evolutionary hypotheses positing that in terms of mating value, current health status is more important than past disease resistance.

All in all, the first sexual selection hypothesis that women are attracted to masculine men is largely inconsistent with the available data, at least as far as faces are concerned. But this hypothesis is about what happened in the distant past, not about what happens now. It is perfectly plausible that the facial cues that mattered in ancestral times matter less in modern times. We cannot directly test this hypothesis, but we can test its best approximation by studying women's preferences not only in industrialized societies but also in small-scale societies. The predictions of the sexual selection hypothesis are straightforward: women in the latter societies should find men with masculine faces more attractive than do women in industrialized societies. A large international team, led by the British evolutionary psychologists Isabel Scott and Ian S. Penton-Voak, studied people from twelve different societies, ranging from highly industrialized ones like Canada and the United Kingdom to small-scale, nonindustrialized ones like the Aka in the Central African Republic and the Miskitu in Nicaragua. The findings were just the opposite of the predictions of the sexual selection hypothesis. The more industrialized the country was, the stronger the women's preferences for men with masculine faces. By the way, the effects for men's preferences were equally inconsistent with the hypothesis. The more industrialized the country was, the stronger the men's preferences for women with feminine faces. The latter finding reminded me of a story from my family's lore. Apparently, my grandfather chose my grandmother not because she was beautiful but because she looked strong and would be able to carry heavy loads in the field. Anecdotal evidence aside, the existing empirical evidence suggests that, if anything, preferences for sexually dimorphic face features emerged in recent times.

●　●　●　●　●

We can safely reject the first sexual selection hypothesis, but there is a second one that may be better supported by the data. The second evolutionary hypothesis is that the development of sexually dimorphic features in men has to do with men's competition over women. In a nutshell, bigger and stronger men are better able to secure women because in a direct fight with smaller and weaker men, they are going to win. It is an exclusively male affair, so to speak. This hypothesis, favored by most evolutionary psychologists, generates the inference that a higher fWHR signals "threat, dominance, and aggressiveness" or in other words, "superiority in intra-sexual conflict." For this hypothesis to be true, at least three assumptions should be verified. The first one is that men with a higher fWHR should have more aggressive qualities. The second is that people—especially men, because this really concerns them—should be able to accurately infer these qualities from faces with a high fWHR. The third is that men from small-scale, nonindustrialized societies should be particularly sensitive to these face qualities. In other words, they should be more likely to associate facial masculinity with aggression than do men from industrialized societies.

The very first empirical papers indicated that men with a higher fWHR are, in fact, more aggressive. Even without the evolutionary hypotheses, this fact is interesting, because it suggests that the physiognomists' promise might not be completely empty. The same researchers who analyzed all published studies for gender differences in the fWHR also analyzed the correlations between this measure and measures of "threat" behaviors, such as self-reports of aggressive behavior and uncooperative behavior in economic games. For men, this correlation was .16 (for women, it was .04). Another group of researchers also analyzed such correlations across studies and found the correlation to be .11. Even with the higher estimate of .16, the relationship is fairly weak, indicating that the fWHR can only predict up to 2.6 percent of the variation in male aggressiveness. And the real relationship, if it even exists, is probably weaker, because the observed correlations between the fWHR and measures of threat behaviors tended to decrease as the sample sizes of the studies increased. This seems to follow a familiar pattern of the history of many interesting and surprising findings. After the first positive results, many other studies follow. Typically, these studies have small samples that are bound to generate more extreme results (the uncertainty of estimation is simply higher). Positive results tend to be published, while negative results remain unpublished until eventually more researchers become skeptical, and failures to replicate the original findings finally get published. Typically, these later studies have larger samples and generate more stable estimates.

But let's assume that the estimated correlation of .16 reflects a true honest signal of the fWHR for aggression. We still need to know whether people are able to perceive this rather weak signal. After all, to act on the value of the signal, people need to be able to perceive it first. Here the evidence is stronger. Both men and women perceive faces with a higher fWHR as more aggressive. The correlation between perceptions of threat and fWHR is about .46. This is very much in the spirit of one of the main arguments of this book: we are heavily influenced by the facial appearance of others. So the second assumption for the male competition hypothesis is established.

But there was no support for the third assumption. Scott, Penton-Voak, and their colleagues found that just as with preferences for sexually dimorphic features, the perceived association between masculinity and aggression was stronger in more industrialized societies. The more industrialized the society was, the more strongly masculine faces were perceived as more aggressive. All studied characteristics of the societies that should have predicted stronger preferences for sexually dimorphic facial features and impressions of aggressiveness from masculine faces—lack of urbanization and high disease, fertility, and homicide rates—predicted weaker preferences and weaker impressions. Like the first sexual selection hypothesis, the second hypothesis is largely inconsistent with the data.

But let's return to the question of accuracy. The expected accuracy of impressions is the product of the correlations of the so-called honest signal (.16) and the perception of this signal (.46). This accuracy is dismally low. For the average perceiver, the correlation between their impression and the aggressive tendencies of the person would be less than .08—that is, their impressions would predict just over one half of 1 percent of the actual variation in aggressiveness. And if we extrapolate from the findings of Scott, Penton-Voak, and their colleagues, this would have been even lower in ancestral times.

Still, to the extent that these tiny accuracy effects are real, they need to be explained. A possible explanation, consistent with the extant data, is what social psychologists call self-fulfilling prophecies. If you proactively distrust a person with a high fWHR, they are probably going to distrust you too. In Chapters 3 and 9 we discussed experimental trust games. Several experiments have reported that men with a higher fWHR seem to be less cooperative in these games. But in the only such experiment in which participants played anonymously with one another, the fWHR did not predict uncooperative behavior. This was the study conducted by the economists from the University of Zurich, Switzerland (see Chapter 9). Charles Efferson and Sonja Vogt took pictures of the participants after they played the game. Although measures of the fWHR did not predict the participants' actual behaviors, if you recall from the previous chapter, when their pictures were shown to other participants (in a different town), the latter participants incorrectly guessed that men with a higher fWHR would be less cooperative. Because social interactions are contingent on the interactants' behaviors, treating people with untrustworthy-looking faces unfairly is bound to generate "unfair" behaviors in response. And there are many demonstrations of this kind of reciprocal negativity in trust games. If the first move against you is unfair, you are likely to retaliate by returning the unfairness. We can evoke the behaviors that we predicted in others by simply acting on our inaccurate beliefs.

· · · · ·

But what makes us see faces with a higher fWHR as more aggressive? The reason the fWHR seems to affect our impressions is because it correlates with more "holistic measures" of the face. Take a look at Figure 10.3. These faces were generated by our model of impressions of threat.

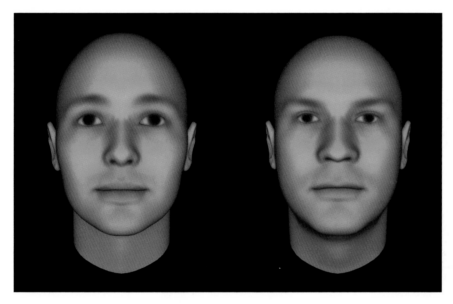

FIGURE 10.3. Faces generated by a model of impressions of threat. As the threat increases, so does the face's width-to-height ratio.

The face perceived as threatening has a higher fWHR than the nonthreatening face. Generally, increasing the perceived threat of faces in the model increases the fWHR of the faces. But does this really mean that people are primarily responding to this ratio as they are judging the threat of the faces? Along with the ratio, many other features change that are much easier to discern. These include the prominence of the brow ridge and the jaw and many other features that are correlated with facial masculinity. Most of Chapter 4 was about the complexity of face perception and how simple measures of distances or single facial features are insufficient to predict our impressions from faces. Töpffer, who invented the comic strip and was the first to demonstrate the holistic nature of face perception, would have been appalled by the fWHR measure. As he put it, "from any sign taken alone you cannot possibly estimate the effect of all together."

As discussed in Chapter 6, impressions of dominance, threat, and physical strength are extremely similar. For all these models, as we change the faces to become more dominant, more threatening, and stronger, the fWHR increases. It is no surprise then that faces with higher ratios are perceived as more dominant, more threatening, and stronger. The fact that this ratio correlates with our impressions doesn't mean that this ratio drives these impressions—it also doesn't mean that the ratio has anything to do with physical formidability. Several lines of evidence suggest that while the fWHR predicts *perceptions* of strength, it doesn't predict *actual* strength.

Some authors have argued that the fWHR reflects levels of testosterone, which is related to physical strength and aggression. But if you simulate the effects of testosterone on faces, as has been done in Figure 10.4, it is not apparent that the fWHR increases with higher levels of testosterone.

FIGURE 10.4. Simulating the effect of testosterone on facial appearance. The image on the left shows a face suggesting a reduced level of testosterone. The image on the right shows a face suggesting an increased level of testosterone.

The most visible effects of testosterone are the increase in face height and the prominence of the lower jaw. The latter is not part of the fWHR, and the former should reduce this ratio.

The most direct evidence against the hypothesis that the fWHR is associated with actual physical strength comes from the work of Iris Holzleitner conducted with David Perrett, one of the most influential face researchers who has trained many evolutionary psychologists working in the field of face perception. Holzleitner scanned the faces of real people and measured their weight, height, and upper body strength. Then she used methods similar to those described in Chapter 6 to build face models of actual and perceived physical strength. The faces in Figure 10.5 visualize the changes in face shape associated with *perceived* strength.

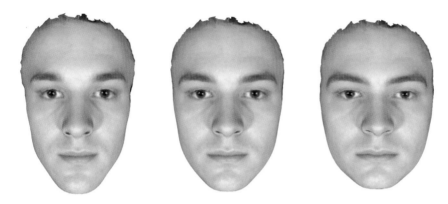

FIGURE 10.5. Models of perceived strength based on faces. The face on the left is perceived as physically weak relative to the average face (in the middle). The face on the right is perceived as physically strong relative to the average face.

The model of perceived strength conforms closely to the hypothesis about the importance of the fWHR. Faces that are perceived to be stronger have a higher fWHR than do faces perceived to be weaker. But these are models of perceived strength, which is not the same as actual strength. Because Holzleitner collected measures of actual strength, she could also build face models of actual strength. The faces in Figure 10.6 visualize the changes in face shape associated with actual strength. Although the physically stronger face becomes wider, it also becomes elongated, which should offset changes in the fWHR. What these findings suggest is that we are primarily responding to body size when judging the strength and by extension the aggressiveness and dominance of others. People with a higher body-mass index (BMI) have a higher fWHR. People with a higher BMI also tend to be stronger.

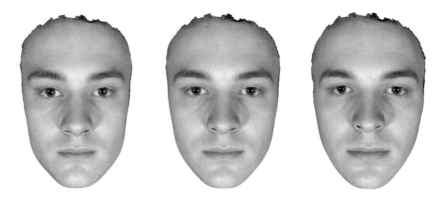

FIGURE 10.6. Models of actual strength of faces. The face on the left is associated with weakness relative to the average face (in the middle). The face on the right is associated with strength relative to the average face.

But notice that although body mass (high BMI) predicts absolute strength, it confounds fat and lean mass. In fact, extremely obese people tend to be physically stronger than people with normal weight. Holzleitner used an electrical impedance scale to estimate the fat and lean masses of their participants. Not surprisingly, actual strength was predicted by lean mass and not by fat mass. More importantly, Holzleitner could build models of faces varying in lean, muscle mass but not fat mass, and of faces varying in fat mass but not muscle mass. You can see an illustration of the latter in Figure 10.7.

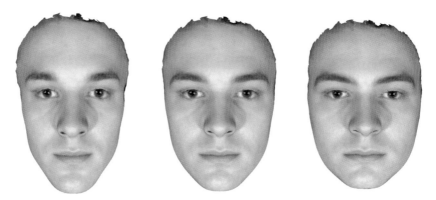

FIGURE 10.7. Models of faces varying in fat mass but not in lean, muscle mass. The face on the left is associated with less fat mass relative to the average face (in the middle). The face on the right is associated with more fat mass relative to the average face.

As in Figure 10.5, the changes in face shape conform to changes in the fWHR. Faces corresponding to bodies with more fat mass, but not more muscle mass, have a higher fWHR than do faces corresponding to bodies with less fat. But this doesn't hold for faces that vary in muscle mass and not in fat mass. This is illustrated in Figure 10.8.

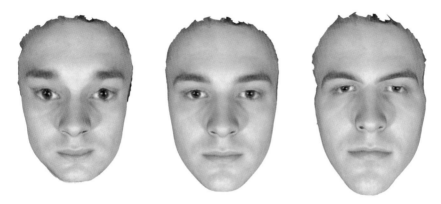

FIGURE 10.8. Models of faces varying in lean, muscle mass but not in fat mass. The face on the left is associated with less lean mass relative to the average face (in the middle). The face on the right is associated with more lean mass relative to the average face.

Faces corresponding to bodies with more lean mass are wider but also more elongated than are faces corresponding to bodies with less lean mass, offsetting possible differences in the fWHR between these faces.

The most parsimonious explanation of these findings is that we simply rely on body size when judging physical formidability. As we will learn in Chapter 11, we are good at judging body weight from faces. But in most situations, particularly in physical competitions, we would have visual information about the body. This would be much more useful than any inferences we can make from the face. And if there are doubts about the sexual dimorphism of faces, especially with respect to the fWHR, there are no such doubts about bodies. Men tend to be larger and stronger. And larger and stronger men would have faces that go with these bodies. The bottom line is that the fWHR is not much of an honest signal of aggressiveness, although it could be a signal of more fat mass and of stereotypes about bigger, heavier men.

This "signal" is not a new psychological invention. Although the fWHR measure is new, related measures have been used in the past. Take a look at the face taken from one of Blackford and Newcomb's books (Figure 10.9).

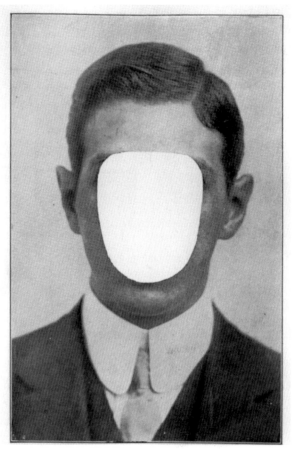

FIGURE 10.9. An illustration from Blackford and Newcomb's *Analyzing Character* (1918). Their logic of reading character from the narrowness/wideness of heads is remarkably similar to the logic of modern studies on the facial width-to-height ratio.

This "narrow head" was meant to indicate "mildness of disposition—an inclination to win way and secure ends by intellect, tact, and diplomacy, rather than by direct conflict." If you reverse these attributions for "wide heads," you would notice the remarkable similarities between Blackford and Newcomb's interpretation of the meaning of the narrowness/wideness of heads and the modern interpretations of the meaning of the fWHR. The fWHR measure is also related to another measure that was extremely popular in the early twentieth century: the cephalic index (the ratio of the maximal head width to maximal head length). The heads of thousands of people were measured, and these data were used by anthropologists, economists, and governmental bureaucrats to classify ethnicities according to this ratio, which they believed was a proxy for intelligence. The U.S. government's interest, in particular, was dictated by the "threat" of what they considered to be the undesirable immigrants at the time: Italians, Eastern Europeans, and especially Jews from Eastern Europe. They were deemed much less intelligent than the northern Teutonic (long-headed) race.

• • • • •

So where does all this leave us? The fact that we cannot find so-called honest signals in the face indicating character does not mean that all evolutionary hypotheses are false: it simply rules out some hypotheses. It also doesn't mean that first impressions are useless, weird quirks. The experimental and modeling work described in Part 2 of this book shows that these impressions serve important social functions: having only information on appearance, we do our best to infer the intentions and capabilities of others. These impressions are an essential part of our social intelligence, part of our quest to know others.

But knowing others in our distant evolutionary past must have been much easier than today. Modern humans have been around for 50,000–70,000 years. For most of this time (and the 2.5 million years before that), people lived in extremely small societies—essentially extended families—consisting of five to eighty individuals. Larger tribal societies started emerging about 13,000 years ago, but they were still relatively small, consisting of hundreds of individuals, all related to one another. In small-scale societies, there is abundant information about others. This information comes from firsthand experiences (like observations of behavior and interactions) and from secondhand experiences (like testimonies of family, friends, and acquaintances). In such small societies, people have no need to rely on appearance information to form character impressions. There is much more reliable and easily accessible information.

The emergence of chiefdoms consisting of thousands of individuals, about 7,500 years ago, and later of modern states, changed the dynamics of human interactions. People had to learn not only "how to encounter strangers regularly without attempting to kill them" but also how to live in large groups where it was no longer possible to have direct information about the character of most others in the group. They had to learn to deal with strangers in situations plagued with uncertainty. It is no coincidence that physiognomy was born at the time that chiefdoms emerged, and that it flourished in the nineteenth century, the time of the biggest industrialized migration. The physiognomists promised an easy, intuitive way to deal with the increased uncertainty of living and interacting with strangers: knowing them from their faces.

We may not be able to know others from their faces, but this doesn't imply that there are no useful signals in the face. The face does carry information about our emotional, mental, and health states, and even our life circumstances. The next chapter is about how traces of our habits, lifestyles, and circumstances can become etched on our faces.

LIFE LEAVES TRACES ON OUR FACES

In *Physiognomica*, the treatise attributed to Aristotle, the author discussed using "the characteristic facial expressions which are observed to accompany different conditions of mind, such as anger, fear, erotic excitement, and all the other passions" to make physiognomic inferences. But he quickly rejected this method as flawed: "permanent bodily signs will indicate permanent mental qualities, but what about those that come and go? How can they be true signs if the mental character does not also come and go?" Lavater took a similar position. For him, physiognomy—"the knowledge of the signs of the power and inclinations of men"—"shows what man is in general." In contrast, pathognomy—"the knowledge of the signs of the passions"—shows "what he becomes at particular moments."

We no longer talk about physiognomy and pathognomy, but modern psychology has preserved the distinction between permanent facial features and transient facial signals. The researchers who study face recognition focus on the former, whereas those who study emotions focus on the latter. But as we saw in the previous chapters, the distinction is not that clear cut when it comes to first impressions. These impressions are influenced by whatever momentary state is expressed on the face. And perhaps frequent expressions of the same states over many years can become imprinted on one's own face.

This idea was first proposed by James Parsons, an English physician, a few decades before the publication of Lavater's *Essay on Physiognomy*. Parsons studied how the muscles work and had already given a lecture on this topic to the Royal Society in London. His second lecture, *Human Physiognomy Explain'd*, was delivered in 1746. This lecture was focused on the facial muscles: "the true agents of every passion of the mind." The first part of the lecture was a detailed description of facial muscles. You can see one of the illustrations in Figure 11.1, showing these muscles in profile.

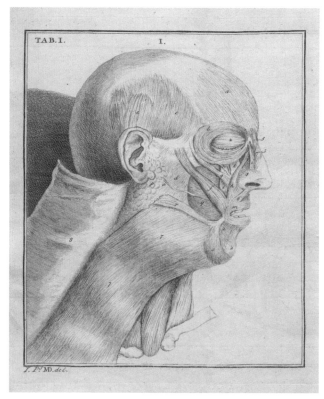

FIGURE 11.1. An illustration from James Parsons's *Human Physiognomy Explain'd* (1746). A view of the muscles of the face in profile. Parsons argued that the facial muscles are responsible for expressions of emotions.

In his lecture, Parsons listed forty-two authors who had written on physiognomy since antiquity to his day. He was not satisfied with the prior work. Much of it relied on the circular logic that Lavater later used when describing famous people: knowledge of their character was projected on their facial features, and then these features were declared as revealing character. Parsons rejected the idea that the form of facial features has any value in revealing the character of the face bearer, "a person with a long chin or nose, etc. may be either of a good or bad turn of mind; and . . . those with the best proportioned faces may be possessed of unhappy as well as happy tempers." For Parsons, "it is the alteration of the muscles alone that is capable of demonstrating the reigning passion of the mind upon every kind of face."

Parsons's lecture is quite remarkable. He had three major insights, none of which has been attributed to him in modern psychology. Parsons's first insight was to describe emotional expressions as movements of facial muscles, an idea taken for granted today. The idea became widely accepted in the nineteenth century—famously tested by the French neurologist G.-B. Duchenne de Boulogne, who applied electrical current to facial muscles—and was later embraced by emotion researchers in the twentieth century. In the 1970s, the psychologists Paul Ekman and Wallace Friesen developed the Facial Action Coding System. This coding system, based on the assumption that each emotion is expressed by a specific set of facial muscle actions, continues to be the most popular tool for classifying emotions in psychology and computer science.

Parsons's second insight was that emotional expressions have a functional, self-preservation value, an idea later attributed to Darwin. Discussing the expression of fear, Parsons noted, "the reason why the eyes and mouth are suddenly opened in frights, seems to be, that the object of danger may be the better perceived and avoided; as if nature intended to lay open all the inlets to the senses for the safety of the animal." Less than 10 years ago, a research group from the University of Toronto obtained direct support for this hypothesis. They found that expressing fear enlarges our visual field, increases the speed of eye movements, and increases the airflow through the nasal passage. As Parsons argued, expressions of fear enhance perception.

Parsons's third and most contentious insight was that continual expression of the same emotions could become imprinted on the face. As he put it, "habitual disposition, causing the muscles of the face, that are destined to express it, frequently to act in obedience to that bent of mind, brings on at length an habitual appearance of that passion in the face, and moulds it into a constant consent with the mind." Figure 11.2 shows his understanding of how frequent expressions of cheerfulness and sorrow can mold the face. The appearance of cheerfulness comes from having a mind that "was happy and glad upon any occasion, where immediate laughter did not seem necessary." All this is expressed by the habitual actions of the muscles moving the mouth and the eyes. As for the appearance of sorrow, "immoderate grief, by keeping those muscles relaxed for a series of time, brings on that hagged gloomy look, which no change of mind afterwards can alter."

Parsons's idea that habitual expressions of emotions could leave their traces on the face also became accepted. Like him, Lichtenberg argued that "patho-

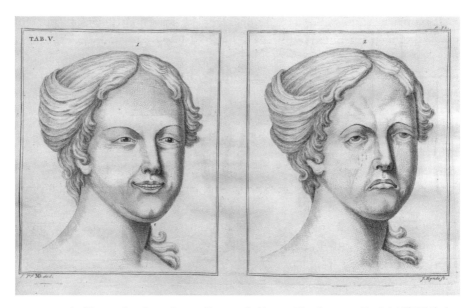

FIGURE 11.2. An illustration from James Parsons's *Human Physiognomy Explain'd* (1746). A countenance of cheerfulness (left image) and sorrow (right image). Parsons believed that repeated expressions of the same emotion can leave permanent traces on the face.

gnomic signs, often repeated, do not disappear again completely, and they leave physiognomic impressions behind." Duchenne, Darwin, and Mantegazza also endorsed the idea. In *The Expression of the Emotions in Man and Animal*, Darwin wrote, "whatever amount of truth the so-called science of physiognomy may contain" depends "on different persons bringing into frequent use different facial muscles, according to their dispositions; the development of these muscles being perhaps thus increased, and the lines or furrows on the face, due to the habitual contraction, being thus rendered deep and more conspicuous."

Parsons's evidence for this idea, as well as the evidence of all those who endorsed it, was anecdotal: "I know some persons who wear on their countenances a continual cheerfulness, complacency, and openness; and, by experience, I know it to be their continual disposition of mind; and, on the other hand, I also know some, on whose faces a settled moroseness always strikes the beholder; and know it to be their own constant plague, and that of those among whom they come." Although the evidence was anecdotal and Parsons's illustrations were not very convincing, his hypothesis was not far-fetched. Frequent exercise of specific muscle groups changes the appearance of your body: if you cycle regularly, your hamstrings and quadriceps will become larger and better defined. Expressing emotions is exercising facial muscle groups. Frequent exercising could leave its permanent traces on your face.

About 250 years after Parsons's lecture, psychologists found support for his hypothesis. They asked elderly people—the average age was 70—to report how frequently they experienced specific emotions, such as anger and guilt, and then to pose for pictures. Whether they posed with angry, happy, sad, fearful, or neutral expressions, students who did not know them tended to perceive one prevalent emotion. The woman in Figure 11.3, for example, was perceived as angry even when posing with a neutral expression.

FIGURE 11.3. An elderly woman who is perceived as angry, although she is posing with a neutral expression.

More importantly, those who were seen as angry reported often experiencing anger. Those who were seen as sad reported often experiencing sadness. The results were the same for contempt and guilt. So if you want to be seen as happy—and hence, trustworthy—in your old age, smile more often now. As Parsons argued, the habits of the mind can find their way to the face, although it might take them considerable time to get there.

● ● ● ● ●

It is not only our expressive habits that get imprinted on our faces. Our lifestyles leave their traces too. After a good night's sleep, not only do we function better, we also look better. In the first controlled study on the topic, participants slept on some days for at least 8 hours (between 11 p.m. and 7 a.m.) and were awake for 7 hours before their pictures were taken; on other days, they slept for 5 hours and were awake for 31 hours before their pictures were taken. The pictures were taken under the same standardized conditions at the same time of day. You can see the two pictures of one of the participants in Figure 11.4. It should be easy to see which picture shows the sleep-deprived participant.

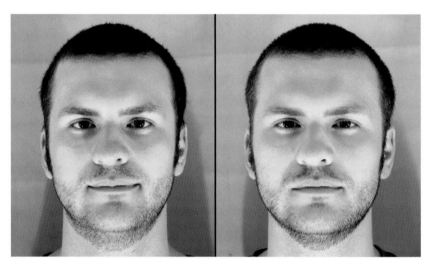

FIGURE 11.4. Pictures of the same person after a good night's sleep (left) and after experiencing sleep deprivation (right).

Not surprisingly, the sleep-deprived people were seen as more fatigued. Observers saw them as having hanging eyelids, swollen and red eyes, dark circles under the eyes, droopy corners of the mouth, and pale skin. Predictably, these changes in appearance influenced impressions. The sleep-deprived people were perceived as less healthy, less attractive, and less intelligent than when they were well rested. These negative impressions can be explained by our tendency to overgeneralize from the immediate facial cues to the face bearer's abilities and character. Sleep deprivation results in a host of negative emotional and cognitive consequences. We just don't perform well when we are sleep deprived. So when we see the signs of sleep deprivation in faces (such as tired-looking eyes) and detect a negative mood, we tend to think of the face-bearers as less intelligent. But all these signs could be a consequence of an anxious night before a job interview.

Like sleep, our diet is also reflected in our faces. Take a look at Figure 11.5. As you move from left to right across each row, do the faces become healthier and more attractive?

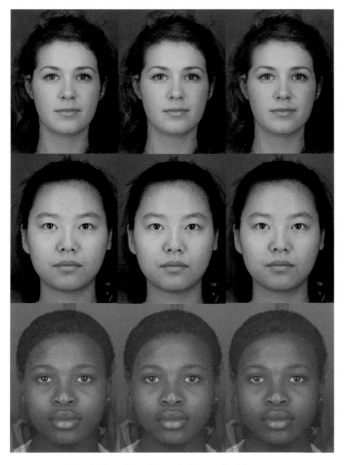

FIGURE 11.5. Simulating the effect of diet on facial appearance. Faces on the left reflect a diet poor in carotenoids. Faces on the right reflect a diet rich in carotenoids.

To most people, the added yellow hues make the faces on the right appear healthier and more attractive. Not only Caucasians but also Africans and Asians are sensitive to these color cues, as they all find faces with a healthy glow more attractive. This effect on attractiveness is different from and stronger than the effect of making the face more suntanned. In Figure 11.5, the "yellow" complexion effect was simulated digitally, but the right diet can have the same effect on your face in 6–8 weeks.

Carotenoids are yellow, orange, and red pigments synthesized by plants. Carrots, pumpkins, tangerines, and spinach (among many other fruits and vegetables) contain carotenoids. Carotenoid pigments accumulate in the skin, and people with a healthy fruit-and-vegetable diet tend to have a more yellowish complexion. If you are a parent and your kids are at the age when attractiveness really matters to them, one way to make them eat more fruits and vegetables is to appeal to their vanity. Participants who were shown how their faces might look with the right diet were able to sustain such a diet for at least 10 weeks. And while on the right diet, it would also be good to start exercising. Exercising can improve the appearance of not only your body but also your face. People who are physically fit have increased blood flow to the skin, which makes the skin redder. We are sensitive to these color cues too. When asked to increase the attractiveness and healthiness of faces by manipulating their color hues, participants increase the redness.

As mentioned in Chapter 10, we are quite good at judging body weight from the face alone. This is not so surprising, because fat accumulates not only in our bodies but also in our faces. Accumulated fat under the cheeks is particularly problematic, as people who have this kind of fat also tend to have visceral fat, the type that collects in the abdominal cavity. Having visceral fat is much worse healthwise than having subcutaneous fat, the kind that collects under the skin, because increased visceral fat is more predictive of obesity complications like type 2 diabetes and hypertension. Given the negative consequences of being overweight—obesity is the second leading cause of death after tobacco use in the United States—it is not surprising that many studies find that weight judgments from the face alone can predict health problems.

In some cases, these judgments can be quite useful. A large study on health-related issues followed more than 10,000 people for a few decades but did not collect measures of their weight and height when the study started in the 1950s. Forty years later, to overcome this omission, researchers managed to get hold of high school yearbook pictures of the participants and had raters estimate their weight from these pictures. These estimates were predictive of the actual BMIs of participants measured decades later and of health symptoms (such as muscle aches), chronic conditions (such as diabetes), and mortality. This is more worrisome than the fact that overweight faces are judged as unattractive.

The use of tobacco, the number one killer, is not good for your face either. Like the poet W. H. Auden, many smokers acquire a "smoker's face" (Figure 11.6), characterized by many wrinkles radiating from the eyes and lips and gray appearance of the skin.

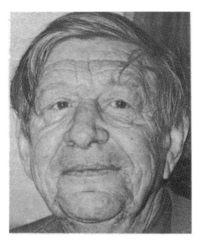

FIGURE 11.6. The poet W. H. Auden had acquired a typical "smoker's face" in his old age.

Smoking, among its other destructive effects, destroys vitamin C. This vitamin is important for producing collagen, the main component of our skin, which makes it flexible and resilient. The reduction in collagen leads to more wrinkles. Smoking also reduces the blood supply to the skin, giving it an unhealthy appearance. All this contributes to an older look, as our age is mostly apparent in the skin condition of our faces. This is illustrated in Figure 11.7.

FIGURE 11.7. Aging of a face. Changing the shape and color of a young face (left image) to the shape and color of an older face (middle image) adds about 15 years to the apparent age of the face. Adding detailed aging texture to the face (right image) adds another 15 years.

Not surprisingly, morphing the shape and color (but not the texture) of a young man's face into those of an older man's face increases the apparent age of the face. In Figure 11.7, the face in the middle is aged by about 15 years. But we can add another 15 years to this face by simply adding a texture with wrinkles (the face on the right).

Looking old is not just a reflection of age. Many physicians use apparent age as an indicator of health. This turns out to be a very good heuristic. Controlling for actual age, looking younger is associated with a number of health indicators, such as maximum breathing capacity and faster speed of motor reactions. In elderly individuals, it is also associated with better physical and cognitive functioning. In a notable study, an international group of researchers followed more than 1,800 Danish twins over many years. These twins were of the same sex, and all were more than 70 years old. The researchers were interested in whether looking older predicts mortality. The design of the study controlled for gender, age, and many other factors, because the comparison was between the twin who looked older and the twin who looked younger. Figure 11.8 illustrates the difference in facial appearance.

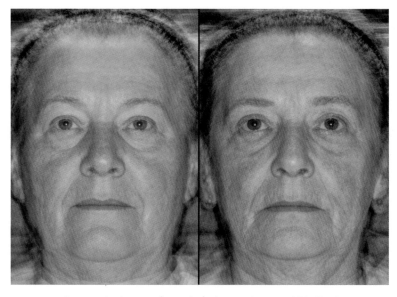

FIGURE 11.8. Composite images (morphs) of ten twins aged 70. The image on the left shows the morph of the younger looking twins. Their average perceived age was 64. The image on the right shows the morph of the older looking twins. Their average perceived age was 74.

In 2001, the researchers took pictures of all the twins. By January 2008, about one-third of the twins had died. You would not be surprised to learn that the best predictor of mortality is actual age. After 70, each year increases the mortality risk by about 11–13 percent. But the effect of perceived age was *just as strong*. The twin who looked older in 2001 was more likely to have died by 2008. No other predictor of mortality has been found to match actual age. As the authors of the study put it, "facial photographs are, currently, likely to be more informative with regard to survival of older people than a DNA sample."

What makes one appear younger besides good genes? The answers are not surprising. Living the good life—having a high socioeconomic status, which typically comes with better education, better nutrition, higher income, and better access to health care; not being depressed; and being (I imagine happily) married—makes you look younger. Smoking, continuous sun exposure (think of occupations like farming and fishing, not vacations on the beach), and disease (asthma for men, cardiovascular disease for women) make you look older. Should we be surprised that older looks predict mortality? What is good for your health is good for your appearance. So take care of your body and mind: eat healthy, exercise, don't smoke, and cut down on needless worries. You won't just feel better; you'll look better too.

• • • • •

Oscar Wilde's *The Picture of Dorian Gray* is about the impossibility of being eternally young and beautiful. After seeing his portrait, Dorian Gray, an extremely handsome young man, is saddened by the thought that he "shall grow old, and horrible, and dreadful" while "this picture will remain always young." He wishes to remain young and for the portrait to grow old. He is ready to give everything for that, including his soul. His wish is granted. Dorian Gray remains eternally youthful and handsome, leading a life of debauchery. As he continues to make morally questionable choices, his portrait becomes more and more loathsome, reflecting his true essence. At one point, once again horrified by seeing his true reflection in the portrait, he decides to change himself for the better. Underlying his motivation is the hope that his portrait would show this positive change. Alas, "in the eyes there was a look of cunning, and in the mouth the curved wrinkle of the hypocrite. The thing was still loathsome—more loathsome, if possible, than before." In his final act of exasperation, he decides to "kill" the portrait, and that is his end. The portrait changes to the original, youthful, and handsome image of Gray, and next to it lies a "withered, wrinkled, and loathsome of visage" dead man.

In some sense, our face is a canvas painted by life. But is it painted by our moral choices or our life circumstances? We can see the goodness or badness of others in their faces only after we have learned what they have done, the way we see any image of Loughner as depicting an evil man (see Figure 8.11). But without this knowledge, all we can see are traces of our lives. These traces need not originate in our characters. As Lichtenberg put it, "our body stands in the middle between the soul and the rest of the world, a mirror of the effects of both; not only our inclinations and abilities but also the whip lashes of fate, climate, disease, food, and a thousand hardships, which are due not always to our own bad decisions but often to chance and imposition." The effects of these hardships accumulate in our faces over our lifetimes. And what we see in these faces may be more informative about these hardships than about character. We might as well draw conclusions from the face about "cold winters, foul diapers, frivolous nurses, damp bedchambers, and childhood diseases."

Perhaps the only "face traces" that are informative about character are the traces of our habitual emotional experience. Parsons, Lichtenberg, and Darwin endorsed this view. But in the end, Lichtenberg remained the reasonable skeptic: "even the lasting traces of previous pathognomic expressions on the face . . . are only to be trusted in extreme cases, where they are so strong that one might call the people marked, and even then only if the traces appear in the company of another indicator that shows the same." Impressions of character from traces of pathognomic expressions are a shaky business: "is someone whose resting face resembles my friend's or mine when I am scoffing therefore someone who scoffs, or is someone whose face when completely awake resembles mine when I am sleepy therefore a sleepy person? No judgments are cruder than these, and none could be more wrong." When it comes to character, faces provide very weak signals.

But this weak informative value doesn't diminish the importance of faces. Faces play an extremely important role in our mental lives, though not the role the physiognomists imagined. The next and final part of the book is about the special status of faces in the mind. Our fascination with faces starts from the moment we are born. Evolution has equipped us with a readiness to attend to faces. This readiness, fueled by an intensive visual experience with faces from the get go, develops into an intricate network of brain regions specialized to process faces. These networks support our extraordinary face skills: recognizing emotional expressions in their situational contexts and recognizing familiar faces. But these skills ironically support the illusion of the accuracy of first impressions. Both the skills and the illusion make us believe that faces provide a wealth of information about the person even when they don't.

PART 4

THE SPECIAL STATUS OF FACES

BORN TO ATTEND TO FACES

I am in a hospital in Monfalcone, a small Italian town between Venice and Trieste, to witness a behavioral experiment. After a couple of hours of waiting, our first participant is brought in. Fabio weights about 7 pounds. He has been out in the world for 33 hours. Although everything is set up for the experiment, one important detail is missing: Fabio's pacifier. The missing pacifier delays the experiment for a minute, which is about one-fourth of the expected alert time of a newborn. The experiment lasts as long as you can push it: 3 minutes. Our second participant is another boy, Dior, who is twice as old as Fabio, at just over 70 hours old. Dior is the perfect participant, not fussy even without a pacifier. Unfortunately, the computer presenting the videos with faces crashes in the middle of the experiment. Half of the data are lost. The third participant is a girl. Emily is rather senior to Fabio and Dior. She has been out in the world for almost 100 hours. After 1 minute and 49 seconds, she starts crying, and this is the end of the experiment.

Teresa Farroni, a developmental psychologist from the University of Padua, and her graduate student, Giulia Orioli, are telling me that we have been extremely lucky. Working with newborns is tough. Their moments of nonfussy alertness are preciously rare. After securing the consent of the mothers, the researchers can wait for hours for the opportune 4 minutes. Some days don't turn out any such minutes. In others like today, you can test three newborns in an hour. And it is not only the difficulty of getting access to the newborns. There are many ways in which you can screw up the experiment besides your computer crashing. How you hold the baby is extremely important. The researchers have a doll on which they can practice. If the baby is lying on you, she is going to quickly fall asleep. This eventually happens even if you are holding the baby "correctly" with her spine straight. Our three participants all dozed off at one moment or another, although Teresa has been doing this for 15 years. During these moments, she was whistling gently or making other sounds to keep them alert.

In this particular experiment, Teresa and Giulia are testing whether newborns can associate tactile and visual sensations. While Teresa is holding the baby, every now and then she gently touches the infant's forehead with a brush. She is sitting in front of a computer monitor with a video camera mounted above the monitor. The camera is locked on the face of the infant, whose behavior is being videotaped. The behavior of interest is the infant's gaze: the researchers are interested in which part of the screen the baby is attending to. In the middle of the black screen, a white circle continuously flashes to attract the attention of the baby. Once the attention is attracted, two baby faces appear on both sides of the screen. One of the faces is shown with a brush touching its forehead. The question is whether the baby would look toward the face with the brush immediately after her own forehead was touched with a brush. Note that there are quite a few assumptions behind this experiment—the most crucial being that newborns' attention is attracted to faces. Is this even possible?

The exploration of such unlikely possibilities is what makes the study of infants fascinating. In the past half century, the findings of many infant studies have continually surprised us. This chapter is about one of the first surprising discoveries: newborns' attraction to faces. The very first finding that newborns prefer to look at facelike stimuli rather than at other objects was incidental, but it spurred more focused studies confirming this finding. In recent years, Teresa, together with the British researcher Mark Johnson and their colleagues have conducted some of the most definitive studies. This is what drew me to Teresa's "field" lab in the hospital in Monfalcone.

Although it may seem unbelievable, newborns with virtually no visual experience are attracted to images that have the basic layout of faces. These early biases channel the infants' attention to the most important stimuli in their life: their caregivers. But the early perceptual biases to faces are not enough. Visual experience plays a tremendous role in shaping which faces infants are attuned to. Within a few months, infants' visual preferences are finely tuned to the faces in their environments. The biases to attend to faces and the massive exposure to faces in the first few months make us believers in the informational value of faces early on in life.

• • • • •

From studies like the ones conducted by Davida Teller, described in Chapter 5, we know that the visual acuity of newborns is incredibly poor. Normal visual acuity is often popularly described as 20/20 vision, which simply means that one can see from 20 feet what a person with a good vision sees from the same distance. People who are legally blind have visual acuity worse than 20/200. That is, from 20 feet they can see what a person with normal vision can see from 200 feet. Newborns' visual acuity is estimated to be about 15 times worse than normal adults' visual acuity; an adult with the visual acuity of a newborn would be declared legally blind. Given newborns' limited vision and their lack of visual experience, one would expect that they possess minimal, if any, capacities to perceive complex stimuli. The idea that faces—the blurred blobs that they see (Figure 12.1)—have a special meaning to them seems preposterous. It is not surprising, then, that the first study that found that newborns prefer to look at faces was not designed to test this possibility.

FIGURE 12.1. How a newborn sees a face from a distance of 12 inches.

Robert Fantz was interested in a much simpler question: do newborns show any sensitivity to visual patterns? At the time, many researchers believed that newborns would not care about any patterns, because they either need to learn these patterns first or because their undeveloped eyes and brains may not register the patterns. In Fantz's study, newborns from 10 hours to 5 days old were placed in a specially constructed chamber. While lying in a hammock crib at the bottom of the chamber, images were shown on the top wall of the chamber 1 foot away from the baby's head. As it happened, one of the patterned images was a schematic face, another one was concentric circles (a "bull's eye"), and a third was a newspaper cutout. The nonpatterned images were colored cards in white, yellow, and red. An adult observer positioned above the chamber observed the infant through a peephole and recorded the length of their gaze at each image from the moment the eyes were directed to the image to the moment the eyes turned away or closed. By now, you are familiar with the logic of the preferential looking paradigm: the length of eye gaze indicates the infant's interest in the image. In fact, it was Fantz who introduced this paradigm to psychology.

Fantz found that newborns spend twice as much time looking at the patterned than at the nonpatterned images. He also found that the patterned image that attracted most attention was the face, but was rightfully careful to point out that "the results do not imply 'instinctive recognition' of a face or other unique significance of this pattern; it is likely that there are other patterns which would elicit equal or greater attention." Fantz's study was published in 1963. In the subsequent years, more reports followed with stronger claims.

In 1975, Carolyn Goren and her colleagues tested whether newborns with no visual experience with faces would show preference for facelike stimuli. Their newborns were 9 minutes old on average. The newborns were literally taken from the womb to the testing room (the mothers had consented to the experiment prior to the delivery). Because the doctors, nurses, and experimenters wore medical gowns, masks, and scrub hats, the only facelike thing the infants could have seen was the eyes of the medical staff or the experimenters. To test the newborns' visual preferences for faces, the researchers used four types of stimuli (Figure 12.2): a schematic face, a partially scrambled schematic face, a fully scrambled schematic face, and a blank schematic face shape.

Each newborn was placed in the lap of one of the experimenters. Once the baby was positioned, her head was aligned with the zeroth degree of a large protractor (just like the ones fourth graders use to measure angles but much larger). The experimenter held one of the four stimuli about 15–30 centimeters from the baby's head. Once the baby fixated on the stimulus, the experimenter rotated it slowly in an ark from 0 to 90 degrees. Two other experimenters independently observed and recorded the degrees of both head and eyes turning of the baby to verify the consistency of the observations. The results were clear. The newborns turned both their head and eyes toward the face most, followed by the moderately scrambled face, the scrambled face, and

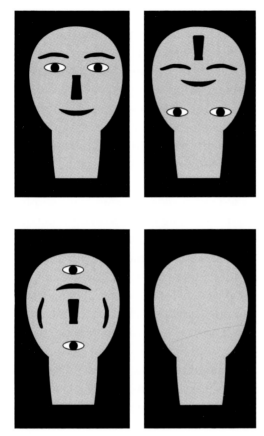

FIGURE 12.2. Stimuli similar to those used by Goren and colleagues in 1975 to test newborns' preferences for facelike stimuli: a face, a moderately scrambled face, a scrambled face, and a blank shape.

the blank shape. The latter was the least interesting to the newborns. Goren and colleagues concluded that "these results suggest that an evolved predisposition to respond selectively to faces may be present at birth."

Surprising findings in science are typically met with skepticism expressed in alternative explanations. There are many things that can go wrong in an experiment. If an observer knows what image the infant is looking at, they can inadvertently bias their measurement in line with their hypothesis. To prevent such biases, Goren and her colleagues designed the experiment so that the experimenters, who recorded the head and eyes turning, were unaware of what the infant was seeing; they were able to see only the reverse side of the stimuli, which was identical for all four stimuli. Yet it is still possible that the experimenters were able to deduce what the infant was seeing. In a subsequent replication, Mark Johnson and his colleagues videotaped the procedure, in which the experimenter (unaware of the stimuli) was showing the stimuli to the infant. The rotations of the head and eye gaze were estimated from the videotapes by two researchers who were not only unaware of the stimuli but also of the purpose of the experiment. These results ruled out experimenter bias as an explanation of the findings.

Still, there could always be other explanations. If the experimental procedures are flawless (although they never are for the skeptic), the skeptic can argue that face and nonface images have different qualities that have nothing to do with the "faceness" of the images. Newborns may be responding not to faces per se but to something simpler that differentiates face from nonface images. This something can refer to low-level visual properties of the stimuli (like different luminance and contrast) or to high-level visual properties (like complexity and symmetry). If the face images are symmetric and the nonface images are not, it is plausible and more parsimonious to argue that babies are responding to symmetry rather than to faces. Such arguments are resolved in subsequent experiments that control for all potentially important differences or confounds. Face and nonface images should have the same luminance and contrast, should be symmetric and equally complex, and so forth.

One of the alternative and simpler explanations of newborns' preferences for facelike stimuli is that they prefer "top-heavy patterns," that is, shapes with more elements on the top (like eyes) and fewer elements on the bottom (like mouths). This kind of preference could explain the observations of multiple experiments with newborns. Although the explanation is unsatisfying—because it is not clear why we should be born with this visual preference as opposed to a preference for "bottom-heavy patterns"—it is simpler than a preference for faces. Simpler though it is, Teresa Farroni, Mark Johnson, and their colleagues showed that this explanation is not only unsatisfying but also insufficient to explain newborns' visual preferences.

Teresa and her colleagues capitalized on the fact that faces are three-dimensional objects and have characteristic shading patterns in the natural environment: the eyes and the mouth tend to be darker than the rest of the face. Think of cavities in an otherwise smooth surface or simply go back and look at Figure 12.1—the visualization of how a newborn sees a face from 12 inches. The simplest possible facelike image consists of an oval with two patches for the eyes positioned above a single patch for the mouth, like the left image in Figure 12.3. This face image is also a "top-heavy pattern." But this is not quite enough to make it look like a face. The patches should appear recessed from the oval.

FIGURE 12.3. A schematic face and its inverted version with dark patches for the eyes and the mouth. Newborns prefer to look at the schematic face rather than at its inverted version.

Making them black and the face white creates this perception. As it happened, all previous studies have used schematic faces with dark patches for the eyes and the mouth. When newborns are presented with the pair of images in Figure 12.3, they look longer at the image that looks like a face than at its inverted version. But what happens if we make the face black and the patches white? Take a look at Figure 12.4.

FIGURE 12.4. A schematic face and its inverted version with light patches for the eyes and the mouth. Newborns show no preference for either stimulus.

The patches now appear as protrusions from the oval violating the "faceness" of the image. With this pair of images, newborns no longer express any detectable visual preference between the facelike configuration and its inversion. And it is not about the blackness or whiteness of the face. Inserting small black patches inside the white patches, as in Figure 12.5, re-creates the illusion of recessed cavities in the oval, and newborns again look longer at the facelike oval.

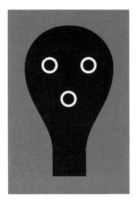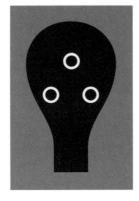

FIGURE 12.5. A schematic face and its inverted version with slits making the eyes and mouth look like recessed cavities. Newborns prefer to look at the schematic face rather than at its inverted version.

Finally, newborns also look longer at a real face when it is illuminated from above (as in normal conditions) than when the same face is illuminated from below, the only angle of illumination that violates the characteristic shading pattern of faces. These visual preferences are fairly specific: the facelike stimulus should not only be "top-heavy," but it should also have the shading pattern of faces viewed in natural conditions. More than 50 years after the publication of Fantz's study, we can be reasonably confident that he found that newborns have preferences for faces. We come to the world equipped to detect faces.

• • • • •

Such early attentional biases to detect faces continue to be present in our adult minds. Adult participants make faster eye movements to upright than to inverted facelike stimuli, but only if the upright stimuli have the right three-dimensional interpretation: the "eyes" and "mouth" look like cavities. These biases are also present in our unconscious. The most common technique to study unconscious visual processes is to present images for extremely brief periods of time, usually less than 30 milliseconds. The problem with this technique is that the rapid presentation puts severe limits on what your mind can do with the presented information. To solve this problem, researchers from the California Institute of Technology in Pasadena (Caltech) invented a new technique—continuous flash suppression—to study the unconscious for a prolonged time. This technique relies on presenting different images to the two eyes. While one eye is bombarded by a rapid succession of different patterns that look like Mondrian paintings, the other eye is presented with a static, stable image. Because the rapid succession of images dominates our conscious awareness, we are unable to see the static image. That is, this image is suppressed from your awareness for durations as long as a second. This is a fairly long time in the world of visual perception. In this experimental setup, the question is how quickly the stable image emerges in your awareness. The speed of this emergence is an indication of what the cognitive unconscious prioritizes for further conscious processing. The psychologist Timo Stein and his colleagues used continuous flash suppression and presented images similar to the ones used to study newborns by Teresa and her colleagues. Ovals that looked like upright faces, such as those in Figure 12.3, emerged faster in awareness than their inverted versions. More importantly, faces lit from above with natural shading patterns also emerged faster than faces lit from below.

If you look back at Figure 12.1, you can see that the contrast polarity—darker patches surrounded by lighter patches—is much more pronounced for the eyes than for the mouth region of the face. Stein and colleagues showed that reversing the contrast polarity of just the eye region (lighter eyes surrounded by darker cheeks and forehead) was sufficient to eliminate the faster emergence of upright faces in awareness. If you have ever worked with film negatives (an extremely rare event in these days of digital cameras), you would know that it is very difficult to recognize faces from the negative. There are many psychology experiments confirming this observation. Can you recognize the face in Figure 12.6?

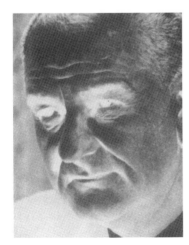

FIGURE 12.6. It is very difficult to recognize images from their negatives. Do you recognize this face?

Pawan Sinha and his colleagues have shown that one can reach almost perfect levels of face recognition from negatives of images as long as the eyes are presented in their normal shading pattern. Restoring the normal contrast polarity of the eyes (but not the mouth) makes the recognition problem easy. Let's do that with the face in Figure 12.6. Take a look at the face with restored contrast polarity in Figure 12.7. This should be a much easier recognition task . . . well, at least if you are an American.

FIGURE 12.7. Restoring the contrast polarity of the eyes makes it easy to recognize former President Lyndon Johnson.

What is so special about the contrast polarity of the eyes? The eyebrows and the eyes remain darker relative to the forehead and the cheeks across a variety of illuminating conditions, except when the face is lit from below. The robustness of this dark-light pattern makes it a great feature for face detection. If the pattern is present in an image, it is very likely that the image contains a face. As it turns out, face-detection algorithms that use this pattern are particularly good at detecting faces. One of the most successful algorithms, Viola-Jones (named after the computer scientists who discovered it), uses simple contrast filters to discover features that are diagnostic for the presence of the face. After training the algorithm on thousands of images, Viola and Jones found that the two best features that distinguish faces from nonfaces are the contrast between the eyes and the cheekbones (dark rectangle above light rectangle) and the contrast between the eyes (two dark rectangles separated by a lighter rectangle). This is shown in Figure 12.8.

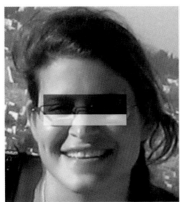

FIGURE 12.8. The two best features for discriminating faces from other objects.

These computer scientists discovered a solution for face detection that had already been "discovered" by evolution. Newborns come into the world with visual biases to detect features that are most likely to distinguish faces from nonfaces.

Knowing how algorithms like the Viola-Jones perform can be used to fool humans. A research group in Germany obtained images that were falsely classified by the Viola-Jones algorithm as faces. These researchers presented participants with pairs of images and asked them to gaze toward the face. The images were flashed on a computer screen for a mere 20 milliseconds. Just like the algorithm, humans were prone to misclassify the illusory faces as faces. This seems puzzling until one sees the average features of the images most likely to be misclassified as faces.

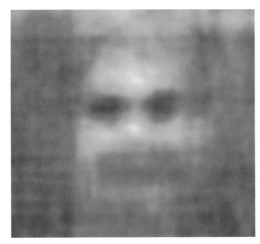

FIGURE 12.9. The average features of images misclassified as faces by people who were presented with the images for extremely brief time intervals.

As shown in Figure 12.9, these images shared the characteristic contrast patterns that are most likely to be present in faces. Of course, participants were most accurate when real faces were paired with nonfaces. The very fast detection of faces after presentations so short that the images remain below the threshold of visual awareness shows that we automatically detect faces. This is not something that suddenly appears in adult vision. The building blocks are already in place when we are born.

●　●　●　●　●

The findings for face preferences in newborns have stood the test of time. Newborns attend to highly specific configurations of features. This is difficult to explain without positing that evolution has equipped the primate brain with the ability to attend to features that distinguish faces from nonfaces. We have been given a jumpstart in life. But this only gets us off the ground for a moment. What pushes us further is the massive exposure to faces in the early days of life and our interest in and dependence on other people.

To find out what the world looks like in the eyes of infants, Canadian researchers recorded the visual perspective of 1- and 3-month-old infants for 2 weeks. The infants wore headbands to which the researchers attached tiny spy cameras. When the infant was awake, the camera was turned on and recorded what was in their field of view. For one quarter of their waking time—on average, 7 hours for 1-month-olds and 9 hours for 3-month-olds—faces populated their visual world.

This massive exposure to faces matters as our perceptual skills get tuned to our social environments. The kinds of faces the infants see are highly predictable. These tend to be from their own race, women, and older faces: the most likely caregivers. This matters, because infants get better at learning about what they see (or hear) and worse at what they don't see (or hear). Developmental psychologists have a term for this: perceptual narrowing. Within the first year of development, our perceptual skills tune to what is relevant in our environments. While 6- to 8-month-old English-learning infants can discriminate similarly sounding consonants from other languages like Hindu, 10- to 12-month-olds cannot do it. If you are a non-native English speaker, you may be able to relate to this experience. I still have not lost my strong Bulgarian accent after living in the United States for 20 years.

Similar processes are at work for face perception. Six-month-old babies are as good at discriminating between faces from other races as they are at discriminating between faces from their own race. But 3 months later, they lose the ability to discriminate between faces from other races. The perceptual narrowing in the first year comes at a cognitive cost. Our recognition difficulties with faces from other races have an early origin in our visual experience. And it is about our visual experience per se, not about our race origins. Korean children adopted by French families are better at discriminating French than Korean faces. Within just a few months of development, our perceptual biases to attend to faces are shaped by experience.

You cannot raise human infants without exposure to faces and then systematically manipulate their exposure to different kinds of faces, but you can do it with infant monkeys. The Japanese researcher Yoichi Sugita reared monkeys without any exposure to faces for as much as 24 months. The infant monkeys were deprived from exposure to faces but not from human contact. The human caregivers wore (flat) masks and played with the monkeys for at least 2 hours per day. The cages of the monkeys were filled with colorful toys but nothing facelike. After the face-deprivation period, using tasks like the preferential looking paradigm, the monkeys were tested for their visual preferences. Although they had never seen a face, the monkeys preferred to look at faces than at other objects. This nicely replicates the findings of human studies. Primates are born with visual biases to detect faces in their environment.

Sugita also manipulated the kinds of faces the monkeys were exposed to after the face-deprivation period. This initial exposure determined what faces the monkeys were best at learning: they discriminated best those faces they were first exposed to. If exposed to monkey faces—which is what would have happened in their natural habitat—for a month and not to human faces, they discriminated monkey faces best. But if exposed to human faces for a month and not to monkey faces, they discriminated human faces best. Our ability to detect faces is broadly tuned: anything that looks like a face will do. But visual experience finely tunes this ability. We need a healthy diet of faces to develop proper face-processing mechanisms. Without such mechanisms, we would not be able to recognize relatives, friends and foes, emotional states and intentions; and we would have a hard time communicating with and learning from others.

There are good reasons to be born with biases to attend to faces. These biases draw newborns' attention to the most motivationally significant stimuli: their caregivers. Without caregivers, infants will not survive. They need to be able to track faces and communicate with them. And newborns prefer not just faces but faces with open eyes and gaze directed toward them. After their first 24 hours, they also prefer to look at happy rather than at fearful faces. After 6–8 weeks, infants start smiling at their caregivers. When I excitedly started recounting the first smiling episodes of my son to a friend, she offered the following explanation: "unless babies start smiling, they would be killed." Exaggerated as this is, everyone who has been a parent knows that babies are an incredible amount of work. The smiling is the tiny reward that we need to overcome the misery of sleepless hours and changing diapers. But our happy face-to-face interactions are more important than simply overcoming our adult misery. The face-to-face communication with caregivers provides the foundations for some of our most important skills: social coordination and language. Not having access to faces can disrupt normal social and cognitive development. Four-month-old infants are already engaged in highly synchronized face-to-face behaviors with their mothers, anticipating and predicting each other's attention. Lapses in this synchronization predict poor developmental outcomes, such as insecure attachment. When face synchronization is completely prevented, the consequences for social and cognitive development must be much more severe.

Our interest in and dependence on other people is what drives the development of our face perception skills. By 6 months, infants spontaneously allocate their attention to dynamic faces. By 7 months, they discriminate among different emotions. But these skills are not fully developed by the end of our first year. Recognition of other individuals continues to improve until our teenage years. And although we might lose the ability to discriminate faces from other races in our first year, we regain such skills once we have accumulated sufficient visual experience with such faces. As discussed in Chapter 7, our face preferences are dynamic: as our social world changes, so do our face preferences. The early attentional biases to faces and our early visual experience do not determine what we end up liking as adults, but they channel our learning in the right direction. These biases and early perceptual experiences, coupled with the motivational significance of faces, lead to the development of an extraordinary, intricate neural system dedicated entirely to the processing of faces. The next chapter is about the discovery of this system.

FACE MODULES IN THE BRAIN

We are extremely visual creatures. One of the distinctive features of the primate brain is the massive expansion of cortex dedicated to vision—more than half of our cortex processes visual information. Primate mammals have more cortical visual areas with much more densely packed neurons than do nonprimate mammals. And some of these areas are exclusively dedicated to the processing of faces. The first insights about the special status of faces in the brain came from studying cases of face blindness. We think of blindness as not being able to see anything, but as odd as this may sound, there are people with fairly normal vision who can recognize all kinds of objects except faces. A few isolated reports of such clinical cases cropped up in the nineteenth century, but the first systematic observations were made by the German neurologist Joachim Bodamer in the 1940s. One of his patients, after receiving a bullet wound in his head during World War II, "recognized a face as such, i.e. as different from other things, but could not assign the face to its owner. He could identify all the features of a face, but all faces appeared equally 'sober' and 'tasteless' to him. Faces had no expression, no 'meaning' for him." This description is as apt today. Bodamer named this condition prosopagnosia (from the Greek words for face, "prosopon," and for not knowing, "agnosia"). After they have had selective brain lesions, prosopagnosics lose the ability to recognize familiar faces, including their own faces. They know they are looking at a face when they are looking at one, but they cannot put it all together and relate this face to memory.

Cases of prosopagnosia provided the first evidence that we may have face-processing modules in our brains: cortical areas that only respond to faces. Soon this unlikely idea would be corroborated by other findings. The key—

and one of the most surprising findings in the history of neuroscience—was the discovery of face neurons. Neurons are the basic units of the brain, and there are billions of them specializing in different functions. Typically, we think of neurons as performing very simple functions like visual neurons responding to spots of light or somatosensory neurons responding to touch. But neurons responding to faces and no other objects were a big surprise. Like the discovery of newborns' attentional biases toward faces, the discovery of face neurons was incidental, a discovery that was even more controversial. But it too stood the test of time. Not only do we have face neurons, but these neurons are clustered in specific regions of the brain that are highly interconnected with each other. This chapter is about the remarkable progress in the study of the face-processing system in the brain, the most studied and the best understood system for the perception of complex categories of stimuli like faces. This system is a gateway to the brain systems underlying our understanding of the social world.

• • • • •

In the 1960s, Charlie Gross, one of my colleagues at Princeton, and his collaborators were working on characterizing the visual properties of neurons in the temporal cortex, part of the temporal lobe that sits above the neck and behind the ears. Until the middle of the twentieth century, it had not even been established that this part of the cortex is involved in vision, although experimental studies with monkeys had shown that lesions in the temporal cortex impair visual learning and discrimination of objects. However, the visual properties of neurons in these cortical areas were unknown. David Hubel and Torsten Wiesel, who received the Nobel Prize in 1981 for their work on the visual system, had characterized the properties of neurons in the occipital cortex, but not much was known about neurons in visual areas outside the occipital cortex.

Working with cats, Hubel and Wiesel would insert electrodes in the cats' primary visual cortex (the first station for visual information in the cortex), present different visual stimuli to the cats, and record the firing rate of single neurons. If the neuron responds to a particular stimulus like a spot of light or a moving bar, it would fire continuously and vigorously. If it doesn't, it would remain silent. You can literally listen to the neuron, because the electrode is connected not only to an oscilloscope, which records the voltage fluctuation of the neuron, but also to an audio amplifier. When the neuron is very active, it sounds like a rapid-fire shooting. Hubel and Wiesel discovered that neurons in the primary visual cortex respond to more complex light patterns than do neurons in the retina or subcortical neurons. Spots of lights would typically activate the latter, but this was not sufficient to activate neurons in the primary visual cortex. These neurons would respond to more complex forms, such as edges and lines. Hubel and Wiesel discovered three types of visual neurons, which they called simple, complex, and hypercomplex cells. Simple cells respond to bars with a particular orientation, complex cells respond to bars moving in a particular direction, and hypercomplex cells respond to parts of bars moving in a particular direction. This was an exciting discovery, as it suggested a possible way of representing the visual world in the brain: the rich stimuli like faces and flowers that we see in the world are gradually built up from simple features—coded in populations of neurons—as signals from the retina move along neuronal pathways in the visual cortex.

Following Hubel and Wiesel's procedures, Charlie Gross and his students would show moving bars to monkeys and record the firing rates of neurons in the temporal cortex. Their objective was to identify the stimulus features that activate these neurons. And they did discover neurons that were activated by moving bars like the one in Figure 13.1. This particular neuron fires vigorously (the tall spikes in the left panel of the figure) when the monkey sees a bar moving downward in the diagonal direction, but it does not fire when the bar is moving in other directions. More importantly, Charlie and his students stumbled on something much more surprising and exciting.

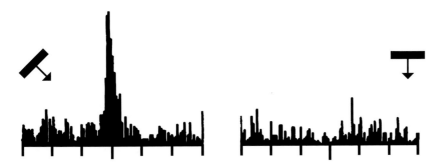

FIGURE 13.1. The firing pattern of a neuron in the temporal cortex. The neuron fires vigorously in response to a bar moving in the diagonal direction but not to one moving in the vertical direction. The arrows indicate the direction of movement.

Their first, and incidental, discovery was of a hand-sensitive neuron. Exasperated after failing to elicit response to any preprogrammed stimulus, they waved "a hand at the stimulus screen" and observed "a very vigorous response." In the same 1972 paper, where they outlined this finding, they noted that for some neurons, "complex colored patterns (e.g., photographs of faces, trees) were more effective than the standard stimuli, but the crucial features of these stimuli were never determined." These findings were reported but did not figure prominently in the paper. In a different lab, the findings may not even have been reported. As Charlie recounts, "when we wrote the first draft of an account of this work for *Science*, we did not have the nerve to include this hand cell until Teuber urged us to do so." Hans-Lukas Teuber was the head of the psychology department at MIT and the person who provided the initial funding for Charlie's research. Responses to edges and bars with particular orientations and directions were fine, but responses to such complex objects as hands and faces seemed out of the ordinary.

● ● ● ● ●

Although the "hand neuron" discovery was incidental, there had been prescient ideas about such neurons. Jerzy Konorski, a Polish neuroscientist, had proposed the existence of "gnostic" neurons in his 1967 book *Integrative Activity of the Brain*. He argued that there are neurons in the brain that respond to complex shapes, like faces, animals, and body parts. Charlie knew Konorski, he had visited his lab in Warsaw, and had written a glowing review of the book in *Science*. But Konorski's ideas were truly ahead of his time with no evidence for such neurons prior to Charlie's work. At the time, there was only a running joke about a "grandmother cell," a cell that responds to different views of only one person, such as one's grandmother. The joke was born in a 1969 MIT course and the term stuck, often used to denote a straw man theory of recognition. Perhaps not surprisingly, in this atmosphere of skepticism, no attempts were made to question or replicate Charlie's findings for about 10 years.

In 1981, Charlie and his students published the first formal description of a face-selective neuron, and a few years later they systematically investigated these neurons. Reports of face-selective neurons started coming out from other labs around the world: Japan, Italy, and Scotland. The lab of David Perrett at the University of Saint Andrews in Scotland was particularly active in this area of research, documenting more and more face selective neurons. A typical face-selective neuron may have a response like the one shown in Figure 13.2.

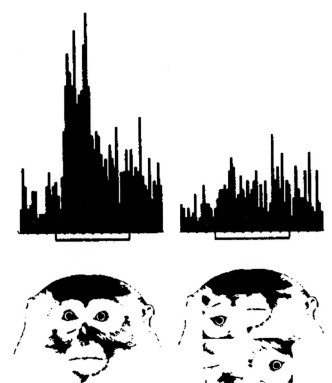

FIGURE 13.2. The firing pattern of a face-selective neuron. The neuron fires vigorously in response to a monkey face but not to the scrambled version of the face.

A monkey face shown for a couple of seconds at the center of vision of the monkey leads to vigorous firing of the neuron. This firing disappears when the features of the monkey face are scrambled. Such neurons respond to both monkey and human faces but not to hands. Removing facial features like the eyes or the mouth reduces but does not eliminate the response. Scrambling the features so that the face no longer looks like a face eliminates the response. Some neurons also prefer particular face orientations, for example, firing vigorously to a profile view of the face but not to a frontal view. Other neurons have holistic responses and, just like newborns, they respond to facelike stimuli with the right contrast polarity. The neuron responds to a circle with two black spots above a black horizontal bar, but it does not respond if any of the features—circle, spots, or bar—is missing or if the spots and the bar are white, appearing as protrusions rather than as cavities. This fairly selective pattern of responses is difficult to explain in terms of low-level visual features that have nothing to do with the face.

Face neurons are not just passively responding to faces. They matter for face perception. To demonstrate the causal significance of face neurons, Iranian researchers first trained monkeys to distinguish between faces and other objects in a difficult perceptual task. Then they stimulated face neurons with electrical current to test whether this would change the monkeys' categorization decisions (face vs. nonface). To make the perceptual task difficult, the researchers degraded the face and nonface images with visual noise (Figure 13.3), just like the images used in the experiments described in Chapter 5.

FIGURE 13.3. Noise-degraded nonface and face images used to study monkeys' perceptual categorization after electrical stimulation of face-selective neurons in the temporal cortex.

By manipulating the difficulty of the task, it is easier to detect changes in the monkeys' categorization decisions. To the extent that face neurons are causally important for face perception, changing their activity should change these decisions. In fact, when the face neurons, but no other neurons, were stimulated, the monkeys were more likely to see faces in the noisy images. This is strong evidence that face neurons are not just responding to faces but are responsible for face perception.

Charlie recently had his festschrift, a festive occasion celebrating his research career. During these events, former students give research talks peppered with personal memories. There was more than one picture of Charlie's lab members holding toilet brushes, the old-fashioned ones that end in a circle covered with long bristles. Apparently, the toilet brush was one of the best stimuli to elicit vigorous responses in neurons in the temporal cortex. Though Charlie could not recall how they came to use this particular object as a stimulus, his tongue-in-cheek explanation for its power to elicit responses in face-selective neurons was that it resembled the members of his lab: most of them, including himself, sported beards and long hair at the time of the experiments. Unfortunately, the beards and long hair were gone 30 years later. Face-selective neurons would often respond not only to toilet brushes but also to other round objects like clocks and apples that resemble the shape of faces. Yet their response tends to be much stronger to faces than to these facelike objects.

If the newborns' sensitivity to faces was controversial, the discovery of face-selective neurons was hypercontroversial. First, it is strictly impossible to prove that these neurons respond to faces, because in principle an infinite number of visual categories may be able to activate these neurons. So logically speaking, we can never be sure that there are no other simpler stimuli that activate these neurons. Second, the leap from neurons responding to moving bars to neurons responding to complex visual categories like faces was too big. Many people who were involved in this research were advised by senior colleagues to pursue other research directions if they really wanted to have research careers. At Charlie's festschrift, Bob Desimone, a professor at MIT and a former student of Charlie's, was recounting how David Hubel was shaking his head in disbelief when learning about their findings. But findings proliferated in many labs, and by the 1990s face-selective neurons were an established fact. We have not found "grandmother cells," but there are many types of neurons that primarily respond to changes in the view of the face, head orientation, emotional expressions, eye gaze, and many other things related to faces. It is the interactions of these neurons that enable us to be so good at perceiving faces. And there might be something akin to "grandmother cells" in the hippocampus—a subcortical region critical for our memories. A recent study recording neuronal responses in the hippocampus of an epilepsy patient who was being evaluated for the source of epileptic seizures found a neuron that seemed to particularly like Halle Berry. The neuron fired to different views of her face but no other faces, a drawing of her face, a picture of her as Catwoman from the 2004 movie, and even a letter string of her name. These kinds of neurons seem to act like memory neurons and are activated by particular visual scenes, not just faces but pictures of famous buildings like the Sydney operahouse or cartoons like *The Simpsons.*

• • • • •

In the 1990s, functional magnetic resonance imaging (fMRI) was introduced as a standard tool in cognitive neuroscience research, a tool that allows us to unobtrusively observe how activity in the normal human brain changes in real time. Functional MRI lacks the precision of recordings from single neurons. It measures the brain's metabolic activity, which luckily is tightly coupled with neuronal activity. Although a rather crude tool relative to recording from single neurons, fMRI provides a large-scale picture of the functions of the brain that cannot be obtained by recordings from single neurons. As long as a person with no metal in their body and no claustrophobia is willing to stay still for an hour or so, lying down in an MRI machine that looks like a time capsule, we can record their brain activity while they engage in a particular task. We can present faces and other objects (like houses or chairs) and observe whether some brain regions are more strongly activated by faces than by other objects.

By the early 1990s, there were reports based on positron emission tomography studies—the predecessor of fMRI that had the unfortunate requirement of injecting participants with a (harmless) radioactive trace—that faces activate regions in the temporal lobe more strongly than did other visual categories like houses. But the scientist who made the most forceful case that there are face-selective regions in the brain was Nancy Kanwisher from MIT. In 1997, using fMRI, she and her colleagues first identified an area in the brain that responded more strongly to faces than to common objects like spoons and cars. Then they showed that the same area responded more strongly to intact than to scrambled faces, and to faces than to hands. They called the area the fusiform face area (FFA), because it was located in the fusiform gyrus, part of the temporal lobe. As in the case of face-selective neurons, this idea was controversial at the time but is now a well-established fact. Although vision scientists argue about many things related to this area (such as how it came about), the finding that it responds to faces more strongly than any other object tested so far is undisputed.

In principle, brain lesions causing prosopagnosia, as in the patients of Bodamer, should overlap with face-selective regions identified in fMRI studies, but lesions that are not induced surgically are messy. Nevertheless, every now and then a patient with a fairly localized lesion allows a causal glimpse at some of the critical parts of the brain's machinery for face perception. Two Japanese neurologists described a 67-year-old patient who suffered a brain lesion from a hemorrhage in the brain. This patient, a retired journalist, suddenly lost his ability to recognize faces. His own reflection in the mirror looked like a stranger. A computed tomography scan, which uses X-rays, of his brain revealed a hemorrhage in the area of the occipital cortex. Subsequent MRI scans established that the hemorrhage damaged an area in the right fusiform gyrus that almost perfectly matched the FFA identified by Kanwisher. There was also damage in the lateral occipital cortex. The patient had normal visual acuity, normal memory, and normal intelligence. None of these were affected by the lesion. Detailed tests showed that his visual impairment was specific to faces. When shown a photograph of the Japanese sumo wrestler champion in front of a famous shrine, he could not recognize the face but immediately named the shrine. Although he could identify all of thirty-eight Japanese celebrities when given their names, he could identify only eight from their pictures. At the same time, he was perfect at identifying nonface objects in pictures, even when they were shown from unconventional views. This is quite striking, as most prosopagnosics show other visual impairments. Apparently, when the lesion is sufficiently localized, only recognition of faces is impaired.

Research on the FFA has come a long way since the initial controversy. A whole scene in the latest James Bond movie, *Spectre*, is based on this research. Bond is captured and about to be tortured by the villain he has been pursuing for most of the movie. The villain, well versed in brain research, is operating a remotely controlled drill with which he intends to drill into Bond's brain: "so James, I'm going to penetrate to where you are. To the inside of your head. Now, the first probe will play with your sight, your hearing, and your balance, just with the subtlest of manipulations." The torture begins. The camera moves from Bond's face with the penetrating drill to his newly found gorgeous love, who is observing the proceedings with horror, and back to him. It is pretty awful. The villain's next target is the FFA. "If the needle finds the correct spot in the fusiform gyrus, you'll recognize no one." The villain mocks Bond: "of course, the faces of your women are interchangeable, aren't they, James? You won't know who she is. Just another passing face on your way to the grave." Then turning to Bond's partner: "he dies not knowing who you are." Somehow the procedure does not work (perhaps because the villain was targeting the left rather than the right fusiform gyrus); Bond recognizes his love and is even able to give her one of his gadgets, which will reverse his uncomfortable situation in 60 seconds.

The FFA is one of many regions in the "face network." Two other face-selective areas have been identified in the human brain: one in the occipital lobe labeled the occipital face area and another in an area of the temporal lobe that integrates auditory and visual information, the superior temporal sulcus. And the face network is continuing to expand in the brain. Recently, Peter Mende-Siedlecki, one of my former graduate students who is now a professor at the University of Delaware, analyzed fMRI scans from hundreds of participants. Comparing the activation by faces with the activation by objects and scenes, he found that regions in the amygdala were consistently more active for faces. You can see these regions in Figure 13.4.

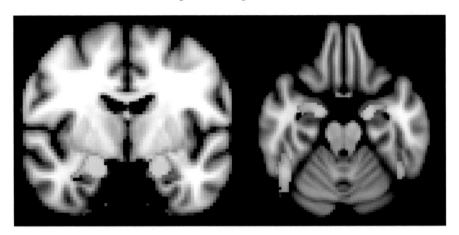

FIGURE 13.4. Face-selective voxels in the amygdala. The image on the left shows a brain slice from the middle. The image on the right shows the brain from below. This image shows not only activation in the amygdala but also in the fusiform face area (the activations in the lower part of the image; the activation in the right hemisphere is larger).

The amygdala and the FFA are not only more strongly activated by faces than by other objects, they also track the motivational significance of faces. When participants in fMRI studies are shown faces generated by our model of trustworthiness, their amygdalas and FFAs are more strongly activated by "trustworthy" and "untrustworthy" faces than by neutral faces. These faces activate the amygdala even if they are presented for an extremely brief amount of time. The role of the amygdala in face processing is not surprising. Earlier studies with monkeys have reported face-selective responses in amygdala neurons, and the amygdala is one of the most interconnected regions in the brain involved in multiple functions related to emotion and vigilance.

In the latest research development, fMRI is helping neurophysiologists identify regions populated by face-selective neurons. The neuroscientists Doris Tsao and Winrich Freiwald did the pioneering work of combining fMRI and recordings from neurons. In their first studies conducted with Margaret Livingstone, a former student and collaborator of David Hubel, they identified face-selective patches in the temporal cortex of monkeys using fMRI. Then they recorded from single neurons in these patches. The findings were nothing short of stunning. In all previous investigations, regardless where in the brain neuronal responses were recorded, at most 20 percent of neurons would be face selective. Using fMRI to cast the right spotlight, Tsao, Freiwald, and their colleagues found patches almost exclusively populated with face-selective neurons. Just as Konorski had predicted 40 years ago, the "gnostic" neurons are clustered in "gnostic fields." There are about six such fields in the posterior cortex of monkeys, and some of them are connected to the amygdala. This is very strong evidence for specialized "modules" in our brains dedicated to the perception of faces. Unlike computers, in which the same processing units compute all kinds of different things, we have processing units computing only face things.

The only circumstances under which we can directly record the neuronal responses in the human brain are when patients with epilepsy resistant to medication are being evaluated for the exact brain source of their epileptic seizures. This evaluation requires implanting electrodes directly in the brain. Studies with such patients have confirmed findings from animal studies. Face-selective neurons have been identified in the fusiform cortex, the amygdala, and the hippocampus. In a recent study, a research group led by Josef Parvizi and Kalanit Grill-Spector first identified face-selective patches in the fusiform cortex of a patient. Then they applied weak electrical charges to these patches to disrupt normal neuronal functions. When that happened, the face of the experimenter suddenly became distorted. The patient reported, "you just turned into somebody else. You metamorphosed. Your nose got saggy, went to the left. You almost looked like somebody I'd seen before, but somebody different." Inquired further about any other perceptual distortions, the patient reported that "only your face changed, everything else was the same." This weird face-distortion effect was obtained only when the electrical stimulation was real rather than sham and only when the stimulation was applied to the face-selective patches. As the patient put it, "that was a trip."

• • • • •

The newborns' readiness to attend to faces develops into a complex network of brain regions specialized to process faces. There is nothing mysterious about this process or the face selectivity of neurons. All faces look alike, yet we have to make fine face discriminations on an everyday basis. Other specialized areas in the brain process scenes, body parts, and words. These areas deal with categories that always mattered in primate history or categories for which we accrue considerable experience during our lifetimes. Literate people like you, dear reader, have a "visual word form area" in the left hemisphere that is adjacent to the left FFA. In just the past few years, Margaret Livingstone and her colleagues have shown that after intensive training that spans a couple of years, monkeys can be trained to discriminate human symbols. Juvenile monkeys, in contrast to adult monkeys, are not only better learners but also develop specialized "symbols" regions in the temporal cortex. The right experience at the right time is what seems to drive the formation of "gnostic" fields in the brain. As for the gnostic units, they need not respond to highly complex configurations of features. Recent work shows that some face-selective neurons simply respond to contrast polarity, the features critical for face detection. Others respond to external features like hair, and others to extreme facial features. An ensemble of millions of interconnected neurons, each one processing relatively simple facial features, goes a long way toward explaining our exquisite face perception skills. And for the record, we primates are not the only ones with such skills and "privileged access" to faces. This access is necessary for all visual, social creatures. Sheep, perhaps undeservingly, have a reputation for being stupid creatures. Yet they have a good recognition of sheep faces and the populations of neurons in their brains that represent sheep faces also seem to represent faces of humans who are good to them.

The face modules in our brains serve a larger function than just processing faces: they provide the input to neural systems that help us understand other people. The face-processing system is embedded in a much larger network of brain regions responsible for attention, emotions, memory, and cognitive control. The mere presence of faces activates multiple regions across the whole brain: not only of perceptual regions in the occipital and temporal cortices but also of affective and memory subcortical regions, and cognitive control regions in the prefrontal cortex. Our brains are doing much more than computing the familiarity of faces and recognizing them. They are automatically computing the social value of faces: the mental and emotional states of the person and their possible intentions.

First impressions are our best attempt to figure out this face value, having only appearance information to rely on. These impressions are automatically computed in the face modules and the extended brain network activated by faces. We can't help but compute this value, however illusory the value might be. The compulsory nature of impressions, coupled with the emotional and social significance of faces, tempts us to believe that faces always provide strong signals of this value. But as we will learn next, faces provide weak signals even for what we believe they are the best source of information for: recognition of emotions and people. We simply overestimate the clarity of facial signals.

14

ILLUSORY FACE SIGNALS

Neue Gallerie is located at 86th Street and 5th Avenue in Manhattan. It specializes in twentieth-century German and Austrian art. If you like Egon Schiele, Oskar Kokoschka, and Gustav Klimt, this is the place to visit. Yet in September 2010, the gallery opened with a show of works by Franz Xaver Messerschmidt. These works were created between 1771 and 1783, preceding German expressionism by more than 100 years. But Messerschmidt's head sculptures, called "Character Heads," were strangely modern. You can see an image of one of them in Figure 14.1.

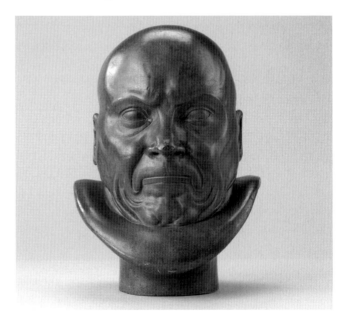

FIGURE 14.1. "Character Head No. 30" by Franz Xaver Messerschmidt.

Messerschmidt was 10 years old when he started his apprenticeship in sculpture. Eventually he was admitted to the Academy of Fine Arts in Vienna, the most prestigious institution for the study of arts in Central Europe, and he soon gained the appreciation and support of the Academy director. He built a successful career in Vienna, where he was often commissioned by the Imperial court to create busts of royalty. In 1769, he became a member of the Academy. Only a couple of years later, his life took an unfortunate turn. Messerschmidt had a mental breakdown and was forced to leave his position at the Academy. Because there were no new commissions and he was unable to support himself financially, he had to leave Vienna. He spent his last 12 years living in isolation and creating the work he is best known for today: the series of striking busts with distorted expressions. There is only one written account of how Messerschmidt created these heads. According to this account, he pinched himself to distort his face, observed his face in the mirror, and re-created his expressions. The more than fifty heads were completely unusual for his time—nobody had ever made or seen such expressive heads—and were never shown while he was alive. Thirteen years after his death, forty-nine of the heads were exhibited in the Communal Hospital of Vienna. Messerschmidt did not name the heads and never discussed their intended meaning. But an anonymous author, who described himself as the "author of candid letters about breeding sheep in Bohemia and Austria," wrote a brochure for the exhibition, describing the sculptures as "Character Heads" and naming all the individual heads.

The heads were shown as a kind of freak entertainment until the end of the nineteenth century, at which time they struck a chord with artists and collectors, who started buying them. Although Messerschmidt did not name his sculptures, the names added after his death stuck. When you looked at the head in Figure 14.1, what did you think the person was expressing? I bet "afflicted with constipation" was not on your mind, but that's what the bust was named. The names were meant to be amusing—"the enraged and vengeful gypsy," "a dismal and sinister man," "the ultimate simpleton"—and to attract crowds. But names have their own disturbing effects. Once you have seen the "afflicted with constipation" head, it is hard to see it any other way. As Andy Warhol put it, "the moment you label something, you take a step—I mean, you can never go back to seeing it unlabeled."

In virtually any research article on faces, including my own, you can read in the opening paragraph that faces are this amazing, rich source of social information about all kinds of things from the obvious, like gender and age, to the less obvious, like focus of attention and emotional states. But the face is a much more ambiguous source of information than we realize. This final chapter is about two skills most of us think we excel at: recognizing emotional expressions—the pathognomy of the face—and recognizing faces. Our everyday experience provides countless confirmations that we can do these two tasks easily. And these confirmations fuel our beliefs about the clear informational value of faces. As a result, we see value in faces even when it is not there. This illusion contributes to our faith in first impressions.

● ● ● ● ●

For Parsons, Lichtenberg, and Darwin, emotional expressions were clear signals of our emotional states. Lichtenberg called them the "involuntary sign language spoken by the passions in all their gradations all across the Earth." Darwin also argued that emotional expressions were universal. Many modern psychologists, following in his footsteps, believe that there is a limited set of universal emotional expressions that are easily recognized. This view has been repeatedly contested by other psychologists and is a perpetual topic of debate among emotion researchers. This debate is hardly new in the history of ideas. Le Brun's seventeenth-century lecture on the expressions of emotions was the first systematic attempt to depict the basic set of emotions with their corresponding set of facial movements. After his death, he was extensively criticized. His system was perceived as too artificial and limited, failing to capture expressions as they occur in real life and the many nuances in the expressions of the passions.

We are not going to resolve this debate here (that would take another whole book), but we will look at how the meaning of the universal emotional expressions can be easily changed. Imagine the following scenario: "A woman wanted to treat her sister to the most expensive, exclusive restaurant in their city. Months ahead, she made a reservation. When she and her sister arrived at the restaurant, they were told that their table would be ready in 45 minutes. Meanwhile, other groups arrived and were seated. A local celebrity arrived and was immediately shown a table. The woman was told that all the tables were now full, and that it might be another hour before anything was available." Now take a look at the woman's face in Figure 14.2. What does this face express?

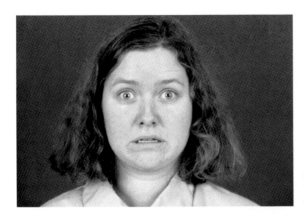

FIGURE 14.2. Do you recognize the expression conveyed by this face?

Most people see the face as enraged. But the face is expressing fear, one of the so-called basic and universally recognized emotions.

We do not need to be told stories to change how we see emotional expressions. The same emotional face transplanted on different bodies can communicate very different emotions. Take a look at Figure 14.3. What does the face express?

FIGURE 14.3. What does the face express?

We instantly see anger. But the face is expressing disgust, another of the basic and presumably universally recognized emotions. You can easily see the expression of disgust in Figure 14.4.

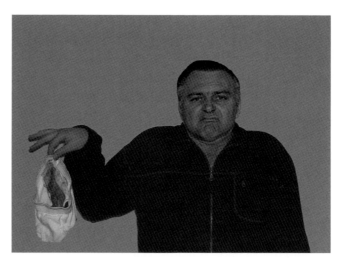

FIGURE 14.4. The face from Figure 14.3 transplanted on a different body. What does the face express?

Telling people to ignore the bodies and only judge the faces does not make any difference. We simply cannot ignore the contextual prompts that guide our interpretation of the face. Just as in the work of Cindy Sherman, these prompts make us see the same face differently.

Great artists know that bodily gestures and contextual prompts are indispensable for understanding the meaning of emotions. Leonardo argued that the painter has two principal things to paint: "man and the intention of his mind." "The first is easy and the second difficult, because the latter has to be represented through gestures and movements of the limbs." Depicting people experiencing emotions was not just about their facial expressions: "[to] show an angry figure hold someone up by the hair—wrenching that person's head against the ground, with one knee upon the person's ribcage—and raising high the fist of his right arm." "Give the despairing man a knife and let him have rent his garments with his hands. One of his hands will be tearing at his wound." These depictions guaranteed that the viewer would understand the intended meaning of the painting: "the motions and postures of figures should display the true mental state of the originator of these motions, in such a way that they could not signify anything else."

Just the shape of bodies, even without any gestures, can change our impressions. Remember the artistic experiments of Töpffer? If not, go back to Chapter 2 and look at Figure 2.4. Töpffer would take the same lower or upper part of a face and change the remaining part to alter our impressions as he desired. He did not limit his experiments to the drawing of faces only. Take a look at Figure 14.5. Here he is experimenting with drawing the same face on different bodies.

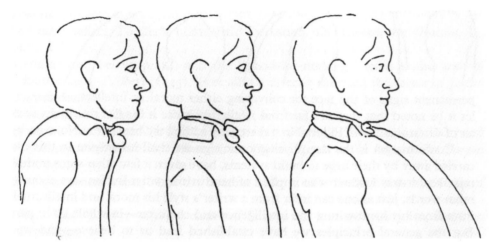

FIGURE 14.5. Illustrations from Rodolphe Töpffer's *Essay on Physiognomy*. By drawing the same face on different bodies, Töpffer can evoke different impressions of the face.

His result: "what strikes me in this series is that the quality of an individual expression (either of character or intelligence) changes as the form of the bust varies, irrespective of any gesture or pose. The first face has lost its determination, both moral and intellectual, compared to the second, and the second has also gained in power and penetration. The third has again lost, if not in determination and power, at least in sensitive and accurate penetration." Just as changing the lower or upper part of the face creates a new impression, changing the body attached to the same face also creates a new impression. It is not just about the face, it is about the whole person. We rapidly integrate information from all person-related sources—face, body, gestures, clothing, paraphernalia, and setting—to create a coherent impression of the person.

• • • • •

One of the criticisms of Le Brun's system of expressions was that the faces were not from nature. This is also one of the criticisms of much modern research on emotional expressions. Nearly all studies use posed expressions of emotions. The expressions in Figures 14.2 and 14.3 are such expressions. The main argument for using posed expressions is that they can be a "cleaner" version of actual emotional expressions. If you instruct people what emotion to express, especially if they are told how to move their faces, the expression may be closer to the ideal, prototypical form. This is all good, but it is difficult to make inferences about the prevalence of prototypical expressions in real life and how good we are at reading them.

Let's look at some extreme real-life situations in which people are experiencing intense positive or negative emotions. Think of losing or winning in sports competitions with high stakes. Or imagine experiencing intense pain like your nipple being pierced, intense pleasure like having an orgasm, intense grief, or intense joy. All theories of emotion recognition predict that as the intensity of the emotion increases, it should be easier to distinguish positive from negative emotions. Well, let's try it. The faces in Figure 14.6 are of tennis players who have just won or lost a point in a high-stakes game. Can you guess who won and who lost?

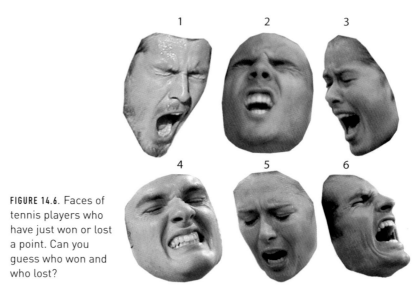

FIGURE 14.6. Faces of tennis players who have just won or lost a point. Can you guess who won and who lost?

Hillel Aviezer, who is now a professor at Hebrew University in Israel, was a post-doctoral fellow in my lab. Hillel was the one to show that the meaning of so-called basic expressions of emotions can be dramatically changed when these expressions are artfully transplanted on bodies communicating different emotional states (see Figures 14.3 and 14.4). He was also the one to suggest that when it comes to extreme emotions like pleasure and pain or winning or losing in a high-stakes game, people can't tell positive from negative emotions in the face. He was right. When participants were shown disembodied faces of tennis players (like the ones in Figure 14.6) or of people experiencing pleasure or pain, they had no idea whether the experience was positive or negative. Everything looked pretty negative. If you are curious about Figure 14.6, faces 1, 4, and 6 are of players after losing a point, and faces 2, 3, and 5 are of players after winning a point. If participants were shown just the bodies of the players, they made pretty good guesses about who won and who lost. Adding the faces to the bodies did not make these guesses better. Transplanting a losing face on a winning body made participants see the face as expressing positive emotions (Figure 14.7). Transplanting a winning face on a losing body made participants see the face as expressing negative emotions (Figure 14.7).

FIGURE 14.7. The same face is seen as expressing positive emotions when imposed on a body after winning a point (images 2 and 3) and as expressing negative emotions when imposed on a body after losing a point (images 1 and 4). Images 1 and 2 are the original (unmanipulated) images. Images 3 and 4 were the manipulated images. The thumbnails show the original images used to create images 3 and 4.

The body information completely dominated the interpretation of the facial expression. It was also the only information leading to an accurate judgment of the experience of the person. Yet participants who were shown intact (face plus body) images of the players thought that their judgments were predominantly based on information from the face. Nobody thought that they would guess the emotion solely from the body. Even when the face does not provide information about the underlying emotion, we think that it does. Our brains rapidly integrate information to disambiguate what we see. These processes are so rapid that we never become aware of them. Because the immediate context—including the situation we are in, bodily gestures, verbal exchanges, and many other less salient cues—helps us disambiguate the meaning of the face, we end up believing that the face is a good source of information, even when it is not. We misattribute the accuracy of our decisions to the natural focus of our attention: the face. And in the process, we "reconfirm" our ability to read faces accurately.

● ● ● ● ●

Perhaps recognition of emotional expressions is a special case, in which the meaning of "distorted" faces is simply illusive, and we need the help of context. Surely we would not run into these kinds of problems when recognizing faces. With the exception of the unfortunate people suffering from prosopagnosia, we excel in face-recognition tasks. Do you recognize the faces in Figure 14.8?

FIGURE 14.8. Low-resolution images of two politicians. Do you recognize them? Despite the low resolution, this is an easy recognition task.

I bet you can, despite the very low resolution of the images. We can easily identify familiar people from extremely degraded images. How about the squashed images in Figure 14.9?

FIGURE 14.9. Do you recognize these celebrities from their squashed images? Despite the deformation of the images, this is an easy recognition task.

This is another easy task for most seeing humans: Donald Trump and Bernie Sanders.

We can reduce the depictions of famous faces to abstractions with little visual similarity to their actual faces and still recognize the celebrities. Can you recognize the three men in Figure 14.10?

FIGURE 14.10. Illustrations by Hanoch Piven. Do you recognize the individuals from these schematic drawings? Images courtesy of Hanoch Piven.

The Israeli artist Hanoch Piven finds the minimal visual and conceptual cues that make the celebrity immediately recognizable. All the faces in Figure 14.10 have the shape of the celebrities' faces, but there are many thousands of people with similarly shaped faces. The same goes for facial hair. What makes Karl Marx (the image on the left) recognizable is the sickle and hammer used to depict his eyebrows. At least for a person who grew up in communist Eastern Europe, there is no mistake. As for Freud, his "eyes" and "nose" give him away. The image on the right, I imagine, would be most recognizable to people from New Jersey. This is the current governor of my state, Chris Christie.

We need remarkably little information to recognize familiar people, but there is a catch. Although recognition of familiar faces is easy, recognition of unfamiliar ones is hard. Just like recognizing emotions in context fools us into thinking that this is easy, recognizing familiar faces fools us into thinking that recognizing unfamiliar faces is easy too. Take a look at Figure 14.11. Are those two different people or two different images of the same person? How about Figure 14.12?

FIGURE 14.11. Are those two different people or two different images of the same person? In contrast to recognizing familiar people, recognizing unfamiliar people is hard.

The psychologist Alice O'Toole and her colleagues used state-of-the-art recognition algorithms to identify pairs of images in which the decision of whether the two images depict the same person or two different people is extremely difficult. These were pairs on which the algorithms consistently failed, deciding inaccurately that pairs like those in Figure 14.11 show two different people and that pairs like those in Figure 14.12 show the same person. How did people do? They did much better than the algorithms on these extremely difficult pairs, but they did so because they relied on information

FIGURE 14.12. Are those two different people or two different images of the same person? In contrast to recognizing familiar people, recognizing unfamiliar people is hard.

from the body and the hair. When shown the internal features of the faces alone, as in the image on the left in Figure 14.13, participants were barely better than chance at making correct identifications.

FIGURE 14.13. When making extremely difficult recognition decisions for unfamiliar faces (see Figure 14.12), we rely on information from the bodies and the hair, but we are not aware of this. We think that we rely on information from the features of the face.

When shown the bodies with the internal features of the faces masked, as in the image on the right in Figure 14.13, participants did much better. Just as in my studies with Hillel Aviezer, the recognition accuracy from these masked face images was as good as from the intact images of faces and bodies. And just as in our studies, participants had no idea that the information from the body was helping them make accurate decisions. When asked to rate what features helped them make decisions, they overwhelmingly reported relying on the internal face features.

Relying on extrafacial features helped recognition but did not make it perfect. Here is a real-life example of how things can go wrong in a very similar task. On April 18, 2013, three days after the bombing of the Boston marathon, the FBI released images of two suspects, later identified as the Tsarnaev brothers. You may be able to recognize the younger Tsarnaev in the image on the left in Figure 14.14. What about the image on the right? Is this another picture of the younger Tsarnaev?

FIGURE 14.14. The image on the left shows Dzhokhar Tsarnaev, one of the two Boston marathon bombers. Does the image on the right also show him?

If your answer is affirmative, you are not alone. Of course, if you have followed the ensuing events, including the Tsarnaev trial, you would be familiar with his face, and it would be obvious to you that the picture on the right doesn't show him. This truth was not obvious to everybody back then, though. Within hours of the FBI posting the pictures of the suspected bombers, Sunil Tripathi was misidentified by social media users as one of the brothers, and the false identification spread widely across the Internet. It all started with a user of Reddit, one of the largest websites in the world, who compared the faces of Tsarnaev and Tripathi. Tripathi was missing, and his family had created a Facebook page, "Help Us Find Sunil Tripathi." After the first hate messages on the Facebook page, the family removed the page, which further fueled beliefs that Tripathi was one of the perpetrators. This false information was retweeted more than 1,000 times in the early hours of the next day. Finally, on the morning of April 19, the FBI revealed Dzhokhar Tsarnaev's name.

It is easy to be angry with the people who propagated this false information and caused additional grief to the Tripathi family. But our incredible ability to recognize familiar faces sharply contrasts with our poor ability to recognize unfamiliar faces. This goes a long way toward explaining why mistaken eyewitness identification is the most frequent cause of false convictions. We assume that our facility with familiar faces extends to unfamiliar faces, and that gives eyewitnesses a false sense of confidence. When jurors decide whether to trust a witness, they heavily rely on the witness's confidence. But how indicative is confidence of accurate testimony? The relationship between confidence and accuracy of eyewitness testimony is as strong as the relationship between height and gender. Yes, men on average are taller than women, but we all know tall women and short men.

• • • • •

Our insensitivity to the differences between familiar and unfamiliar faces matters for first impressions. It contributes to the pernicious assumption that looks correspond to character. Take a look at Figure 14.15. How many different individuals are shown in the images? Take your time.

FIGURE 14.15. How many different individuals are shown in these images?

In a striking demonstration, Mike Burton, the leading researcher on the differences between recognition of familiar and unfamiliar faces, and his colleagues showed British participants many different images of Dutch celebrities who were unfamiliar to people in the United Kingdom. The participants were simply asked to group the images depicting different people. This extremely trivial task for the Dutch was anything but trivial for Britons. Not a single participant correctly categorized the images into two groups. That's right, the images in Figure 14.15 show only two people.

If the images were of celebrities familiar to you like those in Figure 14.16, the task of grouping the images is, indeed, trivial. Once we are familiar with a person, changes in their images like visual angle, illumination, hairstyle, and whether they are shaved or not are irrelevant. We immediately recognize them.

FIGURE 14.16. How many different individuals are shown in these images? This task is trivial when you are familiar with the depicted people.

And this recognition comes with knowledge: memory of familiar faces is interlocked with knowledge about the face bearers. This is what makes the celebrities in Piven's drawings (see Figure 14.10) recognizable. The drawings include cues that unlock this knowledge: the sickle and hammer (Marx), the penis-shaped nose (Freud), and the cars and bridge that make us think of the George Washington Bridge scandal (Christie). The knowledge that comes with face recognition doesn't depend on the particular face image we see. Any image will unlock it. But this is not how it works when we form impressions of strangers. We already saw in Chapter 8 that subtle differences in images of the same person can trigger different impressions. Take another look at the forty images of the two men in Figure 14.15. If you have to form impressions about their friendliness, trustworthiness, or any other characteristics you might think of, would you form the same impressions from their different images?

Our insensitivity to the differences between familiar and unfamiliar faces fuels the illusions of first impressions. For people we know, their images immediately cue a relatively stable face representation in our memory, creating a perfect correspondence between their appearance and their character. But this relation between appearance and character comes from our prior knowledge of them, not from their appearance. Even though we don't have such knowledge of strangers, we nevertheless assume the same (illusory) correspondence between their appearance (at the moment) and their character. It is almost impossible to get rid of this illusion, because we are too egocentric. We have a hard time seeing that two different images of a familiar person that look so alike to us may look bewilderingly different to someone who is unfamiliar with the person. We cannot escape the curse of our knowledge. And so we take what appears to us "the magic path" from appearance to character.

• • • • •

Our excellent recognition of familiar faces and of emotional expressions in contexts makes us believe that we can see the traces of character in the face. We do see traces in appearance, but these traces mainly reflect our circumstances: cultural upbringing, wealth, social class, peer groups, and aspirations. Goethe, who helped Lavater edit the first volume of his *Essays on Physiognomy*, wrote an addendum to one of the essays. In contrast to Lavater, he thought that the character traces were not to be found in the firm parts of the body. As he saw it, "we can draw sure conclusions about man's character from his clothes and household effects. Nature forms human beings, but they in turn transform themselves, and these transformations are once again natural; those who find themselves placed in a wide, expansive world erect fences and walls to create their own small world within it, and they design and furnish this world according to their own image." In their book *Exactitudes*, the photographer Ari Versluis and his creative partner Ellie Uyttenbroek document the self-chosen "uniforms" of more than 100 social types, like "hipsters," "yupstergirls," "ecopunks," "backpackers," "city girls," "skaters," and "intellectuals." The hipsters are shown in Figure 14.17. The uniforms signal to the world our cultural affiliations, tastes, and preferences. These may not constitute our character, but are better traces of it than the firm parts of our faces.

FIGURE 14.17. We all wear a "uniform" signaling our tastes and preferences. Hipsters from *Exactitudes* by Ari Versluis and Ellie Uyttenbroek.

Albeit on a smaller scale, like Cindy Sherman, we are agents of our own appearance transformation. We try to present a face (and put on clothing) that represents how we wish to be seen by the world. Dangin may be right to "look at life as retouching. Makeup, clothes are just a transformation of what you want to look like."

Like Goethe, Lichtenberg believed that the traces of characters were not to be found in the face: "one can infer with greater certainty from orderliness in the living room the orderliness in a person's head, from a sure eye for proportion a powerful understanding, from the color and cut of the clothes people wear at a certain age their character, than one can infer from a hundred silhouettes made from a hundred different perspectives of one and the same head." The personality psychologist Sam Gosling and his colleagues have amassed evidence supporting these ideas. We express ourselves in our environments. Our bedrooms, offices, online profiles, and music preferences are revealing of our personalities. Conscientious people's offices and bedrooms are organized, clean, and uncluttered. People who are open to new experiences have a greater variety of books and magazines in their bedrooms. Their offices are also more distinctive and unconventional. Our first impressions are more accurate if they come from seeing one's office, bedroom, or personal website than from seeing or briefly interacting with the person. The traces of character, if present in the face at all, are extremely faint. We can read more from the traces one leaves in one's physical environment than from one's face. But let's not delude ourselves: even those traces are weak. Predicting personality has always been an uncertain business.

MORE EVOLUTIONARY STORIES

To understand why physiognomy will not disappear from our lives, we need to understand the evolutionary origins of first impressions. And to understand these origins, we need to consider one more type of evidence before you close this book. This evidence comes from comparative primate studies that suggest evolutionary changes in the human face: unique features, such as our hairless faces and elongated eyes with white sclera. We can only speculate how these features evolved, but we can be reasonably confident that they facilitate "reading" of other minds in the service of social communication. The adaptations in our faces are about emitting and reading social signals, about inferring the emotions and intentions of others rather than inferring their characters. First impressions are grounded in these adaptations, in our ability to read the dynamic changes in the face, changes that are informative about the situation here and now.

There is actually a meaningful width-to-height ratio measure in the face, unlike the fWHR discussed in Chapters 9 and 10, that makes us distinctive from other primates. But this ratio is about our eyes, not the width and height of the face per se. The Japanese researchers Hiromi Kobayashi and Shiro Kohshima measured the eyes of more than eighty primate species. They used two ratios, illustrated in Figure E.1, to measure differences among the species. The first ratio—width-to-height of the eye—is an index of the elongation of the eye. The second ratio is an index of exposed sclera. Kobayashi and Kohshima found that humans are the primate with the most elongated eyes and the most exposed sclera. Across primates, the two ratios were correlated with habitat. Primates who live in trees tend to have the least elongated eyes with the least exposed sclera. Primates who live on the ground have the most elongated eyes with the most exposed sclera. Primates who live both in trees and on the ground are in between.

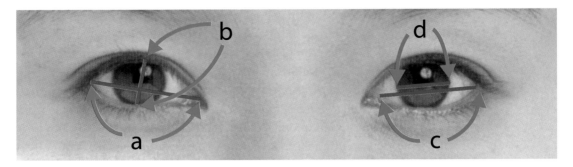

FIGURE E.1. Eye measures used by Kobayashi and Kohshima to compare eye morphology across primate species. The ratio of A to B is the width-to-height ratio. The ratio of C to D is an index of exposed sclera size.

The two eye ratios were also highly correlated with the walking height of primates: the greater the height is, the more elongated the eye and the more exposed the sclera. These relations between eye measurements, habitat, and walking height can be explained by a simple hypothesis: elongated eyes with exposed sclera were optimized for larger upright bodies living on the ground. Terrestrial life requires more horizontal eye scanning than does arboreal life, and for animals with large bodies it is more energy efficient to move their eyes than their heads to scan the environment. Elongated eyes with exposed sclera allow for a greater range of eyeball movements. And these movements extend the visual field in the horizontal direction.

Kobayashi and Kohshima discovered something even more remarkable. We are the only primate with a sclera much lighter than the surrounding skin and the iris. This is illustrated in Figure E.2. This distinctively human pattern cannot be explained by factors like terrestrial habitat and large body size, as these are similar across all great apes.

 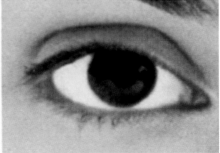

FIGURE E.2. Comparing the color patterns of the eyes of orangutans and humans. We are the only primates with a sclera much lighter than the surrounding skin and the iris.

The one plausible explanation is that human eyes were optimized to facilitate social communication. In contrast to other primates, the unique human eye pattern makes the detection of eye gaze easy. And eye gaze is a highly informative signal—we can establish mutual attention by direct eye gaze, we can direct others' attention by gazing at a specific direction, we can detect others' attention from their eye gaze, and we can even infer their intentions from their eye gaze and the situational context. Our attentiveness to eye gaze starts early: newborns are highly sensitive to eye gaze, preferring faces with direct eye gaze. In fact, the development of our perceptual expertise with faces may be driven by the newborns' attentiveness to eye gaze as a source of social information.

The distinctiveness of our eyes goes along with the distinctiveness of our eyebrows. As we learned in Chapter 4, the eyebrows are critical for both expressions of different emotional states and for recognition of people. The movements of the eyebrows are easily detectable on our hairless faces with prominent and flat foreheads. Most likely, our large, flat foreheads evolved to accommodate our larger brains, particularly the frontal cortex. The foreheads on their own are of no particular significance for reading others' minds, although physiognomists and scientists in the eighteenth and nineteenth centuries used the angle of the forehead to classify the intelligence of races (you can imagine which races they deemed to have the "better" [flatter] foreheads indicating superior intelligence). But our foreheads make the eyebrows more salient, facilitating the reading of social signals.

There are other evolutionary changes in our faces that together with our perceptual abilities facilitate social communication. Take our bare skin faces. In Chapter 11, we learned how changes in the color of faces could be informative about mental and health states. But to get this information, we should be able to perceive these short-term changes. This is easy for most of us who see in the three basic colors (red, green, and blue) but exceedingly difficult for people who lack one of the three basic color receptors in their retinas. Trichromatic vision turned out to be a rare characteristic in mammals. Primates are the only mammals with trichromatic vision, but not all primates have it. Some (typically nocturnal monkeys) are monochromats seeing in only one color, some are dichromats seeing in two colors, and some are trichromats like us and the rest of the Old World monkeys. The kind of color vision primates have is correlated with the amount of bare skin on their faces. Monochromats and dichromats tend to have furry faces, whereas trichromats tend to have bare skin faces. Researchers from Caltech have argued that this correlation is not coincidental. Trichromatic primate vision is much better than dichromatic vision for detection of short-term changes in skin reflectance. These changes can be produced by changes in the oxygenated hemoglobin in the blood. But to detect these changes in skin coloration whether in the face or on the rump for many primates, the skin needs to be bare. The Caltech researchers argued that color vision might have been naturally selected for reading social signals from the changes in the skin of conspecifics.

There are, of course, alternative hypotheses about the origins of trichromatic vision. These hypotheses have to do with fruit and leaf discrimination. The main diet of many primates consists of fruits and leaves. Trichromatic vision is better than dichromatic vision for detecting fruits against a background of foliage. It is also better at detecting leaves with coloring, which indicates a good nutritional value (leaves with high protein-to-toughness ratios, which tend to be young but not too young). Irrespective of which hypothesis turns out to be the right one, our vision makes it easier to read changes in the coloration of faces that could signal different mental and health states.

All these changes in our faces—bare skin, elongated eyes with white sclera, prominent eyebrows—make it easier to read other minds and to communicate and coordinate our actions. Our bigger brains don't just make us smarter, they make us socially smarter, and this might be our most distinctive characteristic. Michael Tomasello and his colleagues compared 2.5-year-old (illiterate and pre-school) children with orangutans and chimpanzees on a number of tasks measuring intelligence in the physical and social domains. Children were just as smart as chimpanzees (and a bit smarter than orangutans) on tasks like locating and tracking a reward or discriminating quantities of objects. But they outsmarted both chimpanzees and orangutans (who were indistinguishable from each other) in social tasks like learning from imitation and following eye gaze. The evolutionary changes in our appearance are about facilitating the reading of social signals, not about the reading of character.

• • • • •

That we find evidence for adaptations in the face facilitating social communication but not inferences of character is not surprising in light of the timeline of human evolution. If you imagine humankind evolving in 24 hours, the time we have been living in large societies populated with strangers amounts to less than 5 minutes—the last 5 minutes of the day. The rest of the time, we lived in small groups in which people did not have to rely on appearance information to draw inferences about character. The reliance on appearance emerged only in the last 5 minutes of our evolutionary history. Substantive person knowledge that was easily accessible in small-scale societies was replaced by appearance stereotypes in large societies. In our quest to know others and in the absence of good information, we are forced to rely on appearance information. This information could be useful as a guide to the intentions and actions of the person in the immediate here and now, but it is misleading as a guide to the person's character. The modern models of visualizing first impressions are mathematical maps of our appearance stereotypes, not of reality. The real map of the face is dynamic and constantly shifting, its interpretation rapidly changing in different situations. As long as we remember that, we will be less likely to fall into the physiognomists' trap of seeing the face as a source of information about character.

ACKNOWLEDGMENTS

This book took more than 5 years to complete. At a point when I was not sure where I was going, I turned to Peter Dougherty from Princeton University Press for advice. Peter immediately saw value in *Face Value* and became a champion of the project. His wisdom, sense of humor, editorial comments, and encouragement were invaluable. Meagan Levinson, my hands-on editor, was always on top of things and super sharp in seeing where the text was lacking. I was lucky to work with her. Generally, working with Princeton University Press was a blessing: I worked with people I completely trusted and who deeply cared about my work.

Many friends and colleagues read drafts of sections of the book, and some read the entire book. I thank them for their generosity and for making the book better: Hillel Aviezer, Ahmet Bayazitoglu, Maarten Bos, Jim Burton, Erik Cheries, Alin Coman, Lisa DeBruine, Ron Dotsch, Virginia Falvello, Friederike Funk, Charlie Gross, Ran Hassin, Daniel Kahneman, Yoshi Kashima, Aaron Kurosu, Katia Mattarozzi, DongWon Oh, Chris Olivola, Susanne Quadflieg, Eldar Shafir, Carmel Sofer, Kimberly Solomon, and Sara Verosky. Katia Mattarozzi not only read sections of the book but also helped with the translation of Italian texts. Aaron Kurosu and DongWon Oh created many of the illustrations. I am grateful to Iris Holzleitner, Xue Lei, David Perrett, Clare Sutherland, and Mirella Walker, who created new images for the book illustrating their work. Keisha Craig provided timely and excellent administrative support. Linda Chamberlin, Julie Mellby, and Neil Nero from the Princeton University Library were always ready to help with tracking the most obscure references. Laura Giles and Veronica White from the Princeton Art Museum were an unending source of information about art history. Melissa Flamson and her team were extremely efficient in obtaining the rights for the many illustrations in the book. Cyd Westmoreland, my terrific copy editor, made the book better.

I started working on this book while on a sabbatical leave at the Russell Sage Foundation in New York in 2010–2011. The Russell Sage Foundation and a fellowship from the John Simon Guggenheim Memorial Foundation supported this initial work. Princeton University provided the perfect environment to do research and be able to work on this book. I thank these institutions for their support.

Finally, I thank my wife, Sasha, and our son, Luca, who were incredibly patient with my incessant talking about the book, especially in the past year. Luca was also one of the best judges of the quality of the illustrations.

NOTES AND REFERENCES

PROLOGUE

p. 1: First impressions from facial appearance predict important elections. See A. Todorov, A. N. Mandisodza, A. Goren, and C. C. Hall (2005). "Inferences of competence from faces predict election outcomes." *Science* 308, 1623–1626. See also C. C. Ballew and A. Todorov (2007). "Predicting political elections from rapid and unreflective face judgments." *Proceedings of the National Academy of Sciences of the USA* 104(46), 17948–17953.

p. 1: International replications of election studies. For a review, see C. Y. Olivola and A. Todorov (2010). "Elected in 100 milliseconds: Appearance-based trait inferences and voting." *Journal of Nonverbal Behavior* 34(2), 83–110. Most of these studies are described in Chapter 3.

p. 1: John Antonakis and Olaf Dalgas's replication of election studies. See J. Antonakis and O. Dalgas (2009). "Predicting elections: Child's play!" *Science* 323, 1183.

p. 3: Seeing faces for less than a second provides enough information to form impressions. See Ballew and Todorov. "Predicting political elections from rapid and unreflective face judgments"; J. Willis and A. Todorov (2006). "First impressions: Making up your mind after 100 ms exposure to a face." *Psychological Science* 17, 592–598.

p. 3: "We look at a person . . ." from p. 258 in S. E. Asch (1946). "Forming impressions of personality." *Journal of Abnormal and Social Psychology* 41, 258–290.

p. 3: "At the first advance of a stranger . . ." from p. 127 in J. C. Lavater (1797). *Essays on Physiognomy; Calculated to Extend the Knowledge and the Love of Mankind*. Translated from the last Paris edition by C. Moore, Volume 1: London.

p. 3: "An ardent disciple of Lavater . . ." from p. 72 in C. Darwin (1969). *The Autobiography of Charles Darwin 1809–1882*. New York: W. W. Norton and Company.

p. 3: C. Lombroso (2006). *Criminal Man*. Durham, NC, and London: Duke University Press; C. Lombroso and G. Ferrero (2004). *Criminal Woman, the Prostitute, and the Normal Woman*. Durham, NC, and London: Duke University Press. These are modern translations by M. Gibson and N. H. Rafter of excerpts from the five different editions of *Criminal Man* and the first full English translation of *Criminal Woman*.

p. 3: F. Galton (1878). "Composite portraits." *Nature* 17, 97–100; F. Galton (1892). Composite portraiture. In *Inquiries into Human Faculty and Its Development*. London: Macmillan. First electronic edition, 2001.

p. 4: "Indicates broad-mindedness, and intellectual powers . . ." from pp. 139–144 in G. H.

LeBarr (1922). A brief analysis of President Warren G. Harding observed from the face alone. In *Why You Are What You Are*. Boston: G. H. LeBarr.

p. 4: Surveys of historians about the greatness of American presidents. See G. M. Maranell (1970). "The evaluation of presidents: An extension of the Schlesinger polls." *Journal of American History* 57, 104–113; R. K. Murray and T. H. Blessing (1983). "The presidential performance study: A progress report." *Journal of American History* 70, 535–555.

p. 5: G. C. Lichtenberg (2012). *Georg Christoph Lichtenberg: Philosophical Writings*. Translated, edited, and with an introduction by S. Tester. Albany, NY: SUNY Press. (Notebook G; G95 on pp. 94–95.)

CHAPTER 1: THE PHYSIOGNOMISTS' PROMISE

p. 9: A. Holland (Director), A. Brauner (Producer), and M. Ménégoz (Producer) (1990). *Europa, Europa* [Motion Picture]. Germany: CCC Film, France: Les Films du Lasange, France: Telmar Film International Ltd., Poland: Zespol Filmowy "Perspektywa."

p. 10: "Profiling people and revealing their personality . . ." from http://www.faception.com/, retrieved on September 4, 2016. See also M. McFarland (2016). "Terrorist or pedophile? This start-up says it can out secrets by analyzing faces." *Washington Post* (May 24), https://www.washingtonpost.com/news/innovations/wp/2016/05/24/terrorist-or-pedophile-this-start-up-says-it-can-out-secrets-by-analyzing-faces/.

pp. 10–11: *Physiognomica*, a treatise attributed to Aristotle. In *Works of Aristotle: Translated into English under the Editorship of W. D. Ross*, Volume VI (first edition 1913). Oxford: Oxford University Press. (Quotations from p. 806[b].)

p. 11: Giovan Battista della Porta (2011). *De Humana Physiognomonia Libri Sex*. Naples: Edizioni Scientifiche Italiane. The introduction to this Latin edition by A. Paolella contains information about the various editions of della Porta's book. The examples in the text were translated from the following Italian edition: Giovan Battista della Porta (1988). *Della Fisonomia Dell'Uomo*. Parma: Ugo Guanda Editore.

pp. 12–14: For Le Brun's work and his influence, as well as the translation of his lecture on emotional expressions, see J. Montagu (1994). *The Expressions of the Passions: The Origin and Influence of Charles Le Brun's Conférence sur l'expression générale et particularé*. New Haven, CT: Yale University Press.

p. 15: J. W. Redfield (1852). *Comparative Physiognomy or Resemblances between Men and Animals*. Clinton Hall, NY: Redfield.

p. 15: "The fanciful Porta . . . " from p. 153 in J. K. Lavater (1789). *Essays on Physiognomy; For the Promotion of the Knowledge and the Love of Mankind*, Volume 2, translated by Thomas Holcroft. London: Printed for G. G. J. and J. Robinson, Paternoster-Row. Despite the many English translations of Lavater, his original four-volume work, *Physiognomische Fragmente zur Beförderung der Menschenkenntniss und Menschenliebe* (Leipzig and Winterthur, 1775–1778), was never completely translated. All translations originated from two abbreviated texts of the original work. The first text was an abbreviated three-volume edition, which was translated into English by Thomas Holcroft in 1789. The second text was an abbreviated three-volume edition first translated into French and approved by Lavater. The French edition was first translated into English by Henry Hunter between 1788 and 1799. George Moore seemed to have largely plagiarized the Hunter translation, although his translation from 1797 is slightly expanded. Because of these different sources, there is no perfect correspondence between the original four-volume work and various translations. When I quote Lavater in the text, I use either translations (from excerpts of the original work) from scholarly articles on Lavater or the translations of Holcroft and Moore. For the history of translations of Lavater, see M. L. Johnson (2004). "Blake's engravings for Lavater's *Physiognomy*: Overdue credit to Chodowiecki, Schellenberg, and Lips." *Blake: An Illustrated Quarterly* 38, 52–74.

p. 15: "Pretending to have skill in physiognomy" from p. 550 in A. MacAliste (1911). Physiognomy. *Encyclopaedia Britannica* (eleventh edition) 21, 550–552.

p. 15: P. Mantegazza (1891). *Physiognomy and the Expression of Emotions.* New York: Scribner and Welford. (Quotations from p. 13 and p. 17.)

p. 16: "Had it printed wholly . . ." from p. 10 of J. K. Lavater (1775–1778). *Physiognomische Fragmente zur Beförderung der Menschenkenntniss und Menschenliebe,* Volume 1. Leipzig and Winterthur: Weidmanns Erben & Reich. Quotation translation from p. 72 in S. Frey (1993). "Lavater, Lichtenberg, and the suggestive power of the human face." In E. Shookman (ed.), *The Faces of Physiognomy: Interdisciplinary Approaches to Johann Caspar Lavater.* Columbia, SC: Camden House. The quoted episode is not mentioned in Holcroft's translation of Lavater, but it is mentioned in Moore's translation: "Mr. Zimmermann put them to the press without my knowledge; and thus was I suddenly and undesignedly brought forward, the avowed champion of the science of Physiognomies." from p. xiii in Lavater (1797). *Essays on Physiognomy; Calculated to Extend the Knowledge and the Love of Mankind.* Translated from the last Paris edition by C. Moore, Volume 1: London: H. D. Symonds.

p. 16: For the biography of Lavater and the success of his *Essays on Physiognomy,* see J. Graham (1961). "Lavater's *Physiognomy*: A checklist." *Papers of the Bibliographical Society of America,* January 1, 1961, 297–308; J. Graham (1979). *Lavater's Essays on Physiognomy: A Study in the History of Ideas.* Berne, Switzerland: Peter Lang Publishers; G. Tytler (1982). *Physiognomy in the European Novel: Faces and Fortunes.* Princeton, NJ: Princeton University Press; M. Shortland (1986). "The power of a thousand eyes: Johann Caspar Lavater's science of physiognomical perception." *Criticism* 28, 379–408; S. Frey. "Lavater, Lichtenberg, and the suggestive power of the human face."

p. 16: "A typographical splendor with which no German book . . ." translation by S. Frey (see previous note) from p. 173 of Georg Gustav Fülleborn (1797). *Abriss einer Geschichte und Litteratur der Physiognomik,* in *Beyträge zur Geschichte der Philosophie,* revised edition, Achtes Stück. Züllichau and Freystadt, Germany: Fromann.

p. 16: Lavater obituary: anonymous (1801). Untitled obituary, *Gentleman's Magazine.* London: Printed by Nichols and Son (February 1801); quotation from p. 184.

p. 16: "The talent of discovering, the interior man . . ." from p. 12 of Moore's translation of Lavater (Volume 1).

p. 17: "Universal axioms and incontestible principles" from p. 10 of Moore's translation of Lavater (Volume 1).

p. 17: "Who could have the temerity to maintain . . ." from p. 22 of Moore's translation of Lavater (Volume 1).

p. 17: "It is certain that every man of the smallest judgment . . ." from p. 221 of Moore's translation of Lavater (Volume 1).

p. 17: "I revel in this silhouette! . . ." original from pp. 243–244 of Lavater (Volume 1), *Physiognomische Fragmente zur Beförderung der Menschenkenntniss und Menschenliebe;* translation from p. 319 in A. Altman (1973). *Moses Mendelssohn: A Biographical Study.* Tuscaloosa: University of Alabama Press. The relationship of Lavater and Mendelssohn was complicated: see pp. 194–263, 426–427 in Altman; and pp. 83–106, 115 in S. Feiner (2010). *Moses Mendelssohn: Sage of Modernity*. New Haven, CT: Yale University Press. Impressed by a book by the Geneva philosopher Charles Bonnet on the evidence for Christianity, Lavater quickly translated the relevant parts into German. Inexplicably, in his preface to the translation, Lavater challenged Mendelssohn either to refute this evidence or to convert to Christianity. Lavater's public challenge, which appalled many of the leading intellectuals of the day, including Goethe, forced Mendelssohn to discuss in public what he was reluctant to discuss in private. Mendelssohn's reply advocating religious tolerance is as relevant today as it was back then. The dispute was eventually resolved, and Lavater retracted his public challenge, but the episode would cast a long shadow on the rest of Mendelssohn's life. Altman referred to Lavater as the "most sinister figure in Mendelssohn's life" (p. 731). Yet when asked by a Jewish community in Switzerland—facing legislation limiting the number of Jews with residential rights—to intervene on their behalf, Mendelssohn turned to Lavater. Lavater promptly did the right thing, and the legislation was stopped.

p. 18: "It is not virtue which that horrible face announces . . ." from p. 148 of Moore's translation of Lavater (Volume 1). The same plate is described on p. 207 in Holcroft's translation of Lavater (Volume 1).

p. 18: Letter to Lavater "so as not to have the entire local population . . ." from p. 60 in G. Tytler (1982). *Physiognomy in the European Novel: Faces and Fortunes*. Princeton, NJ: Princeton University Press.

p. 18: "The fact that you can see into people's hearts . . ." from p. 61 in Tytler. *Physiognomy in the European Novel*.

p. 18: For the interactions between Emperor Joseph II and Lavater, see pp. 86–88 in S. Frey. "Lavater, Lichtenberg, and the suggestive power of the human face." Quotation is from pp. 87–88.

p. 18: For the biography of Lichtenberg, see C. Brinitzer (1960). *A Reasonable Rebel*. New York: Macmillan; J. P. Stern (1959). *Lichtenberg: A Doctrine of Scattered Occasions*. Bloomington: Indiana University Press; Introduction by Steven Tester in *Georg Christoph Lichtenberg: Philosophical Writings*; Introduction by Frantz H. Mautner and Henry Hatfield (1959). *The Lichtenberg Reader: Selected Writings of Georg Christoph Lichtenberg*. Boston: Beacon Press; Introduction by R. J. Hollingdale in *The Waste Book: Georg Christoph Lichtenberg*. New York: New York Review of Books.

pp. 18–19: "This shallow and passionate youthful declamation . . ." from p. 11 in G. C. Lichtenberg, *On Physiognomy, against the Physiognomists, for the Promotion of the Love and Knowledge of Man*, translated by Steven Tester for Princeton University Press. Translation courtesy of Steven Tester, University of Göttingen.

p. 19: "I just want to put in a word for the Negro, . . ." from Lichtenberg, *On Physiognomy, against the Physiognomists, for the Promotion of the Love and Knowledge of Man*, quotation from p. 97 in S. Frey. "Lavater, Lichtenberg, and the suggestive power of the human face."

p. 19: "From my early youth, . . ." from p. 4 in Lichtenberg. *On Physiognomy, against the Physiognomists, for the Promotion of the Love and Knowledge of Man*. Translation courtesy of Steven Tester, University of Göttingen.

p. 19: "Instead of cultivating the intellect, . . ." from p. 576 in G. C. Lichtenberg (1968), *Schriften und Briefe*, ed. Wolfgang Promies, Erster Band, Heft F 813. Munich: Carl Hanser Verlag; translation from p. 89 in Frey. "Lavater, Lichtenberg, and the suggestive power of the human face."

p. 19: "Antiphysiognomics would be *roughly* and *forcefully* refuted." from p. 565 (Dritter Band) G. C. Lichtenberg (1972). *Schriften und Briefe*, edited by Wolfgang Promies. Munich: Carl Hanser Verlag; translation from p. 94 in Frey. "Lavater, Lichtenberg, and the suggestive power of the human face."

p. 19: "What do you hope to conclude . . ." from pp. 9–10 in Lichtenberg. *On Physiognomy, against the Physiognomists, for the Promotion of the Love and Knowledge of Man*. Translation courtesy of Steven Tester, University of Göttingen.

p. 19: "About people, who are always changing" from p. 2 in Lichtenberg. *On Physiognomy, against the Physiognomists, for the Promotion of the Love and Knowledge of Man*.

p. 19: "Beautiful rogues" and "smooth swindlers" from p. 10 in Lichtenberg. *On Physiognomy, against the Physiognomists, for the Promotion of the Love and Knowledge of Man*.

p. 20: Pocket editions dedicated to reading character from noses; one example is G. Jabet (1852). *Notes on Noses*. London: Richard Bentley, New Burlington Street.

p. 20: On the popularity of physiologie in Paris, see pp. 31–39 in J. Wechsler (1982). *A Human Comedy: Physiognomy and Caricature in 19th Century Paris*. Chicago: University of Chicago Press.

p. 20: Consumed with "the news and the morning coffee," from p. 15 in Wechsler. *A Human Comedy*.

p. 20: On the influence of physiognomy on the visual arts and caricatures, see M. Cowling (1989). *The Artist as Anthropologist: The Representation of Type and Character in Victorian Art*. Cambridge: Cambridge University Press; Wechsler. *A Human Comedy*. When caricatures were used to criticize authorities, they were also dangerous. Honoré Daumier, one of the most talented French caricaturists, was jailed for 6 months for one of his many caricatures of King Louis-Philippe. In 1835, the French authorities went so far as to issue a charter banning the pictorial treatment of political subjects: "Frenchmen have the right to circulate their opinions in published form," but "when opinions are converted into actions by the circulation of drawings, it is a question of speaking to the eyes. That is something more than the expression of an opinion. It is an incitement to action not covered by Article 3." See chapter 3 in Wechsler. *A Human Comedy*.

p. 20: On the influence of physiognomy on European writers in the eighteenth and nineteenth centuries, see J. Graham (1961). "Lavater's physiognomy in England." *Journal of the History of Ideas* 22, 561–572; J. Graham (1966). "Character description and meaning in the romantic novel." *Studies in Romanticism* 5, 208–218; Tytler. *Physiognomy in the European Novel*; S. Pearl (2010). *About Faces: Physiognomy in Nineteenth-Century Britain*. Cambridge, MA: Harvard University Press; Cowling. *The Artist as Anthropologist*.

p. 20: "A style of head and set of features, . . ." from p. 201 in C. Dickens (1994). *Sketches by Boz and Other Early Papers 1833–39*. Edited by M. Slater, new edition. London: J. M. Dent.

p. 20: "Perhaps more than in any other science, . . ." from p. 59 in Lavater. *Essays on Physiognomy*. Translated by C. Moore (Volume 1).

p. 20: For the links between Lavater's physiognomy and Gall's phrenology, see G. P. Brooks and R. W. Johnson (1980). "Contributions to the history of psychology: XXIV. Johan Caspar Lavater's *Essays on Physiognomy*." *Psychological Reports* 46, 3–20.

pp. 20–21: For biographies of Galton, see N. W. Gillham (2001). *A Life of Sir Francis Galton: From African Exploration to the Birth of Eugenics*. Oxford University Press; M. Brookes (2004). *Extreme Measures: The Dark Visions and Bright Ideas of Francis Galton*. New York: Bloomsbury.

p. 21: L. Terman (1917). "The intelligence quotient of Francis Galton in childhood." *American Journal of Psychology* 28, 209–215. (Quotations from pp. 209 and 211.)

p. 21: E. J. Webb, D. T. Campbell, R. D. Schwartz, and L. Secherest (1966). *Unobtrusive Measures: Nonreactive Research in the Social Sciences*. Chicago: Rand McNally and Company.

p. 21: "Inclination of one person toward another, . . ." from p. 151 in Webb et al. *Unobtrusive Measures*.

p. 21: "Let this suggest to observant philosophers, . . ." from p. 174 in F. Galton (1885). The measure of fidget. *Nature* 32, 174–175.

pp. 21–22: "A needle mounted as a pricker, . . ." from pp. 315–316 in F. Galton (1909). *Memories of My Life*. New York: E. P. Dutton and Company.

p. 22: For Galton's work "Kantsaywhere," see pp. 342–344 in Gillham. *A Life of Sir Francis Galton*.

p. 22: For the endorsement of eugenics by the Left, see D. Paul (1984). "Eugenics and the Left." *Journal of the History of Ideas* 45, 567–590.

p. 22: "Each type of crime is committed by men . . ." from p. 51 in C. Lombroso (2006). *Criminal Man*. Durham, NC, and London: Duke University Press.

p. 22: For Lombroso as a court witness, see chapter 5 of part III in C. Lombroso (1911). *Crime: Its Causes and Remedies*. London: William Heinemann; Little, Brown, and Company.

pp. 22–23: "The first group included murder, . . ." from p. 346 in F. Galton (1877). "Address. Section D.—Biology. Department of Anthropology." *Nature* 16, 344–347.

p. 23: "The physiognomical difference between different men . . ." from p. 4 in F. Galton (1892). *Inquiries into Human Faculty and Its Development*. London: Macmillan. First electronic edition, 2001.

p. 23: For correspondence between L. A. Austin and Darwin, see F. Galton (1878). "Composite portraits." *Nature* 17, 97–100. (Quotation from letter on p. 98.)

p. 23: For studies on improving composite photography, see F. Galton (April 17, 1885). "Photographic composites." *Photographic News*, 243–245; J. T. Stoddard (1886). "Composite portraiture." *Science* 8, 89–91; J. T. Stoddard (1887). "Composite photography." *Century* 33, 750–757.

p. 24: "Method of discovering the central physiognomical type . . ." from p. 10 in Galton. *Inquiries into Human Faculty and Its Development*.

p. 24: "When the photographer had his head . . ." from p. 263 in Galton. *Memories of My Life*.

p. 24: "With this great contribution of Galton . . ." from p. 374 in anonymous (1886). "Comment and Criticism." *Science* 5, 373–374.

p. 24: "The faces give to me an idea of perfect equilibrium, . . ." from p. 378 in R. Pumpelly (1885). "Composite portraits of members of the National Academy of Sciences." *Science* 5, 378–379.

pp. 24–25: "I have made numerous composites of various groups of convicts, . . ." from p. 11 in Galton. *Inquiries into Human Faculty and Its Development*.

p. 25: For Nancy Burson's work, see N. Burson (2002). *Seeing and Believing: The Art of Nancy Burson*. Santa Fe, NM: Twin Palms Publishers.

p. 26: "The new face of America;" see the *Time* cover from November 18, 1993.

p. 26: For modern studies on creating composites of different character types, see I. S. Penton-Voak, N. Pound, A. C. Little, and D. I. Perrett (2006). "Personality judgments from natural and composite facial images: More evidence for a 'kernel of truth' in social perception." *Social Cognition* 24, 607–640; A. C. Little and D. I. Perrett (2007). "Using composite images to assess accuracy in personality attribution to faces." *British Journal of Psychology* 98, 111–126; L. G. Boothroyd, B. C. Jones, D. M. Burt, L. M. DeBruine, and D. I. Perrett (2008). "Facial correlates of sociosexuality." *Evolution and Human Behavior* 29, 211–218; A. L. Jones, R. S. S. Kramer, and R. Ward (2012). "Signals of personality and health: The contributions of facial shape, skin texture, and viewing angle." *Journal of Experimental Psychology: Human Perception and Performance* 38, 1353–1361. There are several things to be noted about these studies: (a) the results of different groups are inconsistent (compare Jones et al. with Penton-Voak et al.); (b) the composites are based on self-reports of personality traits rather than on objective criteria; (c) the composite images are always created from a small subset of images on the extremes of the self-reports, which should maximize any differences; and (d) the results are computed on aggregated data (averaged across participants) rather than on data from individual participants, which inflates correlations between self-reports and images. The methodological problems facing studies on accuracy from judgments of facial images are discussed in Part 3 of this book.

p. 26: On the founding of organized eugenics societies around the world and eugenic policies in Nazi Germany and the United States, see chapter 22 and the epilogue in Gillham. *A Life of Sir Francis Galton*; for eugenics-inspired economic policies in the United States, see T. C. Leonard (2016). *Illiberal Reformers: Race, Eugenics, and American Economics in the Progressive Era*. Princeton, NJ: Princeton University Press.

p. 26: On H. F. K. Günther, see chapter 6 in R. T. Gray (2004). *About Face: German Physiognomic Thought from Lavater to Auschwitz*. Detroit: Wayne State University Press.

p. 27: "I wanted to prevent people from practicing physiognomy . . ." from p. 2 in Lichtenberg. *On Physiognomy, against the Physiognomists*. Translation courtesy of Steven Tester, University of Göttingen.

p. 27: "If physiognomy becomes what Lavater expects of it, . . ." from Notebook F (F521 on p. 81) in G. C. Lichtenberg (2012). *Georg Christoph Lichtenberg: Philosophical Writings*. Translated, edited, and with an introduction by S. Tester. Albany, NY: SUNY Press.

p. 27: "Anthropological examination, by pointing out the criminal type, . . ." from pp. 438–439 in Lombroso. *Crime: Its Causes and Remedies*.

Chapter 2: Single-Glance Impressions

p. 28: "one of the most popular . . ." Two reviews of the game of first impressions by T. Vasel (2007). "Ugly faces, fun game." G. J. Schloesser (2007). "A picture really is worth a thousand words!" From https://www.funagain.com/control/product/~product_id=016091/~affil =MFUN, retrieved on June 17, 2015.

p. 28: Early studies on matching pictures of people to "social types." S. A. Rice (1926). "'Stereotypes': A source of error in judging human character." *Journal of Personnel Research* 5, 267–276; O. F. Litterer (1933). "Stereotypes." *Journal of Social Psychology* 4, 59–69. Litterer's study is described in the chapter.

p. 29: "Pictures in our heads." This phrase was introduced by Walter Lipmann (1922) in his book, *Public Opinion*. New York: Macmillan.

p. 29: A study conducted half a century later: A. G. Goldstein, J. E. Chance, and B. Gilbert (1984). "Facial stereotypes of good guys and bad guys: A replication and extension." *Bulletin of the Psychonomic Society* 22, 549–552. For other papers on occupational stereotypes for faces, see R. Klatsky, G. L. Martin, and R. A. Kane (1982). "Semantic interpretation effects on memory for faces." *Memory and Cognition* 10, 195–206; J. A. Oldmeadow, C. A. M. Sutherland, and A. W. Young (2012). "Facial stereotype visualization through image averaging." *Social Psychological and Personality Science* 4, 615–623. The last study is also interesting because it uses methods derived from Galton's composite photography to create face morphs of occupational stereotypes.

pp. 29–30: On Darwin's thoughts about Lavater, see C. Darwin (1987). *Charles Darwin's Notebooks, 1836–1844, Geology, Transmutation of Species, Metaphysical Inquiries*, transcribed and edited by P. H. Barrett, P. J. Gautrey, S. Herbert, D. Kohn, and S. Smith. Ithaca, NY: Cornell University Press. The quotations are from notebook M, comment 145e on p. 556 and notebook N, comment 10 on pp. 565–566.

p. 30: M. O. Stanton (1890). *A System of Practical and Scientific Physiognomy; On How to Read Faces*. Philadelphia and London: F. A. Davis; K. M. H. Blackford and A. Newcomb (1916). *Analyzing Character: The New Science of Judging Men; Misfits in Business, the Home, and Social Life*, third edition. New York: Review of Reviews Company; L. H. McCormick (1920). *Characterology: An Exact Science*. Chicago: Rand McNally and Company; L. A. Vaught (1902). *Vaught's Practical Character Reader*. Chicago: L. A. Vaught.

p. 30: "Accurately, quickly, scientifically . . ." See G. C. Brandenburg (1926). "Do physical traits portray character?" *Industrial Psychology* 1, 580–588. The quotation is from an ad reprinted in the paper on p. 586. See also chapter 7 in D. A. Laird (1927). *The Psychology of Selecting Men*. New York: McGraw-Hill.

p. 30: "The results as a whole certainly look very bad . . ." from p. 119 in C. L. Hull (1928). *Aptitude Testing*. New York: World Book. See also the references in the previous note and R. W. Husband (1934). "The photograph on the application blank." *Personnel Journal* 13, 69–72.

p. 30: "It is noteworthy that casual observation . . ." from p. 224 in G. U. Cleeton and F. B. Knight (1924). "Validity of character judgments based on external criteria." *Journal of Applied Psychology* 8, 215–231.

p. 30: S. W. Cook (1939). "The judgment of intelligence from photographs." *Journal of Abnormal and Social Psychology* 34, 384–389.

pp. 31–32: W. Bevan, P. F. Secord, and J. M. Richards (1956). "Personalities in faces: V. Personal identification and the judgment of facial characteristics." *Journal of Social Psychology* 44, 289–291; P. F. Secord (1958). "Facial features and inference processes in interpersonal perception." In R. Tagiuri and L. Petrullo (eds.), *Person Perception and Interpersonal Behavior*. Stanford, CA: Stanford University Press; P. F. Secord and W. Bevan (1956). "Personalities in faces: III. A cross-cultural comparison of impressions of physiognomy and personality in faces." *Journal of Social Psychology* 43, 283–288; P. F. Secord, W. Bevan, and W. F. Dukes (1953). "Occupational and physiognomic stereotypes in the perception of photographs." *Journal of Social Psychology* 37, 261–270; P. F. Secord, W. Bevan, and B. Katz (1956). "The negro stereotype and perceptual accentuation." *Journal of Abnormal Social Psychology* 53, 78–83; P. F. Secord, W. F. Dukes, and W. Bevan (1954). "Personalities in faces: I. An experiment in social perceiving." *Genetic Psychology Monographs* 49, 231–279; P. F. Secord and J. E. Muthard (1955). "Personalities in faces: IV. A descriptive analysis of the perception of women's faces and the identification of some physiognomic determinants." *Journal of Psychology* 39, 269–278.

p. 31: "We respond to a face as a whole . . ." from p. 334 in E. H. Gombrich (2000). *Art and Il-*

lusion: *A Study in the Psychology of Pictorial Representation*. Princeton, NJ: Princeton University Press.

p. 32: For a physiognomic interpretation of Leonardo's grotesque heads, see P. D. G. Britton (2002). "The signs of faces: Leonardo on physiognomic science and the 'Four Universal States of Man.'" *Renaissance Studies* 16, 143–162.

p. 33: On Leonardo's intentions to write a book on physiognomy, see Britton. "The signs of faces," as well as F. Caroli (2015). *Leonardo Studi di Fisiognomica*, ninth edition. Milan: BibliotecaElectra; M. W. Kwakkelstein (1994). *Leonardo da Vinci as a Physiognomist: Theory and Drawing Practice*. Leiden: Primavera Press.

p. 33: "I will not enlarge upon false physiognomy and chiromancy . . ." from p. 147 in Martin Kemp (ed.) (1989). *Leonardo on Painting*. New Haven, CT: Yale University Press.

p. 33: For a nonphysiognomic interpretation of Leonardo's grotesque heads, see p. 362 in J. Nathan (2012). "Profile studies, character heads and grotesque." In F. Zöllner (ed.), *Leonardo da Vinci 1452–1519: The Complete Paintings and Drawings*. Cologne: Taschen.

p. 33: "How to make a portrait in profile . . ." from pp. 207–208 in Martin Kemp (ed.). *Leonardo on Painting*.

p. 33: A. Cozens (1778). *Principles of Beauty, Relative to the Human Head*. London: Printed by James Dixwell.

p. 33: "That a set of features may be combined . . ." from p. 2 in Cozens. *Principles of Beauty*.

p. 34: F. Grose (1788). *Rules for Drawing Caricaturas: With an Essay on Comic Painting*. London: Printed by A. Grant.

p. 34: "Whereby he will produce a variety of odd faces . . ." from pp. 7–8 in Grose. *Rules for Drawing Caricaturas*.

p. 34: "Convex faces, prominent features, and large aquiline noses, . . ." from note on p. 7 in Grose. *Rules for Drawing Caricaturas*.

p. 34: "Has never yielded one immediate, dependable result . . ." from p. 16 in R. Töpffer (1965). *Essay on Physiognomy. In Enter: The Comics. Rodolphe Töpffer's Essay on Physiognomy and the True Story of Monsieur Crépin*, translated and edited by E. Wiese. Lincoln, NE: University of Nebraska Press. The essay was originally published in 1845.

p. 35: "Any human face, however poorly and childishly drawn . . ." from p. 11 in Töpffer. *Essay on Physiognomy*.

p. 35: "The style of schoolboys," from p. 11 in Töpffer. *Essay on Physiognomy*.

p. 35: "Can modify, transform, or diminish the intellectual faculties . . ." from p. 26 in Töpffer. *Essay on Physiognomy*.

pp. 35–36: "In art you can combine these signs among themselves . . ." from p. 30 in Töpffer. *Essay on Physiognomy*.

p. 36: "The ultimate decision of the principles . . ." from p. 10 in Cozens. *Principles of Beauty*.

p. 36: E. Brunswick and L. Reiter (1938). "Eindruckscharactere schematisierter Gesichter." *Zeitshrift für Psychologie* 142, 67–134.

p. 37: M. R. Samuels (1939). "Judgments of faces." *Character & Personality* 8, 18–27.

pp. 38–39: D. S. Berry and L. Zebrowitz McArthur (1985). "Some components and consequences of a babyface." *Journal of Personality and Social Psychology* 48, 312–323; D. S. Berry and L. Zebrowitz McArthur (1986). "Perceiving character in faces: The impact of age-related craniofacial changes on social perception." *Psychological Bulletin* 100, 3–18; L. Zebrowitz McArthur and K. Apatow (1983). "Impressions of baby-faced adults." *Social Cognition* 2, 315–342; J. M. Montepare and L. Zebrowitz McArthur (1986). "The influence of facial characteristics on children's age perceptions." *Journal of Experimental Child Psychol-*

ogy, 42, 303–314. For reviews of this work, see J. M. Montepare and L. A. Zebrowitz (1998). "Person perception comes of age: The salience and significance of age in social judgments." *Advances in Experimental Social Psychology* 30, 93–161; L. A. Zebrowitz (2011). "Ecological and social approaches to face perception." In A. Calder, J. V. Haxby, M. Johnson, and G. Rhodes (eds.), *Handbook of Face Perception*. Oxford: Oxford University Press.

p. 39: "The significance of the pure convex type is energy . . ." from pp. 154–156 in K. M. H. Blackford and A. Newcomb (1917). *The Job, The Man, The Boss*. New York: Doubleday, Page and Company.

p. 39: For Hull's instrument to measure the convexity of face profiles, see pp. 127–130 in Hull. *Aptitude Testing*.

p. 40: "A small deficient chin stands . . ." from pp. 73–74 in LeBarr. *Why You Are What You Are*.

p. 40: "Perhaps the strongest of any of our Presidents . . ." from chapter 16 in LeBarr. *Why You Are What You Are*.

p. 40: K. Lorenz (1971). "Part and parcel in animal and human societies (1950). A methodological discussion." In K. Lorenz, *Studies in Animal and Human Behavior*, translated by Robert Martin, Volume 2. Cambridge, MA: Harvard University Press.

p. 40: L. A. Zebrowitz, H. A. Wadlinger, V. X. Luevano, B. M. White, C. Xing, and Y. Zhang (2011). "Animal analogies in first impressions of faces." *Social Cognition* 29, 486–496.

p. 40: S. J. Gould (1980). "A biological homage to Mickey Mouse." In *The Panda's Thumb: More Reflections in Natural History*. New York: W. W. Norton and Company.

p. 42: N. N. Oosterhof and A. Todorov (2008). "The functional basis of face evaluation." *Proceedings of the National Academy of Sciences of the USA* 105, 11087–11092; A. Todorov and N. N. Oosterhof (2011). "Modeling social perception of faces." *Signal Processing Magazine, IEEE* 28, 117–122; A. Todorov, R. Dotsch, J. M. Porter, N. N. Oosterhof, and V. B. Falvello (2013). "Validation of data-driven computational models of social perception of faces." *Emotion* 13, 724–738. This work is discussed in detail in Chapter 6.

p. 42: A. Todorov, A. N. Mandisodza, A. Goren, and C. C. Hall (2005). "Inferences of competence from faces predict election outcomes." *Science* 308, 1623–1626; J. Willis and A. Todorov (2006). "First impressions: Making up your mind after 100 ms exposure to a face." *Psychological Science* 17, 592–598.

p. 43: M. Bar, M. Neta, and H. Linz (2006). "Very first impressions." *Emotion* 6, 269–278.

p. 43: For subsequent replications of impressions from brief exposure to faces, see C. C. Ballew and A. Todorov (2007). "Predicting political elections from rapid and unreflective face judgments." *Proceedings of the National Academy of Sciences of the USA* 104(46), 17948–17953; P. Borkenau, S. Brecke, C. Möttig, and P. Paelecke (2009). "Extraversion is accurately perceived after a 50-ms exposure to a face." *Journal of Research in Personality* 43, 703–706; S. Porter, L. England, M. Juodis, L. ten Brinke, and K. Wilson (2008). "Is the face the window to the soul?: Investigation of the accuracy of intuitive judgments of the trustworthiness of human faces." *Canadian Journal of Behavioural Science* 40, 171–177; N. O. Rule, N. Ambady, and R. B. Adams (2009). "Personality in perspective: Judgmental consistency across orientations of the face." *Perception* 38(11), 1688–1699; A. Todorov, V. Loehr, and N. N. Oosterhof (2010). "The obligatory nature of holistic processing of faces in social judgments." *Perception* 39, 514–532; A. Todorov, M. Pakrashi, and N. N. Oosterhof (2009). "Evaluating faces on trustworthiness after minimal time exposure." *Social Cognition* 27, 813–833.

p. 43: E. Cogsdill, A. Todorov, E. Spelke, and M. R. Banaji (2014). "Inferring character from faces: A developmental study." *Psychological Science* 25, 1132–1139.

p. 43: For judgments of trustworthiness of model-generated faces after 33 milliseconds of presentation, see Todorov, Loehr, and Oosterhof. "The obligatory nature of holistic processing of faces in social judgments."

p. 44: S. Jessen and T. Grossmann (2016). "Neural and behavioral evidence for infants' sensitivity to the trustworthiness of faces." *Journal of Cognitive Neuroscience* 28, 1728–1736.

p. 45: E. W. Cheries, A. B. Lyons, R. L. Rosen, and A. Todorov (2016). "Infants' and toddlers' social evaluations of trustworthy- and untrustworthy-looking faces." Working manuscript. University of Massachusetts Amherst.

p. 46: Infants' sensitivity to faces and facial expressions is discussed in Chapter 12.

p. 46: On the importance of faces in perception, see M. Cerf, E. P. Frady, and C. Koch (2009). "Faces and text attract gaze independent of the task: Experimental data and computer model." *Journal of Vision* 9(12), 1–15; S. M. Crouzet, H. Kirchner, and S. J. Thorpe (2010). "Fast saccades toward faces: Face detection in just 100 ms." *Journal of Vision* 10(4), 1–17.

CHAPTER 3: CONSEQUENTIAL IMPRESSIONS

p. 48: K. M. H. Blackford and A. Newcomb (1917). *The Job, The Man, The Boss.* New York: Doubleday, Page and Company.

p. 48: "Does not know what you are writing . . ." from p. 85 in Blackford and Newcomb. *The Job, The Man, The Boss.*

pp. 48–50: "Filled out in cipher so that . . ." from p. 85 in Blackford and Newcomb. *The Job, The Man, The Boss.*

p. 50: "Walking quickly through the hundred or more men . . ." from p. 74 in Blackford and Newcomb. *The Job, The Man, The Boss.*

p. 50: On character analysts working as business consultants, see chapter 1 in E. H. Brown (2008). *The Corporate Eye: Photography and the Rationalization of American Commercial Culture, 1884–1929.* Baltimore, MD: Johns Hopkins University Press.

p. 50: "Apply the principles and laws of the science . . ." from p. 353 in K. M. H. Blackford and A. Newcomb (1916). *Analyzing Character: The New Science of Judging Men; Misfits in Business, the Home, and Social Life*, third edition. New York: Review of Reviews Company.

p. 50: "That some insight may be gained . . ." from p. 429 in D. A. Laird and H. Lemmers (1924). "A study of intelligence from photographs." *Journal of Experimental Psychology* 7, 429–446.

p. 50: K. Randall (December 25, 2014). "Teams turn to a face reader, looking for that winning smile." *New York Times.*

p. 51: Things were not better for the Milwaukee Bucks in the next season: they won 33 games, lost 49 games, and did not qualify for the playoffs.

p. 51: "What begins as a failure of the imagination . . ." from p. 115 in M. Lewis (2004). *Moneyball.* New York: W. W. Norton and Company.

p. 52: A. Todorov, A. N. Mandisodza, A. Goren, and C. C. Hall (2005). "Inferences of competence from faces predict election outcomes." *Science* 308, 1623–1626.

p. 53: G. S. Lenz and C. Lawson (2011). "Looking the part: Television leads less informed citizens to vote based on candidates' appearance." *American Journal of Political Science* 55, 574–589.

p. 53: On predicting Finnish elections, see P. Poutvaara, H. Jordahl, and N. Berggren (2009).

"Faces of politicians: Babyfacedness predicts inferred competence but not electoral success." *Journal of Experimental Social Psychology* 45, 1132–1135.

p. 53: On predicting Bulgarian elections, see A. B. Sussman, K. Petkova, and A. Todorov (2013). "Competence ratings in US predict presidential election outcomes in Bulgaria." *Journal of Experimental Social Psychology* 49, 771–775.

pp. 53–54: On predicting Mexican and Brazilian elections, see C. Lawson, G. S. Lenz, A. Baker, and M. Myers (2010). "Looking like a winner: Candidate appearance and electoral success in new democracies." *World Politics* 62, 561–593.

p. 54: Lenz and Lawson. "Looking the part."

p. 54: Estimated advantage of "better"-looking candidate from Lenz and Lawson. "Looking the part."

pp. 54–55: D. J. Ahler, J. Citrin, M. C. Dougal, and G. S. Lenz (2016). "Face value? Experimental evidence that candidate appearance influences electoral choice." *Political Behavior*, doi: 10.1007/s11109-016-9348-6.

pp. 55–56: "Have come to the candid determination . . ." from p. 70 in H. Holzer, G. S. Boritt, and M. E. Neely (1984). *The Lincoln Image: Abraham Lincoln and the Popular Print*. New York: Scribner Press.

p. 56: For analyses pitting attractiveness vs. competence, see C. Y. Olivola and A. Todorov (2010). "Elected in 100 milliseconds: Appearance-based trait inferences and voting." *Journal of Nonverbal Behavior* 34(2), 83–110.

p. 56: D. S. Martin (1978). "Person perception and real-life electoral behavior." *Australian Journal of Psychology* 30, 255–262. We probably missed this study, because up to that point, the study was cited only once in a paper on German elections published in a German journal.

p. 56: S. W. Rosenberg, L. Bohan, P. McCafferty, and K. Harris (1986). "The image and the vote: The effect of candidate presentation on voter preference." *American Journal of Political Science* 30, 108–127. Quotation from p. 112.

p. 56: On the importance of characteristics for political leaders, see Todorov et al. "Inferences of competence from faces predict election outcomes"; C. C. Hall, A. Goren, S. Chaiken, and A. Todorov (2009). "Shallow cues with deep effects: Trait judgments from faces and voting decisions." In E. Borgida, J. L. Sullivan, and C. M. Federico (eds.), *The Political Psychology of Democratic Citizenship*. Oxford: Oxford University Press.

p. 57: For attribute substitution in decisions, see D. Kahneman (2003). "A perspective on judgment and choice: Mapping bounded rationality." *American Psychologist* 58, 697–720.

p. 57: D. Kahneman (2011). *Thinking, Fast and Slow*. New York: Farrar, Straus, and Giroux.

p. 57: C. C. Ballew and A. Todorov (2007). "Predicting political elections from rapid and unreflective face judgments." *Proceedings of the National Academy of Sciences of the USA* 104(46), 17948–17953.

p. 58: "So it looked to me like it would be either Romney . . ." from p. 88 in J. M. Laskas (2012). "Bob Dole: Great American." *GQ* July, 88–90.

p. 58: A. C. Little, R. P. Burriss, B. C. Jones, and S. C. Roberts (2007). "Facial appearance affects voting decisions." *Evolution and Human Behavior* 28, 18–27.

p. 60: L. Laustsen and M. B. Petersen (2016). "Winning faces vary by ideology: How nonverbal source cues influence election and communication success in politics." *Political Communication* 33, 188–211. In my lab, we have obtained similar findings for the United States: politicians with more stereotypically Republican looks gain votes among conservative voters. See C. Y. Olivola, A. B. Sussman, K. Tsetsos, O. E. Kang, and A. Todorov (2012). "Republicans prefer Republican-looking leaders: Political facial stereotypes predict candidate electoral success among right-leaning voters." *Social Psychological and Personality Science* 3, 605–613. The accuracy of visual stereotypes of politicians is discussed in Chapter 9.

p. 61: "A man I do not trust could not get money from me . . ." quoted in C. Farrell (June 7, 2002). "J. P. Morgan's character lesson." Bloomberg. Available from http://www.bloomberg .com/news/articles/2002–06–06/j-dot-p-dot-morgans-character-lesson.

pp. 62–63: C. Rezlescu, B. Duchaine, C. Y. Olivola, and N. Chater (2012). "Unfakeable facial configurations affect strategic choices in trust games with or without information about past behavior." *PLoS ONE* 7(3), e34293.

p. 63: L. Ewing, F. Caulfield, A. Read, and G. Rhodes (2014). "Perceived trustworthiness of faces drives trust behaviour in children." *Developmental Science* 18, 327–334.

p. 63: M. Bertrand, D. Karlan, S. Mullainathan, E. Shafir, and J. Zinman (2010). "What's advertising content worth? Evidence from a consumer credit marketing field experiment." *Quarterly Journal of Economics* 125, 263–305.

p. 64: J. Duarte, S. Siegel, and L. Young (2012). "Trust and credit: The role of appearance in peer-to-peer lending." *Review of Financial Studies* 25, 2455–2484.

p. 64: For studies claiming that CEO appearance predicts firms' performance, see N. O. Rule and N. Ambady (2008). "The face of success: Inferences from chief executive officers' appearance predict company profits." *Psychological Science* 19, 109–111; N. O. Rule and N. Ambady (2009). "She's got the look: Inferences from female chief executive officers' faces predict their success." *Sex Roles* 61, 644–652.

p. 64: For studies showing that CEO appearance doesn't predict firms' performance, see J. R. Graham C. R. Harvey, and M. Puri (2016). "A corporate beauty contest." *Management Science*. http://dx.doi.org/10.1287/mnsc.2016.2484; J. I. Stoker, H. Garretsen, and L. J. Spreeuwers. (2016). "The facial appearance of CEOs: Faces signal selection but not performance." *PLoS ONE* 11 (7), e0159950.

p. 64: "What you see is not necessarily what you get" from p. 13 in Graham, Harvey, and Puri. "A corporate beauty contest."

p. 65: E. A. Hooton (1939). *The American Criminal: An Anthropological Study. Volume 1: The Native White Criminal of Native Parentage.* Cambridge, MA: Harvard University Press.

p. 65: "A desperately dull statistical work . . ." from p. vii in Hooton. *The American Criminal.*

p. 65: E. A. Hooton (1939). *Crime and the Man.* Cambridge, MA: Harvard University Press.

p. 65: On the eminence of Hooton, see H. L. Shapiro (1954). "Earnest A. Hooton: 1887–1954." *Science* 119, 861–862.

pp. 65–66: "No one but an anthropological ignoramus . . ." from p. 104 in Hooton. *Crime and the Man.*

p. 66: "A skillful and experienced anthropological observer" from p. 104 in Hooton. *Crime and the Man.*

p. 66: "The degenerative trends in human evolution . . ." from p. 393 in Hooton. *Crime and the Man.*

p. 66: "Habitual criminals who are hopeless constitutional inferiors . . ." from p. 392 in Hooton. *Crime and the Man.*

p. 66: "Direct and control the progress of human evolution . . ." from pp. 396–397 in Hooton. *Crime and the Man.*

p. 67: For components of the criminal stereotype, see H. D. Flowe (2012). "Do characteristics of faces that convey trustworthiness and dominance underlie perceptions of criminality? *PLoS ONE* 7(6), e37253.

p. 67: Model of criminal appearance: see F. Funk, M. Walker, and A. Todorov (2016). "Modeling perceived criminality and remorse in faces using a data-driven computational approach." *Cognition & Emotion*, doi.org/10.1080/02699931.2016.1227305. For a different approach to visualizing criminal stereotypes, see R. Dotsch, D. H. J. Wigboldus, and A. van Knippenberg (2011). "Biased allocation of faces to social categories." *Journal of Personality and Social Psychology* 100, 999–1014. This approach is discussed in Chapter 5.

p. 67: R. H. C. Bull and J. Greene (1980). "The relationship between physical appearance and criminality." *Medicine, Science, and the Law* 20, 79–83.

pp. 67–68: D. J. Shoemaker, D. R. South, and J. Lowe (1973). "Facial stereotypes of deviants and judgments of guilt or innocence." *Social Forces* 51, 427–433.

p. 68: For replications and extensions of the "face-to-crime fit" effect, see C. N. Macrae (1989). "The good, the bad, and the ugly: Facial stereotyping and juridic judgments." *Police Journal* 62, 195–199; C. N. Macrae and J. W. Shepherd (1989). "Do criminal stereotypes mediate juridic judgements?" *British Journal of Social Psychology* 28, 189–191; R. Dumas and B. Testé (2006). "The influence of criminal facial stereotypes on juridic judgments." *Swiss Journal of Psychology* 65, 237–244.

p. 68: H. D. Flowe and J. E. Humphries (2011). "An examination of criminal face bias in a random sample of police lineups." *Applied Cognitive Psychology* 25, 265–273.

p. 68: L. A. Zebrowitz and S. M. McDonald (1991). "The impact of litigants' babyfacedness and attractiveness on adjudication in small claims courts." *Law and Human Behavior* 15, 603–623.

p. 68: J. P. Wilson and N. O. Rule (2015). "Facial trustworthiness predicts extreme criminal-sentencing outcomes." *Psychological Science* 26, 1325–1331. These findings were replicated on a smaller sample in Arkansas: see J. P. Wilson and N. O. Rule (2016). "Hypothetical sentencing decisions are associated with actual capital punishment outcomes: The role of facial trustworthiness." *Social Psychological and Personality Science* 7, 331–338.

p. 69: "In the Middle Ages there was a law . . ." from p. 87 in H. Ellis (1895). *The Criminal*. London: Walter Scott.

p. 69: On facial dominance and military rank attainment, see U. Mueller and A. Mazur (1996). "Facial dominance of West Point cadets as a predictor of later military rank." *Social Forces* 74, 823–850.

p. 69: For reviews of studies on first impressions predicting important outcomes, see C. Y. Olivola, F. Funk, and A. Todorov (2014). "Social attributions from faces bias human choices." *Trends in Cognitive Sciences* 18, 566–570; A. Todorov, C. Y. Olivola, R. Dotsch, and P. Mende-Siedlecki (2015). "Social attributions from faces: Determinants, consequences, accuracy, and functional significance." *Annual Review of Psychology* 66, 519–545.

Chapter 4: The Psychologist's Trade

p. 73: "The most entertaining surface on earth . . ." from p. 473 in G. C. Lichtenberg (1968). *Schriften und Briefe*, edited by Wolfgang Promies (Erster Band, Heft F 88). Munich: Carl Hanser Verlag; translation from p. 25 in C. Siegrist (1993). "Letters of the divine alphabet"—Lavater's concept of physiognomy. In E. Shookman (ed.), *The Faces of Physiognomy: Interdisciplinary Approaches to Johann Caspar Lavater*. Columbia, SC: Camden House.

p. 73: "The human face is a slate . . ." from p. 290 in G. C. Lichtenberg (1968). *Schriften und Briefe*, edited by Wolfgang Promies (Dritter Band). Munich: Carl Hanser Verlag; translation from p. 98 in S. Frey (1993). "Lavater, Lichtenberg, and the suggestive power of the human face. In Shookman." *The Faces of Physiognomy*.

p. 73: "On a slight investigation . . ." from footnotes on pp. 7–8 in F. Grose (1788). *Rules for Drawing Caricaturas: With an Essay on Comic Painting*. London: Printed by A. Grant.

p. 73: "A stupid stammering fellow" from p. 11 in R. Töpffer (1965), "Essay on Physiognomy." In *Enter: The Comics. Rodolphe Töpffer's Essay on Physiognomy and the True Story of Monsieur Crépin*, translated and edited by E. Wiese. Lincoln, NE: University of Nebraska Press. Originally published in 1845.

p. 73: P. F. Secord, W. F. Dukes, and W. Bevan (1954). "Personalities in faces: I. An experiment in social perceiving." *Genetic Psychology Monographs* 49, 231–279.

p. 75: "The eyebrow is the part of the face where . . ." from p. 128 in J. Montagu (1994). *The Expressions of the Passions: The Origin and Influence of Charles Le Brun's Conférence sur l'expression générale et particularé*. New Haven, CT: Yale University Press. This is the Montagu's translation of Le Brun's lecture on emotions.

p. 75: For modern research on the importance of eyebrows for expressing emotions, see P. Ekman (1979). "About brows: Emotional and conversational signals." In M. Von Cranach, K. Foppa, W. Lepenies, and D. Ploog (eds.), *Human Ethology: Claims and Limits of a New Discipline*. Cambridge: Cambridge University Press; P. Ekman and W. V. Friesen (1978). *The Facial Action Coding System: A Technique for Measurement of Facial Movement*. Palo Alto, CA: Consulting Psychologists Press; C. J. Linstrom, C. A. Silverman, and W. M. Susman (2000). "Facial-motion analysis with a video and computer system: A preliminary report." *American Journal of Otology* 21, 123–129.

p. 76: J. Sadr, I. Jarudi, and P. Sinha (2003). "The role of eyebrows in face recognition." *Perception* 32, 285–293.

p. 77: "Frequent cross-outs and blank spaces . . ." from p. 23 in M. R. Samuels (1939). "Judgments of faces." *Character & Personality* 8, 18–27.

p. 77: R. E. Nisbett and T. D. Wilson (1977). "Telling more than we can know: Verbal reports on mental processes." *Psychological Review* 84, 231–259.

p. 78: The example in the chapter is from pp. 543–544 in M. S. Gazzaniga, R. B. Ivry, and G. R. Mangun (1998). *Cognitive Neuroscience: The Biology of the Mind*. New York: W. W. Norton and Company. See also M. S. Gazzaniga (1975). "Review of the split brain." *Journal of Neurology* 209, 75–79; K. Baynes and M. S. Gazzaniga (2000). "Consciousness, introspection, and the split brain: The two minds/one body problem." In M. S. Gazzaniga (ed.), *The New Cognitive Neurosciences*, second edition. Cambridge, MA: MIT Press.

p. 78: P. Johansson, L. Hall, S. Sikström, and A. Olsson (2005). "Failure to detect mismatches between intention and outcome in a simple decision task." *Science* 310, 116–119.

pp. 80–81: For research on schematic faces, see S. J. McKelvie (1973). "The meaningfulness and meaning of schematic faces." *Perception & Psychophysics* 14, 343–348; D. Lundqvist, F. Esteves, A. Öhman (1999). "The face of wrath: Critical features for conveying facial threat." *Cognition & Emotion* 13, 691–711; D. Lundqvist, F. Esteves, and A. Öhman (2004). "The face of wrath: The role of features and configurations in conveying social threat." *Cognition & Emotion* 18, 161–182.

p. 81: For the "scheming" label, see McKelvie. "The meaningfulness and meaning of schematic faces."

p. 82: Figure 4.7 (the smiling eyes illusion) is from M. C. Mangini and I. Biederman (2004). "Making the ineffable explicit: Estimating the information employed for face classification." *Cognitive Science* 28, 209–226. This illusion was first reported by O. Schwartz, H. Bayer, and D. Pelli (1998). "Features, frequencies, and facial expressions" [Abstract]. *Investigative Ophthalmology and Visual Science* 39, 173.

p. 83: For research on the composite face illusion, see B. Rossion (2013). "The composite face illusion: A whole window into our understanding of holistic face perception." *Visual Cognition* 21, 139–253.

p. 84: The composite face effect is particularly powerful when we align parts from different faces horizontally, most likely because identity information is coded in horizontal stripes of face information rather than in vertical stripes. See S. C. Dakin and R. J. Watt (2009). "Biological 'bar codes' in human faces." *Journal of Vision* 9(4), 1–10.

p. 85: For the discovery of the composite face illusion, see A. W. Young, D. Hellawell, and D. C. Hay (1987). "Configurational information in face perception." *Perception* 16, 747–759.

p. 85: "Permanent signs are changeable . . ." from p. 17 in Töpffer, *Essay on Physiognomy*.

pp. 85–86: A. Todorov, V. Loehr, and N. N. Oosterhof (2010). "The obligatory nature of holistic processing of faces in social judgments." *Perception* 39, 514–532.

p. 87: For the gender illusion, see R. Russell (2009). "A sex difference in facial contrast and its exaggeration by cosmetics." *Perception* 38, 1211–1219.

p. 88: For Nancy Burson's work, see N. Burson (2002). *Seeing and Believing: The Art of Nancy Burson*. Santa Fe, NM: Twin Palms Publishers.

pp. 88–89: For the hair/race effect, see O. H. MacLin and R. S. Malpass (2003). "The ambiguous-race face illusion." *Perception* 32, 249–252.

p. 91: "Many thousands of different combinations . . ." from p. 5 in A. Cozens (1778). *Principles of Beauty, Relative to the Human Head*. London: Printed by James Dixwell.

p. 91: For the proliferation of combinations of features in testing hypotheses about face perception, see A. Todorov, R. Dotsch, D. Wigboldus, and C. P. Said (2011). "Data-driven methods for modeling social perception." *Social and Personality Psychology Compass* 5, 775–791.

p. 91: "The empirical approach requires . . ." from p. 319 in A. Altman (1973). *Moses Mendelssohn: A Biographical Study*. Tuscaloosa: University of Alabama Press. See pp. 317–322 for the relationships among Mendelssohn, Lavater, Zimmermann, and Lichtenberg.

pp. 91–92: "These results suggest that the conventional . . ." from p. 273 in Secord, Dukes, and Bevan. "Personalities in faces: I. An experiment in social perceiving."

CHAPTER 5: MAKING THE INVISIBLE VISIBLE

p. 93: T. Nagel (1974). "What is it like to be a bat?" *Philosophical Review* 83, 435–450.

p. 93: D. Y. Teller, R. Morse, R. Borton, and D. Regal (1974). "Visual acuity for vertical and diagonal gratings in human infants." *Vision Research* 14, 1433–1439. For a review of the procedure, see also D. Y. Teller (1979). "The forced-choice preferential looking procedure: A psychophysical technique for use with human infants." *Infant Behavior and Development* 2, 135–153.

p. 95: For spatial frequency illusions, see P. G. Schyns and A. Oliva (1999). "Dr. Angry and Mr. Smile: When categorization flexibly modifies the perception of faces in rapid visual presentations." *Cognition* 69, 243–265; A. Oliva (2013). "The art of hybrid images: Two for the view of one." *Art & Perception* 1, 65–74.

p. 97: N. D. Haig (1985). "How faces differ—a new comparative technique." *Perception* 14, 601–615.

p. 98: For one example of blending of faces and visual noise, see J. Sadr and P. Sinha (2004). "Object recognition and random image structure evolution." *Cognitive Science* 28, 259–287.

p. 99: F. Gosselin and P. G. Schyns (2001). "Bubbles: A technique to reveal the use of information in recognition tasks." *Vision Research* 41, 2261–2271.

p. 100: M. L. Smith, G. W. Cottrell, F. Gosselin, and P. G. Schyns (2005). "Transmitting and decoding facial expressions." *Psychological Science* 16, 184–189.

p. 101: For Leonardo's technique of painting *Mona Lisa*, see pp. 301–303 in E. H. Gombrich (2012). *The Story of Art*, sixteenth edition. London: Phaidon.

p. 101: L. L. Kontsevich and C. W. Tyler (2004). "What makes Mona Lisa smile?" *Vision Research* 44(13), 1493–1498.

p. 102: M. S. Livingstone (2001). "Is it warm? Is it real? Or just low spatial frequency?" *Science* 290, 1299.

p. 103: For the experimental demonstration of Livingstone's hypothesis, see I. Bohrn, C.-C. Carbon, and F. Hutzler (2010). "Mona Lisa's smile—perception or deception?" *Psychological Science* 21, 378–380.

p. 104: M. C. Mangini and I. Biederman (2004). "Making the ineffable explicit: Estimating the information employed for face classification." *Cognitive Science* 28, 209–226. Mangini and Biederman showed similar effects for identity. Participants were presented with a morph of Tom Cruise and John Travolta and asked to decide whose face they were seeing. Just as in the gender decisions, described in the main text, the underlying image was the same face—a morph of Cruise and Travolta—and the only difference was the noise masks superimposed on the morph. Yet participants constructed the images of Tom Cruise and John Travolta from this visual noise. Unfortunately, I was not able to obtain high-resolution images to show this part of the experiment.

p. 104: I was not able to obtain a high-resolution image from the study of Mangini and Biederman. The images in Figure 5.13 are from a similar study conducted by Loek Brinkman and Ron Dotsch from the University of Utrecht, the Netherlands.

p. 105: F. Gosselin and P. G. Schyns (2003). "Superstitious perceptions reveal properties of internal representations." *Psychological Science* 15, 505–509.

p. 106: R. Dotsch, D. H. Wigboldus, O. Langner, and A. van Knippenberg (2008). "Ethnic outgroup faces are biased in the prejudiced mind." *Psychological Science* 19, 978–980.

p. 107: R. Imhoff, R. Dotsch, M. Bianchi, R. Banse, and D. H. Wigboldus (2011). "Facing Europe: Visualizing spontaneous in-group projection." *Psychological Science* 22, 1583–1590; A. I. Young, K. G. Ratner, and R. H. Fazio (2014). "Political attitudes bias the mental representation of a presidential candidate's face." *Psychological Science* 25, 503–510.

p. 108: R. Dotsch and A. Todorov (2012). "Reverse correlating social face perception." *Social Psychological and Personality Science* 3, 562–571.

CHAPTER 6: THE FUNCTIONS OF IMPRESSIONS

pp. 112–113: The two faces in Figures 6.1 and 6.2 were rated by experimental participants in studies conducted by Oosterhof and Todorov; the data in the text are based on these empirical ratings; see N. N. Oosterhof and A. Todorov (2008). "The functional basis of face evaluation." *Proceedings of the National Academy of Sciences of the USA* 105, 11087–11092. Note though that the specific ratings would depend on the individual rater and the set of faces in which the rated faces are embedded.

pp. 114–115: For the structure of impressions from faces, see Oosterhof and Todorov. "The functional basis of face evaluation"; A. Todorov, C. P. Said, A. D. Engell, N. N. Oosterhof

(2008). "Understanding evaluation of faces on social dimensions." *Trends in Cognitive Sciences* 12, 455–460.

pp. 116–122: The models of impressions are based on the following research: Oosterhof and Todorov." The functional basis of face evaluation"; A. Todorov and N. N. Oosterhof (2011). "Modeling social perception of faces." *Signal Processing Magazine, IEEE* 28, 117–122; A. Todorov, R. Dotsch, J. M. Porter, N. N. Oosterhof, and V. B. Falvello (2013). "Validation of data-driven computational models of social perception of faces." *Emotion* 13, 724–738.

p. 122: For impressions of dominance and physical strength, see H. Toscano, T. W. Schubert, R. Dotsch, V. Falvello, and A. Todorov (2016). "Physical strength as a cue to dominance: A data-driven approach." *Personality and Social Psychology Bulletin*, doi:10.1177 /0146167216666266.

p. 123: For studies on ratings of untrustworthiness, dominance, threat, and criminal appearance, see H. D. Flowe (2012). "Do characteristics of faces that convey trustworthiness and dominance underlie perceptions of criminality?" *PLoS ONE* 7(6), e37253.

p. 124: For the dependence of impressions of trustworthiness on emotion cues, and the dependence of impressions of dominance on masculinity and facial maturity cues, see Oosterhof and Todorov. "The functional basis of face evaluation"; A. Todorov (2011). "Evaluating faces on social dimensions." In A. Todorov, S. T. Fiske, and D. Prentice (eds.), *Social Neuroscience: Toward Understanding the Underpinnings of the Social Mind*. Oxford: Oxford University Press.

p. 126: For removing (subtracting) one model of impressions from another, see Todorov et al. "Validation of data-driven computational models of social perception of faces."

pp. 127–130: C. A. M. Sutherland, J. A. Oldmeadow, I. M. Santos, J. Towler, D. M. Burt, and A. W. Young (2013). "Social inferences from faces: Ambient images generate a three-dimensional model." *Cognition* 127, 105–118.

CHAPTER 7: THE EYE OF THE BEHOLDER

p. 132: For adaptation experiments, see G. Rhodes, L. Jeffery, T. L. Watson, C. W. G. Clifford, and K. Nakayama (2003). "Fitting the mind to the world: Face adaptation and attractiveness aftereffects." *Psychological Science* 14, 558–566; M. A. Webster, D. Kaping, Y. Mizokami, and P. Duhamel (2004). "Adaptation to natural facial categories." *Nature* 428, 557–561; M. A. Webster and O. H. MacLin (1999). "Figural aftereffects in the perception of faces." *Psychonomic Bulletin & Review* 6, 647–653. For a general review, see G. Rhodes and D. A. Leopold (2011). "Adaptive norm-based coding of face identity." In A. Calder, J. V. Haxby, M. Johnson, and G. Rhodes (eds.), *Handbook of Face Perception*. Oxford: Oxford University Press.

p. 133: "The law of our thinking . . ." from p. 18 in G. C. Lichtenberg, *On Physiognomy, against the Physiognomists, for the Promotion of the Love and Knowledge of Man*, translated by Steven Tester for Princeton University Press. Translation courtesy of Steven Tester, University of Göttingen.

p. 134: "some ideal typical form" from p. 10 in F. Galton (1892). *Inquiries into Human Faculty and Its Development*. London: Macmillan. First electronic edition, 2001.

p. 135: "People had to learn, . . ." from p. 273 in J. Diamond (1999). *Guns, Germs, and Steel: The Fates of Human Societies*. New York: W. W. Norton and Company.

p. 135: C. Sofer, R. Dotsch, M. Oikawa, H. Oikawa, D. H. J. Wigboldus, and A. Todorov (in press).

"For your local eyes only: Culture-specific face typicality influences perceptions of trust-worthiness." *Perception.*

p. 136: For studies on prototype extraction, see R. L. Solso and J. E. McCarthy (1981). "Prototype formation: Central tendency model vs. attribute-frequency model." *Bulletin of the Psychonomic Society* 17, 10–11; D. Inn, K. J. Walden, and R. Solso (1993). "Facial prototype formation in children." *Bulletin of the Psychonomic Society* 31, 197–200; R. Cabeza, V. Bruce, T. Kato, and M. Oda (1999). "The prototype effect in face recognition: Extension and limits." *Memory & Cognition* 27, 139–151. Many of these studies are reviewed in Rhodes and Leopold. "Adaptive norm-based coding of face identity."

p. 136: M. de Haan, M. H. Johnson, D. Maurer, and D. I. Perrett (2001). "Recognition of individual faces and average face prototypes by 1- and 3-month-old infants." *Cognitive Development* 16, 659–678.

pp. 136–139: R. Dotsch, R. Hassin, and A. Todorov (2016). Statistical learning shapes face evaluation. *Nature Human Behavior*, doi:10.1038/s41562-016-0001.

p. 139: "There is no physiognomy for one people to another . . ." from p. 16 in Lichtenberg, *On Physiognomy, against the Physiognomists, for the Promotion of the Love and Knowledge of Man*. Translation courtesy of Steven Tester, University of Göttingen.

p. 139: "The face of an enemy . . ." from p. 11 in Lichtenberg, *On Physiognomy, against the Physiognomists, for the Promotion of the Love and Knowledge of Man*. Translation courtesy of Steven Tester, University of Göttingen.

p. 139: S. M. Andersen and A. Baum (1994). "Transference in interpersonal relations: Inferences and affect based on significant-other representations." *Journal of Personality* 62, 459–497; S. M. Andersen and S. W. Cole (1990). "Do I know you?: The role of significant others in general social perception." *Journal of Personality and Social Psychology* 59, 384–399.

p. 139: For resemblance to significant others as a trigger of impressions, see M. W. Kraus and S. Chen (2010). "Facial-feature resemblance elicits the transference effect." *Psychological Science* 21, 518–522; G. Günaydin, V. Zayas, E. Selcuk, and C. Hazan (2012). "I like you but I don't know why: Objective facial resemblance to significant others influences snap judgments." *Journal of Experimental Social Psychology* 48, 350–353.

pp. 139–140: S. C. Verosky and A. Todorov (2010). "Generalization of affective learning about faces to perceptually similar faces." *Psychological Science* 21, 779–785.

p. 140: For the ability to learn evaluatively charged facts about people, see V. B. Falvello, M. Vinson, C. Ferrari, and A. Todorov (2015). "The robustness of learning about the trustworthiness of other people." *Social Cognition* 33, 368–386.

p. 140: For the automaticity of the influence of face similarity, see S. C. Verosky and A. Todorov (2013). "When physical similarity matters: Mechanisms underlying affective learning generalization to the evaluation of novel faces." *Journal of Experimental Social Psychology* 49, 661–669.

p. 141: For the effect of face similarity on hiring decisions, see B. von Helversen, S. M. Herzog, and J. Rieskamp (2013). "Haunted by a doppelgänger: Irrelevant facial similarity affects rule-based judgments." *Experimental Psychology* 61, 12–22.

p. 141: For the effect of face similarity on consumer choices, see R. J. Tanner and A. Maeng (2012). "A tiger and a president: Imperceptible celebrity facial cues influence trust and preference." *Journal of Consumer Research* 39, 769–783.

pp. 141–142: "The very soul which rules . . ." from p. 204 in Martin Kemp (ed.) (1989). *Leonardo on Painting*. New Haven, CT: Yale University Press.

p. 142: For effects of self-similarity, see J. N. Bailenson, P. Garland, S. Iyengar, and N. Yee (2006). "Transformed facial similarity as a political cue: A preliminary investigation." *Political Psychology* 27, 373–385; J. N. Bailenson, S. Iyengar, N. Yee, and N. A. Collins (2008). "Facial similarity between voters and candidates causes influence." *Public Opinion Quarterly* 72, 935–961; L. M. DeBruine (2002). "Facial resemblance enhances trust." *Proceedings of the Royal Society B: Biological Sciences* 269, 1307–1312; L. M. DeBruine (2005). "Trustworthy but not lust-worthy: Context-specific effects of facial resemblance." *Proceedings of the Royal Society B: Biological Sciences* 272, 919–922; D. B. Krupp, L. M. Debruine, and P. Barclay (2008). "A cue of kinship promotes cooperation for the public good." *Evolution & Human Behavior* 29, 49–55.

p. 142: For findings of face resemblance of partners, see L. Alvarez and K. Jaffe (2004). "Narcissism guides mate selection: Humans mate assortatively, as revealed by facial resemblance, following an algorithm of 'self seeking like.'" *Evolutionary Psychology* 2, 177–194; R. W. Griffiths and P. R. Kunz (1973). "Assortative mating: A study of physiognomic homogamy." *Biodemography and Social Biology* 20, 448–453; V. B. Hinsz (1989). "Facial resemblance in engaged and married couples." *Journal of Social and Personal Relationships* 6, 223–229. R. Zajonc, P. Adelmann, S. Murphy, and P. Niendenthal (1987). "Convergence in the physical appearance of spouses." *Motivation and Emotion* 11, 335–346.

p. 142: For effects of self-similarity on choices of purebred dogs, see C. Payne and K. Jaffe (2005). "Self seeks like: Many humans choose their dog pets following rules used for assortative mating." *Journal of Ethology* 23, 15–18; M. M. Roy and N. J. S. Christenfeld (2004). "Do dogs resemble their owners?" *Psychological Science* 15, 361–363; M. M. Roy and N. J. S. Christenfeld (2005). "Dogs still do resemble their owners." *Psychological Science* 16, 743–744.

p. 142: For the tendency of people to recognize themselves in trustworthy morphs, see S. C. Verosky and A. Todorov (2010). "Differential neural responses to faces physically similar to the self as a function of their valence." *NeuroImage* 49, 1690–1698.

p. 142: For effects of positive interactions on assessment of self-similarity, see H. Farmer, R. McKay, and M. Tsakiris (2014). "Trust in me: Trustworthy others are seen as more physically similar to the self." *Psychological Science* 25, 290–292.

p. 143: For the cultural variation of the meaning of smiling, see M. Rychlowska, Y. Miyamoto, D. Matsumoto, U. Hess, E. Gilboa-Schechtman et al. (2015). "Heterogeneity of long-history migration explains cultural differences in reports of emotional expressivity and the functions of smiles." *Proceedings of the National Academy of Sciences of the USA* 112, E2429–E2436.

p. 143: For the cultural variation in the association between masculinity in faces and perceptions of aggressiveness, see I. M. L. Scott, A. P. Clark, S. C. Josephson, A. H. Boyette, I. C. Cuthill et al. (2014). "Human preferences for sexually dimorphic faces may be evolutionarily novel." *Proceedings of the National Academy of Sciences of the USA* 111, 14388–14393.

p. 143: For higher agreement among people from the same race, see J. Hönekopp (2006). "Once more: Is beauty in the eye of the beholder? Relative contributions of private and shared taste to judgments of facial attractiveness." *Journal of Experimental Psychology: Human Perception and Performance* 32, 199–209.

p. 143: For higher agreement among close others, see P. M. Bronstad and R. Russell (2007). "Beauty is in the 'we' of the beholder: Greater agreement on facial attractiveness among close relations." *Perception* 36, 1674–1681.

pp. 143–144: For the study of twins, see L. Germine, R. Russell, P. M. Bronstad, G. A. M. Blokland, J. W. Smoller et al. (2015). "Individual aesthetic preferences for faces are shaped mostly by environments, not genes." *Current Biology* 25, 2684–2689.

p. 144: "Individual life history and experience . . ." from p. 2687 in L. Germine et al. "Individual aesthetic preferences for faces." But note that these findings do not rule out genetic contributions to face preferences. For such contributions to women's preferences for masculine men's faces, see B. P. Zietsch, A. J. Lee, J. M. Sherlock, and P. Jern (2015). "Variation in women's preferences regarding male facial masculinity is better explained by genetic differences than by previously identified context-dependent effects." *Psychological Science* 26, 1440–1448.

CHAPTER 8: MISLEADING IMAGES

p. 147: C. Lombroso (2006). *Criminal Man*. Durham, NC, and London: Duke University Press. Quotations from pp. 51–53.

p. 147: For similarities between the description of Count Dracula and Lombroso's description of the born criminal, see p. 300 in L. Wolf (1975). *Annotated Dracula*. London: New English Library. Here is the first description of Dracula in the novel: "His face was a strong—a very strong—aquiline, with high bridge of the thin nose and peculiarly arched nostrils; with lofty domed forehead, and hair growing scantily round the temples, but profusely elsewhere. His eyebrows were very massive, almost meeting over the nose, and with bushy hair that seemed to curl in its own profusion. The mouth, so far as I could see it under the heavy mustache, was fixed and rather cruel-looking, with peculiarly sharp white teeth; these protruded over the lips, whose remarkable ruddiness showed astonishing vitality in a man of his years. For the rest, his ears were pale and at the tops extremely pointed; the chin was broad and strong, and the cheeks firm though thin. The general effect was one of extraordinary pallor," from pp. 21–22 in Wolf. *Annotated Dracula*.

pp. 147–148: On the transformation of the images depicted in Figure 8.1, see p. 23 in the editors' introduction by M. Gibson and N. H. Rafter (p. 23) in Lombroso. *Criminal Man*.

p. 148: For the relation between perceptions of criminality and face distinctiveness, see H. D. Flowe and J. E. Humphries (2011). "An examination of criminal face bias in a random sample of police lineups." *Applied Cognitive Psychology* 25, 265–273.

p. 148: "The influence of *L'Uomo Delinquente* . . ." from pp. 38–39 in H. Ellis (1895). *The Criminal*. London: Walter Scott.

p. 148: "Illustrating in a very remarkable manner . . ." from p. 53 in Ellis. *The Criminal*.

p. 149: C. Goring (1972). *The English Convict: A Statistical Study*. Montclair, NJ: Patterson Smith. The work was first published in 1913.

p. 149: For Lombroso's challenge at the Congress of Criminal Anthropology, see E. D. Driver (1972). Introductory Essay. In Goring. *The English Convict*.

p. 149: "No evidence has emerged confirming . . ." from p. 173 in Goring. *The English Convict*. Needless to say, Lombroso's disciples questioned these conclusions, and years later Hooton would openly disparage Goring's work.

pp. 149–150: "An examination of these contrasted outlines . . ." from p. 1 in Goring. *The English Convict*.

p.150: "Swayed by exceptional and grotesque features . . ." from p. 4 in F. Galton (1892). *Inquiries into Human Faculty and Its Development*. London: Macmillan.

p. 151: For studies on guesses of sexual, political, religious orientations, mental health problems, and criminal inclinations, see S. Kleiman and N. O. Rule (2012). "Detecting suicidality from facial appearance." *Social Psychological and Personality Science* 4, 453–460; S. Porter, L. England, M. Juodis, L. ten Brinke, and K. Wilson (2008). "Is the face the window to the soul?: Investigation of the accuracy of intuitive judgments of the trustworthiness of human faces." *Canadian Journal of Behavioural Science* 40, 171–177; N. O. Rule and N. Ambady (2008). "Brief exposures: Male sexual orientation is accurately perceived at 50 ms." *Journal of Experimental Social Psychology* 44, 1100–1105; N. O. Rule and N. Ambady (2010). "Democrats and Republicans can be differentiated from their faces." *PLoS ONE* 5, e8733; N. O. Rule, N. Ambady, and K. C. Hallett (2009). "Female sexual orientation is perceived accurately, rapidly, and automatically from the face and its features." *Journal of Experimental Social Psychology* 45, 1245–1251; N. O. Rule, J. V. Garrett, and N. Ambady (2010). "On the perception of religious group membership from faces." *PLoS ONE* 5(12), e14241; J. Samochowiec, M. Wänke, and K. Fiedler (2010). "Political ideology at face value." *Social Psychology and Personality Science* 1, 206–213; N. J. Scott, A. L. Jones, R. S. S. Kramer, and R. Ward (2015). "Facial dimorphism in autistic quotient scores." *Clinical Psychological Science* 3, 230–241; J. M. Valla, S. J. Ceci, and W. M. Williams (2011). "The accuracy of inferences about criminality based on facial appearance." *Journal of Social, Evolutionary, and Cultural Psychology* 5, 66–91.

p. 151: R. Highfield, R. Wiseman, and R. Jenkins (February 11, 2009). "How your looks betray your personality." *New Scientist* (February 11), https://www.newscientist.com/article/mg20126957-300-how-your-looks-betray-your-personality/.

p. 151: D. M. Johns (2009). "Facial profiling: Can you tell if a man is dangerous by the shape of his mug?" *Slate* (October 14), http://www.slate.com/articles/health_and_science/science/2009/10/facial_profiling.html.

p. 151: "We imagine that photographs . . ." from p. 92 in E. Morris (2011). *Believing Is Seeing (Observations on the Mysteries of Photography)*. New York: Penguin Press.

pp. 151–153: For Cindy Sherman's work, see E. Respini (ed.) (2012). *Cindy Sherman*. New York: Museum of Modern Art.

p. 153: On Pascal Dangin, see L. Collins (2008). "Pixel perfect: Pascal Dangin's virtual reality." *New Yorker* (May 12), http://www.newyorker.com/magazine/2008/05/12/pixel-perfect.

p. 153: "Just by the fact that he works . . ." from p. 3 in Collins, "Pixel perfect: Pascal Dangin's virtual reality."

p. 154: Applying mathematical models of first impressions to images of real faces: see M. Walker and T. Vetter (2009). "Portraits made to measure: Manipulating social judgments about individuals with a statistical face model." *Journal of Vision* 9(11), 1–13; M. Walker and T. Vetter (2016). "Changing the personality of a face: Perceived big two and big five personality factors modeled in real photographs." *Journal of Personality and Social Psychology* 110, 609–624.

p. 155: K. Robinson, C. Blais, J. Duncan, H. Forget, and D. Fiset (2014). "The dual nature of the human face: There is a little Jekyll and a little Hyde in all of us." *Frontiers in Psychology* 5, 139, doi: 10.3389/fpsyg.2014.00139.

p. 157: R. Jenkins, D. White, X. Van Montfort, and A. M. Burton (2011). "Variability in photos of the same face." *Cognition* 121, 313–323.

p. 157: "No face casts the same image twice" from p. 314 in Jenkins, White, Van Montfort, and Burton. "Variability in photos of the same face."

p. 158: A. Todorov and J. Porter (2014). "Misleading first impressions: Different for different images of the same person." *Psychological Science* 25, 1404–1417.

p. 159: For studies that purport to show accurate inferences of sexual orientation, see Rule and Ambady. "Brief exposures"; Rule, Ambady, and Hallett. "Female sexual orientation."

p. 159: For photograph quality confounds in studies on guesses of sexual orientation, see W. T. L. Cox, P. G. Devine, A. A. Bischmann, and J. S. Hyde (2016). "Inferences about sexual orientation: The roles of stereotypes, faces, and the gaydar myth." *Journal of Sex Research* 53, 157–171. The authors suggest a plausible explanation of this confound: because the pool of potential partners is much smaller for gay men and lesbian women, they need to be more competitive than straight men and women. One consequence is that they may be more selective when it comes to their dating online profiles.

p. 159: For studies on the accuracy of impressions of criminal inclinations, see Porter et al. "Is the face the window to the soul?" Valla, Ceci, and Williams. "The accuracy of inferences about criminality based on facial appearance."

p. 159: "You will not find any comments . . ." from p. 11 in R. Pellicer (2010). *Mug Shots*. New York: Abrams.

p. 160: C. Landis and L. W. Phelps (1928). "The prediction from photographs of success and of vocational aptitude." *Journal of Experimental Psychology* 11, 313–324.

p. 160: "Any study conducted along . . ." from p. 321 in Landis and Phelps, "The prediction from photographs."

p. 161: "It was intense and arresting . . ." from P. Farhi (2011). "Publications grapple with Jared Loughner mug shot." *Washington Post* (January 11), http://www.washingtonpost.com /wp-dyn/content/article/2011/01/11/AR2011011106921.html.

p. 163: "The consumptive patients consisted of . . ." from pp. 12–13 in F. Galton (1892). *Inquiries into Human Faculty and Its Development*. London: Macmillan. First electronic edition 2001.

p. 163: S. C. Verosky and A. Todorov (2010). "Generalization of affective learning about faces to perceptually similar faces." *Psychological Science* 21, 779–785; S. C. Verosky and A. Todorov (2013). "When physical similarity matters: Mechanisms underlying affective learning generalization to the evaluation of novel faces." *Journal of Experimental Social Psychology* 49, 661–669.

p. 164: A. Kayser (1985). *Heads*. New York: Abbeville Press.

p. 164: You can see the video of the experiment of The Lab group of Canon Australia at: https://www.youtube.com/watch?v=F-TyPfYMDK8. You can see the resulting images at: http://www.diyphotography.net/6-portrait-photographers-demonstrate-the-power-of-our -own-perspective/.

p. 164: "Every movement of the soul corresponds . . ." from p. 23 in G. C. Lichtenberg, *On Physiognomy, against the Physiognomists, for the Promotion of the Love and Knowledge of Man*, translated by Steven Tester for Princeton University Press. Translation courtesy of Steven Tester, University of Göttingen.

pp. 164–165: P. F. Secord (1958). "Facial features and inference processes in interpersonal perception." In R. Tagiuri and L. Petrullo (eds.), *Person Perception and Interpersonal Behavior*. Stanford, CA: Stanford University Press.

p. 165: For studies showing that we perceive smiling people as more trustworthy and angry people as less trustworthy, see B. Knutson (1996). "Facial expressions of emotion influence interpersonal trait inferences." *Journal of Nonverbal Behavior* 20, 165–181; J. M. Montepare and H. Dobish (2003). "The contribution of emotion perceptions and their overgeneralizations to trait impressions." *Journal of Nonverbal Behavior* 27, 237–254; N. N. Oosterhof and A. Todorov (2009). "Shared perceptual basis of emotional expressions and trustworthiness impressions from faces." *Emotion* 9, 128–133.

pp. 165–166: C. Said, N. Sebe, and A. Todorov (2009). "Structural resemblance to emotional expressions predicts evaluation of emotionally neutral faces." *Emotion* 9, 260–264.

p. 166: For effects of sleep on appearance, see J. Axelsson, T. Sundelin, M. Ingre, E. J. W. Van Someren, A. Olsson, and M. Lekander. (2010). "Beauty sleep: Experimental study on the perceived health and attractiveness of sleep deprived people." *BMJ* 341: c6614; T. Sundelin, M. Lekander, G. Kecklund, E. J. W. Van Someren, A. Olsson, and J. Axelsson (2013). "Cues of fatigue: Effects of sleep deprivation on facial appearance." *Sleep* 36, 1355–1360.

p. 166: For effects of clothing on appearance, see M. Lõhmus, L. F. Sundström, and M. Björklund (2009). "Dress for success: Human facial expressions are important signals of emotions." *Annales Zoologici Fennici* 46, 75–80.

p. 166: For effects of head tilt and visual angle, see A. Mignault and A. Chaudhuri (2003). "The many faces of a neutral face: Head tilt and perception of dominance and emotion." *Journal of Nonverbal Behavior* 27, 111–132; C. A. M. Sutherland, A. W. Young, and G. Rhodes (2016). "Facial first impressions from another angle: How social judgements are influenced by changeable and invariant facial properties." *British Journal of Psychology*, doi: 10.1111/bjop.12206; R. J. W. Vernon, C. A. M. Sutherland, A. W. Young, and T. Hartley (2014). "Modeling first impressions from highly variable face images." *Proceedings of the National Academy of Sciences* 111, E3353–E3361.

CHAPTER 9: SUBOPTIMAL DECISIONS

p. 168: You can watch Colbert's interview of David Brooks at: http://tlab.princeton.edu /about/mediacoverage/.

pp. 168–169: "Are so horrendously mistaken . . ." from p. 22 in G. C. Lichtenberg, *On Physiognomy, against the Physiognomists, for the Promotion of the Love and Knowledge of Man*, translated by Steven Tester for Princeton University Press. Translation courtesy of Steven Tester, University of Göttingen.

p. 169: The discussed study is study 2 in N. O. Rule and N. Ambady (2008). "Brief exposures: Male sexual orientation is accurately perceived at 50 ms." *Journal of Experimental Social Psychology* 44, 1100–1105.

p. 169: For Gallup surveys, see F. Newport (May 21, 2015). "Americans greatly overestimate percent gay, lesbian in U.S. Gallup." Available from http://www.gallup.com/poll/183383 /americans-greatly-overestimate-percent-gay-lesbian.aspx.

pp. 171–172: C. Y. Olivola and A. Todorov (2010). "Fooled by first impressions? Re-examining the diagnostic value of appearance-based inferences." *Journal of Experimental Social Psychology* 46, 315–324.

p. 171: The website "What's my image?" is no longer functional.

p. 173: C. Y. Olivola, A. B. Sussman, K. Tsetsos, O. E. Kang, and A. Todorov (2012). "Republicans prefer Republican-looking leaders: Political facial stereotypes predict candidate electoral success among right-leaning voters." *Social Psychological and Personality Science* 3, 605–613.

p. 173: For comparing dumb algorithms with human judges, see C. Y. Olivola, D. Tingley, A. Bonica, and A. Todorov (2016). "The donkey in elephant's clothing: The prevalence, impact, and (in)validity of political facial stereotypes." Working manuscript. Carnegie Mellon University.

pp. 174–175: J. F. Bonnefon, A. Hopfensitz, and W. De Neys (2013). "The modular nature of trustworthiness detection." *Journal of Experimental Psychology: General* 142, 143–150.

p. 176: Recent research by economists suggests that behavior in experimental games is practically unrelated to actual behavior outside the lab. See M. M. Galizzi and D. Navarro-Martinez (2016). "On the external validity of social-preference games: A systematic lab-field study." Working manuscript. London School of Economics and Political Science.

p. 176: R. T. LaPiere (1934). "Attitudes vs. actions." *Social Forces* 13, 230–237.

p. 177: C. Efferson and S. Vogt (2013). "Viewing men's faces does not lead to accurate predictions of trustworthiness." *Scientific Reports* 3, 1047, doi: 10.1038/srep01047.

p. 177: H. Hartshorne and M. A. May (1928). *Studies in the Nature of Character, I: Studies in Deceit.* New York: Macmillan.

p. 178: For the low generalizability from one situation to another, see W. Mischel (1968). *Personality and Assessment.* New York: Wiley; chapter 4 in L. Ross and R. E. Nisbett (1991). *The Person and the Situation: Perspectives on Social Psychology.* New York: McGraw-Hill; Y. Shoda, W. Mischel, and J. C. Wright (1994). "Intraindividual stability in the organization and patterning of behavior: Incorporating psychological situations into the idiographic analysis of personality." *Journal of Personality and Social Psychology* 67, 674–687.

p. 178: "Very difficult, and perhaps impossible . . ." from p. 9 in Lichtenberg, *On Physiognomy, against the Physiognomists, for the Promotion of the Love and Knowledge of Man.* Translation courtesy of Steven Tester, University of Göttingen.

p. 179: M. P. Haselhuhn and E. M. Wong (2012). "Bad to the bone: Facial structure predicts unethical behavior." *Proceedings of the Royal Society of London B* 279, 571–576.

p. 179: J. M. Carré and C. M. McCormick (2008). "In your face: Facial metrics predict aggressive behaviour in the laboratory and in varsity and professional hockey players." *Proceedings of the Royal Society of London: Biological Sciences* 275, 2651–2656.

p. 179: R. O. Deaner, S. M. Goetz, K. Shattuck, and T. Schnotala (2012). "Body weight, not facial width-to-height ratio, predicts aggression in pro hockey players." *Journal of Research in Personality* 46, 235–238.

p. 180: "It was like running into Nosferatu . . ." from B. McCall (2015). "When you meet the star you hate." *New Yorker* (April 19). Bruce McCall/The New Yorker, © Conde Nast. Reprinted by permission.

p. 181: On the fundamental attribution error, see L. Ross (1977). "The intuitive psychologist and his shortcomings." In L. Berkowitz (ed.), *Advances in Experimental Social Psychology,* Volume 10. New York: Academic Press; R. E. Nisbett and L. Ross (1980). *Human Inference: Strategies and Shortcomings of Social Judgment.* Englewood Cliffs, NJ: Prentice-Hall.

p. 181: L. A. Zebrowitz, C. Andreoletti, M. A. Collins, S. Y. Lee, and J. Blumenthal (1998). "Bright, bad, babyfaced boys: Appearance stereotypes do not always yield self-fulfilling prophecies." *Journal of Personality and Social Psychology* 75, 1300–1320.

p. 182: "He [the job interviewer] is not interested in . . ." from p. 89 in K. M. H. Blackford and A. Newcomb (1917). *The Job, The Man, The Boss.* New York: Doubleday, Page and Company.

p. 182: For the weak predictability of interviews, see J. E. Hunter and R. F. Hunter (1984). "Validity and utility of alternative predictors of job performance." *Psychological Bulletin* 96, 72–98.

p. 182: For the interview illusion, see Z. Kunda and R. E. Nisbett (1986). "The psychometrics of everyday life." *Cognitive Psychology* 18, 195–224; and pp. 136–138 in L. Ross and R. E. Nisbett (1991). *The Person and the Situation: Perspectives on Social Psychology*. New York: McGraw-Hill.

p. 183: "Emanates directly from . . ." from p. 35 in T. Töpffer (1965). *Essay on Physiognomy. In Enter: The Comics. Rodolphe Töpffer's Essay on Physiognomy and the True Story of Monsieur Crépin*, translated and edited by E. Wiese. Lincoln, NE: University of Nebraska Press, 1965. Originally published in 1845.

p. 183: For Anna Lelkes, see J. Perlez (1997). "Vienna Philharmonic lets women join in harmony." *New York Times* (February 28), http://www.nytimes.com/1997/02/28/world /vienna-philharmonic-lets-women-join-in-harmony.html?_r=0; H. Roegle (1997). "Notes on 26 years as official non-entity." *Los Angeles Times* (March 5), http://articles .latimes.com/1997-03-05/news/mn-35044_1_vienna-philharmonic-orchestra.

p. 183: On the effect of "blind" auditions, see C. Goldin and C. Rouse (2000). "Orchestrating impartiality: The impact of 'blind' auditions on female musicians." *American Economic Review* 90, 715–741.

p. 183: "The boy had a body . . ." from p. 7 in M. Lewis (2004). *Moneyball*. New York: W. W. Norton and Company.

p. 184: "To be victimized by what we see." from p. 37 in Lewis. *Moneyball*.

p. 184: "Those guys who for their whole career . . ." from pp. 117–118 in Lewis. *Moneyball*.

p. 184: "The smallest possible knowledge . . ." from p. 3 in Lichtenberg, *On Physiognomy, against the Physiognomists*. Translation courtesy of Steven Tester, University of Göttingen.

p. 184: "Consider someone wise who acts wisely . . . "from p. 13 in Lichtenberg, *On Physiognomy, against the Physiognomists*. Translation courtesy of Steven Tester, University of Göttingen.

Chapter 10: Evolutionary Stories

p. 185: "Based upon three very simple . . ." from p. 432 in K. M. H. Blackford and A. Newcomb (1916). *Analyzing Character: The New Science of Judging Men, Misfits in Business, the Home, and Social Life*, third edition. New York: Review of Reviews Company.

p. 186: For the correlation between the shape of noses and the climate of one's ancestors, see R. G. Franciscus, and J. C. Long (1991). "Variation in human nasal height and breadth." *American Journal of Physical Anthropology* 85, 419–427; M. L. Noback, K. Harvati, and F. Spoor. (2011). "Climate-related variation of the human nasal cavity." *American Journal of Physical Anthropology* 145, 599–614; T. R. Yokley (2009). "Ecogeographic variation in human nasal passages." *American Journal of Physical Anthropology* 138, 11–22.

p. 186: "The low, flat nose is everywhere . . ." from p. 433 in Blackford and Newcomb. *Analyzing Character*.

p. 186: "Slow, easy-going, hateful of change, . . ." from pp. 432–433 in Blackford and Newcomb. *Analyzing Character*.

p. 186: For the correlation between skin color and climate, see N. G. Jablonski and G. Chaplin (2000). "The evolution of human skin coloration." *Journal of Human Evolution* 39, 57–106.

p. 188: E. M. Weston, A. E. Friday, and P. Liò (2007). "Biometric evidence that sexual selection has shaped the hominin face." *PLoS ONE* 2(8), e710.

p. 188: Measuring the fWHR from photographs has a number of problems, because different images of the same person can generate different fWHRs. The British researcher Robin Kramer measured the fWHR of the same actor from different (frontal) screen shots of movies. On average, Matt Damon, as it happened, has a higher fWHR than John Cusack and Ben Affleck, but for many screen shots Damon appears to have a lower fWHR than Cusack and Affleck. This occurred even when the expressions of the actors were neutral. These differences arise from lack of control of cameras and camera angles. Kramer also found that emotional expressions can change the fWHR. See R. S. S. Kramer (2016). "Within-person variability in men's facial width-to-height ratio." *Peer Journal* 4, e1801, doi: 10.7717/peerj.1801.

p. 188: For reviews of studies using the fWHR, see S. N. Geniole, T. F. Denson, B. J. Dixson, J. M. Carré, and C. M. McCormick (2015). "Evidence from meta-analyses of the facial width-to-height ratio as an evolved cue of threat." *PLoS ONE* 10(7), e0132726; M. P. Haselhuhn, M. E. Ormiston, and E. M. Wong (2015). "Men's facial width-to-height ratio predicts aggression: A meta-analysis." *PLoS ONE* 10(4), e0122637.

p. 188: "Part of an evolved cueing system . . ." from p. 15 in Geniole et al. "Evidence from meta-analyses of the facial width-to-height ratio."

p. 188: "An honest signal of superiority . . ." from p. 1 in M. P. Haselhuhn, Ormiston, and Wong. "Men's facial width-to-height ratio predicts aggression."

pp. 188–189: J. Gómez-Valdés, T. Hünemeier, M. Quinto-Sánchez, C. Paschetta, S. de Azevedo et al. (2013). "Lack of support for the association between facial shape and aggression: A reappraisal based on a worldwide population genetics perspective." *PLoS ONE* 8(1), e52317.

p. 189: Geniole et al. "Evidence from meta-analyses of the facial width-to-height ratio."

p. 189: For correlations between gender and height, body, and muscle mass, see W. D. Lassek and S. J. C. Gaulin (2009). "Costs and benefits of fat-free muscle mass in men: Relationship to mating success, dietary requirements, and native immunity." *Evolution and Human Behavior* 30, 322–328.

p. 189: For the complex version of this hypothesis, see S. W. Gangestad and J. A. Simpson (2000). "The evolution of human mating: Trade-offs and strategic pluralism." *Behavioral and Brain Sciences* 23, 573–644.

p. 189: For the immunocompetence hypothesis, see I. Folstad and A. J. Karter (1992). "Parasites, bright males, and the immunocompetence handicap." *American Naturalist* 139, 603–622. For its application to human faces, see R. Thornhill and S. W. Gangestad (1993). "Human facial beauty: Averageness, symmetry, and parasite resistance." *Human Nature* 4, 237–269.

p. 189: For a critique of the immunocompetence hypothesis from an evolutionary point of view, see I. M. L. Scott, A. P. Clark, L. G. Boothroyd, and I. S. Penton-Voak (2013). "Do men's faces really signal heritable immunocompetence?" *Behavioral Ecology* 24, 579–589.

p. 190: For alternative views of the role of testosterone, see S. Braude, Z. Tang-Martinez, and G. Taylor (1999). "Stress, testosterone, and the immunoredistribution hypothesis." *Behavioral Ecology* 10, 345–350.

p. 190: C. P. Said and A. Todorov (2011). "A statistical model of facial attractiveness." *Psychological Science* 22, 1183–1190.

p. 191: I. M. L. Scott, N. Pound, I. D. Stephen, A. P. Clark, and I. S. Penton-Voak (2010). "Does masculinity matter? The contribution of masculine face shape to male attractiveness in humans." *PLoS ONE* 5(10), e13585.

p. 191: For gender differences in skin reflectance, see N. G. Jablonski and G. Chaplin (2000). "The evolution of human skin coloration." *Journal of Human Evolution* 39, 57–106.

p. 191: For the importance of current health status for mating, see Scott et al. "Does masculinity matter?"; and I. D. Stephen, I. M. L. Scott, V. Coetzee, N. Pound, D. I. Perrett, and I. S. Penton-Voak (2012). "Cross-cultural effects of color, but not morphological masculinity, on perceived attractiveness of men's faces." *Evolution and Human Behavior* 33, 260–267.

p. 192: I. M. L. Scott, A. P. Clark, S. C. Josephson, A. H. Boyette, I. C. Cuthill et al. (2014). Human preferences for sexually dimorphic faces may be evolutionarily novel. *Proceedings of the National Academy of Sciences of the USA, 111*, 14388–14393.

p. 192: For the second evolutionary hypothesis, see D. Puts (2010). "Beauty and the beast: Mechanisms of sexual selection in humans." *Evolution and Human Behavior* 31, 157–175.

p. 193: The estimate of .16 is from Geniole et al. "Evidence from meta-analyses of the facial width-to-height ratio."

p. 193: The estimate of .11 is from Haselhuhn et al. "Men's facial width-to-height ratio predicts aggression."

p. 193: The estimate of .46 is from Geniole et al. "Evidence from meta-analyses of the facial width-to-height ratio."

p. 194: C. Efferson and S. Vogt (2013). "Viewing men's faces does not lead to accurate predictions of trustworthiness." *Scientific Reports* 3, 1047, doi:10.1038/srep01047.

p. 195: M. P. Haselhuhn, E. M. Wong, and M. E. Ormiston (2013). "Self-fulfilling prophecies as a link between men's facial width-to-height ratio and behavior." *PLoS ONE* 8(8), e72259.

p. 195: For the correlation between the faces from our model of threat and the fWHR, see J. M. Carré, M. D. Morrissey, C. J. Mondloch, and C. M. McCormick (2010). "Estimating aggression from emotionally neutral faces: Which facial cues are diagnostic?" *Perception* 39, 356–377.

p. 196: "From any sign taken alone . . ." from p. 17 in R. Töpffer (1965). "Essay on Physiognomy." In *Enter: The Comics. Rodolphe Töpffer's Essay on Physiognomy and the True Story of Monsieur Crépin*, translated and edited by E. Wiese. Lincoln, NE: University of Nebraska Press. Originally published in 1845.

p. 196: For the potential connection between the fWHR and testosterone, see M. Stirrat and D. I. Perrett (2010). "Valid facial cues to cooperation and trust: Male facial width and trustworthiness." *Psychological Science* 21, 349–354; C. E. Lefevre, G. J. Lewis, D. I. Perrett, and L. Penke (2013). "Telling facial metrics: Facial width is associated with testosterone levels in men." *Evolution and Human Behavior* 34, 273–279. However, this evidence has been questioned recently. See C. R. Hodges-Simeon, K. N. H. Sobraske, T. Samore, M. Gurven, and S. J. C. Gaulin (2016). "Facial width-to-height ratio (fWHR) is not associated with adolescent testosterone levels. *PLoS ONE* 11(4), e0153083.

p. 196: For simulating the effect of testosterone on face shape, see J. P. Swaddle and G. W. Reierson (2002). "Testosterone increases perceived dominance but not attractiveness in human males." *Proceedings of the Royal Society B* 269(1507), 2285–2289.

pp. 197–199: I. J. Holzleitner (2015). "Linking 3D face shape to social perception." Doctoral dissertation, University of St Andrews, Scotland; see also I. J. Holzleitner and D. I. Perrett (2016). "Perception of strength from 3D faces is linked to facial cues of physique." *Evolution and Human Behavior* 37, 217–229.

p. 198: For the strength of obese people, see C. L. Lafortuna, N. A. Maffiuletti, F. Agosti, and A. Sartorio (2005). "Gender variations of body composition, muscle strength and power output in morbid obesity." *International Journal of Obesity* 29, 833–841. Of course, obese people are stronger than people with normal weight only in terms of absolute strength, not in terms of relative strength measured per kilogram of body weight.

p. 200: "Mildness of disposition . . ." from p. 319 in Blackford and Newcomb. *Analyzing Character.*

p. 200: For the use of the cephalic index in the beginning of twentieth century, see T. C. Leonard (2016). *Illiberal Reformers: Race, Eugenics, and American Economics in the Progressive Era.* Princeton, NJ: Princeton University Press.

p. 201: For the wealth of personal information in small-scale societies, see C. Von Rueden, M. Gurven, and H. Kaplan (2008). "The multiple dimensions of male social status in an Amazonian society." *Evolution and Human Behavior* 29, 402–415.

p. 201: "How to encounter strangers regularly . . ." from p. 273 in J. Diamond (1999). *Guns, Germs, and Steel: The Fates of Human Societies.* New York: W. W. Norton and Company.

Chapter 11: Life Leaves Traces on Our Faces

p. 203: "The characteristic facial expressions . . ." from 805a and 806a in *Physiognomica*, a treatise attributed to Aristotle. In *Works of Aristotle: Translated into English under the Editorship of W. D. Ross.* Volume VI (First edition 1913). Oxford University Press.

p. 203: "The knowledge of the signs of the power . . ." from p. 20 in J. K. Lavater (1789). *Essays on Physiognomy; For the Promotion of the Knowledge and the Love of Mankind*, Volume 1, translated by Thomas Holcroft. London: Printed for G. G. J. and J. Robinson, Paternoster-Row.

p. 203: J. Parsons (1746). *Human Physiognomy Explain'd: In the Crounian Lectures on Muscular Motion. Read before the Royal Society, Being a Supplement to the Philosophical Transactions for That Year.* London: Printed for C. Davis.

p. 203: "The true agents of every passion of the mind" from p. ii in Parsons. *Human Physiognomy Explain'd.*

p. 204: "A person with a long chin or nose, . . ." from p. 37 in Parsons. *Human Physiognomy Explain'd.*

p. 205: G.-B. Duchenne de Boulogne (1990). *The Mechanism of Human Facial Expression.* New York: Cambridge University Press. Originally published in 1862.

p. 205: P. Ekman and W. V. Friesen (1978). *The Facial Action Coding System: A Technique for Measurement of Facial Movement.* Palo Alto, CA: Consulting Psychologists Press.

p. 205: "The reason why the eyes and mouth . . ." from p. 60 in Parsons. *Human Physiognomy Explain'd.*

p. 205: For the test of Parsons's insight, see J. M. Susskind, D. H. Lee, A. Cusi, R. Feiman, W. Grabski, and A. K. Anderson (2008). "Expressing fear enhances sensory acquisition." *Nature Neuroscience* 11, 843–850.

p. 205: "Habitual disposition, causing the muscles of the face . . ." from p. 43 in Parsons. *Human Physiognomy Explain'd.*

p. 205: "Was happy and glad upon any occasion . . ." from p. 73 in Parsons. *Human Physiognomy Explain'd.*

p. 205: "Immoderate grief, by keeping those muscles relaxed . . ." from p. 78 in Parsons. *Human Physiognomy Explain'd.*

pp. 205–206: "Pathognomic signs, often repeated, . . ." from p. 17 in G. C. Lichtenberg. *On Physiognomy, against the Physiognomists, for the Promotion of the Love and Knowledge of*

Man, translated by Steven Tester for Princeton University Press. Translation courtesy of Steven Tester, University of Göttingen.

p. 206: See pp. 31 and 36 in de Boulogne. *The Mechanism of Human Facial Expression*; and p. 276 in P. Mantegazza (1891). *Physiognomy and the Expression of Emotions*. New York: Scribner and Welford.

p. 206: "Whatever amount of truth the so-called science . . ." from p. 359 in C. Darwin (1998). *The Expression of the Emotions in Man and Animal*, third edition. New York: Oxford University Press.

p. 206: "I know some persons . . ." from p. 47 in Parsons. *Human Physiognomy Explain'd*.

p. 207: For support of Parsons's hypothesis, see C. Z. Malatesta, M. J. Fiore, and J. J. Messina (1987). "Affect, personality, and facial expressive characteristics of older people." *Psychology and Aging* 2, 64–69.

pp. 207–208: For effects of sleep deprivation on apperance, see J. Axelsson, T. Sundelin, M. Ingre, E. J. W. Van Someren, A. Olsson, and M. Lekander (2010). "Beauty sleep: Experimental study on the perceived health and attractiveness of sleep deprived people." *BMJ* 341, c6614; T. Sundelin, M. Lekander, G. Kecklund, E. J. W. Van Someren, A. Olsson, and J. Axelsson (2013). "Cues of fatigue: Effects of sleep deprivation on facial appearance." *Sleep* 36, 1355–1360; as well as pp. 187–188 in D. Perrett (2012). *In Your Face: The New Science of Human Attraction*. London: Palgrave Macmillan.

p. 209: For effects of diet on apperance, see C. E. Lefevre and D. I. Perrett (2015). "Fruit over sunbed: Carotenoid skin colouration is found more attractive than melanin colouration." *Quarterly Journal of Experimental Psychology* 68, 284–293; C. Pezdirc, M. Hutchesson, R. Whitehead, G. Ozakinci, D. Perrett, and C. E. Collins (2015). "Can dietary intake influence perception of and measured appearance? A systematic review." *Nutrition Research* 35, 175–197; I. D. Stephen, V. Coetzee, and D. I. Perrett (2011). "Carotenoid and melanin pigment coloration affect perceived human health." *Evolution & Human Behavior* 32, 216–227; R. D. Whitehead, D. Re, D. Xiao, G. Ozakinci, and D. I. Perrett (2012). "You are what you eat: Within-subject increases in fruit and vegetable consumption confer beneficial skin-color changes." *PLoS ONE* 7, e32988. See also R. D. Whitehead, G. Ozakinci, I. D. Stephen, and D. I. Perrett (2012). "Appealing to vanity: Could potential appearance improvement motivate fruit and vegetable consumption?" *American Journal of Public Health* 102, 207–211; R. D. Whitehead, V. Goetzee, G. Ozakinci, and D. I. Perrett (2012). "Cross-cultural effects of fruit and vegetable consumption on skin color." *American Journal of Public Health* 102, 212–213.

p. 209: For Figure 11.5, recent evidence suggests that only Caucasians and Africans, but not Asians, find faces with yellow hues more attractive (personal communication with Lisa M. DeBruine).

p. 210: For effects on diet within 6–8 weeks, see Whitehead et al. "You are what you eat." However, it should be noted that this effect might not generalize to non-Caucasians. A study with participants in South Africa showed that a 10-week course of carotenoid supplements produced detectable effects only on areas of the skin with low sun exposure, like the palm of the hand; see V. Coetzee and D. I. Perrett (2014). "Effect of beta-carotene supplementation on African skin." *Journal of Biomedical Optics* 19(2), 025004.

p. 210: Sustaining a diet for at least 10 weeks: see R. D. Whitehead, G. Ozakinci, and D. I. Perrett (2014). "A randomized control trial of an appearance-based dietary intervention." *Health Psychology* 33, 99–102.

p. 210: For the effect of physical training on skin blood flow, see J. M. Johnson (1998). "Physical training and the control of skin blood flow." *Medicine & Science in Sports & Exercise* 30, 382–386.

p. 210: For the effect of redness on perceptions of health and attractiveness, see I. D. Stephen, V. Coetzee, M. J. Law Smith, and D. I. Perrett (2009). "Skin blood perfusion and oxygenation colour affect perceived human health." *PLoS ONE* 4(4), e5083; I. D. Stephen, M. J. Law Smith, M. R. Stirrat, and D. I. Perrett (2009). "Facial skin coloration affects perceived health of human faces." *International Journal of Primatology* 30, 845–857; see also pp. 142–144 in Perrett. *In Your Face.*

p. 210: For judging body weight from the face, see V. Coetzee, D. I. Perrett, and I. D. Stephen (2009). "Facial adiposity: A cue to health?" *Perception* 38, 1700–1711; R. M. Tinlin, C. D. Watkins, L. M. Welling, E. A. S. Al-Dujaili, and B. C. Jones (2013). "Perceived facial adiposity conveys information about women's health." *British Journal of Psychology* 104, 235–248.

p. 210: J. A. Levine, A. Ray, and M. D. Jensen (1998). "Relation between chubby cheeks and visceral fat." *New England Journal of Medicine* 339, 1946–1947.

p. 210: For weight judgments from faces predicting health problems, see Coetzee, Perrett, and Stephen. "Facial adiposity: A cue to health?"; Tinlin et al. "Perceived facial adiposity conveys information about women's health."

p. 210: A large study on health-related issues: see E. N. Reither, R. M. Hauser, and K. C. Swallen (2009). "Predicting adult health and mortality from adolescent facial characteristics in yearbook photographs." *Demography* 46, 27–41.

p. 211: For "smoker's face," see D. Model (1985). "Smoker's face: An underrated clinical sign?" *British Medical Journal* 291, 1760–1762; see also pp. 140–141 in Perrett. *In Your Face.*

p. 211: On the effects of skin condition on perceptions of age, see B. Tiddeman, M. Burt, and D. I. Perrett (2001). "Prototyping and transforming facial textures for perception research." *IEEE Computer Graphics and Applications* 21, 42–50; see also pp. 163–165 and 167–169 in Perrett. *In Your Face.*

p. 212: For relations between looking younger and health indicators, see G. A. Borkan and A. H. Norris (2009). "Assessment of biological age using a profile of physical parameters." *Journal of Gerontology* 35, 177–184; K. Christensen, M. Thinggaard, M. McGue, H. Rexbye, J. v. B. Hjelmborg et al. (2009). "Perceived age as clinically useful biomarker of ageing: Cohort study." *BMJ* 339, b5262.

p. 212: For the study of Danish twins, see Christensen et al. "Perceived age as clinically useful biomarker of ageing."

p. 213: "facial photographs are, . . ." from p. 7 in Christensen et al. "Perceived age as clinically useful biomarker of ageing."

p. 213: For environmental determinants of looking younger, see H. Rexbye, I. Petersen, M. Johansen, L. Klitkou, B. Jeune, and K. Christensen (2006). "Influence of environmental factors on facial ageing." *Age and Ageing* 35, 110–115.

p. 213: "Shall grow old, . . ." from p. 29 in O. Wilde (2004). *The Picture of Dorian Gray.* New York: Modern Library.

p. 213: "In the eyes there was a look . . ." from p. 252 in Wilde. *The Picture of Dorian Gray.*

p. 214: "Our body stands in the middle . . ." from p. 8 in Lichtenberg. *On Physiognomy, against the Physiognomists, for the Promotion of the Love and Knowledge of Man.* Translation courtesy of Steven Tester, University of Göttingen.

p. 214: "cold winters, foul diapers, . . ." from p. 8 in Lichtenberg. *On Physiognomy, against the*

Physiognomists, for the Promotion of the Love and Knowledge of Man. Translation courtesy of Steven Tester, University of Göttingen.

p. 214: "Even the lasting traces . . ." from p. 23 in Lichtenberg. *On Physiognomy, against the Physiognomists, for the Promotion of the Love and Knowledge of Man.* Translation courtesy of Steven Tester, University of Göttingen.

p. 214: "Is someone whose resting face resembles . . ." from p. 18 in Lichtenberg. *On Physiognomy, against the Physiognomists, for the Promotion of the Love and Knowledge of Man.* Translation courtesy of Steven Tester, University of Göttingen.

Chapter 12: Born to Attend to Faces

p. 221: For research on newborns' visual acuity, see F. Acerra, Y. Burnod, and S. de Schonen (2002). "Modelling aspects of face processing in early infancy." *Developmental Science* 5, 98–117; J. Atkinson, O. Braddick, and F. Braddick (1974). "Acuity and contrast sensitivity of infant vision." *Nature* 247, 403–404; M. S. Banks and P. Salapatek (1978). "Acuity and contrast sensitivity in 1-, 2-, and 3-month-old human infants." *Investigative Ophthalmology and Visual Science* 17, 361–365; V. Dobson and D. Y. Teller (1978). "Visual acuity in human infants: A review and comparison of behavioral and electrophysiological studies." *Vision Research* 18, 1469–1483; A. Slater and M. Sykes (1977). "Newborn infants' visual responses to square wave gratings." *Child Development* 48, 545–554.

p. 221: R. L. Fantz (1963). "Pattern vision in newborn infants." *Science* 140, 296–297.

p. 222: "The results do not imply . . ." from p. 297 in Fantz. "Pattern vision in newborn infants."

p. 222: C. C. Goren, M. Sarty, and P. J. K. Wu (1975). "Visual following and pattern discrimination of face-like stimuli by newborn infants." *Pediatrics* 56, 544–549.

p. 223: "These results suggest . . ." from p. 548 in Goren, Sarty, Wu. "Visual following and pattern discrimination of face-like stimuli by newborn infants."

pp. 223–224: M. H. Johnson, S. Dziurawiec, H. D. Ellis, and J. Morton (1991). "Newborns' preferential tracking of face-like stimuli and its subsequent decline." *Cognition* 40, 1–19.

p. 224: For "top-heavy pattern" explanation, see V. Macchi Cassia, C. Turati, and F. Simion (2004). "Can a non-specific bias toward top-heavy patterns explain newborns' face preference?" *Psychological Science* 15, 379–383.

pp. 224–225: T. Farroni, M. H. Johnson, E. Menon, L. Zulian, D. Faraguna, and G. Csibra (2005). "Newborns' preferences for face-relevant stimuli: Effects of contrast polarity." *Proceedings of the National Academy of Sciences of the USA* 102, 17245–17250.

p. 226: For adults' eye movements to upright stimuli with the right three-dimensional interpretation, see P. Tomalski, G. Csibra, and M. H. Johnson (2009). "Rapid orienting toward face-like stimuli with gaze-relevant contrast information." *Perception* 38, 569–578.

p. 226: For continuous flash suppression, see N. Tsuchiya and C. Koch (2005). "Continuous flash suppression reduces negative afterimages." *Nature Neuroscience* 8, 1096–1101.

p. 227: T. Stein, M. V. Peelen, and P. Sterzer (2011). "Adults' awareness of faces follows newborns' looking preferences." *PLoS ONE* 6(12), e29361.

p. 227: For the difficulty of recognizing faces from negatives, see R. E. Galper (1970). "Recognition of faces in photographic negative." *Psychonomic Science* 19, 207–208; N. George, R. J. Dolan, G. R. Fink, G. C. Baylis, C. Russell, and J. Driver (1999). "Contrast polarity and face recognition in the human fusiform gyrus." *Nature Neuroscience* 2, 574–580; T. Hayes, M.

C. Morrone, and D. C. Burr (1986). "Recognition of positive and negative bandpass-filtered images." *Perception* 15, 595–602; M. Nederhouser, X. Yue, M. C. Mangini, and I. Biederman (2007). "The deleterious effect of contrast reversal on recognition is unique to faces, not objects." *Vision Research* 47, 2134–2142; M. White (2001). "Effect of photographic negation on matching the expressions and identities of faces." *Perception* 30, 969–981.

p. 228: S. Gilad, M. Meng, and P. Sinha (2009). "Role of ordinal contrast relationships in face encoding." *Proceedings of the National Academy of Sciences of the USA* 106, 5353–5358.

p. 228: P. Viola and M. J. Jones (2004). "Robust real-time face detection." *International Journal of Computer Vision* 57, 137–154.

p. 229: B. M. 't Hart, T. G. J. Abresch, and W. Einhäuser (2011). "Faces in places: Humans and machines make similar face detection errors." *PLoS ONE* 6(10), e25373.

p. 230: N. A. Sugden, M. I. Maohamed-Ali, and M. C. Moulson (2014). "I spy with my little eye: Typical, daily exposure to faces documented from a first-person infant perspective." *Developmental Psychobiology* 56, 249–261.

p. 230: For perceptual narrowing, see D. J. Lewkowicz and A. A. Ghazanfar (2009). "The emergence of multisensory systems through perceptual narrowing." *Trends in Cognitive Sciences* 13, 470–478.

pp. 231–232: For perceptual narrowing in face perception, see D. J. Kelly, P. C. Quinn, A. M. Slater, K. Lee, L. Ge, and O. Pascalis (2007). "The other-race effect develops during infancy: Evidence of perceptual narrowing." *Psychological Science* 18, 1084–1089; O. Pascalis, M. de Haan, and C. A. Nelson (2002). "Is face processing species-specific during the first year of life?" *Science* 296, 1321–1323; O. Pascalis and D. J. Kelly (2009). "The origins of face processing in humans: Phylogeny and ontogeny." *Perspectives on Psychological Science* 2(2), 200–209.

p. 231: S. Sangrigoli, C. Pallier, A.-M. Argenti, V. A. G. Ventureyra, and S. de Schonen (2005). "Reversibility of the other-race effect in face recognition during childhood." *Psychological Science* 16, 440–444.

p. 231: Y. Sugita (2008). "Face perception in monkeys reared with no exposure to faces." *Proceedings of the National Academy of Sciences of the USA* 105, 394–398.

p. 232: For newborns' preferences for faces with open eyes, see T. Farroni, G. Csibra, F. Simion, and M. H. Johnson (2002). "Eye contact detection in humans from birth." *Proceedings of the National Academy of Sciences of the USA* 99, 9602–9605.

p. 232: For newborns' preferences to look at happy rather than at fearful faces, see T. Farroni, E. Menon, S. Rigato, and M. H. Johnson (2007). "The perception of facial expressions in newborns." *European Journal of Developmental Psychology* 4, 2–13.

p. 232: For mother-infant synchronized face-to-face behavior, see B. Beebe, J. Jaffe, S. Markese, K. Buck, H. Chen et al. (2010). "The origins of 12-month attachment: A microanalysis of 4-month mother-infant interaction." *Attachment & Human Development* 12, 3–141.

p. 232: For infants' spontaneous allocation of attention to dynamic faces, see M. C. Frank, E. Vul, and S. P. Johnson (2009). "Development of infants' attention to faces during the first year." *Cognition* 110, 160–170.

p. 232: For infants' discrimination of emotions see, E. Kotsoni, M. De Haan, and M. H. Johnson (2001). "Categorical perception of facial expressions by 7-month-old infants." *Perception* 30, 1115–1125; C. A. Nelson and K. Dolgin (1985). "The generalized discrimination of facial expressions by 7-month-old infants." *Child Development* 56, 58–61; M. J. Peltola, J. M. Leppänen, S. Mäki, and J. K. Hietanen (2009). "Emergence of enhanced attention to fearful faces between 5 and 7 months of age." *Social Cognitive and Affective Neuroscience* 4, 134–142; M. J. Peltola, J. K. Hietanen, L. Forssman, and J. M. Leppänen (2013). "The emergence and stability of the attentional bias to fearful faces in infancy." *Infancy* 18, 905–926.

CHAPTER 13: FACE MODULES IN THE BRAIN

p. 233: For primates' cortical visual areas, see J. H. Kaas (2014). The evolution of the visual system in primates. In J. S. Werner and L. M. Chapula (eds.), *The New Visual Neurosciences*. Cambridge, MA: MIT Press.

p. 233: H. D. Ellis and M. Florence (1990). "Bodamer's (1947) paper on prosopagnosia." *Cognitive Neuropsychology* 7, 81–105. This is a partial translation of Bodamer's paper.

p. 233: "Recognized a face as such . . ." from p. 86 in Ellis and Florence. "Bodamer's (1947) paper on prosopagnosia."

p. 234: For the history of research on the visual functions of temporal cortex, see C. G. Gross (1994). "How inferior temporal cortex became a visual area." *Cerebral Cortex* 4, 455–469; see also C. G. Gross (1998). *Brain, Vision, Memory: Tales in the History of Neuroscience*. Cambridge, MA: MIT Press.

p. 234: Hubel and Wiesel's work is collected in D. H. Hubel and T. N. Wiesel (2005). *Brain and Visual Perception: The Story of a 25-Year Collaboration*. Oxford: Oxford University Press.

pp. 235–236: C. G. Gross, D. B. Bender, and C. E. Rocha-Miranda (1969). "Visual receptive fields of neurons in inferotemporal cortex of the monkey." *Science* 166, 1303–1306; C. G. Gross, C. E. Rocha-Miranda, and D. B. Bender (1972). "Visual properties of neurons in inferotemporal cortex of the macaque." *Journal of Neurophysiology* 35, 96–111.

p. 236: "A hand at the stimulus screen" from p. 103 in Gross, Rocha-Miranda, and Bender. "Visual properties of neurons in inferotemporal cortex of the macaque."

p. 236: "Complex colored patterns . . ." from p. 103 in Gross, Rocha-Miranda, and Bender. "Visual properties of neurons in inferotemporal cortex of the macaque."

p. 236: "When we wrote the first draft . . ." from p. 199 in Gross. *Brain, Vision, Memory*.

p. 236: J. Konorski (1967). *Integrative Activity of the Brain: An Interdisciplinary Approach*. Chicago: University of Chicago Press.

p. 236: C. G. Gross (1968). "Review of J. Konorski, *Integrative Activity of the Brain* (1967)." *Science* 160, 652–653.

p. 236: For the history of the "grandmother cell" joke, see C. G. Gross (2002). "Genealogy of the 'grandmother cell.'" *Neuroscientist* 8, 84–90.

p. 236: C. Bruce, R. Desimone, and C. G. Gross (1981). "Visual properties of neurons in a polysensory area in superior temporal sulcus of the macaque." *Journal of Neurophysiology* 46, 369–384.

p. 236: For early replications of findings of face-selective neurons, see D. I. Perrett, E. T. Rolls, and W. Caan (1982). "Visual neurons responsive to faces in the monkey temporal cortex." *Experimental Brain Research* 47, 329–342; E. T. Rolls (1984). "Neurons in the cortex of the temporal lobe and in the amygdala of the monkey with responses selective for faces." *Human Neurobiology* 3, 209–222; S. Yamane, S. Kaji, and K. Kawano (1988). "What facial features activate face neurons in the inferotemporal cortex of the monkey?" *Experimental Brain Research* 73, 209–214. For a review of the early findings, see R. Desimone (1991). "Face-selective cells in the temporal cortex of monkeys." *Journal of Cognitive Neuroscience* 3, 1–8.

p. 237: For neurons with holistic responses, see E. Kobatake and K. Tanaka (1994). "Neuronal selectivities to complex object features in the ventral visual pathway of the macaque cerebral cortex." *Journal of Neurophysiology* 71, 856–867.

p. 238: For the causal significance of face neurons, see S.-R. Afraz, R. Kiani, and H. Esteky (2006). "Microstimulation of inferotemporal cortex influences face categorization." *Nature* 442, 692–695.

pp. 238–239: For responses of face-selective neurons to round objects, see D. Y. Tsao, W. A. Freiwald, R. B. H. Tootell, and M. S. Livingstone (2006). "A cortical region consisting entirely of face-selective cells." *Science* 311, 670–674.

p. 239: R. Q. Quiroga, L. Reddy, G. Kreiman, C. Koch, and I. Fried (2005). "Invariant visual representation by single neurons in the human brain." *Nature* 435, 1102–1107.

p. 240: For studies using positron emission tomography, see J. V. Haxby, C. L. Grady, B. Horwitz, J. A. Salerno, L. G. Ungerleider et al. (1993). "Dissociation of object and spatial visual processing pathways in human extrastriate cortex." In B. Gulyas, D. Ottoson, P. E. Roland (eds.), *Functional Organization of Human Visual Cortex*. Oxford: Pergamon; J. Sergent, S. Ohta, and B. MacDonald (1992). "Functional neuroanatomy of face and object processing. A positron emission tomography study." *Brain* 115, 15–36.

p. 240: N. Kanwisher, J. McDermott, and M. M. Chun (1997). "The fusiform face area: A module in human extrastriate cortex specialized for face perception." *Journal of Neuroscience* 17, 4302–4311; for a subsequent review of related findings, see N. Kanwisher, and G. Yovel (2006). "The fusiform face area: A cortical region specialized for the perception of faces." *Philosophical Transactions of the Royal Society of London B* 361, 2109–2128.

p. 240: Y. Wada and T. Yamamoto (2001). "Selective impairment of facial recognition due to a haematoma restricted to the right fusiform and lateral occipital region." *Journal of Neurology, Neurosurgery, and Psychiatry* 71, 254–257.

p. 241: "So, James, I'm going to . . ." S. Mendes (Director), M. G. Wilson (Producer), and B. Broccoli (Producer) (2015). *Spectre* [Motion Picture]. United Kingdom: Eon Productions.

pp. 241–242: P. M. Mende-Siedlecki, S. C. Verosky, N. B. Turk-Browne, and A. Todorov (2013). "Robust selectivity for faces in the human amygdala in the absence of expressions." *Journal of Cognitive Neuroscience* 25, 2086–2106.

p. 242: For fMRI studies of responses to "trustworthy" and "untrustworthy" faces, see A. Todorov, C. P. Said, N. N. Oosterhof, and A. D. Engell (2011). "Task-invariant brain responses to the social value of faces." *Journal of Cognitive Neuroscience* 23, 2766–2781. For reviews, see A. Todorov and P. M. Mende-Siedlecki (2013). "The cognitive and neural basis of impression formation." In K. Ochsner and S. Kossyln (eds.), *The Oxford Handbook of Cognitive Neuroscience*, Volume 2. New York: Oxford University Press; A. Todorov, P. M. Mende-Siedlecki, and R. Dotsch (2013). "Social judgments from faces." *Current Opinion in Neurobiology* 23, 373–380.

p. 242: J. B. Freeman, R. M. Stolier, Z. A. Ingbretsen, and E. Hehman (2014). "Amygdala responsivity to high-level social information from unseen faces." *Journal of Neuroscience* 34, 10573–10581.

p. 242: For findings of face-selective responses in amygdala neurons, see K. M. Gothard, F. P. Battaglia, C. A. Erickson K. M. Spitler, and D. G. Amaral (2007). "Neural responses to facial expression and face identity in the monkey amygdala." *Journal of Neurophysiology* 97, 1671–1683; K. Kuraoka and K. Nakamura (2006). "Responses of single neurons in monkey amygdala to facial and vocal emotions." *Journal of Neurophysiology* 97, 1379–1387; C. M.

Leonard, E. T. Rolls, F. A. W. Wilson, and G. C. Baylis (1985). "Neurons in the amygdala of the monkey with responses selective for faces." *Behavioural Brain Research* 15, 159–176; K. Nakamura, A. Mikami, and K. Kubota (1992). "Activity of single neurons in the monkey amygdala during performance of a visual discrimination task." *Journal of Neurophysiology* 67, 1447–1463; F. A. W. Wilson and E. T. Rolls (1993). "The effects of novelty and familiarity on neuronal activity recorded in the amygdala of monkeys performing recognition memory tasks." *Experimental Brain Research* 93, 367–382. For a review, see E. T. Rolls (2000). "Neurophysiology and function of the primate amygdala, and neural basis of emotion." In J. P. Aggleton (ed.), *The Amygdala: A Functional Analysis*. Oxford: Oxford University Press.

p. 242: D. Y. Tsao, W. A. Freiwald, R. B. H. Tootell, and M. S. Livingstone (2006). "A cortical region consisting entirely of face-selective cells." *Science* 311, 670–674. For a review of their work, see W. A. Freiwald and D. Y. Tsao (2011). "Taking apart the neural machinery of face processing." In A. Calder, J. V. Haxby, M. Johnson, and G. Rhodes (eds.), *Handbook of Face Perception*. Oxford: Oxford University Press.

p. 243: For studies with patients, see I. Fried, K. A. MacDonald, and C. Wilson (1997). "Single neuron activity in human hippocampus and amygdala during recognition of faces and objects." *Neuron* 18, 753–765; G. Kreiman, C. Koch, and I. Fried (2000). "Category-specific visual responses of single neurons in the human medial temporal lobe." *Nature Neuroscience* 3, 946–953; R. Q. Quiroga, L. Reddy, G. Kreiman, C. Koch, and I. Fried (2005). "Invariant visual representation by single neurons in the human brain." *Nature* 435, 1102–1107; U. Rutishauser, O. Tudusciuc, D. Neumann, A. N. Mamelak, A. C. Heller et al. (2011). "Single-unit responses selective for whole faces in the human amygdala." *Current Biology* 21, 1654–1660; I. V. Viskontas, R. Q. Quiroga, and I. Fried (2009). "Human medial temporal lobe neurons respond preferentially to personally relevant images." *Proceedings of the National Academy of Sciences of the USA* 106, 21329–21334.

p. 243: J. Parvizi, C. Jacques, B. L. Foster, N. Withoft, A. Rangarajan, K. S. Weiner, and K. Grill-Spector (2012). "Electrical stimulation of human fusiform face-selective regions distorts face perception." *Journal of Neuroscience* 32, 14915–14920.

p. 243: For a movie of the patient's experience, see http://www.jneurosci.org.ezproxy.princeton.edu/content/32/43/14915.full#media-1.

p. 244: For literacy and the "visual word form area," see S. Dehaene, F. Pedago, L. W. Braga, P. Ventura, G. N. Filho et al. (2010). "How learning to read changes the cortical networks for vision and language." *Science* 330, 1359–1364.

p. 244: For trainings of monkeys to discriminate symbols, see K. Srihasam, J. B. Mandeville, I. A. Morocz, K. J. Sullivan, and M. S. Livingstone (2012). "Behavioral and anatomical consequencesof early versus late symbol training in macaques." *Neuron* 73, 608–619; K. Srihasam, J. L. Vincent, and M. S. Livingstone (2014). "Novel domain formation reveals proto-architecture in inferotemporal cortex." *Nature Neuroscience* 17, 1776–1783.

p. 244: For face-selective neurons responding to contrast polarity, see S. Ohayon, W. A. Freiwald, and D. Y. Tsao (2012). "What makes a cell face selective: The importance of contrast." *Neuron* 74, 567–581. For face-selective neurons responding to features, see W. A. Freiwald, D. Y. Tsao, and M. S. Livingstone (2009). "A face feature space in the macaque temporal lobe." *Nature Neuroscience* 12, 1187–1196.

p. 244: For face-selective neurons in sheep, see K. M. Kendrick and B. A. Baldwin (1987). "Cells in the temporal cortex of conscious sheep respond preferentially to the sight of faces." *Sci-*

ence 238, 1497–1499; K. Kendrick, A. P. da Costa, A. E. Leigh, M. R. Hinton, and J. W. Peirce (2001). "Sheep don't forget a face." *Nature* 414, 165–166.

p. 244: For recent research on how the face-processing system is embedded in other brain networks, see C. M. Schwiedrzik, W. Zarco, S. Everling, and W. A. Freiwald (2015). "Face patch resting state networks link face processing to social cognition." *PLoS Biology* 13(9), e1002245.

CHAPTER 14: ILLUSORY FACE SIGNALS

p. 246: For the work of Messerschmidt, see M. Pötzl-Malikova and G. Scherf (eds.) (2010). *Franz Xaver Messerschmidt 1736–1783: From Neoclassicism to Expressionism*. New York: Neue Galerie. For the biographical facts, see M. Pötzl-Malikova, "The life and work of Franz Xaver Messerschmidt." In Pötzl-Malikova and Scherf (2010). *Franz Xaver Messer-schmidt 1736–1783*.

p. 247: "Author of candid letters . . ." from p. 23 in Pötzl-Malikova. "The life and work of Franz Xaver Messerschmidt."

p. 247: "The moment you label something . . ." from p. 50 in A. Warhol and P. Hackett (1980). *POPism: The Warhol Sixties*. Orlando, FL: Harcourt.

p. 248: "Involuntary sign language . . ." from p. 15 in G. C. Lichtenberg, *On Physiognomy, against the Physiognomists, for the Promotion of the Love and Knowledge of Man*, translated by Steven Tester for Princeton University Press. Translation courtesy of Steven Tester, University of Göttingen.

p. 248: The story description of the "fear/rage" face is adapted from J. M. Carroll and J. A. Russell (1996). "Do facial expressions signal specific emotions? Judging emotion from the face in context." *Journal of Personality and Social Psychology* 70, 205–218. The complete story is on p. 208.

p. 249: For the same emotional face transplanted on different bodies, see H. Aviezer, R. Hassin, J. Ryan, C. Grady, J. Susskind, A. Anderson et al. (2008). "Angry, disgusted or afraid? Studies on the malleability of emotion perception." *Psychological Science* 19, 724–732; H. Aviezer, S. Bentin, V. Dudareva, and R. Hassin (2011). "Automaticity in contextualized emotion perception." *Emotion* 11, 1406–1414.

p. 250: "Man and the intention of his mind . . ." from pp. 144–146 in Martin Kemp (ed.) (1989). *Leonardo on Painting*. New Haven, CT: Yale University Press.

p. 251: "What strikes me in this series . . ." from pp. 33–34 in R. Töpffer (1965). "Essay on Physiognomy." In *Enter: The Comics. Rodolphe Töpffer's Essay on Physiognomy and the True Story of Monsieur Crépin*, translated and edited by E. Wiese. Lincoln, NE: University of Nebraska Press. First published in 1845.

pp. 252–254: H. Aviezer, Y. Trope, and A. Todorov (2012). "Body cues, not facial expressions, discriminate between intense positive and negative emotions." *Science* 338, 1225–1229.

pp. 254–255: Figures 14.8 and 14.9 are based on research described in P. Sinha, B. Balas, Y. Ostrovsky, and R. Russell (2006). "Face recognition by humans: Nineteen results all computer vision researchers should know about." *Proceedings of the IEEE* 94, 1948–1962.

pp. 255–256: For Hanoch Piven's work, see www.pivenworld.com.

pp. 256–257: A. Rice, P. J. Phillips, X. Natu, X. An, and A. J. O'Toole (2013). "Unaware person recognition from the body when face identification fails." *Psychological Science* 24, 2235–2243.

p. 258: On the misidentification of Sunil Tripathi for Dzhokhar Tsarnaev, see J. C. Kang (2013). "Should Reddit be blamed for the spreading of a smear?" *New York Times Magazine* (July 25), http://www.nytimes.com/2013/07/28/magazine/should-reddit-be-blamed-for-the-spreading-of-a-smear.html?_r=0.

p. 259: For the relation between confidence and accuracy of eyewitness testimony, see G. L. Wells, E. Olson, and S. Charman (2002). "The confidence of eyewitnesses in their identifications from lineups." *Current Directions in Psychological Science* 11, 151–154.

p. 260: R. Jenkins, D. White, X. Van Montfort, and A. M. Burton (2011). "Variability in photos of the same face." *Cognition* 121, 313–323.

p. 261: For failing to see that we underestimate the differences in images of familiar people, see K. L. Ritchie, F. G. Smith, R. Jenkins, M. Bindemann, D. White, and A. M. Burton (2015). "Viewers base estimates of face matching accuracy on their own familiarity: Explaining the photo-ID paradox." *Cognition* 141, 161–169.

p. 261: "We can draw sure conclusions . . ." from p. 15 (Volume 1) in J. K. Lavater (1775–1778). *Physiognomische Fragmente zur Beförderung der Menschenkenntniss und Menschenliebe.* Leipzig and Winterthur: Weidmanns Erben & Reich; quotation translation from p. 34 in R. T. Gray (2004). *About Face: German Physiognomic Thought from Lavater to Auschwitz.* Detroit: Wayne State University Press. This quotation appears in Lavater's first volume of *Essays on Physiognomy*, but historical research suggests that it was written by Goethe (see pp. 32–34 in Gray. *About Face*).

p. 261: A. Versluis and E. Uyttenbroek (2011). *Exactitudes.* Rotterdam: 010 Publishers.

p. 263: "Look at life as retouching . . ." from L. Collins (2008). "Pixel perfect: Pascal Dangin's virtual reality." *New Yorker* (May 12), http://www.newyorker.com/magazine/2008/05/12/pixel-perfect.

p. 263: "One can infer with greater certainty . . ." from Lichtenberg, *On Physiognomy, against the Physiognomists*, quotation translation from p. 88 in Gray. *About Face*.

p. 263: M. D. Back, J. M. Stopfer, S. Vazire, S. Gaddis, S. C. Schmukle, B. Egloff, and S. D. Gosling (2010). "Facebook profiles reflect actual personality not self-idealization." *Psychological Science* 21, 372–374; S. D. Gosling, S. J. Ko, T. Mannarelli, and M. E. Morris (2002). "A room with a cue: Judgments of personality based on offices and bedrooms." *Journal of Personality and Social Psychology* 82, 379–398; L. P. Naumann, S. Vazire, P. J. Rentfrow, and S. D. Gosling (2009). "Personality judgments based on physical appearance." *Personality and Social Psychology Bulletin* 35, 1661–1671; P. J. Rentfrow and S. D. Gosling (2003). "The do re mi's of everyday life: The structure and personality correlates of music preferences." *Journal of Personality and Social Psychology* 84, 1236–1256; S. Vazire and S. D. Gosling (2004). "e-perceptions: Personality impressions based on personal websites." *Journal of Personality and Social Psychology* 87, 123–132.

EPILOGUE: MORE EVOLUTIONARY STORIES

pp. 264–265: H. Kobayashi and S. Kohshima (1997). "Unique morphology of the human eye." *Nature* 387, 767–768; H. Kobayashi and S. Kohshima (2001). "Unique morphology of the human eye and its adaptive meaning: Comparative studies on external morphology of the primate eye." *Journal of Human Evolution* 40, 419–435; H. Kobayashi and K. Hashiya (2011). "The gaze that grooms: Contribution of social factors to the evolution of primate eye morphology." *Evolution and Human Behavior* 32, 157–165.

p. 266: For the hypothesis that the development of face expertise is driven by newborns' attentiveness to eye gaze, see T. Gliga and G. Csibra (2007). "Seeing the face through the eyes: A developmental perspective on face expertise." *Progress in Brain Research* 164, 323–339.

p. 266: The idea to use the angle of the forehead to classify races was originally proposed by the Dutch scientist, Petrus Camper. See P. Camper (1794). *The Works of the Late Professor Camper, on The Connexion between the Science of Anatomy and The Arts of Drawing, Painting, Statuary.* Translated from the Dutch by T. Cogan. London: Printed for C. Dilly.

p. 266: For types of color vision in mammals, see G. H. Jacobs and J. Nathans (2009). "The evolution of primate color vision." *Scientific American* (April), 56–63.

p. 267: M. A. Changizi, Q. Zhang, and S. Shimojo (2006). "Bare skin, blood, and the evolution of primate colour vision." *Biology Letters* 2, 217–221.

p. 267: For alternative hypotheses, see P. W. Lucas, N. J. Dominy, P. Riba-Hernandez, K. E. Stoner, N. Yamashita et al. (2003). "Evolution and function of routine trichromatic vision in primates." *Evolution* 57, 2636–2643; B. C. Regan, C. Julliot, B. Simmen, F. Vienot, P. Charles-Dominque, and J. D. Mollon (2001). "Fruits, foliage and the evolution of primate colour vision." *Philosophical Transactions of the Royal Society London B* 356, 229–283.

p. 267: E. Herrmann, J. Call, M. V. Hernández-Lloreda, B. Hare, and M. Tomasello (2007). "Humans have evolved specialized skills of social cognition: The cultural intelligence hypothesis." *Science* 317, 1360–1366.

IMAGE CREDITS

Fig. 0.1 Social Perception Lab, Princeton University. Morphs adapted from Capitol Advantage images.

Fig. 0.2 Moffett Studios, Chicago. Portrait of President Warren Harding. Library of Congress, Prints and Photographs Division, Washington, DC.

Figs. 1.1 and 1.2 G. Battista della Porta (1586). *De Humana Physiognomia*. Naples: Apud Iosephum Cacchium. Digitized by Internet Archive from The Getty Research Institute. Courtesy of Hathi Trust.

Fig. 1.3 After Charles Le Brun (1619–1690). "Two lion heads and two related male heads." Etching by André Le Grand (known 1806/1820), 43 × 31.6 cm., INV28153-Bis-recto. Musée du Louvre, Paris, France. © Musée du Louvre, Dist. RMN-Grand Palais/Art Resource, NY.

Fig. 1.4 Charles Le Brun (1619–1690). "Two heads of Antoninus Pius." INV28246-recto-folio16. Photo by M. Urtado. © RMN-Grand Palais/Art Resource, NY.

Fig. 1.5 Charles Le Brun (1619–1690). "Album I: A head of horse and a head of lion." Seventeenth century. © RMN-Grand Palais/Art Resource, NY.

Fig. 1.6 J. C. Lavater (1789). *Essays on Physiognomy: For the Promotion of the Knowledge and the Love of Mankind*, translated by T. Holcraft. London: Printed for G.G.J. and J. Robinson. Rare Book Division, Department of Rare Books and Special Collections, Princeton University Library.

Fig. 1.7 F. Galton (1878). "Composite portraits." *Nature* 17, 97–100.

Fig. 1.8 R. Pumpelly (1885). "Composite Portraits of Members of the National Academy of Sciences." *Science* 5(118).

Fig. 1.9 N. Burson (1982). "Warhead I." Reproduced by permission of Nancy Burson.

Fig. 2.1 Leonardo da Vinci (1452–1519). "Study for five grotesque heads." In C. L. Hind (1907). *Drawings of Leonardo da Vinci*. London: G. Newnes. Photo by C. Braun. Marquand Library of Art and Archaeology, Princeton University, presented by Frank Jewett Mather, Jr.

Fig. 2.2 A. Cozens (1778). *Principles of Beauty*. London: J. Dixwell. British Library, via *Eighteenth Century Collections Online*. Gale. Princeton University Library. 10 Jan. 2017. Arranged by Social Perception Lab, Princeton University.

Figs. 2.3 and 2.4 R. Töpffer (1845). *Essay on Physiognomy*. In M. Giuffredi (2001). Fisiognomica rate e psicologia tea ottocento e novecento. Bologna: CLUEB Cooperativa Libraria Universitaria Editrice Bologna.

Fig. 2.5 Social Perception Lab, Princeton University. Based on figure 1, p. 20 from Samuels, M. R. (1939). "Judgments of faces." *Character & Personality* 8, 18–27.

Figs. 2.6 and 2.7 J. M. Montepare and L. Zebrowitz McArthur (1986). "The influence of facial characteristics on children's age perceptions." *Journal of Experimental Child Psychology* 42, 303–314. Copyright 1986. Reproduced by permission from Elsevier.

Fig. 2.10 S. Jessen and T. Grossmann (2016). "Neural and behavioral evidence for infants' sensitivity to the trustworthiness of faces," *Journal of Cognitive Neuroscience* 28(11), 1728–1736. Copyright © 2016 Massachusetts Institute of Technology. Reproduced by permission of MIT Press.

Fig. 2.11 © François Robert Photography.

Fig. 3.1 K. M. H. Blackford and A. Newcomb (1919). *The Job, The Man, The Boss.* Garden City, NY: Doubleday, Page & Company.

Figs. 3.2 and 3.3 A. C. Little, R. P. Burriss, B. C. Jones, and S. C. Roberts (2007). "Facial appearance affects voting decisions." *Evolution and Human Behavior* 28, 18–27. Copyright 2007. Reproduced by permission of Elsevier.

Fig. 3.5 L. Laustsen and M. B. Petersen (2016). "Winning faces vary by ideology: How nonverbal source cues influence election and communication success in politics." *Political Communication* 33, 188–211. Reproduced by permission of the publisher, Taylor & Francis Ltd, www.tandfonline.com. Adapted from a photograph by Steen Brogaard. Portrait of Ole Haekkerup. Courtesy The Folketing. Reproduced by permission of Ole Haekkerup.

Fig. 3.7 E. A. Hooton (1939). *Crime and the Man.* Cambridge, Mass.: Harvard University Press. Copyright © 1939 by the President and Fellows of Harvard College. Copyright renewed 1967 by Mary C. Hooton. Reproduced by permission of Harvard University Press.

Fig. 3.9 Images from the Basel Face Database, courtesy of M. Walker. M. Walker, S. Schönborn, R. Greifeneder, and T. Vetter (2017). "The Basel Face Database: A validated set of photographs reflecting systematic differences in Big Two and Big Five personality dimensions." Manuscript under review. Based on F. Funk, M. Walker, and A. Todorov (2016). "Modeling perceived criminality and remorse in faces using a data-driven computational approach." *Cognition & Emotion*, http://dx.doi.org/10.1080/02699931.2016.1227305.

Figs. 4.2 and 4.3 Social Perception Lab, Princeton University. Adapted from a portrait of President Richard Nixon. National Archives and Records Administration.

Fig. 4.4 P. Johansson, L. Hall, C. S. Silkstrom and A. Olsson (2005). "Failure to detect mismatches between intention and outcome in a simple decision task." *Science* 310, 116–119. Reproduced by permission of AAAS.

Fig. 4.5 Social Perception Lab, Princeton University. Based on Figure 1, p. 695 from D. Lundqvist , F. Esteves and A. Ohman (1999). "The Face of Wrath: Critical Features for Conveying Facial Threat." *Cognition & Emotion* 13(6), 691–711.

Fig. 4.7 M. C. Mangini and I. Biederman (2004). "Making the ineffable explicit: estimating the information employed for face classification." *Cognitive Science* 28, 209–226. © 2004 Cognitive Science Society, Inc. All rights reserved. Reproduced by permission of John Wiley & Sons, Inc.

Figs. 4.8 and 4.9 B. Rossion, "The composite face illusion: A whole window into our understanding of holistic face perception." *Visual Cognition* 21, 139–253. Copyright © 2013 by Routledge. Reproduced by permission of Taylor and Francis, Inc.

Fig. 4.10 Social Perception Lab, Princeton University. Adapted from images © DFree/Shutterstock.com.

Figs. 4.13 and 4.14 R. Russell (2009). "A sex difference in facial contrast and its exaggeration by cosmetics." *Perception* 38, 1211–1219. Reproduced by permission of Richard Russell.

Fig. 4.15 N. Burson (1996). "He with She. She with He." Reproduced by permission of Nancy Burson.

Fig. 4.16 Social Perception Lab, Princeton University. Adapted from images © CURAphotography/Shutterstock and © Dean Drobot/Shutterstock.

Fig. 4.17 © CURAphotography/Shutterstock.

Fig. 4.18 © United Archives GmbH/Alamy Stock Photo.

Fig. 5.1 D. Y. Teller and J. A. Movshon (1986). "Visual development." *Vision Research* 26(9), 1483–1506. Reproduced by permission from Elsevier (top). Social Perception Lab, Princeton University (bottom).

Fig. 5.2 P. Souza. Official White House portrait of President Barack Obama. www .whitehouse.gov/administration/president-obama (center). Adapted images by Social Perception Lab, Princeton University (left and right).

Fig. 5.3 A. Oliva (2013). "The art of hybrid images: Two for the view of one." *Art & Perception* 1, 65–74. Reproduced by permission of Koninklijke Brill NV. booksandjournals .brillonline.com/content/journals/22134913/1/1-2.

Fig. 5.4 Social Perception Lab, Princeton University. Adapted through tinyeyes.com from an author photo by E. Shur of Mindy Kaling for M. Kaling (2015). *Why Not Me?* New York: Crown Archetype.

Fig. 5.5 Social Perception Lab, Princeton University. Adapted from images © Tinseltown/Shutterstock.com.

Fig. 5.6 J. Sadr and P. Sinha (2004). "Object recognition and Random Image Structure Evolution." *Cognitive Science* 28, 259–287. © 2003 Cognitive Science Society, Inc. All rights reserved. Reproduced by permission of John Wiley & Sons, Inc.

Figs. 5.7 and 5.8 F. Gosselin and P. G. Schyns (2001). "Bubbles: A technique to reveal the use of information in recognition tasks." *Vision Research* 41(17), 2261–2271. © 2001. Reproduced by permission from Elsevier.

Fig. 5.9 M. L. Smith, G. W. Cottrell, F. Gosselin, and P. G. Schyns (2005). "Transmitting and decoding facial expressions." *Psychological Science* 16(3), 184–189. © 2005 by Sage Publications. Reproduced by Permission of SAGE Publications, Inc.

Figs. 5.10 and 5.11 L. L. Kontsevich and C. W. Tyler (2004). "What makes Mona Lisa smile?" *Vision Research* 44(13), 1493–1498, Copyright (2004). Reproduced by permission from Elsevier.

Fig. 5.12 M. S. Livingstone (2001). "Is it warm? Is it real? Or just low spatial frequency?" *Science* 290, 1299. Reproduced with permission from AAAS.

Fig. 5.13 Images courtesy of L. Brinkman and R. Dotsch from the University of Utrecht, the Netherlands.

Fig. 5.14 R. Dotsch and A. Todorov (2012). "Reverse correlating social face perception." *Social Psychological and Personality Science* 3, 562–571. Reproduced by permission from SAGE. Base face is neutral male mean from D. Lundqvist and J. E. Litton (1998). *The Averaged Karolinska Directed Emotional Faces - AKDEF*. CD ROM from Department of Clinical Neuroscience, Psychology section, Karolinska Institutet, ISBN 91-630-7164-9. Reproduced by permission.

Fig. 5.15 R. Dotsch and A. Todorov (2012). "Reverse correlating social face perception." *Social Psychological and Personality Science* 3, 562–571. Reproduced by permission from SAGE. Adapted from neutral male mean image in D. Lundqvist and J. E. Litton (1998).

Figs. 5.16 and 5.17 R. Dotsch, D. H. Wigboldus, O. Langner, and A. van Knippenberg (2008). "Ethnic out-group faces are biased in the prejudiced mind." *Psychological Science* 19, 978–980. Reproduced by permission of SAGE Publications, Inc.

Figs. 5.18–5.20 R. Dotsch and A. Todorov (2012). "Reverse correlating social face perception." *Social Psychological and Personality Science* 3, 562–571. Reproduced by permission from SAGE.

Figs. 6.3 and 6.14 Social Perception Lab, Princeton University. Adapted from D. Lundqvist, A., Flykt, and A. Öhman (1998). *The Karolinska Directed Emotional Faces - KDEF.* CD ROM from Department of Clinical Neuroscience, Psychology section, Karolinska Institutet, ISBN 91-630-7164-9. Reproduced by permission.

Figs. 6.19–6.21 Social Perception Lab, Princeton University. Adapted from C. A. M. Sutherland, J. A. Oldmeadow, I. M. Santos, J. Towler, D. M. Burt, and A. W. Young (2013). "Social inferences from faces: Ambient images generate a three-dimensional model." *Cognition* 127, 105–118. Copyright © 2012 by Elsevier B. V. All rights reserved. Reproduced by permission.

Fig. 7.4 Social Perception Lab, Princeton University. Adapted from base images provided by Carmel Sofer. Based on C. Sofer, R. Dotsch, M. Oikawa, H. Oikawa, D. H. J. Wigboldus, and A. Todorov (In press). "For your local eyes only: Culture-specific face typicality influences perceptions of trustworthiness." *Perception.*

Fig. 7.9 Photos © Alex Kayser, from the book *Heads by Alex Kayser*, Abbeville Press, 1985, permission for republication in Face Value: The Irresistible Influence of First Impressions granted by the Estate of Alex Kayser, Switzerland.

Fig. 7.10 Base photos © Alex Kayser, from the book *Heads by Alex Kayser*, Abbeville Press, 1985, permission for republication in Face Value: The Irresistible Influence of First Impressions granted by the Estate of Alex Kayser, Switzerland. Adapted in S. C. Verosky and A. Todorov (2010). "Generalization of affective learning about faces to perceptually similar faces." Psychological Science 21, 779–785. Reproduced by permission of Alexander Todorov.

Fig. 7.11 R. J. Tanner and A. Maeng (2012). "A Tiger and a President: Imperceptible Celebrity Facial Cues Influence Trust and Preference." *Journal of Consumer Research* 39(4), 769–783. Reproduced by permission of Oxford University Press.

Fig. 7.12 C. Payne and K. Jaffe (2005). "Self seeks like: Many humans choose their dog-pets following rules used for assortative mating." *Journal of Ethology* 23 (1), 15–18. Copyright © 2005 C. Payne, K. Jaffe. Reproduced by permission.

Fig. 8.1 C. Lombroso (1876). Drawings from Editors' introduction. In C. Lombroso (2006). *Criminal Man*, translated by M. Gibson and N. H. Rafter. Durham and London: Duke University Press.

Fig. 8.2 C. Goring (1972). *The English Convict: A Statistical Study.* Montclair, NJ: Patterson Smith.

Fig. 8.6 Images from the Basel Face Database, courtesy of M. Walker. M. Walker, S. Schönborn, R. Greifeneder, and T. Vetter (2017). "The Basel Face Database: A validated set of photographs reflecting systematic differences in Big Two and Big Five personality dimensions." Manuscript under review. Based on M. Walker and T. Vetter (2016). "Changing the personality of a face: Perceived Big Two and Big Five personality factors modeled in real photographs." *Journal of Personality and Social Psychology*, 110(4), 609–624. doi:http://dx.doi.org/10.1037/pspp0000064.

Fig. 8.7 K. Robinson, C. Blais, J. Duncan, H. Forget and D. Fiset (2014). "The dual nature of the human face: there is a little Jekyll and a little Hyde in all of us." *Frontiers in Psychology* 5, 139. doi:10.3389/fpsyg.2014.00139. Photos licensed under the Creative Commons Attribution 4.0 license (CC BY 4.0). creativecommons.org/licenses/by/4.0/.

Fig. 8.8 K. Robinson, C. Blais, J. Duncan, H. Forget and D. Fiset (2014). "The dual nature of the human face: there is a little Jekyll and a little Hyde in all of us." *Frontiers in Psychology* 5, 139. doi:10.3389/fpsyg.2014.00139. Adapted photos licensed under the Creative Commons Attribution 4.0 license (CC BY 4.0) creativecommons.org/licenses/by/4.0/. Original photo by P. Souza (2008). Official White House portrait of President Barack Obama.

Fig. 8.9 R. Jenkins, D. White, X. Van Montfort and A. M. Burton (2011). "Variability in photos of the same face," *Cognition* 121, 313–323. Copyright © 2011 by Elsevier B. V. All rights reserved. Reproduced by permission of Elsevier.

Fig. 8.10 National Institute of Standards and Technology. Reproduced by permission of NIST. In A. Todorov and J. Porter (2014). "Misleading first impressions: Different for different images of the same person." *Psychological Science* 25, 1404–1417.

Fig. 8.11 Courtesy Pima County Sheriff's Office.

Fig. 8.12 Courtesy Arizona Daily Star.

Fig. 8.13 Photos © Alex Kayser, from the book *Heads by Alex Kayser*, Abbeville Press, 1985, permission for republication in Face Value: The Irresistible Influence of First Impressions granted by the Estate of Alex Kayser, Switzerland.

Fig. 8.14 Social Perception Lab, Princeton University. Adapted from D. Lundqvist, A., Flykt, and A. Öhman (1998). *The Karolinska Directed Emotional Faces - KDEF*. CD ROM from Department of Clinical Neuroscience, Psychology section, Karolinska Institutet, ISBN 91-630-7164-9. Reproduced by permission.

Fig. 9.3 J. M. Carré, C. M. McCormick, and C. J. Mondloch, (2009). "Facial structure is a reliable cue of aggressive behavior." *Psychological Science* 20, 1194–1198. © 2009 by Psychological Science. Reproduced by permission of SAGE Publications, Inc.

Fig. 10.4 J. B. Swaddle and G. W. Reiserson (2002). "Testosterone increases perceived dominance but not attractiveness in human makes." *Proceedings of the Royal Society B* 269 (1507), 2285–2289. Copyright © 2002 by The Royal Society. Reproduced by permission.

Figs. 10.5–10.8 Social Perception Lab, Princeton University. Adapted from I. J. Holzleitner (2015). "Linking 3D face shape to social perception." Doctoral dissertation. University of St Andrews, Scotland. Copyright © 2015. Reproduced by permission.

Fig. 10.9 K. M. H. Blackford and A. Newcomb (1916). *Analyzing Character: The New Science of Judging Men, Misfits in Business, the Home, and Social Life*. New York: The Review of Reviews Company. Digitized by Google from Harvard University. Courtesy of Hathi Trust.

Figs. 11.1 and 11.2 J. Parsons, (1746). "Human Physiognomy Explain'd: in the Crounian Lectures on Muscular Motion." Read before the Royal Society, being a Supplement to the Philosophical Transactions for that year. London: Printed for C. Davis. Yale Historical Medical Libray.

Fig. 11.3 C. Z. Malatesta, M. J. Fiore, and J. J. Messina (1987). "Affect, personality, and facial expressive characteristics of older people." *Psychology and Aging* 2, 64–69. Reproduced by permission of Carol Z. Malatesta.

Fig. 11.04 J. Axelsson, T. Sundelin, M. Ingre, E. J. W. Van Someren, A. Olsson, and M. Lekander (2010). "Beauty sleep: experimental study on the perceived health and attractiveness of sleep deprived people." *British Medical Journal* 341, c6614. Copyright © 2010 by British Medical Journal Publishing Group. Reproduced by permission.

Fig. 11.5 Xue Lei, The Perception Lab, University of St Andrews. Reproduced by permission.

Fig. 11.6 Wystan H. Auden (1985). "Smokers' faces: who are the smokers?" In D. Model (1985). "Smoker's face: an underrated clinical sign?" *British Medical Journal* 291, 1760–1762. Copyright © 1985 by BMJ Publishing Group Ltd. Reproduced by permission from BMJ Publishing Group. Ltd.

Fig. 11.7 B. P. Tiddeman, D. M. Burt, and D. I. Perrett, "Phototyping and transforming facial textures for perception research." *IEEE Computer Graphics and Applications* 21, 42–50. Copyright © 2001 by IEEE. Reproduced by permission.

Fig. 11.8 K. Christensen, et al. (2009). Composite of photos from The Longitudinal Study of Aging Danish Twins (LSADT). In "Perceived age as clinically useful biomarker of ageing: cohort study." *British Medical Journal* 339, b5262. Copyright © 2009 by Unilever R&D. Reproduced by permission of Unilever R&D.

Fig. 12.1 Social Perception Lab, Princeton University. Adapted through tinyeyes.com from an author photo by E. Shur of Mindy Kaling for M. Kaling (2015). *Why Not Me?* New York: Crown Archetype.

Fig. 12.2 Social Perception Lab, Princeton University. Based on Figure 1, p. 545 from C. C. Goren, M. Sarty and P. J. K. Wu (1975). "Visual following and pattern discrimination of face-like stimuli by newborn infants." *Pediatrics* 56, 544–549. Reproduced by permission.

Fig. 12.6 Social Perception Lab, Princeton University. Negative image adapted from a photo of President Lyndon Johnson from the White House, courtesy of the Library of Congress. Based on Figure 3a, page 5356 from S. Gilad, M. Meng, and P. Sinha (2009). "Role of ordinal contrast relationships in face encoding." *Proceedings of the National Academy of Sciences of the USA* 106, 5353–5358.

Fig. 12.7 Social Perception Lab, Princeton University. Contrast chimera image adapted from a photo of President Lyndon Johnson from the White House, courtesy of the Library of Congress. Based on Figure 3a, page 5356 from S. Gilad, M. Meng, and P. Sinha (2009). "Role of ordinal contrast relationships in face encoding." *Proceedings of the National Academy of Sciences of the USA* 106, 5353–5358.

Fig. 12.8 S. Gilad, M. Meng, and P. Sinha (2009). "Role of ordinal contrast relationships in face encoding." *Proceedings of the National Academy of Sciences of the USA* 106, 5353–5358. Reproduced by permission of PNAS and P. Sinha.

Fig. 12.9 B. M. 't Hart, T. G. J. Abresch and W. Einhäuser (2011). "Faces in places: Humans and machines make similar face detection errors." *PLoS ONE* 6(10), e25373. doi:10.1371/journal.pone.0025373 © 2011 't Hart et al. Used and available under the Creative Commons Attribution 4.0 International license (http://creativecommons.org/licenses/by/4.0/).

Fig. 13.1 C. G. Gross, C. E. Rocha-Miranda, and D. B. Bender (1972). "Visual properties of neurons in inferotemporal cortex of the macaque." *Journal of Neurophysiology* 35, 96–111. © The American Physiological Society (APS). All rights reserved. Reproduced by permission.

Fig. 13.2 R. Desimone, T. D. Albright, C. G. Gross, and C. Bruce (1984). "Stimulus-selective properties of inferior temporal neurons in the macaque." *Journal of Neuroscience* 4(8), 2051–2062.

Fig. 13.3 S. R. Afraz, R. Kiani, and H. Esteky, "Microstimulation of inferotemporal cortex influences face categorization." *Nature* 442, 692–695. Copyright © 2006 by Nature Publishing Group. Reproduced by permission.

Fig. 14.1 Franz Xaver Messerschmidt (ca. 1771–1783). *Character Head No. 30.* Pl.O.2539. Germanisches NationalMuseum, Nürnberg. Reproduced with permission.

Fig. 14.2 D. Matsumoto and P. Ekman (1988). "Japanese and Caucasian facial expressions of emotion (JACFEE)." Unpublished slide set and brochure, Department of Psychology, San Francisco State University. In J. M. Carroll and J. A. Russell (1996). "Do facial expressions signal specific emotions? Judging emotion from the face in context." *Journal of Personality and Social Psychology* 70, 205–218. Reproduced by permission of Humintell.

Figs. 14.3 and 14.4 H. Aviezer, R. Hassin, J. Ryan, C. Grady, J. Susskind, A. Anderson, M. Moscovitch and S. Bentin (2008). "Angry, disgusted or afraid? Studies on the malleability of emotion perception." *Psychological Science* 19, 724–732. Reproduced by permission of Hillel Aviezer and the Paul Ekman Group.

Fig. 14.5 R. Töpffer (1845). Essay on Physiognomy. In M. Giuffredi (2001). *Fisiognomica rate e psicologia tea ottocento e novecento.* Bologna: CLUEB Cooperativa Libraria Universitaria Editrice Bologna.

Fig. 14.6 © REUTERS/Alamy Stock Photo; © REUTERS/Francisco Seco; © REUTERS/Alamy Stock Photo; © REUTERS/Alamy Stock Photo; © REUTERS/Alamy Stock Photo; © REUTERS/Mike Segar (left to right from top). Adapted in H. Aviezer, Y. Trope, and A. Todorov (2012). "Body cues, not facial expressions, discriminate between intense positive and negative emotions." *Science* 338, 1225–1229. Reproduced by permission of AAAS.

Fig. 14.7 © REUTERS/Alamy Stock Photo; © REUTERS/Alamy Stock Photo; © REUTERS/Francisco Seco; © REUTERS/Alamy Stock Photo (left to right from top). Adapted in H. Aviezer, Y. Trope, and A. Todorov (2012). "Body cues, not facial expressions, discriminate between intense positive and negative emotions." *Science* 338, 1225–1229. Reproduced by permission of AAAS.

Fig. 14.8 Social Perception Lab, Princeton University. Adapted from E. Draper. Official White House portrait of President George W. Bush (left). Adapted from portrait of Secretary of State Hillary Rodham Clinton. U.S. Department of State (right).

Fig. 14.9 Social Perception Lab, Princeton University. Adapted from Michael Vadon. Photograph of Donald Trump. www.flickr.com/photos/80038275@N00/20724666936. Photo licensed under the Creative Commons Attribution Share-Alike 2.0 Generic license (CC BY-SA 2.0). creativecommons.org/licenses/by-sa/2.0/ (left). Adapted from Official Senate portrait of Bernie Sanders. United States Senate Historical Archives (right).

Fig. 14.10 Hanoch Piven. Reproduced by permission.

Figs. 14.11–14.13 A. Rice, P. J. Phillips, V. Natu, X An, and A. J. O'Toole (2013). "Unaware person recognition from the body when face identification fails," *Psychological Science* 24, 2235–2243. Copyright © 2013 by Association for Psychological Science. Reprinted by permission of SAGE Publications, Inc.

Fig. 14.14 FBI, U.S. Department of Justice (left). Courtesy of the Tripathi family (right).

Fig. 14.15 R. Jenkins, D. White, X. Van Montfort and A. M. Burton (2011). "Variability in Photos of the same face," *Cognition* 121, 313–323. Copyright © 2011 by Elsevier B. V. All rights reserved. Reproduced by permission of Elsevier.

Fig. 14.16 (Top row, left to right) © Denis Makarenko/Shutterstock.com; © Featureflash

Photo Agency/Shutterstock.com; © Everett Collection/Shutterstock.com; © Helga Esteb/Shutterstock.com; © Helga Esteb/Shutterstock.com; © Featureflash Photo Agency/Shutterstock.com; © Tinseltown/Shutterstock.com; © Everett Collection/Shutterstock.com; © Featureflash Photo Agency/Shutterstock.com; © Joe Seer/Shutterstock.com; (bottom row, left to right) © Tinseltown/Shutterstock.com; © Featureflash Photo Agency/Shutterstock.com; © Tinseltown/Shutterstock.com; © Featureflash Photo Agency/Shutterstock.com; © Featureflash Photo Agency/Shutterstock.com; © s_bukley/Shutterstock.com; © Featureflash Photo Agency/Shutterstock.com; © s_bukley/Shutterstock.com; © Featureflash Photo Agency/Shutterstock.com; © Featureflash Photo Agency/Shutterstock.com.

Fig. 14.17 A. Versluis and E. Uyttenbroek (2011). *Exactitudes*. Rotterdam, the Netherlands: 010 Publishers. Image 102. Reproduced with permission of EXACTITUDES.

Fig. E.1 H. Kobayashi and K. Hashiya (2011). "The gaze that grooms: Contribution of social factors to the evolution of primate eye morphology." *Evolution and Human Behavior* 32, 157–165. Copyright © 2011 Elsevier Inc. All rights reserved. Adapted with permission of Elsevier.

Fig. E.2 H. Kobayashi and S. Kohshima (2001). "Unique morphology of the human eye and its adaptive meaning: Comparative studies on external morphology of the primate eye." *Journal of Human Evolution* 40, 419–435. Copyright © 2001 Elsevier Inc. All rights reserved. Reproduced by permission of Elsevier.

INDEX

Note: Illustrations are indicated with *italic* page numbers.

babies (*cont.*)

22; synchronization of expression with care-givers, 232; and trustworthiness, impressions of, 44–46; visual acuity of, 93–94, 96, 221

"babyfaced" appearance, 75; characteristics associated with, 38–41, 120, 181; and legal decisions, 68–69; and submissive appearance, 120

badness/goodness, impressions of, 114–15, 122–24, 144, 214

Ballew, Chas, 57

Banaji, Mahzarin, 43

Bar, Moshe, 43

baseball, 50–51, 183–84

basketball, 74–75

Beane, Billy, 51, 183–84

beauty: composites and, 23; Cozens' "simple *vs.* complex," 33–34, 90–91; digital retouching and, 153; Galton's "beauty maps," 21–22; gender and beauty standards, 189–92; and innocence, 69; racism and beauty standards, 9

behavioral psychology, 31

Beyoncé, 84

biases: attentional bias to faces, 44–47, 220–27, 231–32; idiosyncratic experience and, 5, 134–39, 143–44; image-selection bias, 156–60; projected knowledge and, 17–18, 24, 161–64, 204; self-fulfilling prophecies, 194–95

Bieber, Justin, 84

Biederman, Irving, 104

biometrics, 178–79; applied to real faces, 154; body-mass index (BMI), 197–98, 210; cephalic index, 200; development of, 111–14; eye measures, 246–66; physiognomy and, 9–10, 20, 64–65, 178–79. *See also* facial width-to-height ratio (fWHR)

Blackford, Katherine, 39–40, 48–50, 182, 185–86, 200

Blanchett, Cate, 89, *90*

"Blank No. 3" character analysis form, *49*

Bodamer, Joachim, 233

bodies, gestures as contextual prompt, 249–51

brain: amygdala and face processing, 241–43; face-selective neurons in, 236–39, 244; fMRI (functional magnetic resonance imaging), 239–43; hand-sensitive neurons in, 235–36; hippocampus, 239, 243; "network" for face processing, 6, 214–15, 241–44; prosopagnosia and brain injury, 233–34, 240–41; split-brain patients, 78–79

Brooks, David, 166

Brunswick, Egon, 36–37, 80

"bubbles" technique, 99–101, 154–55

Burson, Nancy, 25, 88

Burton, Mike, 157, 260

Bush, George W., 58–60, *59, 254*

Campbell, Donald, 21

caricatures, 20, 23, 73, 150

Carré, Justin, 179

cats, 234–35

celebrities: recognizing facial composites of, 84

cephalic index, 200

character: agreement on impressions of, 31–32; clothing and environment as expression of, 261–63; employment and "scientific character analysis," 48–51; faces as weak information source, 214, 245; and "face traces" of habitual emotional expressions, 205–7, 214; facial cues and, 144; "honest signals" and, 187; image-based impressions of, 30–31; physiognomy and character evaluation, 3, 10, 19–20, 22–27, 30, 48; prediction of, 178; and resemblance to animals, 10–15; scientific analysis of, 185

"Character Heads" (Messerschmidt), 246–47

cheating, 173–78, 180

cheeks or cheekbones, 130, 210, 227–28. *See also* facial width-to-height ratio (fWHR)

Cheries, Erik, 45

children: cheating behavior among, 177–78; elections predicted by, 53; facial stereotypes and impressions formed by, 1–2; physiognomy and judgments about intelligence of, 159–60; social communication and, 267. *See also* babies

Christie, Chris, *255–56, 260*

Clark, Vance, 148

Clinton, Hillary, *254*

cognitive psychology, 31

Cogsdill, Emily, 43

Colbert, Stephen, 168

color, facial hues, 191, 209–10, 266–67

color, trichromatic vision and perception of, 266–67

competence, impressions of, 69; accuracy of, 166, 168; appearance effect and, 56; and attractiveness, 126–27; children and, 1–2, 43–46; and economic decisions, 61–64; situation or context and, 58–59, 69; and voter choice, 42, 56–58

composite face illusion, *83*, 83–86, *84*

consensus. *See* agreement on impressions

contextual prompts: bodily gestures as, 249–54; clothing as, 261–63; cross-cultural effect, 135,

139; culture, as context for impressions, 133–34, 142–43, 192–94; and illusory face signals, 246–48

contrast polarity, facial recognition and, 227–30, 237

Cook, Stuart, 30–31

Cozens, Alexander, 33–34, 36, 90–91; drawing by, *34*

Crime and the Man (Hooton), 65–66

criminal anthropology, 3, 22, 149

The Criminal (Ellis), 148–49

criminality: composite images and, 149–50; death sentences and appearance of prisoner, 68–69; distinctive faces and perception of, 148; "face-to-crime fit" effect, 67–69; image selection and, 159; and image-selection bias, 159–62; impressions of, 64–69; and perception of prestige or status, 29; physiognomy and identification of, 3–4, 22–23; untrustworthiness and dominance and impressions of, 67, 123–24

Criminal Man (Lombroso), 147–48

cross-cultural effect, 135, 139

cues, facial: babies and discrimination among, 46; as constituents of impressions, 127–30, 133–34; cultural context and meaning of, 142–43, 192; idiosyncratic experience and meaning of, 133–35, 143; and models of impressions, 116–17, 127, 133–34; and shared stereotypes, 30–31, 144–45

culture, as context for impressions, 133–34; cross-cultural effect, 135, 139; gender perception and, 143; and meaning of facial cues, 142–43, 192; sensitivity to facial masculinity, 192–94

Curry, Stephen, 75

Dalgas, Olaf, 1–2, 53

Dangin, Pascal, 153, 263

Darwin, Charles, 3, 23, 29–30, 148, 206, 214, 248

Da Vinci, Leonardo, 32–33, 141–42; drawing by, *32*; and emotional expression in *Mona Lisa*, 101–3

Deaner, Bob, 179–80, 188

decision processes: elections and political (*See* politics); impressions prioritized over knowledge during, 173; optimal, 172–73. *See also* economic decisions

DeGeneres, Ellen, *97*

Della Porta, Giovannie Battista, 11, 15; illustrations by, *11, 12*

Descartes, René, 75

Desimone, Bob, 239

Diamond, Jared, 135

DiCaprio, Leonardo, 260

diet, facial hues and, 209–10

disgust, expressions of, 100, 166, 249

dogs, resemblance to owners, 142

Dole, Bob, 58

dominance, impressions of, 60–61, 69, 108–10; facial masculinity and, 143, 187; gender and, 60–61, 120–22, 128; manipulation of facial features and, 61; and physical strength, 122; power evaluation and, 114; trustworthiness and impressions of, 67, 123–24, 128–30; war, preference for dominant faces during, 58–61

Dotsch, Ron, 105–8, 135–39

Du Cane, Edmund, 22–23

Duchenne de Boulogne, G.-B., 205, 206

economic decisions: face similarity and, 141–42; games and, 173–77; hiring decisions, 48–51, 182–83; impressions and, 61–64, 125–26; legal decisions and, 64–69; trustworthiness and, 173–76

economic games, 173–77

Einstein, Albert, 95

Ekman, Paul, 205

election prediction, 1–3, 42, 51–58, 168

"elementalizing" approach, 91–92, 130

Ellis, Havelock, 69, 148–49

Emerson, Harrington, 50

emotional overgeneralization hypothesis, 164–65

emotions, expression of: ambiguous facial expressions and, 101–3, 248–54; bodily gestures and identification of, 251–54; cultural contexts and, 142–43; emotion overgeneralization hypothesis, 164–65; eyes or eyebrows and, 75–77; facial features and identification of, 100; facial muscles and, 164–65, 203–7, *204*; habitual, 205–7; incongruent facial features and, 80–82; as involuntary, 248; neutral or resting faces and, 165–66, 203–7; permanent traces of, 203–7, 214; and social communication by babies, 230–31; and transient facial signals, 203; as universal, 248

employment: gender bias and, 183; "scientific character analysis" and, 48–51

The English Convict (Goring), 149–50

Essays on Physiognomy (Lavater), 16–17, 26, 203–4, 261; illustration from, *17*

impressions of, 126–27; cultural variations in impressions of, 143; and dominance, impressions of, 60–61, 120–22, 128; facial features and identification of, 98–99; f WHR as measure of sexual dimorphism, 188–89; gender illusion, 87, 104, 121; happy expressions and impressions of, 128; inference of sexual orientation, 159; male bias and impressions of, 126–27; manipulation of facial features and impressions of, 86–89; reflectance (skin surface and texture) and impressions of, 86–87, 118; stereotypes of, 181; and trustworthiness, impressions of, 118–19, 128–30; visual noise and impressions of, 104

generalization. *See* overgeneralization

Gingrich, Newt, 58

Goethe, Johann Wolfgang von, 16, 18–19, 261, 263

Gombrich, Ernst, 31

goodness/badness, impressions of, 114–15, 122–24, 144, 214

Goren, Carolyn, 222–23

Goring, Charles, 148–49

Göring, Hermann, 26

Gosling, Sam, 262

Gosselin, Frederic, 99–101

Gould, Steven Jay, 40

Grill-Spector, Kalanit, 243

Grose, Francis, 34, 39

Gross, Charlie, 235–38

Grossmann, Tobias, 44–45

Günther, H.F.K., 26

Haig, Nigel, 97–98

hair: as external feature, 244, 256–57; face-selective neurons and, 244; faces of bald individuals, 163–64; facial hair and reflectance, 121; and perceived ethnicity, 88, 88–89; and perceived gender, 100

happiness, expressions of: dominance and perceived gender linked to, 128; mouth as cue, 37, 100–103; trustworthiness and, 116–17, 128

Harding, Warren, 4

Hartshorne, Hugh, 177–78

Hassin, Ran, 135–38

Heads (Kayser), *140, 163,* 163–64

health: age as indicator of, 211–12; "face traces" and, 214; facial hue as indicator of, 191, 209–10; facial masculinity and genetic health (immunocompetence), 189–90; "smoker's face," 211

"He with She" (photograph, Burson), 88

hippocampus, 239, 243

Hitler, Adolph, 26

hockey, 179–80

holistic nature of face perception, 82–83, 85, 130, 196, 237

Holland, Agnieszka, 9

Holzleitner, Iris, 197–99

honest signals, 184, 187, 189–90, 194, 201

Hooton, Earnest, 64–66

Hubel, David, 234–35, 239

Hull, Clark, 30, 39

Human Physiognomy Explain'd (lecture, Parsons), 203–7; illustration from, *204, 206*

ideology: appearance effect and, 60–61; impressions of political affiliation, 172–73

illusory face signals: emotional expressions and, 248–50; susceptibility to projected knowledge, 246–48

image-based impressions, 30–31, 156–60, 167

immunocompetence theory, 189–90

I'm Not There (film), 89, *90*

impressions, formation of first: accuracy of (*See* accuracy of impressions); and atypical faces, 131–33; as automatic and unconscious process, 6, 42, 57–58, 77, 136, 226–27, 230, 244–45; combinations of facial features and, 73–75, 124–25; consensus and, 30–31, *41,* 42; context and, 181, 184; decisions influenced by (*See* decision processes); experience and, 131–39, 201; function of, 144; generalization and, 140; as "intuitive," 31–32; "objective," 142–43; prioritized over other information, 182, 183–84; resemblance and, 133, 139; "rules" of, 5; time required to form, 3, 10, 42–43, 57–58, 77, 226–28, 254

infants. *See* babies

insanity, physiognomy and, 63–64

Integrative Activity of the Brain (Konorski), 236

intelligence, 36–37, 159–60, 166; cephalic index and, 200–201; physiognomy and evaluation of, 17, 24; shared stereotype of, 30–31; sleep deprivation and perceived, 166, 208; social, 167, 201; trustworthiness and, 114

interview illusion, 182

introversion/extroversion, 41–42, 56–57, 154

intuition, 36; faultiness of, 74–79, 91

"intuitive" impressions, 31–32

Jenkins, Rob, 157

Jessen, Sarah, 44–45

Johnson, Lyndon B., 227–28
Johnson, Mark, 220, 223–24
Jones, M. J., 228–29

Kahneman, Daniel, 57
Kantsaywhere (Galton), 22, 66
Kanwisher, Nancy, 240
Kayser, Alex, 163–64; photos by, *140, 163*
Keller, Bill, 161
Kerry, John, 58–60, *59*
Kibby, William, 50
knowledge, 214; impressions prioritized over
    other, 173, 182, 183–84; low-information vot-
    ers and election prediction, 54; projected, 17–
    18, 24, 161–64, 204; self-fulfilling prophecies,
    194–95. *See also* experience
Kobayashi, Hiromi, 264
Kohshima, Shiro, 264
Konorski, Jerzy, 236, 243
Kontsevich, Leonid, 101–4

Laird, Donald, 50
Landis, Carney, 159–60, 182
LaPiere, Richard, 176–77
Laustsen, Lasse, 60–61
Lavater, Johann Kaspar: critiques of physiognomy
    as practiced by, 5, 18–19, 26–27, 29–30, 91–
    92, 168–69; illustration by, *17*; physiognomy
    as popularized by, 3, 15–18, 20, 24, 162, 203,
    204
Lawson, Chapel, 53–55, 166
Le Brun, Charles, 12–14, 75, 248; illustrations by,
    13, 14
Leibovitz, Annie, 153
Lelkes, Anna, 183
Lenz, Gabriel, 53–55, 166
Lewis, Michael, 51, 183
Lichtenberg, Georg Chistoph: critiques of La-
    vater's physiognomy, 5, 18–19, 26–27, 139,
    168–69, 178; on faces as entertaining, 73; on
    face traces, 204–5, 214; on overgeneralization,
    133, 164–65, 181–82, 184
Lincoln, Abraham, 55–56
literature, physiognomy and, 19–20
Little, Anthony, 58
Livingstone, Margaret, 242–43, 242–44
Lombroso, Cesare, 3, 22, 27, 147–49
Loughner, Jared Lee, 160–62
L'Uomo Delinquente (Lombroso), 147–48
Lyons, Ashley, 45

Madoff, Bernie, 173–74
makeup, 87
Mangini, Michael, 104
manipulation of facial features, 77; artists and ex-
    perimentation with, 32–36; in combination,
    73–75, 79–86, 91, 130; and effect on impres-
    sions, 32, 36–41, 77; and impressions of eth-
    nicity, 88–89, 105–7; and perceived criminal-
    ity, 67–68; and perceived dominance, 61; and
    perceived gender, 86–89; visual noise and, 98–
    99. *See also* morphing/facial morphs
Mantegazza, Paolo, 15, 206
Martin, D. S., 56
Marx, Karl, 255–56, 260
masculinity, facial: and dominance, 143, 187; fe-
    male preference for, 189–92; and fWHR, 187–
    88, 194–201; and genetic health (immuno-
    competence), 189–90; linked to threat, 123,
    187; and perceived threat, 123, 187; reflec-
    tance (skin surface and texture) and, 190–91;
    testosterone, 196
masculinity/femininity, 130
mathematical measures. *See* biometrics
May, Mark, 177–78
McCall, Bruce, 179–80
McCormick, Cheryl, 179
McDonald, S. M., 68–69
Mendelssohn, Moses, 91, 130
Merton, Holmes, 50
Messerschmidt, Franz Xaver, 246–47
Mickey Mouse, 40
models of impressions, building: agreement (con-
    sensus) and, 42, 134; atypical faces, 131–33;
    computer-generated, 42, 86, 127, 129, 131–33;
    emotion and, 116–17; and gender bias, 126–
    27; and identification of meaningful facial
    cues, 116, 127, 133–34, 143; and manipulation
    of real faces, 67–68; morphing and, 26,
    128–29
Mona Lisa (Da Vinci), 101–3
Moneyball (Lewis), 51
monkeys, 231, 234–35, 237–38, 242–43, 244, 266–
    67; face-deprivation studies, 231
Monroe, Marilyn, *95*
Morgan, J. P., 61
morphing/facial morphs, 3–4, 26; atypical faces
    and, 131–33; and composite photography,
    3–4, 25; composite photography and, 127–28;
    gender and, 88, 104; as "pictorial averages,"
    127–28

mortality, facial predictors of, 212–13

mouths: as cue when perceiving emotional expressions, 82, 100–103; eyebrow/mouth combinations and impressions, 80–82; height of placement, 36–37; physiognomy and analysis of, 17–18

muscles, facial: emotional expressions and, 164–65, 203–7, *204*; Facial Action Coding System (FACS) and emotions, 205

Nagel, Thomas, 93

"neutral" expressions, 165–66, 203–7

Newcomb, Arthur, 39, 48–50, 182, 185–86, 200

Nisbett, Richard, 77–78, 182

Nixon, Richard, *76*, 77

noise masks, 98–110

noses, 20, 185–86

Obama, Barack, *95*, 155–56

Olivola, Chris, 62–63, 171–73

Oosterhof, Nick, 42, 117–18

optimal decision making, 172–73

Orioli, Giulia, 219–20

O'Toole, Alice, 256–58

overgeneralization, 39, 181, 208; emotion overgeneralization hypothesis, 164–65; situation or context and risk of, 178

Parsons, James, 203–7, 214

Parvizi, Josef, 243

Pellicer, Raynal, 159

Penton-Voak, Ian S., 192

perceptual masking, 42–43

perceptual narrowing, 230–31

Perrett, David, 197, 236

personality: agreement on impressions of, 31; attributed to inanimate objects, 46–47; expressed through environment, 263. *See also* character

Petersen, Michael, 60–61

Petkova, Kristina, 53

Phelps, L. W., 159–60, 182

photography: accuracy of photographs, 151–52; composite, 3–4, 20–25, 64, 150 (*See also* morphing/ facial morphs); digital retouching, 153; image-selection bias, 156–62; negatives and facial recognition, 227–28; pictures on loan applications, 63–64

phrenology, 20, 26, 30, 34

physiognomy, 3–5, 144; accuracy of, 91, 168–69; comparative (resemblance between humans and animals), 11–15; and identification of criminality, 3–4, 22–23, 64–65; mathematical measurement and, 9–10, 20, 64–65, 178–79; in popular culture, 4–5, 19–20, 30; profile analysis and, 16–17, 39, 148–49; psychology and, 10, 30; racism and, 9–11, 17–19; social contexts for appeal of, 201–2

physiologie, 20

Physionomica, 10–11, 203

The Picture of Dorian Gray (Wilde), 213–14

Pitt, Brad, 260

Piven, Hanoch: illustrations by, *255*, *256*

politics: appearance effect and elections, 51–61; candidate photos on ballots, 54–55; election prediction, 1–3, 42, 51–58, 168; ideology and voter preferences, 60–61; image-induced bias and, 158; impressions and evaluation of politicians, 4, 51–53; impressions of political affiliation, 172–73; voters and impressions of competence, 4, 55–57, 61–62, 168; war and voter preferences, 60–61

power, impressions of, 114–15. *See also* dominance, impressions of

primates: development of visual cortex in, 233, 244; eye morphology in, 264–66; face detection as innate in, 230–31; trichromatic vision (color vision) and, 266–67

Principles of Beauty, Relative to the Human Head (Cozens), 33–34

profiles, facial, 39, 73, 90; age and shape of, 38–39; combination of facial features and, 33, 90–91; concave and convex, 38–39, 65; neurons and processing of, 237; physiognomy and analysis of, 16–17, 39, 148–49

projected knowledge, 17–18, 24, 161–64, 204; susceptibility to labels, 246–48

prosopagnosia, 233–34

Prosper (peer-to-peer lending site), 63–64

pychophysics, 97

race: and agreement on impressions, 143; facial features and perception of, 106–7; hair and perception of, 88–89; infants and perception of, 230–31

racism, 9–11, 106–7, 176–77; physiognomy and, 9–11, 17–19; racist assumptions applied to character analysis, 186. *See also* eugenics

Sugita, Yoichi, 231
"superstitious perception," 105–7
surprise, expressions of, 100
Sussman, Abby, 53
symmetry, 224

Teller, Davida, 93–94, 96
Terman, Lewis, 21
Teuber, Hans-Lukas, 235
Thinking, Fast and Slow (Kahneman), 57
threat, perceived, 114, 122–24; angry expressions
    and, 166; fWHR and perception of, 187–88,
    192–96; gender, masculine faces and, 123, 187;
    racial or ethnic prejudice and perceived, 200–
    201; and untrustworthiness, 109–11
time required to form impressions, 42–43, 57–58,
    77, 226–28, 254
"Token Quest" (game), 63
Töpffer, Rodolphe, 34–36, 73, 85, 130, 166, 183;
    drawings by, *35, 36*
Toscano, Hugo, 122
Tripathi, Sunil, 258
Trump, Donald, *255*
trustworthiness, impressions of, 43–46, 80–82,
    105, 107–9, 110; amygdala and, 242; babies
    and, 44–46; children and, 63; and criminal
    sentencing, 68–69; and economic decisions,
    62–63; gender and, 118–19, 128–30; good-
    ness/badness evaluation and, 114; influence of
    culture and personal experience, 131–39;
    morphing model and, 127–29
Tsao, Doris, 242–43
Tsarnaev, Dzhokhar, 258
twin studies, 142–43, 212–13
Tyler, Christopher, 101–4

uniformity and variation of human faces,
    73–74

*Unobtrusive Measures: Nonreactive Research in the
    Social Sciences* (Webb et al.), 21
Uyttenbroek, Ellie, 261–62

Verosky, Sara, 139–40, 142
Versluis, Ari, 261–62
Vetter, Thomas, 154
Viola, P., 228–29
vision: development of visual cortex, 233, 244; ex-
    pression of fear and enhanced visual percep-
    tion, 205; faces and newborn visual prefer-
    ence, 222–26; peripheral, 102–3; in primates,
    233, 244, 266–67; spatial frequencies and, 94–
    96; speed of visual processing, 226–28;
    trichromatic (color) vision, 266–67; visual
    acuity of infants, 93–94, 96, 221

Walker, Mirella, 154
war, preference for dominant faces during,
    58–61
"Warhead I" (Burson), *25*
Warhol, Andy, 247
Webb, Eugene, 21
"What's my image?" website, 171
Wiesel, Torsten, 234–35
Wigboldus, Daniel, 135
Wilde, Oscar, 213–14
Willis, Janine, 42, 57
Wilson, John Paul, 68–69
Wilson, Timothy, 77–78
Woods, Tiger, 141
wrinkles, 211–12

Young, Andrew (Andy), 84–85, 127–30

Zebrowitz, Leslie, 38–41, 68, 120, 181
Zimmermann, Johann George Ritter von, 15–16,
    19